T0060030

CHILDREN
OF THE NIGHT

ALSO BY PAUL KENYON

Dictatorland

CHILDREN OF THE NIGHT

THE STRANGE AND EPIC STORY OF MODERN ROMANIA

PAUL KENYON

An Apollo Book

Head of Zeus Ltd
First Floor East
5–8 Hardwick Street
London EC1R 4RG

WWW.HEADOFZEUS.COM

For Flavia

CONTENTS

Land of Dracula

POLAND

KINGDOM OF
HUNGARY

o Budapest

Carpathian Mts.

MOLDAVIA

TRANSYLVANIA

o Sighişoara

Sibiu o

Fǎgǎraş Mts. ⚔ Poenari Castle

Târgovişte o

Lake Snagov

WALLACHIA
o Bucharest

o Giurgiu

R. Danube

SERBIA

OTTOMAN

BULGARIA

Black Sea

Constantinople o

EMPIRE

Gallipoli
Peninsula

Eğrigöz o

Aegean
Sea

------ Border of present day Romania

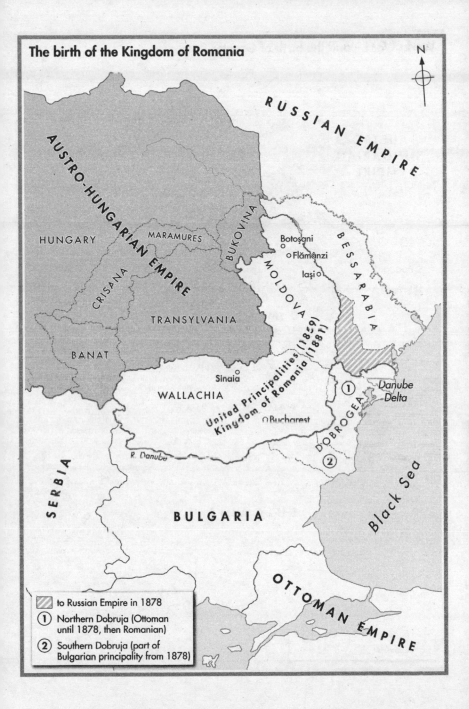

The birth of the Kingdom of Romania

N

RUSSIAN EMPIRE

AUSTRO-HUNGARIAN EMPIRE

HUNGARY

MARAMURES

BUKOVINA

BESSARABIA

Botoşani

○ Flămânzi

Iaşi

MOLDOVA

CRISANA

TRANSYLVANIA

BANAT

United Principalities (1859)
Kingdom of Romania (1881)

Sinaia ○

WALLACHIA

DOBROGEA

① Danube
Delta

○ Bucharest

R. Danube

②

SERBIA

BULGARIA

Black Sea

OTTOMAN EMPIRE

to Russian Empire in 1878

① Northern Dobruja (Ottoman
until 1878, then Romanian)

② Southern Dobruja (part of
Bulgarian principality from 1878)

World War I – and the birth of Greater Romania

N

AUSTRO
HUNGARIAN
EMPIRE

RUSSIAN EMPIRE
(until 1917)

Carpathian Mts

BUKOVINA

MOLDOVA

BESSARABIA

TRANSYLVANIA

ROMANIA

Iaşi

Odessa

Sibiu

Făgăraş

Braşov

×Mărăşti

Târgovişte

Ploiştei

WALLACHIA

Bucharest

Turtucaia

NORTHERN
DOBRUJA

Constanţa

R. Danube

SOUTHERN DOBRUJA

SERBIA

BULGARIA

Black Sea

OTTOMAN EMPIRE

····· Eastern front 7 January 1917
◫ Oilfields

World War II and the Three Rivers

N

LATVIA

LITHUANIA

EAST PRUSSIA

GERMANY

Berlin

SOVIET UNION

Warsaw

Brest-Litovsk

Prague

POLAND

CZECHOSLOVAKIA

AUSTRIA

Vienna

Lvov

Kiev

Dniester

SOVIET UKRAINE

N. BUKOVINA

Budapest

Cernăuţi

Yampol

TRANSNISTRIA

Bershad

HUNGARY

S. BUKOVINA

Southern Bug

Prut

BESSARABIA

Iaşi

ROMANIA

Sibiu

Braşov

Odessa

Belgrade

Ploiştei

YUGOSLAVIA

Bucharest

Danube

Danube Delta

Black Sea

Sofia

BULGARIA

TURKEY

Area occupied by Romania

Oilfields

Istanbul

DRAMATIS PERSONAE

Antonescu, Ion (14 June 1882 – 1 June 1946). Brilliant and fierce military tactician and patriot. Ally of Hitler. Romania's *Conducător* during the Second World War. Architect of the Romanian Holocaust. Executed by firing squad.

Bodnăraş, Emil (10 February 1904 – 24 January 1976). Soviet agent and communist politician who was present in the royal palace on the night of the coup against Antonescu. Later became minister of war and deputy prime minister.

Brătianu, Ion (20 August 1864 – 24 November 1927). Leader of the National Liberal Party. Five-time prime minister.

Carol I, King of Romania (20 April 1839 – 27 September 1914). The country's first monarch. Stolid, dutiful, German-born soldier and diplomat, held in high esteem by Romanians.

Carol II, King of Romania (3 October 1893 – 4 April 1953). Eldest son of King Ferdinand and Queen Marie. Corrupt womanizer who became a fascist-leaning dictator-king, and fled the country with some of Romania's national treasures. Died in exile in Portugal.

Ceauşescu, Elena (7 January 1916 – 25 December 1989). Wife of Nicolae. Deputy prime minister. Bogus doctor of chemistry.

Ceauşescu, Nicolae (23 January 1918 – 25 December 1989). President of Romania. Former apprentice cobbler.

Codreanu, Corneliu Zelea (13 September 1899 – 30 November 1938). Charismatic leader of the far-right Iron Guard. Ideologically a fascist, he was also a devout Christian. Founder of the Legionary movement and admirer of Hitler. Assassinated by strangulation.

Cuza, Alexandru C. (8 November 1857 – 3 November 1947). Professor at the University of Iaşi, and far-right politician. Early mentor to Codreanu. Founder of the far-right National Christian Defence League. Minister of state in the fascist government of Octavian Goga.

Cuza, Alexandru Ioan (20 March 1820 – 15 May 1873). Dashing boyar and colonel who became the first ruler of the United Principalities. Overthrown in a coup.

Dracul, Vlad II (1395–1447). Prince of Wallachia. Shrewd diplomat, famed crusader against the Ottoman Turks, member of the Order of the Dragon, and father to Dracula. Bludgeoned to death in a coup.

Princess Helen of Greece and Denmark (2 May 1896 – 28 November 1982). Long-suffering wife of the mentally unstable King Carol II. Stoical and somber. Mother to King Michael. Divorced in 1928. Lived much of her life in exile near Florence.

Iorga, Nicolae (17 January 1871 – 27 November 1940). Brilliant historian, right-wing politician, and briefly prime minister of Romania. Anti-Semitic inspiration to Romania's early fascists, but also a fierce protector of peasants' rights and a revered patriot. His politics mellowed in later years. Murdered by a fascist death squad.

Lambrino, Zizi (3 October 1898 – 11 March 1953). First wife of the future King Carol II. Mother of Carol's disowned son (Carol Lambrino). Died in exile in France.

Lupescu, Elena (16 September 1899 – 29 June 1977). Mistress and, later, wife of Carol II. Also known as Magda. Self-styled Princess Elena of Romania.

Maniu, Iuliu (8 January 1873 – 5 February 1953). Popular elder statesman who tried to clean up Romanian politics. President of the left-leaning National Peasants' Party. Prime minister on three occasions in the early 1930s. Devout Christian and anti-corruption campaigner. Died in Sighet Prison.

Marie, Queen of Romania (1875–1938). British-born princess, and later queen. Wife of King Ferdinand I, mother of King Carol II. Aesthete, writer of fairy tales, and 'Mother of Romania'.

Maurer, Ion Gheorghe (23 September 1902 – 8 February 2000). Communist politician. Long-serving prime minister under Ceaușescu.

Mehmed II, Sultan – 'the Conqueror' (30 March 1432 – 3 May 1481). Sultan of the Ottoman Empire. Son of Sultan Murad II. School friend of Dracula, and later his nemesis. Alleged lover of Radu the Handsome.

Moța, Ion (5 July 1902 – 13 January 1937). Deputy leader of the Iron Guard, closest friend of Codreanu. Nationalist, anti-Semite, lawyer.

Murad II, Sultan (1404–1451). Sultan of the Ottoman Empire. Father of Mehmed II.

Pacepa, Ion Mihai (28 October 1928 – 14 February 2021). Chief of Romania's foreign intelligence service, and advisor to Nicolae Ceausescu. The highest-ranking defector of the Cold War.

Pătrășcanu, Lucrețiu (4 November 1900 – 17 April 1954). Lawyer, intellectual, and communist politician. Minister of law under Gheorghiu-Dej. Executed in Jilava Prison.

Pauker, Ana (13 February 1893 – 3 June 1960). Communist, Jewish intellectual and politician. The world's first female foreign minister.

Pintilie, Gheorghe (1902 – 11 August 1985). First head of Romania's Securitate. He bludgeoned to death Ștefan Foriș.

Radu III of Wallachia – 'Radu the Handsome' (1437–1475). Younger brother of Dracula. Alleged lover of Sultan Mehmed II. Dracula's rival for the Wallachian throne.

Rakovksy, Christian (13 August 1873 – 11 September 1941). Romanian/Bulgarian socialist revolutionary, Bolshevik politician, physicist and journalist. Life-long collaborator of Leon Trotsky.

Știrbey, Barbu (4 November 1872 – 24 March 1946). Prince, landowner, intellectual, advisor to King Carol I. Queen Marie's lover, and the father to at least one of her children. Prime minister.

Tőkés, László (1 April 1952 –). Ethnic Hungarian pastor from Transylvania whose peaceful resistance to Ceaușescu's regime sparked the Romanian revolution of 1989.

INTRODUCTION

I arrived in Bucharest in August 1994, rather fancying myself as an adventurer-correspondent of the old school, scribbling notes in the back of taxis, drinking into the small hours with former Cold War spies, poring over a coded document or two, anything that might conjure the intrigue of a John le Carré novel. I was on assignment for the BBC, investigating Romania's post-revolution trade in babies, and was trying to set up an interview with the British ambassador. On a humid Friday evening, I was told he was attending a party at a grand stucco-fronted villa in the centre of town, and duly made my way there. Gypsy violinists played soaring rhapsodies among the dripping ferns and apricot trees. Fairy lights flickered sherbet white among the vines above the marble terraces. The air was filled with the aroma of Turkish cigarettes and cooked spices. Some of the guests had managed to get their hands on faded old tuxedos, and stood around smoking nonchalantly in small groups, bowing gracefully at the arrival of diplomats and government ministers. Young, cultured women were dressed in their grandmothers' silks and antique shawls and any scraps of jewellery they could find. They swayed easily to the galloping Ottoman tunes, sipping martinis and chatting excitedly. I never did find the ambassador, but I did meet the girl I would later marry.

It was as if I'd stepped back into a Belle Époque soirée but as we sparkled on the terraces, the city beyond was in near darkness. Horses and carts rattled along the once grand boulevards, weaving dangerously through garbage fires and yawning pot holes. I remember one man riding what appeared to be a giant, oily sewing machine, laughing madly as he zipped through Revolution Square. Earlier I had been approached by a woman pleading for milk-powder for her emaciated baby. The only snatched conversations I had managed were in the stairwells of communist blocks, where people whispered warnings about the supposedly omnipresent secret police. Romania was still staggering out of the dust of revolution.

For almost half a century, the country had endured a primitive form of Stalinism, latterly under the cruel dictatorship of Nicolae Ceauşescu and his psychotic wife, Elena, and before that by a club-fisted rail worker by the name of Gheorghe Gheorghiu-Dej. Intellectuals were jailed or consigned to labour camps. The bourgeoisie were all but exterminated. Normal social convention was turned on its head. Cleverness was mocked, ignorance rewarded. Uniformity was the ultimate expression of beauty. And yet here, on the terraces of the baroque villa, I found a pocket of old-world Romanian sophistication, a glimpse into the true essence of the country; exotic, daring, cosmopolitan, a crossroads between East and West, a kaleidoscopic mix of cultures and ethnicities whose most ancient peoples could trace their blood back to Ancient Rome.

I had packed my bags for Heathrow with, I am ashamed to say, little knowledge of Romania other than its location behind the old Iron Curtain. Like everyone else I had seen the television images of its bewildered ruling couple being marched out of a makeshift courtroom and shot against a wall. My only pre-communist reference point was a vague notion that Dracula might have once stalked the ramparts of a castle somewhere high in the mountains of Transylvania.

In terms of excitement and disorder, the country did not disappoint. Aid workers were everywhere, rushing down from the mountains with tales of dancing bears, gambling dens, Gypsy weddings, and even a tiger on a leash. Seedy Western businessmen bought tracts of city-centre land over bottles of Johnnie Walker in the capital's dimly lit bars. Evidence of Ceaușescu's scorched-earth totalitarianism was all around, from his grotesque city-centre palace, to the soulless rows of communist blocks that dominated every identical neighbourhood.

I met my future wife, Flavia, on the terrace of the old baroque mansion as the Gypsy musicians played Brahms's *Hungarian Dance No. 5*. We walked that night through the deserted streets of Bucharest, and I felt strangely at home.

In the months that followed, I spent all my savings travelling back and forth to Romania. Flavia showed me the palace where Romania's British-born queen had hosted sumptuous soirées between the wars, the mountain resorts where nineteenth-century princes had built spectacular villas, the Black Sea coast where the poet Ovid had been exiled from ancient Rome, the oil fields of Ploiești that Hitler had depended on during the Second World War, and, of course, the old quarter of Târgoviște where Dracula had once impaled his enemies.

Flavia and I were married two years later. I still return often to Romania. For me it is the most beautiful and misunderstood country in all of Europe, a land of adventure and romance, where it still feels possible to unearth new history and new drama. I have watched the country change and grow, researching as I travelled, for a book which, I now realize, has been twenty-seven years in the making.

Paul Kenyon
London, April 2021

CHAPTER ONE

'I am Dracula; and I bid you welcome, Mr. Harker, to my house. Come in; the night air is chill, and you must need to eat and rest.'

Dracula, Bram Stoker

The waters around the fortified Ottoman peninsula of Gallipoli flashed emerald green and peacock blue. Out in the deep water, a spring breeze lifted the surface into fields of shimmering ribs but in the coves and the sandy bays beneath the fort's turreted walls, the Aegean Sea was dead calm. From the water emerged a rocky shoreline that climbed steeply into sharp ridges, breaking through the coarse grasslands to form strange bald peaks, bleached bone-white by the sun. Into this harsh landscape, in the year 1442, rode a party of three on horseback. One of the group was a twelve-year-old boy who would later become known as Dracula.

He was a gaunt, sensitive child, no taller than a riding cane, with a bramble of auburn hair and penetrating green eyes. Alongside him rode his father, Vlad II, Prince of Wallachia, and Dracula's six-year-old brother, Radu. The three had travelled from a country of snow and ice to this barren western tip of the Ottoman Empire in order to meet the imperial ruler, Sultan Murad II.

For young Dracula, the visit seemed destined for dullness. There would be diplomatic meetings, endless ceremonies, treaties to be signed. If he was fortunate, he might get a ride on a Turkish cavalry horse. If not, he would ask if he might swim in the sea or fire a few arrows. Dracula was a keen sportsman, trained in the knightly skills of archery and fencing.

They had set off in mid-April, riding south-east from the ancient beech forests of Wallachia – a land that would one day become part of Romania – crossing the mighty River Danube into Ottoman-held Bulgaria on the other side. The river was the border that represented the southern edge of Prince Vlad's territory. Wallachia was still semi-independent, having halted the Ottomans' otherwise irresistible push north, but only just. This small, lozenge-shaped piece of eastern Europe, a bucolic landscape that was baked by hot summers and pounded by polar-style blizzards in winter, had become an Ottoman vassal, with all the bowing and scraping that Vlad deplored. He was a fierce protector of his princely throne, a strong and charismatic leader of Wallachia's Christian army, whose young recruits came from farming families who tilled the region's unusually rich soils. A vassal because he had no choice, Vlad would not allow control to slip any further.

He and his two sons arrived at the heavily fortified Gallipoli peninsula, in what is now modern Turkey, at the start of May 1442, exhausted and covered in dust. Prince Vlad brushed down his red silk cape, smoothed his long moustache and announced to the guards that they had an appointment to see Sultan Murad II. In fact, it was more like a summons.

As a vassal of the pre-eminent empire of the age, Vlad had always paid 'tribute' to the Sultan in return for a promise that he would not be invaded. The price was hefty – 10,000 ducats a year. The embarrassing truth was that Vlad was only allowed to remain on Wallachia's throne at Murad's sufferance. Break the agreement and Murad would march in, seize Wallachia and install his own choice of leader.

Vlad was forty-seven years old at the time, with large almond-shaped eyes, a curtain of dark hair swept back over his head, and delicate, pursed lips. He dressed in opulent red silks, jewel-encrusted furs and capes stitched with golden threads. A hat of ivory-coloured silk was often balanced precariously on his head like a jauntily squashed fez. His costumes were a fusion of Ottoman and European styles, made from costly cloths transported along the Silk Road from the Far East.

Beside him, the boy who would become famous in Romanian history and world mythology was, for the moment, still known as Vlad, just like his father, but we will call him Dracula to avoid confusion. Dracula was the middle son. In his teens, he dressed in ornate Byzantine silks, billowing cotton trousers tucked into high leather boots, and a tunic with golden buttons. His hair was unkempt and when he grew it long, it would fall around his shoulders in corkscrew curls. The third member of the royal party – Dracula's younger brother, Radu – was tiny, with innocent round eyes and a sunny disposition. He seemed, at times, more like a girl than a boy. Dracula found him tiresome and fragile, and the two never got along.

Slowly, the gates to the fort swung open and out marched a unit of the Sultan's guards. They surrounded Vlad, wrestled him to the ground, bound him in chains and carried him into the castle. At the same time, his two sons were led, crying and shouting, to a horse-drawn wooden cart. A Turkish soldier leapt on board, pulled the reigns sharply and off they went. Dracula and Radu were taken to the distant mountain fortress of Eğrigöz in Asia Minor. On arrival they were thrown into a dungeon.

*

We need to retrace their steps, though, before the kidnap, back northwards through Bulgaria, into the smoky villages and cornfields of ancient Wallachia and to the modest palace where their story begins.

A decade earlier, Vlad had not been the princely ruler but part of a powerful clan that fought regular battles in factional struggles for the Wallachian throne. At the time, his half-brother, Alexander, was in charge – holding a position known in the region as Voievod – and Vlad was his bitter rival. Alexander, realizing that his grip on power was perilous, had approached the powerful Ottoman Sultan and requested his protection. It was then that Wallachia had become an Ottoman vassal. These were violent times, characterized by assassinations and grisly family feuds, but even in that environment, the contest for Wallachia's throne was notoriously bloody.

Vlad had watched events unfold from across the border, in exile in the mountainous Hungarian region of Transylvania, where he lived the privileged life of a successful knight. He fought for the Byzantine Empire against the Muslims and would return after battle to his young family in the picturesque Transylvanian city of Sighişoara, where he kept a small court of servants, soldiers and noblemen, all of whom were waiting for him to break back into Wallachia and seize the throne from his half-brother.

For much of the time, Vlad and his men were away on campaign and young Dracula was raised by the women of the clan. But on one occasion, in 1431, when Dracula was still a toddler, his father had an altogether more enticing reason to leave home. He was invited to Nuremberg, the unofficial capital of the Holy Roman Empire, as an honoured guest of the Emperor Sigismund. At dawn on 8 February 1431, in the chapel of the imperial fortress – before rows of kneeling monks and some of Europe's most famous knights – Vlad was beckoned to Sigismund's feet and a golden necklace hung around his bowed head. On its pendant was the delicately etched image of a winged dragon, along with the motto *O Quam Misericors Est Deus* – Oh, how merciful is God! It also carried a red cross on a white background, a reference to the famous dragon slayer, St George, symbol of the medieval crusaders.

Vlad was asked to make a holy vow to protect Christianity from all invading forces. In particular, he would fight to the death against the Islamic armies of the Ottoman Turks. That vow inducted Vlad into what was known as the Order of the Dragon, a secret chivalric society comprising just twenty-four illustrious members from Europe's most prominent royal families, including, at one time, England's King Henry V. Vlad's inclusion was remarkable. Not only was Wallachia an obscure backwater but Vlad still had no idea how he was going to oust his half-brother from the throne.

When he returned from Nuremberg, he could not resist telling his courtiers about the exotic rituals of the secret Order. From then on, they named him Vlad the Dragon. In old Romanian, Dragon translates as 'Dracul'. So, he became Vlad Dracul, a term of great honour. But the word had a secondary meaning – and that was 'Devil'. Vlad passed the honourable title to his son, at which point it was changed to the diminutive by adding an 'a', and thus the boy became known as Dracula.

Five years after entering the Order of the Dragon, Vlad II had a stroke of good fortune. News reached him that his half-brother was seriously ill. With the help of his Hungarian hosts, Vlad raised an army and invaded Wallachia from the north. By the time he arrived, Alexander was already dead. The Wallachian throne now belonged to Vlad. He and his family moved into the princely palace from which Wallachia was ruled, in the trading hub of Târgoviște fifty miles north-west of the Citadel of Bucharest. This is where the young Dracula was raised; an austere fort-like palace of thick stone walls, roaring fires, high ceilings, sparse oak furniture and deep cellars in which his father kept wine. There were formal gardens, with vegetables and flowers and bees for honey. Beside the palace was a church that Vlad and his family attended daily. Vlad's court, made up of noblemen known as boyars, lived in smaller properties encircling the palace, and the whole community was protected by a moat and high stone walls.

Fortified living quarters, personal guards, armies of patriotic Wallachian soldiers billeted all around, this was the life that young Dracula grew to know. His father worked hard to minimize the possibility of attack and decided, reluctantly, that a continuation of vassal status to the Ottoman Empire was the best way of ensuring peace. The arrangement required not only annual payments, but a guarantee that he would never raise a sword against the Ottoman army, and it could have remained in place had it not been for the Sultan's regular incursions into neighbouring European territory. Whenever a Christian ruler was under Ottoman attack, Vlad would arrive secretly and with his Wallachian army help fight off the Sultan's attack. Memories of that sombre ritual in the candlelit Nuremberg chapel never left him. He was a member of the Order of the Dragon and would fight to protect his land and his faith.

Vlad's double-dealing had gone undetected for several years, until the Sultan's spies witnessed him fighting on the frontline during a battle in Bulgaria. It was then that the Sultan had summoned Vlad to the showdown in Gallipoli, along with Dracula and Radu, on that May afternoon in 1442.

But once detained by the Sultan's guards, instead of being tortured and killed, the three received unexpectedly generous treatment. Vlad was wined and dined and given his own well-appointed quarters. Dracula and Radu were provided with elite schooling alongside the Sultan's own son and were treated like family. The aim was to gently indoctrinate them into supporting the Ottoman Empire. A year later, Sultan Murad decided that Vlad was ready to return home as his obedient servant. He sent him back to rule Wallachia but kept Dracula and Radu behind as collateral, to be executed should Vlad ever break his peace.

The two boys spent the next five years in Turkish captivity, albeit in regal style. Dracula undertook lessons in philosophy, theoretical mathematics, Aristotelian logic, Greek and Latin literature, and the Koran. He learned to speak fluent Turkish and to recite poetry, and he excelled in military history and the tactics of war. But he was prone to outbursts of temper and was regularly whipped. Radu had an easier time. He and the Sultan's son – Mehmed – became close friends and, according to legend, even lovers, with Radu eventually earning the sobriquet Radu the Handsome and becoming a fully-fledged officer of the Ottoman court at the age of just twelve.

Dracula's captivity was to end in dramatic fashion. News reached the Ottoman Empire that his father, Vlad, had been murdered in a bloody coup in November 1447, along with Dracula's elder brother, Mircea. Dracula was released and sent home with the Sultan's blessing to seize the Wallachian throne and to rule the country with Ottoman backing. The story of his return has become part of popular Romanian folklore. It is said that Dracula and a unit of Ottoman soldiers stormed the palace at Târgoviște, killing everyone they encountered. Dracula found the body of Mircea, tortured and buried alive. His father's corpse was discovered nearby in marshland, his head bludgeoned to a pulp. From that moment on, Dracula's mission was to find and punish the killers. He knew exactly who they were – his father's own noblemen boyars. But revenge had to be put on hold. Dracula himself was ousted from the throne after just thirty days in power and spent the next few years drifting around Europe in restless exile.

*

A bright star with a long silver tail lit the night sky over Europe in the summer of 1456. Many years later it would become known as Halley's Comet, but to fifteenth-century eyes it represented a divine message, a celestial warning of great and lasting change.

Vlad Dracula observed it from the affluent Transylvanian city of Sibiu in eastern Hungary, a hub for aspiring artists and silversmiths, and a place he had made his home after years of roaming. His neighbours were unsure as to the identity of the mysterious stranger. An expert horseman, they could see. Probably of noble descent. A keen Christian, they had no doubt. He rode to church on the finest of horses, dressed in scarlet silk and bear-fur capes. He prayed dutifully, luxurious curls falling around his tanned face, a red silk hat on the crown of his head, decorated with precious pearls, golden thread and peacock feathers. There was something of the Ottoman about him, certainly in the way he dressed, but he spoke Romanian, a language that was still evolving in Wallachia and the neighbouring principality of Moldavia. It was said to have been passed down from ancient times, a wild-child derivative of Latin (*Latin Vulgaris*) – a link, claimed Wallachians, to the mighty Roman Empire in the East and the centurions who had once occupied these parts, and from whom Wallachians were descended. Like a lost historical tribe, these were said to be the proud blood relatives of Romans who had refused to return home. The folk of Sibiu knew that this was a powerful man and believed he had fought in many Crusades. But he was a silent, enigmatic figure who seemed in perpetual transit, always gazing southwards over the Carpathian Mountains to Wallachia on the other side.

When Dracula observed the Transylvanian skies that June of 1456, the question was not whether the comet was a heavenly sign. He was sure that it was. The question was whether it would bring good fortune or catastrophe.

*

Transylvania was a wild and beautiful land dominated by the curved spine of the Carpathian Mountains which, in Dracula's day, separated Wallachia from the powerful Kingdom of Hungary to the north-west. The region's deposits of gold and silver were the richest in Europe, making it a highly coveted territory that Hungary and Romania would fight over for centuries to come. Controlled by Hungary at the time – a pre-eminent power in central Europe – Transylvania had become the chosen home in exile for a succession of pretenders to the Wallachian throne, who used the region's inaccessible peaks as a base from which to plot their coups. Dracula was the latest, waiting for an opportune moment to storm down the mountainsides and reclaim his homeland.

During the summer of the comet, events turned unexpectedly in his favour. He was approached by the famous Hungarian military commander, John Hunyadi, with a proposal. The essence of it was this: as Dracula knew, the old Sultan was dead, replaced by his son Mehmed, who had similarly expansionist ambitions to those of his father. Sultan Mehmed was intent on driving his borders right into central Europe, with Hungary an important strategic target. Ottoman troops were already massing in Bulgaria and an unprecedented invasion would soon be underway. They might invade from the south of Hungary, via Serbia, or from the east, across the mountains of Transylvania. One of the few people who might predict the Sultan's tactics was his old school friend, Dracula. Had the two not studied military science together? Had they not sat side-by-side, learning how to organize armies and seize territory? If Dracula were to protect the Transylvanian corridor from the coming onslaught, Hunyadi promised him a most generous reward. He would be provided with an army to help him break into Wallachia and seize back his throne.

Mehmed launched his historic invasion of Europe in the summer of 1456, choosing to gain access via the southern route, and the fortified Serbian city of Belgrade. Over on the eastern side, in Transylvania, Dracula surveyed the mountain passes for signs of an invasion but all was quiet. The Ottomans did not come. Hunyadi, meanwhile, had a fierce fight on his hands, attempting to defend Belgrade with a ragtag army of untrained Christian recruits. As fighting intensified, news of his brave resistance reached Dracula 250 miles away and the would-be Wallachian Prince realized that this was his opportunity.[1] Every army for miles around would be distracted by events in Belgrade, including that of his old adversary – Vladislav, the ruling Prince of Wallachia.

In mid-July, Dracula raised a small guerrilla unit and set off south, sweeping across the high Carpathian peaks and down into Wallachia, heading for the princely capital of Târgoviște.

There, he and his men spotted a column of royal guards moving stealthily through the woods. At its head was Prince Vladislav himself. Dracula's men laid an ambush, attacking with such speed and surprise that Vladislav was thrown from his horse. It is said that Dracula dismounted and engaged the Prince in a swordfight. The twenty-six-year-old challenger was the stronger. He fatally wounded his rival and Vladislav's royal guard immediately surrendered.

On 22 August 1456, Vlad III Dracula entered the high, wooden-ceilinged throne room of his late father's princely palace – the ruins of which one can still visit today – and reinstated himself as Prince of Wallachia. Astonished boyars who, just days earlier, had paid homage to Vladislav, now found themselves singing hymns of praise to their new leader. Dracula was not impressed. He knew that among them were the men who had turned against his father, and who might well turn against him. One of his priorities was to decisively curtail their power and end their plotting.

But first, he commissioned a new coin. It was to be made of gold, with Dracula's face on one side and an image of Halley's Comet on the other – gratitude for the divine intervention and celestial power that had guided his path to the throne.

Dracula is said to have struck against the boyars at a banquet on Easter morning 1457 – nine months into his rule. Contemporary chroniclers claim that he had them dragged away, with the older noblemen impaled on sharpened beech-wood stakes that were then erected as a terrible warning to others around the city walls. The younger boyars were marched into the Făgăraș Mountains and forced to labour on restoring the citadel of Poenari, an impregnable fortress on the edge of a precipice. Then they too were impaled.

After this terrible revenge, Vlad Dracula acquired another lasting nickname. He became Vlad Țepeș – a word that, in Romanian, means 'the Impaler'. He would also acquire a legendary reputation for decisive, ruthless action that would appeal to Romanian nationalists of a much later generation.

*

In Wallachia, the massacre of the boyars was greeted with celebration. The much-hated noblemen who had exploited the poor were gone. Dracula replaced them with far more malleable and grateful courtiers.

Wallachians were equally impressed with Dracula's bold approach to foreign affairs. He was supposedly a vassal to both the Ottoman Turks and the Hungarians but he was daringly defiant towards both. The Ottomans had instructed him not to build any military positions or defences. Dracula's reconstruction of the crow's-nest castle at Poenari had been intentionally subversive. In domestic affairs too, he pursued his own uncompromising reforms, savagely suppressing dishonesty and theft, and punishing even mild misdemeanours with impalement.

It was around this time, during the first couple of years of Dracula's rule, that he organized a notorious feast for all the beggars of Târgoviște. The event appeared to be a great humanitarian gesture. A hall was hired and tables were filled with food and wine. Invitations were put out around the city to cripples, the blind, the diseased and the destitute. They all congregated in a large wooden hall, toasting Dracula's generosity. But towards the end of the meal someone noticed smoke coming from the walls. They ran to the door, only to find Dracula's troops had locked it from the outside and set the place ablaze. Many hundreds were trapped and a bonfire of souls was left burning into the dark Wallachian sky.

The Bonfire of the Beggars, as it became known, was a warning: begging would not be tolerated. It was a drain on the finances of the most decent and generous in society, said Dracula, a crime as evil as theft. Wallachians were uneasy. It was one thing killing the rich, but to massacre the poor in such violent circumstances? On the other hand, Dracula's tactics did seem to be working, and crime fell. It was said that Dracula's guards would test the townsfolk by leaving a purse full of gold coins in a busy market place. When the guards came to collect it in the evening, the purse was always left untouched. This admiration for authoritarian solutions would also resonate down the centuries.

*

Payment of the Sultan's annual tribute was an obligation that Dracula treated with undisguised contempt. He was a proud nationalist and a warrior, and having to grovel to foreign leaders was a humiliation he could not endure. Mehmed had also upped his price. In addition to the usual 10,000 ducats, he insisted that 500 elite Wallachian soldiers be transferred each year to his personal Janissary corps. Dracula ignored Sultan Mehmed's demands and, by 1460, Wallachia was three years in arrears.

In the autumn of that year, two Ottoman emissaries were sent to collect the debt. They were ushered into Dracula's presence, and made the fatal mistake of refusing to remove their turbans. Dracula ordered his guards to fetch some nails. The two emissaries were then forced to the ground, and their headwear nailed to their skulls, as Dracula looked on, cursing them for their bad manners. Despite appearances, the murder of the Ottoman debt collectors was not an uncontrolled outburst, but a deliberate provocation designed to lure Sultan Mehmed into war. Dracula's rationale was this: if Mehmed invaded Wallachia, all Europe's Christian armies would join forces to inflict an almighty defeat on the Ottomans, ending Dracula's humiliating vassal status once and for all, and unifying Christian Europe. Mehmed, however, did not take the bait.

The following year, Dracula appeared to change tactics. He sent a letter of apology to the Sultan, something entirely out of character, offering to meet and pay the tribute in person. He would like very much, he said, to arrange the summit in Mehmed's cosmopolitan capital, Constantinople, but he was reluctant to leave the Wallachian throne even for a day. By return, Mehmed thanked Dracula for his kind offer but said he did not want to trouble his old friend with such a long and hazardous journey. He would send an agent to simply collect the debt instead. That man would be the regal Hamza Pasha, former commander of the Ottoman fleet, feted by the Ottoman public for his role in the conquest of Constantinople and for his brave leadership of many an expeditionary force. But no sooner had Hamza Pasha set off for Wallachia than Mehmed learned through his spies that the meeting was a ruse and that Dracula intended to kidnap the Sultan's envoy.

Mehmed hurriedly sent his apologies, saying Hamza Pasha would not be able to make it after all but would wait for him at the border town of Giurgiu, beside the Danube. This new location could not have been more dangerous for Dracula. Giurgiu was an ancient and strategic port situated on mudflats and marshes, and home to a fiercely contested fort. The town was on the north bank and was therefore part of Wallachian territory but it had been captured by the Sultan and established as an Ottoman salient in Dracula's territory, a forward position consistent with a planned attack against Wallachia.

To ensure that Dracula did not try to back out of the arrangement, Mehmed sent a lower-ranking envoy, a Greek by the name of Thomas Catavolinos, together with a unit of fighters to collect Dracula from Târgoviște and escort him down to Giurgiu for the meeting. Now it was Dracula's turn to feel uneasy. Wasn't this just a straightforward kidnap attempt? He pondered for a while and came up with a plan to outwit his old school friend.

In the winter of 1461, Catavolinos and his armed guard arrived in Târgoviște as arranged. Dracula obediently saddled up his horse and went with them, travelling a hundred miles through frozen forests and farmland in what was one of the coldest Decembers in living memory. As the party approached Giurgiu fort, a unit of the Sultan's men suddenly appeared from the forest and ambushed them. This was the first stage of a plan to install Dracula's brother, Radu the Handsome, on the Wallachian throne. Among the kidnappers that day was the stately Hamza Pasha, the nobleman whom Dracula was supposed to be meeting.

At that same moment, the air was filled with the sound of galloping hooves. From an opening in the forest emerged a hundred-strong unit of Wallachian cavalry, who quickly surrounded the smaller Ottoman force. Dracula had guessed Mehmed's scheme and had arranged to have himself followed all the way from Târgoviște. Dracula's men killed the Ottomans on the spot, apart from two of them. Special arrangements were made for Hamza Pasha and Thomas Catavolinos. They were escorted all the way back to Târgoviște, where stakes had been prepared. In recognition of Hamza's lofty status, he was skewered on a particularly high piece of timber. Catavolinos died next to him, at a more modest level. The two Ottoman noblemen hung like grisly trophies above the walls of Târgoviște, clouds of cawing rooks circling in the snowy Wallachian sky.

But before leaving the area of Giurgiu, Dracula had another score to settle. The fort out there on the mudflats had been constructed by his beloved grandfather, Mircea I of Wallachia, yet here it was, occupied by the enemy. He stormed the fort and massacred the garrison and then launched a large-scale raid across the frozen Danube into Ottoman-held territory, an assault that has gone down in Romanian history for its spontaneous ferocity against a more powerful adversary. Soldiers, civilians, farmers, slaves, everyone in their path was slaughtered. Entire villages were torched. Soldiers were locked into their barracks and engulfed by flames.

In Rome, Pope Pius II was overjoyed. The long-awaited crusade that he had urged upon Europe for three years was finally taking place. The King of Hungary, Matthias Corvinus, was just as ecstatic, and received a letter from Dracula in the midst of battle on 11 February 1462. 'I have killed men and women, old and young,' reported the Wallachian Prince, 'those who lived at Oblucitza and Novoselo where the Danube flows into the sea, up to Rahova, which is located near Chilea, from the lower Danube up to such places as Samovit and Ghighen. We killed 23,884 Turks and Bulgars without counting those whom we burned in homes or whose heads were not cut by our soldiers.' Just in case the Hungarian king was unable to understand the significance of the attack for Wallachian–Ottoman relations, Dracula ended with the words: 'Thus, your Highness must know that I have broken the peace with him (the Sultan).'

News of further Wallachian victories spread quickly across Europe. Dracula was toasted in the Venetian Senate. In the Hungarian Diet, politicians spoke of his bravery and his commitment to the Christian church. In Rome, the Pope thanked God for the life of the Wallachian Prince, and sent Dracula his personal blessings. On the Greek island of Rhodes, where guerrilla fighters were engaged in combat with the Ottoman army, Christian fighters set up long tables and feasted the night away in Dracula's honour.

Mehmed was in Constantinople at the time, studying reports of the bloodshed. He had lost at least 10,000 men. Civilian deaths were far higher. The Sultan understood his old adversary well and knew there would be no end to the slaughter until he took the principality of Wallachia by force.

*

In summertime the Danube was transformed into a fast-flowing river carrying broken branches and beds of weed from the interior down to the Black Sea. The currents were strong, the water deep, the banks hazardous with sinking sand and marsh. It would require an oarsman of rare expertise to navigate from one side to another, particularly if they were trying to do so undetected by Dracula's scouts. But across this closely watched river, in June 1462, Mehmed launched a vast army on barges and pontoons, a force larger than the one he had mobilized to conquer Constantinople nine years before.

Dracula's own army comprised just 30,000 men, most of them trained in guerilla warfare. They were scattered the length of the Danube, unsure where the attack might begin. When they spotted Mehmed's camp being constructed, they launched an assault on the periphery with just a handful of men, silently by cover of night, wiping out hundreds of Ottoman soldiers in a matter of minutes before spiriting themselves away into the woods. But this was just a pinprick on such a huge military leviathan.

Dracula ordered his army into strategic retreat, because even retreats can be devastating to the enemy. As his troops withdrew northwards towards Târgoviște, they destroyed every Wallachian village that lay in their path. Houses were burned, rivers and streams contaminated with sewage, crops destroyed, every head of cattle killed and poisoned. These were the resources that Mehmed's advancing troops were relying on to survive. But Dracula's scorched-earth policy left nothing behind. Any morsels of meat the Turks managed to scavenge had to be cooked on their metal shields – even pots and pans had been destroyed.

Whenever Dracula's retreating army came upon a stream, they made dams that spread mud and water across nearby fields, thus forcing Mehmed to abandon his heavy cannons early in the advance. Every few miles, Dracula would pause and commandeer local men to dig pits that were lined with spikes and covered over with leaves.

On the evening of 17 June 1462, Mehmed's army finally arrived, hungry and terrorized, in fields to the south of Târgoviște. Tens of thousands of men and horses cannot be hidden in open countryside and so Mehmed's tactic was to construct a high wooden fence with watchtowers encircling the camp in the manner of a walled city. In the centre was erected Mehmed's tent, surrounded by thousands of others. It was domed like a pavilion, with linking arches and ornate silk panels.

Dracula made another of his daring guerilla assaults on the encampment, sending a cavalry force into the heart of the besieging army that seems to have come close to killing the Sultan. It was an attack that has gone down in legend as the epitome of patriotism and valour against all the odds. Despite Dracula losing 5,000 men, he inflicted three times the casualties on Mehmed's supposedly world-beating army. Psychologically, it was a stunning victory. The Ottoman enemy were terrified by the seemingly supernatural abilities of Dracula's men, who attacked from all directions, unseen like the wind. What devil of a man, they asked, could inflict such terror on the Ottoman war machine? Nevertheless, Mehmed insisted on one final push.

His traumatized army set off the next day for Târgoviște. Still forty miles from the princely capital, they are said to have spotted a line of trees on the horizon. It seemed to be the start of a forest but as they drew closer, the soldiers realized these were not trees at all. They were stakes and skewered on each was the body of an Ottoman hostage. Some historians, like the Byzantine Greek chronicler Laonikos Chalkokondyles, tell us that 20,000 had been erected on that hillside. Many of the corpses were months old, carried from Târgoviște to join Dracula's growing forest of the dead. It is said that some had rooks nesting inside their bellies and their heads. Right at the front, greeting the approaching Ottomans, were the horribly decayed bodies of their celebrated commander, Hamza Pasha, and the Greek envoy, Catavolinos.

Legend has it that Mehmed never did fight that battle. Chalkokondyles tells us that the Sultan was seized with amazement and said that it was not possible to deprive a country of 'a man who had such a diabolical understanding of how to govern his realm and his people'. We are told that he ordered the Ottoman army into retreat. But Radu the Handsome, Dracula's renegade brother who had prospered in his Ottoman captivity, stayed behind. From his base on an inhospitable plain in the south-east of Wallachia, he let it be known that he was available to run the principality. Radu offered Wallachians a close friendship with the Sultan and a guarantee of peace. His messengers travelled the country warning that if Dracula remained Prince, the Sultan would invade again. Even Dracula's faithful boyars began to survey the flattened villages and burnt-out towns and realized that desolation on this scale did not look like victory.

Soon, they turned against Dracula and he was forced to flee north, across the border into Hungary, where he was first a prisoner and then became a member of the Hungarian gentry. He married a cousin of King Matthias Corvinus and the couple moved into a fine mansion in Budapest, where Dracula mixed in royal circles and was sometimes consulted on diplomatic issues. But there was to be one, final, comeback.

In autumn 1476, King Matthias decided he needed an ally on the Wallachian throne and asked the forty-six-year-old Dracula to return home and re-take his crown. The incumbent was no longer Radu the Handsome – he had died of syphilis the previous year – but a bitter rival called Basarab Laiotă, an Ottoman puppet and brother of Vladislav, the Prince who Dracula had killed twenty years earlier. Supported by Hungarian soldiers, Dracula raided the country from the north, chasing Laiotă from the palace and re-establishing himself as Prince after a fourteen-year absence. For his third and final reign, his capital would be the Citadel of Bucharest, where a new generation of Wallachians were about to discover what it was like living under an uncompromising leader obsessed with discipline, order and punishment.

Shortly before Christmas of 1476, Dracula was paying a visit to his favourite monastery on Snagov Lake, accompanied by a guard of 2,000 men, when he was attacked by the returning forces of Basarab Laiotă (whom Dracula had uncharacteristically failed to kill while seizing his throne). A battle was fought and Dracula's men seemed to be winning. At some point, it is said that the Prince took a rest, wandering a fair distance from the action to reflect on the courage of his men. As he did so, a young servant approached. Dracula assumed he was running a message from the field of battle. Legend has it that the man was actually a Turkish assassin in disguise, and that he took out a sword and slew Vlad III Dracula, cutting off his head as a trophy, and ending the life of Romania's most celebrated son.

*

Today in Târgovişte, a little cake shop beside the walls of the old princely palace sells Vlad Dracula cream buns with a splash of blood-red strawberry ice. You can drink a cappuccino and stare up at Dracula's Chindia Tower, the original structure from where he observed impalements taking place in the square below. Groups of excited school children dash around the ruins of his palace, looking for secret tunnels and leaping out from dark corners.

Over at the monastery in Snagov, the mood is more sombre. Tourists drift through a candlelit Byzantine chapel and pose for pictures beside a rust-coloured tombstone, beneath which are supposedly Dracula's remains. The disappointing truth is that archaeologists excavated the grave in the 1930s and found nothing but horse bones. But Dracula must lie somewhere, and not too far away.

The morning after his final battle, which did indeed take place near Snagov, monks arrived to pick up the dead. It is said that Dracula's head was already on its way to Constantinople, where it was presented to Sultan Mehmed as confirmation of victory. The rest of his body parts were scooped up and taken for burial. Dracula's remains may as well be scattered everywhere in the Wallachian soil. His spirit imbues the earth and the air of this ancient wooded land, and its people too, through folklore and historical memory.

For centuries, there was little interest in where he lay. His name, like his mortal remains, had been forgotten by the outside world. But gradually, Dracula was resurrected as the embodiment of Romanian nationalism, the authoritarian Prince who defended Romania from the Ottomans and who triumphed over his enemy against all odds.

But he was still unheard of outside the country until, in 1890, an Irish writer called Abraham 'Bram' Stoker began leafing through a book about Transylvanian history and came across a character who might lend his name to Stoker's new Gothic novel.

CHAPTER TWO

'We are in Transylvania; and Transylvania is not England. Our ways are not your ways, and there shall be to you many strange things. Nay, from what you have told me of your experiences already, you know something of what strange things there may be.'

Dracula, Bram Stoker

Bram Stoker was born in the affluent coastal suburb of Clontarf on the north side of Dublin in 1847. A restless civil servant with an interest in Gothic literature, by the time he moved to London at the age of thirty-two, he was already writing short stories and nursing aspirations to become a famous novelist. Stoker's other passion was theatre and he soon became manager of London's Lyceum, working closely with the most respected stage actor of the day, Henry Irving – a haunted, gaunt-looking man with peculiarly arched nostrils, a lofty domed forehead and a pair of unnaturally thick black eyebrows. Irving could be deeply melancholic and then burst into fits of hysterical laughter. He could swing from being an outrageous egoist to intense moments of rather intrusive affection. Stoker found him mesmerizing and began to wonder if he could use Irving's personality as the basis for a character in a book.

The author had only the vaguest idea for a plot when he began researching possible themes in 1890, but fantastical, dark adventure stories and Gothic novels were all the rage. His old friend, Oscar Wilde, was just about to publish *The Picture of Dorian Gray* while Robert Louis Stevenson's *The Strange Case of Dr Jekyll and Mr Hyde* was a great success. Stoker admired it so much that he had even put on a stage production based on the novel. By the mid-1890s, the Irishman was spending most of his evenings in the London Library, a converted townhouse of labyrinthine passageways and shadowy reading rooms tucked away in St James's Square. It was here that he began exploring a collection of little-read texts among the rare and dusty volumes.

Stoker immersed himself in lurid, though supposedly factual, accounts of vampires and the un-dead, most of them from remote villages in Austria and Germany. Eventually his research drew him to a region still less travelled. He happened upon a book called *An Account of the Principalities of Wallachia and Moldavia* (1820) by William Wilkinson, finding it first in the subscription library in Whitby, where he spent his holidays, and then discovering another copy back in London.[1] On page seventeen, Stoker came across a name he had not encountered before. 'Wallachia continued to pay [the tribute]', wrote Wilkinson, 'until the year 1444, when Ladislas, King of Hungary, preparing to make war against the Turks, engaged the Voivode Dracula...' Wilkinson's note at the foot of page nineteen provided a revelation: 'Dracula, in the Wallachian language, means Devil.'

Stoker was hooked. In the Whitby edition of the book, he underscored the name Dracula with a heavy pencil mark and when he returned to the London Library, folded the corner of the same page. He began to read more widely about Dracula, not particularly for facts about the actual historical figure but to try to capture the essence of the Prince who battled, burned, and impaled his way through this mysterious land, Wallachia, after his exile in the equally enthralling Transylvania. Never able to visit eastern Europe himself, the author had to rely on others for portraits of the culture and landscape. At the time he was writing, Wallachia had just been unified with its neighbour to the east, Moldavia, to form Europe's newest independent state – Romania – and it seemed to Stoker a dark, remote and supernatural land.

Over the following months he scrawled, in dreadful handwriting, crosses and marginalia in several books, among them Sabine Baring-Gould's *The Book of Were-Wolves* (1865), Charles Bonner's *Transylvania; Its Products and its People* (1865) and Emily Gerard's *The Land Beyond the Forest* (1888). It was the latter that provided the realistic setting combined with ghoulish folklore that would inform the pages of the world's most famous Gothic horror story.

Even today, Gerard's book makes for a haunting read. She was the Scottish wife of a diplomat based in the remote Transylvanian outpost of Sibiu, where Dracula had lived in exile not far from the Wallachian border, and attempted a factual account of what she encountered beyond the consulate walls. These were the superstitions and 'Devilish practices' she discovered in the towns and villages of 'Roumania' and Transylvania – a name that itself has an eerie derivation. In ancient Latinate Romanian, *Trans* means 'beyond' and *sylvan* means 'trees' – 'the land beyond the trees'.

Gerard reported her findings in meticulous detail, providing a chilling snapshot of the region's superstitions at the end of the nineteenth century: 'The crow is a bird of evil omen, and is particularly ominous when it flies over the head of a man...', 'a shrieking magpie denotes death...', 'it is never permissible to kill a spider, but a toad taking up residence in a cow-byre, should be stoned to death...', 'the skull of a horse, placed over a gate is a preservation against ghosts...' She describes witches and malevolent spirits, toothless old hags, alluring virgins and, of course, vampires, or *nosferatu*, which she says every Romanian peasant believes in. One passage that particularly interested Bram Stoker is worth quoting at length. Nosferatu, writes Gerard:

... will continue to suck the blood of other innocent people till the spirit has been exorcised either by opening the grave of the person suspected and driving a stake through the corpse, or firing a pistol shot into the coffin. In very obstinate cases it is further recommended to cut off the head and replace it in the coffin with the mouth filled with garlic, or to extract the heart and burn it, strewing the ashes over the grave.

Devilish decapitations such as these, Gerard tells us, were still occurring in remote villages in both Transylvania and Romania when her husband was ambassador. It would require a courageous traveller to take a trip to either region.

*

Marie was seventeen years old, with silky fair hair, impish blue eyes and the kind of breezy country-house manner that was more suited to London's debutante balls than a train journey across the Carpathians. She had little idea what to pack and had brought ball gowns and riding boots, high-collared dresses and swimming costumes. Twenty trunks of her belongings were piled into the freight carriage, while her new husband had brought with him just a couple of discreet cases. His name was Ferdinand, or Nando as she liked to call him, ten years older than Marie, meticulously groomed, overly serious and painfully shy. Married just a week earlier, the couple were unused to spending time alone and Nando found the journey a strain. He spent his time staring silently from the window, while Marie squealed with excitement at the snow-capped peaks and picture-book valleys.

In January 1893, while Stoker was still in the throes of writing *Dracula*, Marie was on a journey to meet her in-laws in Romania. When the train passed near to Braşov, in Transylvania, a spectacular castle loomed from the trees. It sat high on a piece of solid rock, with brooding battlements and candle-shaped towers. This had been a look-out post when Dracula was in charge of protecting the Transylvanian border against the Ottomans in the fifteenth century. Known as Bran Castle, it is said that Bram Stoker had seen sketches of the building back in London and that its haunted appearance helped inspire his description of Castle Dracula, 'a vast ruined castle, from whose tall black windows came no ray of light, and whose broken battlements showed a jagged line against the moonlit sky'.

Before catching sight of Bran, Marie had only seen castles in England and at Coburg in Bavaria, where she had spent her teens. With their cuckoo-clock windows and sun-dappled terraces, they had been filled with laughter and light, in contrast with the unsettling Gothic citadel that stood before her now. The newly-weds' train flew through town after town. These high Carpathian peaks were all part of Transylvania – still a province of Hungary, still claimed by Romania. Soon the altitude dropped, the air thickened and they were speeding through mountain passes, following a similar route to that of Bram Stoker's newly qualified solicitor, Jonathan Harker, as he entered the region by horse and carriage. 'There were dark rolling clouds overhead,' wrote Stoker, 'and in the air the heavy, oppressive sense of thunder. It seemed as though the mountain range had separated two atmospheres, and that now we had got into the thunderous one.' The wooded landscape that Marie observed was one of steep rocks, pine forests and deep valleys, whose bottoms seemed cloaked in perpetual darkness. This wild landscape was home to Europe's largest population of wolves (as well as bears and lynx) and Stoker had done his homework well. 'Just then the moon, sailing through the black clouds', he wrote, 'appeared behind the jagged crest of a beetling, pine-clad rock, and by its light I saw around us a ring of wolves with white teeth and lolling red tongues, with long sinewy limbs and shaggy hair. They were a hundred times more terrible in the grim silence which held them than ever when they howled.'

Finally, Marie and Nando's train emerged from a mountain

pass to see the plains of Romania below. Endless snowy fields were dotted with huts and barns. Peasants rode through open countryside on horse-drawn sleighs. From the chimneys of wattle-and-daub houses came threads of fire smoke. It could not have been more different from Eastwell Park, the Kent country estate where Marie grew up. She was more used to formal gardens and well-stocked lakes, picnics on manicured lawns and riding bareback through the local woods. Her summers had been spent swimming in the sea off the Isle of Wight alongside her much-loved grandmother, Queen Victoria – because the woman on the train was, in fact, Princess Marie of Edinburgh, daughter of Prince Alfred, granddaughter of the Queen of the United Kingdom and Ireland. And Nando, her new husband, was Prince Ferdinand of Romania, heir to the country's throne.

When the train reached the station at the Transylvanian border town of Predeal, a cheer broke out on the platform. Homemade flags of blue, yellow, and red – Romania's national colours – were waved alongside freshly made Union Jacks. A brass band struck up stirring music. Locals were expecting a speech. After all, it was not every day that Crown Prince Ferdinand passed through town. Certainly, it was the first time anyone had seen his English wife. The couple would one day become King and Queen of Romania. Their arrival was an historic event. The crowd applauded, hoping to coax Nando and Marie to the top of the train steps, but the couple sat, bashfully, behind the glass, waving and, in Marie's case, smiling. Nando managed little more than a frown.

In Bucharest, the winter streets were blanketed in snow. When Nando and Marie arrived in January 1893, the historic Ottoman-style layout of the city, with its narrow winding streets and wooden abodes, had gone. Romania had begun to view itself as a modern European nation and its old buildings, with timber lattice-work and ornate stone arches, were unwanted reminders of its past as a vassal to the Ottomans. Now the people looked to France for architectural and cultural inspiration, turning Bucharest into what would become known as 'Little Paris'.

Nando and Marie descended onto a packed platform at Bucharest's Gara de Nord, into a sea of top hats and flowers. In the melee, Marie found herself pressed against Nando's chest and was surprised to discover that his whole body was shaking. The couple wheeled through the crowds, endless bouquets thrust at Marie until all she could do was push them over her shoulder into the arms of her ladies-in-waiting. In the street outside, a beautiful golden stagecoach awaited, pulled by six strong horses decorated with bobbing, red feather plumes.

Marie's first impression of the Romanian royal residence, *Palatul Regal*, was unfavourable: '... not very imposing,' she wrote later, 'squat, low, and of no distinctive style'. In fact, its façade was French-style stucco but the ungainly roof resembled an upturned barge. Overall, the impression was one of drab formality, a soulless government building very different from the hearty country houses she was used to. A marble staircase led to the upper floors, lined with schoolgirls who threw bouquets at Marie's feet. She was relieved to get into her room and close the door, but even there the décor was black marble and dark wood without a warm fire in sight.

Let's leave Marie for a moment, sitting there on the cold, unwelcoming sheets of her funereal bed, and explore how she had come to cross paths with a prince from such a remote and unexplored kingdom.

Marie was one of Queen Victoria's forty-two grandchildren, and securing her marriage into the right European family had been a pre-occupation of her relatives since her early teens. Royal marriages were seen as instruments of foreign relations and, ultimately, insurance against war. The last three decades of the nineteenth century – the age of imperialism – was a particularly fraught time for ensuring familial links with all the important monarchies. Marie's father, Prince Alfred, was the half-German

Duke of Saxe-Coburg and Gotha. Her mother was Grand Duchess Maria Alexandrovna, the only daughter of Emperor Alexander II of Russia. Her favourite cousin, Nick, would one day become Czar Nicholas II. For Britain to forge ties with the embryonic Kingdom of Romania, a country poised strategically between East and West, was seen as shrewd politics.

The creation of the Kingdom had come about in fits and starts over a twenty-year period, born from a unification of Wallachia and Moldavia – an event that had happened almost by accident, at least from the perspective of the Great Powers. Wallachia had remained a (nominal) vassal of the Ottoman Empire into the late nineteenth century and had wished to unite with Moldavia for years, but the Great Powers would not allow it. They were worried that a new and potentially troublesome country might pose a threat to peace when thrown into the already explosive Balkan mix. Britain was particularly hostile. London had wanted the two territories controlled by the combined tutelage of the Great Powers and the Ottomans, but had been outfoxed by a privileged boyar in the Moldavian army, Alexandru Ioan Cuza. The dashing young colonel had made himself a popular figure in Moldavia and was elected as its 'Prince' in 1859. The Great Powers had granted such a title to Moldavia, and one to Wallachia in the Treaty of Paris, allowing them autonomy as separate states. But the sharp-witted Cuza noticed an ambiguity in the legal text. Nowhere did it say that the two could not elect *the same* prince. Cuza persuaded the Wallachians to vote for him as well, becoming prince of both and cleverly merging the two as a single autonomous state known as the 'United Principalities'.

Styling himself the *'Domnitor'*, a sort of benevolent authoritarian ruler, Cuza had soon become bogged down in the incendiary issue of land reforms. Rich, fertile soils were the United Principalities' best asset, but a quarter of the land was owned by the corrupt Orthodox Church, which paid no tax and spirited money away to its revered monks at Mount Athos, while three-quarters was owned by the even more corrupt boyars. Peasant farmers, who made up ninety per cent of the population, were exploited whichever way they turned. While attempting to resolve the problem, Cuza ended up at war with all sides and became so unpopular that he managed to achieve the near-impossible, briefly uniting Conservatives and Liberals on the single issue of ejecting him from power. The anti-Cuza coalition became known as 'The Monstrous Alliance'.

In the early hours of 22 February 1866, armed conspirators hired by both sides broke into Cuza's bedchamber. The rakish *Domnitor* was famed for his seduction of women and, on the night in question, did not disappoint these unwelcome visitors. They found him in bed alongside his young mistress and suggested that Cuza's formidable and wealthy wife, Elena, a member of the Rosetti family, might not approve. With rifles pointed at his head, Cuza was offered his abdication papers to sign and duly agreed. The next morning, he was whisked across the border into exile. The first leader of the unified country had fallen victim to Romania's first coup.

Leaderless and desperate for a touch of class, the 'Monstrous Alliance' then set about finding a monarch instead – someone who might bring stability and longevity to the country – and sent scouts abroad to poach a tame royal. Their first choice, Prince Philippe of Belgium, was not interested. Their second, the grandly named Prince Karl Eitel Friedrich Zephyrinus Ludwig, was tracked down to Berlin. A Prussian officer from the royal house of Hohenzollern-Sigmaringen, the normally dour, disciplined twenty-seven-year-old was so enthusiastic he jumped on the next train to Bucharest, taking a second-class compartment for the sake of discretion.

On arrival in May 1866, he was met by members of a welcoming committee who led their new sovereign through a busy neighbourhood of the city and then paused. 'Where are we?' asked the disorientated Prince Karl.

'This', announced one of them excitedly, 'is your new palace!'

'Where?' asked the Prince, looking around.

They pointed, embarrassed, to a building beside a Gypsy camp where pigs wallowed in the mud. But things had soon started to look up after that. The principality was re-named Romania that very year, 1866, and the palace was extended and improved by a famous French architect. Prince Karl learned to speak a little Romanian and even endeared himself to his new country by adopting the Romanian spelling of his name, becoming Prince Carol I. He loathed the notion that his new country was still a vassal of the Ottoman Empire and determined to bring that to an end. But the dawn of Romania's full independence as a Kingdom was not without controversy.

Its roots were in the rebuilding of the Balkan region after the Ottomans were driven from Europe during the Russo–Turkish War of 1878. When the spoils were divided, Romania did rather well. Although it was forced to give up a sliver of land on its far south-eastern border (southern Bessarabia) to the Russian Empire, it was awarded the former Ottoman territory of northern Dobruja, a hundred-mile strip of spectacular coastline that included the commercially important Danube Delta, the gateway to Europe for cargo ships plying their trade on the Black Sea. Territorially, all was agreed but the West had a problem with Romania's domestic politics.

The Great Powers warned that full sovereignty would only be granted if Romania agreed to recognize members of its Jewish and Muslim population as full citizens. Romania was unhappy, particularly about the Jews, announcing that 'there were not, and there have never been, any Romanian Jews; there were merely Jews, who had been born in the Principality, but who had never been assimilated, either in speech or in custom, by the Romanian nation'.[2] It was an ugly turn of events that displeased the West, exposing a streak of anti-Semitism in the new country that would persist and grow. In the end, Romania compromised, allowing the assimilation of a small proportion of its 300,000 Jews on a case-by-case basis but only after they could prove residence in Romania for at least ten years.

With all that finally settled, and the West hesitantly welcoming Romania into the fold, the newly independent state was declared a Kingdom in 1881, with King Carol I on its throne. This was the political landscape that greeted Princess Marie when she hurried up that marble staircase into her 'rich, dark, pompous, unhomelike, inhospitable room' in *Palatul Regal* in January 1893.

Her first few weeks in Bucharest were spent in a sort of royal confinement, imposed by King Carol. Worried that the newly-weds might be contaminated by the already filthy intrigues of the Romanian political class, the over-protective monarch forbade them from fraternizing, confining them to formal receptions at the palace. Marie spent her days with a 'hideous lot of uninteresting monsters' and her evenings watching her new husband and King Carol play billiards, while she drifted off to sleep in a chair.

Ferdinand was not Carol's biological heir. The king had no surviving children of his own and had shopped around his extended family, finally settling on his young, impressionable nephew, confident that although not bright, he was a doggedly dependable soul who would do whatever he was told.

In those first few months of marriage, Ferdinand seemed as sad and bored as Marie. On the few occasions he was allowed out of the palace to attend public events, he crept around as if avoiding predators, muttering apologies under his breath and fiddling with the broad moustache that he had grown to disguise a drooping lower lip. Foreign visitors noticed that his hands shook when he was introduced and that he was so nervous, he would repeat the same sentences again and again while backing towards the door. The only time Marie saw Ferdinand relaxed and happy was when he was picking wild flowers in the sub-Carpathian meadows or reading books about botany. They did, though, gradually fall in love.

When their first child was born in October 1893, the little boy was immediately removed from their care by the king and queen (the overweening, German-born novelist Carmen Sylva) and placed with a series of indulgent nannies. Christened Carol, after the king, he was pampered and never disciplined, becoming obstinate, demanding, and sometimes violent. Still insisting that a parentless upbringing was best, the queen employed a prickly Swiss intellectual, Mr M. Mohrlen, to tutor the boy when he turned twelve years old. Unfortunately, pupil and master got along a little too well. Mohrlen fell passionately and unhealthily in love with the child – as he later, tearfully confessed – and tried to isolate him from the rest of the family, taking young Carol on overnight field trips outside Bucharest where it seems likely that sexual abuse took place. The relationship continued for six years, right through Carol's teens. At first Marie treated the friendship lightly, referring to the pair as 'the two old maids'. But eventually she called a doctor. Mohrlen was sacked and ran weeping from the palace. Carol was sent to school in England. But the damage was already done. His mental instability would later affect Romania's politics for a generation.

As the pressures of an inhospitable Romanian royal court wore Marie down, she took to foreign travel, visiting relations in London and Germany and at the Winter Palace in St Petersburg. She immersed herself in letter-writing and developed a code when describing her despised in-laws. King Carol was *Dombey*, a cruel and cantankerous old man from the pages of Dickens. Even Ferdinand was out of favour. He was *Dombey's nephew*. On one occasion, Marie threw caution to the wind, writing to one of her sisters, 'There is no bigger bore than Nando.' The Princess started looking elsewhere for excitement.

She arrived in Moscow in May 1896 to attend the coronation of her beloved cousin Nick, the new Czar of Russia, and stayed for two weeks, attending a string of wild and exotic parties. Roving between city mansions and aristocratic rural estates, she was pursued by a circus of dukes and assorted noblemen. 'Brilliant, dashing, sentimental, daring, full of Russian ardour,' she wrote in her diary. Nando was less enthused. Tired and uninterested, he left each party almost as soon as it began. Marie, on the other hand, would remain until sunrise. At one picnic, the Princess accepted a dare from a dashing officer of the Imperial Guard to race an untrained Cossack horse against members of the cavalry. A keen horsewoman, she ignored Nando's protestations and leapt aboard the saddleless beast, flying off across the countryside. First across the finish line, Marie draped herself around the horse's neck, kissing it lavishly while the young men watched in delight. 'I rejoice in my own beauty,' she wrote of herself later, 'men have taught me to.' But her marital frustrations would not be cured by a short break in Russia.

In London, the following spring, Bram Stoker's final manuscript was almost ready for the printers. Until just a few weeks before publication, it had been called *The Un-Dead* but a canny editor decided that *Dracula* was a far more alluring title. In May 1897 the distinctive bumble-bee yellow jacket with blood-red lettering hit the book stands. The first press reviews boded well. The *Daily Mail* proclaimed it a classic of Gothic horror, comparing it favourably with Shelley's *Frankenstein* and Edgar Allan Poe's *The Fall of the House of Usher*. Sir Arthur Conan Doyle sent Stoker his personal congratulations: 'I write to tell you how very much I have enjoyed reading *Dracula*. I think it is the very best story of diablerie which I have read for many years.'

It is inconceivable that Marie did not read a copy of the book. She loved Romanian folklore and would soon become a published author of magical fairy tales herself. News of Stoker's fantastical story featuring a Romanian historical figure, as well as locations in Transylvania and old Wallachia, would not have escaped her attention, particularly as Dracula's name had only recently been rediscovered and politicized by nationalist scholars. They had been smarting over Romania's treatment at the hands of the Great Powers, and invoked Dracula's determination to stand up to powerful foreign armies as an example of true patriotism. Domestically, too, they wanted Dracula-style solutions. Both the Conservative and Liberal parties at the time were mired in bribery, nepotism, fraud and intimidation, and the more right-wing elements in the country saw Dracula's zero-tolerance approach as the answer.

Writing just after the coup against Cuza, and while politicians squabbled for favours and privilege under King Carol, Romania's most revered Romantic poet, Mihai Eminescu, wrote a famous stanza that alluded to the famous 'Bonfire of the Beggars':

> Why not come back Vlad the Impaler, to gather them up again,
> Herding them into two cages; villains and the insane
> You could drive them all in a fury til they reach the dungeon's wall.
> Then in prison or asylum – just set fire to them all.

Back in London, Bram Stoker's *Dracula* was not the commercial success he had hoped. Sales dipped and the book quietly vanished. But like the tale's fictional Count, it would soon resurrect itself.

*

On a winter morning in 1907, a young Romanian peasant called Ioan Dolhescu – a thin, underfed young man who survived on maggot cheese and pickled root vegetables – was hit in the eye by a flying stone outside the mayor's office in Flămânzi. We would know nothing of Dolhescu, nor the missile, were it not for the violence that followed the assault. Within six weeks, many thousands would be dead and Romania would be close to revolution.

The conflict had been provoked, as usual, by rich landowners and their exploitation of near-starving peasants, but this time there was also an undercurrent of something more toxic. The man who threw the stone at young Dolhescu was a local estate manager by the name of Gheorghe Constantinescu. He had been surrounded by a mob of screaming peasants demanding wages that had not been paid for three months. The peasants were cold, hungry and so comprehensively exploited that they were effectively paying their landlords for the privilege of working. It was hardly Constantinescu's fault. He was just the messenger, sent to shoo them away, the lowest figure in a hierarchy of ownership that ran Romania's antiquated feudal system.

The private Flămânzi estate where Dolhescu worked was enormous, growing wheat and corn on a scale equivalent to all the vineyards in France. It was owned by the aristocratic Sturdza family, who had begun acquiring land during the time of Dracula 400 years earlier. The Sturdzas were one of the most influential families in Romania, variously providing prime ministers, Royal Academicians, and advisors to the king. They had little time for running their enormously lucrative estate and leased it out to a group of middlemen who the Sturdzas called 'aliens', by which they meant Jews.

After the stone-throwing incident at the town hall, and still without any pay, the bedraggled peasants collected their axes and spades and marched through town looking for trouble. They ended up at the Sturdza estate office, which just happened to be managed by two Jews. The mob set upon them and beat them to within an inch of their lives. Then they barricaded the road and set up a picket, which grew to a crowd of thousands within days.

Newspaper editorials encouraged the view that Jews were to blame. 'The anti-Yid uprising has begun in the extreme north of Romania', said one, 'because it is the area which is most overwhelmed by this scourge of humanity!' With no mention of the real culprits – the Romanian aristocracy – the paper implored patriotic citizens to take to the streets and stop the theft of Romania's most precious asset. 'All true Romanians will give their assistance', it said, 'and will struggle until they have achieved such a crucial victory so as to save our ancestral land and our race from the plague and the infernal plans of the Yids.'[3]

The combination of journalistic provocation, winter cold, hungry children and the apparent insouciance of the urban elite was explosive. Three days after the stone-throwing, 2,000 peasants took to the streets of the nearest big city, Botoșani, armed with burning torches and farm tools. They made for the Jewish quarter where they dragged inhabitants onto the streets, pillaged all they could find and set fire to their homes. Similar violence erupted in other towns and cities across Romania's north-east corner. Then the ringleaders gathered a large contingent of men and began marching south.

Watching events unfold from Bucharest was an erudite young anti-Semite called Nicolae Iorga, who would one day become Romania's most famous historian as well as an influential politician. Immediately recognizable for his waist-long beard, Iorga would write forty books a year and still had time to publish his own newspaper. Entitled *Neamul Romanesc* – The Romanian People – it was ostensibly a celebration of Romania's ancient peasant culture but was really a mouthpiece for violent anti-Semitic nationalists in search of intellectual justification for their actions. Iorga used arguments from metaphysics, international affairs and history to justify his views. Jews were, he said, 'agents of the enemy' (meaning foreign powers, and in particular Russia), 'parasites' and 'an obstacle to the creation of a Romanian middle class'.

In fact, Jews had been in Wallachia and Moldavia since Roman times, and had first begun arriving in significant numbers during the fourteenth century as refugees from anti-Semitic regimes in Hungary and Poland. More arrived on trade routes from the Ottoman Empire to the Black Sea, from the Austro-Hungarian Empire and from Russia, where, in the mid-nineteenth century, Czar Nicholas I had endeavored to destroy Jewish life in accordance with the wishes of the Russian Orthodox Church.

Jews had been grudgingly tolerated in old Wallachia and Moldavia but when the principalities united, a more intense anti-Semitism developed, born of Romania's perceived vulnerability as a newly recognized state and its desire to re-ignite a national identity that stretched all the way back to the Roman Empire. The appalling poverty suffered by the peasant population was more conveniently blamed on the Jews than their own rapacious aristocracy.

Paradoxically, it was Romania's own anti-Semitic laws that were responsible for creating the tensions of 1907. First under Cuza and then Carol I, Jews had been barred from public office and from becoming lawyers, teachers, chemists, stockbrokers and practically every other profession. They were not allowed to trade in alcohol, tobacco or even salt, nor were they allowed to own land. Lending money and leasing land were some of the few commercial activities still open to them.

By early March, violence against Jews, under the guise of a revolt against land inequity, had spread across all of eastern Romania (the region of Moldova). Jewish-run estates were torched, Jewish-owned houses looted. In town after town, entire Jewish quarters were raised to the ground. Then the uprising began moving towards Bucharest, at a rate of fifty miles a day.

In the second week of March, the 'Peasant Revolt' began to broaden its aims, becoming more politicized. Groups of Russian revolutionaries had seen what was happening and judged Bucharest a more promising target than St Petersburg. They swarmed across the border, carrying Marxist texts. Some of the Russian infiltrators were part of the crew of the *Battleship Potemkin* who had rebelled against their imperial officers two years before and taken sanctuary in Romania. The largely uneducated Romanian peasant armies gladly imbibed the propaganda and were soon blaming anyone with wealth, power and property for their predicament.

Princess Marie seemed oblivious to these events. Sitting in her salon at the beautiful baroque Cotroceni Palace, where she and Nando had moved to escape the in-laws, she wrote to friends that – having visited several peasant communities during the previous summer – she could report 'contentment and happiness all round'. There had, she said, been a 'wonderful harvest' and everyone was 'rich and well off'. Even as she was writing, the peasant armies had reached the outskirts of Bucharest. The capital was under siege. 120,000 soldiers were mobilized, with troops taking over the centre of the city and residents subjected to a curfew. Marie had to concede that the spreading violence represented more than a protest from a few disgruntled farm-hands. 'Certainly, it is due to Socialistic influence', she wrote, 'but of course the peasants *are* badly off and a great deal remains to be done for them.'

Then, on 25 March 1907, the king ordered Marie to leave the capital for her own safety and relocate to the royal summer house in the mountains, along with other aristocratic wives. He sacked the entire Conservative government for being too soft and replaced them with the opposition Liberals, who promised to use force to put down the revolt. Their new leader was one Dimitrie Sturdza, from the same land-owning Sturdza family upon whose estate the violence had begun.

One of the largest confrontations took place in Teleorman County, south of Bucharest, where 6,000 peasants gathered with knives and axes, chanting for the redistribution of land. Under instruction from the Liberal government, the Romanian army prepared artillery and ordered the peasants to disperse. When they refused, soldiers launched a ferocious attack, firing indiscriminately upon the crowds. Late that afternoon, when the smoke finally lifted, 600 bodies were found scattered across the soil.

The Peasant Revolt finally came to a precarious end on 5 April 1907, with terrorized peasants returning to their homes having failed to score any meaningful concessions. Romania's Liberal government was so worried about international condemnation of its multiple massacres that it announced an official death toll of just 419. The actual figure was 11,000 and Romania had come very close to civil war.

Marie was socializing at a friend's villa in the mountain resort of Sinaia when she heard the news. Since her arrival in Romania, fourteen years earlier, the Princess had gathered around her a coterie of chic, fashionable women who her in-laws considered too wild to be confidantes of a royal. She had created a *fin de siècle* haven of poetry, music, champagne and gossip, entertaining clever women with absent husbands, who spent their evenings in candle-lit salons smoking cigarettes while draped upon velvet divans. Many indulged in love affairs with princes, writers, and actors. Just like the French, the Romanians viewed infidelity as both healthy and natural. At aristocratic funerals, a man's wife and lovers would embrace like family.

One of Marie's dearest friends was the rather intimidating style-icon and socialite Marta Bibescu. She was married to the wealthy aviation pioneer and adventurer, Prince George Bibescu, who was rarely in the country and allowed Marta to live as she pleased. It was at their villa in the mountains that the wives had met during the Peasant Revolt, and where Marie first encountered a rich, young aristocrat by the name of Barbu Știrbey.

Știrbey had burst into the room while the women were dining to report that the peasant army had destroyed some of his properties. Born into a long line of boyars, Știrbey's estates were so large that he had constructed a private railway to move produce from one side to the other. Even as his farms and houses were being wrecked, he told those present, he sympathized with the cause of the peasants, though not their tactics. Intelligent, humble and entirely lacking the Byzantine scheming that oiled much of Romania's political and social class, Barbu Știrbey was admired by all the wives. Marie was entranced. Though Știrbey's wife and daughters were among the house guests that day, it was

Marie who would spend the day consoling him. Ştirbey was so taken with the Princess that he ended up staying for a week.

As their relationship deepened during the coming months, Ştirbey had a word with his friend King Carol. The young boyar had found Marie to be intellectually sharp and hungry for a more fulfilling role in her adopted country. He knew Carol had sidelined her, believing the young British princess too flighty, unreliable and disorganized, so he set about trying to convince Carol that she might be a great asset for Romania. 'It is essential not to break her spirit,' he advised. 'If we can persuade her to take herself and her duties more seriously, her natural intelligence will do the rest.' The normally gruff, unapproachable monarch responded to the advice in unexpected fashion. Always reluctant to consult his dithering nephew Ferdinand about affairs of state, he turned to Marie instead, inviting her to meetings and asking advice about international affairs.

It had not gone unnoticed, of course, that Marie and Barbu Ştirbey were having an affair but instead of Carol warning Ştirbey off, he promoted him to his chief advisor. The new role meant that Ştirbey had an excuse to meet the Princess every day, alone and in an official capacity. Carol was, in effect, sanctioning their relationship. Over the coming months and years, Ştirbey spent much of his free time tutoring Marie in Romanian arts, culture and heritage. He read her the works of the Romantic poet Mihai Eminescu, played her music by the internationally renowned Romanian composer George Enescu ('pure gold' said Marie) and led her proudly through the country's strange and turbulent history.

Most surprising for Marie was the depth of Ştirbey's national pride in what was, she learned, among the most ancient countries in all Europe. Only its name had changed but its people had remained constant. She was actually living in what was once the ancient Kingdom of Dacia, a territory created almost 200 years before the birth of Christ. It had been invaded by the Romans, under Emperor Trajan, in AD 101 and rechristened *Dacia Felix,* or *Happy Dacia.* At its heart had been the mountainous region of Transylvania, with its fortress capital, Ulpia Traiana Sarmizegetusa, the ruins of which are still visible today and considered a place of deep spirituality.

The indigenous people of Dacia had intermingled with the Roman invaders and after the Romans left in AD 275, those who remained behind had gradually become known as Romanians. Give or take invasions by Goths, Huns, Lombards, Eurasian nomads and Slavs, most Romanians still consider themselves descended from Ancient Rome today, and have done for generations – indeed this conviction is at the root of a rare and intense nationalism – and it is this alluring identity, true or not, that has dominated Romanian politics since the time of Vlad Dracula and beyond. Yet, during Marie's time, Transylvania was part of the Austro-Hungarian Empire. It seemed to her a terrible historic injustice. The majority of the Transylvanian population were ethnic Romanian (55 per cent), but they were under the discriminatory rule of the Hungarians, and had been since the tenth century. The more she read, the more Marie was horrified by their plight. The struggle of little Romania to become Greater Romania – to expand to the size of old Dacia – was the pre-occupation of all Romanian nationalists.

*

Marie still needed to overcome the suspicions of a proudly nationalistic population. To Romanians, she was a self-indulgent, detached foreigner, a flighty princess who preferred French champagne to homemade plum brandy. Her opportunity to change perceptions arrived during the monsoon summer of 1913, when Romania seized an opportunity to try to expand its borders.

On 10 July that year, a column of Romanian soldiers scrambled onto a hastily constructed pontoon bridge across the Danube, close to where Dracula's army had once launched its celebrated attack against Ottoman-controlled lands. Among the 50,000-strong invasion force were several famous faces. The polymath and anti-Semite Nicolae Iorga was there, waist-length beard proudly brushed, notepad and pen in his knapsack. So too was five-time prime minister Ion Brătianu, leader of the National Liberal Party, and future Conservative prime minister Constantin Argetoianu. Everyone who was anyone crossed the bridge that day. Their mission was to reclaim a stretch of spectacular Black Sea coastline from the Bulgarians, who were being mauled from all sides after a failed attempt at expansion themselves in the aftermath of the First Balkan War. Romania had cunningly taken advantage of the chaos and, with the Bulgarians engaged in bigger battles elsewhere, fully expected to march in and plant their flag in southern Dobruja without encountering any resistance at all. This was more jamboree than invasion. By the side of the pontoon, wearing a curious pair of flying goggles, was King Carol himself, seventy-four years of age and waving his cheering men through.

But the celebrations ended abruptly. Within days, Romanian soldiers were dying like flies, not through war but from cholera. The villages they entered were filled with rotting corpses. Instead of shooting at the enemy, the Romanians needed to bury them to stop the disease spreading. Huge graves were dug and scattered with lime. But heavy rains and contaminated drinking water saw the outbreak turn into an epidemic.

Into that deadly environment came a young woman with no medical training, dressed in riding boots and a tailored jacket, insistent that she should nurse Romania's dying troops. When Princess Marie arrived at the cholera camps on 12 July 1913, she was shocked at the conditions she discovered. The sick were housed in leaking tents surrounded by stinking swamps of feces and waste. Volunteer nurses attempted to treat soldiers without medicine or any sort of organization. Most were the wives of Romanian aristocrats, good-natured but entirely ill-equipped.

Marie watched in horror as dying soldiers were put on pieces of board and laid out in front of the tents, in the vain hope that fresh air might resuscitate them.

Arriving at the same time was her old friend Elise Brătianu (wife of the prime minister and sister of Marie's lover, Barbu Ştirbey). She and Marie soon took control. Marie organized rations and supplies but was concerned about the Romanian soldiers on the more dangerous south bank of the Danube, in old Bulgarian territory, where conditions were said to be even worse. Banned from crossing the river by military commanders, she waited until nightfall and scurried across under cover of darkness.

In the third week of July, Marie made it to a cholera camp in southern Dobruja, where she was greeted by two exhausted doctors. 'It was', she wrote later, 'my first initiation into suffering on a large scale.' The place was submerged in days of monsoon rain so Marie waded around in riding boots, administering help to patients on pallets of straw. She knelt beside the dying, holding them with ungloved hands and refusing to wear a face mask – they deserved dignity, she said, in their final moments.

At the close of the Second Balkan War in August 1913, Romania had gained southern Dobruja but lost 6,000 men – all of them to cholera. For Marie the field tents had provided an epiphany. She had found herself a role. Romania had replaced Britain as her emotional homeland. She felt an 'immense urge towards service,' she said, 'a great wish to be of use, even to sacrifice myself if necessary, to put myself entirely at the disposal of my people.'

*

King Carol was in torment. With world war looming in the early summer of 1914, the German-born monarch was going to have to choose sides. There was no doubt that the majority of Romanians would want to join the conflict on the side of the Triple Entente – Britain, France and Russia – rather than the Central Powers of Germany and Austria-Hungary. They despised the Hungarians for their oppression of ethnic Romanians in Transylvania, and despised the Germans for supporting them. If Carol were to respond to Romanian public opinion, that was the way he would have to leap. But fighting against the country of his birth, against his own family, was unthinkable.

By late September, with much of Europe already declared for one side or another, Romania remained curiously silent. Leaders of the Central Powers were dumbfounded. They sent the Austrian ambassador to see Carol in Bucharest and chivvy him along. 'Honour obliges you to unsheathe your sword,' urged the ambassador. Carol was so overcome with indecision he is said to have thrown himself across his desk, weeping and shaking.

Romania's geographical position had always left it teetering on the fault line between East and West. Whenever there was conflict, it was besieged by alternating threats and enticements from all sides. Romania was a buffer state not just between warring countries, but between cultures, languages and ideologies. It was also enigmatic and unpredictable, a capricious ally capable of lightning changes of heart.

King Carol continued to agonize over which side to join, and on 3 August called a meeting of his Crown Council at Peleş Castle, the royal summer house in the mountain resort of Sinaia. Invitees included the leaders of the Liberal and Conservative parties, as well as Marie's lover, Barbu Ştirbey. As they arrived at the grand front entrance and were ushered to the state rooms, guests reported seeing members of the royal household in tears. Seventy-five-year-old Carol had been rendered ill with stress. Every meal time erupted into arguments, Marie counselling for a declaration on the side of Britain, Ferdinand trying to stay neutral, while the German-born queen scoffed at both, saying that London would be defeated and that the Germans '*must* become lords of the world for the good of humanity'.

The conference room at Peleş was like the officer's mess on

a naval ship, all wood panels and stale tobacco. Carol spoke first. Noticeably drawn and pale, he used French since he was unwilling to trust his Romanian when under pressure. He immediately went on the attack. Anyone present who supported the Entente was doing so out of sentiment, he said, and anyway, the Romanian public would never stomach an alliance that included the Russians, their centuries-old foe who regularly invaded the country's eastern flank. Romania, he said, should support the Central Powers. At the end of his speech, the room fell ominously silent.

It was left to the Liberal prime minister, Ion Brătianu, to respond. The most well-known politician in the land, polished, confident and clearly savouring the moment, declared that the king was wrong. Romania should not join the Austro-Hungarians. These were the very people oppressing Romanians in Transylvania. They might well make offers to be kinder in the future in return for Bucharest's support, but could they really be trusted after centuries of animosity? Britain and, in particular, France were Romania's cultural allies, he said. If they defeated the Austro-Hungarians, then Romania could be expected to be gifted Transylvania as a gesture of gratitude for its support. In the end, Brătianu recommended that Romania should stay neutral but that the public be gradually prepared to enter the war on the side of the Entente. His speech was greeted with enthusiastic applause.

All eyes turned to the crumpled figure of the king. 'Gentlemen,' he sobbed, 'you cannot imagine how bitter it is to find oneself isolated in a country of which one is not a native.' As he was assisted out of the chamber, his wife ran over and shouted, 'How dare they!' The king should abdicate, she cried, and 'shake the dust of this ungrateful country' from his feet.

Two months later, Romania was still neutral and Princess Marie was attending a horse race with Ferdinand in Bucharest. The couple had left the king in the mountain resort of Sinaia to take the air and try to recuperate. The horses were a welcome distraction both from his illness and the war. That night, 9 October 1914, Marie stayed at a friend's villa in the commune of Mogosoaia, just north of the capital. She was awoken at dawn by a telephone call. It was her lover, Barbu Ştirbey. King Carol had died. The girl from Kent fell silent while she took in the news. 'I was Queen,' she wrote later. 'I felt wholly capable of being Queen.'

The following afternoon, she stood beside Ferdinand in Parliament as he swore his oath to God and to country. Marie watched from behind a black mourning veil, as her husband addressed a room full of politicians who knew that his German roots predisposed him to siding with the Central Powers. His hands shook and he broke into sobs on several occasions. A polite round of applause followed.

Attention then turned to Marie. Shouts of 'Regina Maria' echoed around the chamber, at which point the new queen lifted her veil to smile and to thank them. 'And that was *my* hour,' she wrote later, 'mine – for at that moment it was not only an idea, not only a tradition or a symbol they were acclaiming, but a woman; a woman they loved.'⁴

CHAPTER THREE

Never did tombs look so ghastly white. Never did cypress, or yew, or juniper so seem the embodiment of funeral gloom. Never did tree or grass wave or rustle so ominously. Never did bough creak so mysteriously, and never did the far-away howling of dogs send such a woeful presage through the night.

Dracula (Dr Seward's Diary), Bram Stoker

It was slippery manoeuvring the Rolls-Royce around the shell craters near the battle front, particularly in the rain. The French countryside had been churned into sticky mud by the marching boots of soldiers and the heavy vehicles that supplied them, and the big old hulk slid uncontrollably, often requiring a winch to help it out of the deeper ruts. Behind the wheel was one Major John Norton-Griffiths, a raffish aristocrat with a passion for wild adventures. The forty-three-year-old British baronet was delivering fine French wines to his troops in the pitiful mud and cold on the Western Front to try to raise their spirits.

Norton-Griffiths was already a veteran of conflict and colonial derring-do. He had fought for the British South Africa Company in Matabeleland, mined diamonds and gold in the Congo, built harbours in Canada and dug aqueducts in Baku. He was, for some, the very definition of a dashing British officer, and had even found time to serve as a member of parliament, a tradition that was later passed down to his grandson, Jeremy Thorpe, the dandyish and controversial leader of Britain's Liberal party in the 1970s. But the unique skill that Norton-Griffiths possessed, and which would become invaluable in the First World War, was his extraordinary ability to dig tunnels.

Norton-Griffiths created a company of specialist engineers, known as the Manchester Moles, who burrowed deep beneath the Somme to lay explosives under German positions. It was extremely dangerous work, crawling under no man's land carrying tonnes of dynamite through dark tunnels, but Norton-Griffiths' corps of sewer men killed hundreds of Germans and were toasted across Whitehall. When a particularly perilous mission arose in 1915, requiring similar clandestine skills using high explosives not far from the Eastern Front, Norton-Griffiths seemed like the man for the job. His presence was required in Romania, where Europe's largest deposits of oil – a potentially decisive resource – were being eyed by the Germans.

By autumn 1915, Romania under King Ferdinand had still not chosen a side in the war. When the newly installed monarch examined the latest war charts, his was the only undeclared space on the map. The Eastern Front stretched a thousand miles, from the Baltic Sea in the north to the Black Sea in the south, and was alarmingly fluid, shifting tens of miles a day and leaving little time to dig trenches. In the southern portion, near Romania, the landscape was one of open steppes and thinly populated villages. Supply lines were unreliable, as were communications. The density of soldiers was low and the distances huge. Both sides were having to ghost around Romania's northern borders in a way that was causing resentment among military commanders. The pressure for Ferdinand to declare for one side or the other was intensifying.

In Bucharest, Romanian officials were engaged in a merry-go-round of deceit. They would lunch with the German delegation at the grand Athénée Palace Hotel, promising an imminent declaration for the Central Powers, before heading off to the

Café Moderne to meet the French, where similar promises of loyalty would be made to the Entente. Queen Marie was busier than ever, juggling her royal connections and trying to firm up promises of territorial gains – particularly Transylvania – in return for a declaration of military support. 'My dear George,' she wrote to her cousin, the king of England, 'Nando is placed in a very difficult position... he cannot launch into an adventure cutting himself away from his old moorings unless he can absolutely count upon the new ones...' Britain's ally, Russia, had made what appeared to be promises of vast swathes of territory, including Transylvania, but Marie was unconvinced. 'Russia can be a big bully,' she warned King George, referring to her cousin Nick, the Russian Czar, 'if England and France don't countersign her promises.'

Distrust between Romania and Russia was deep and long-standing. The Czars had repeatedly invaded their smaller neighbour through the ages, viewing it as a little Latin-speaking aberration in a vast sea of loyal Slavs. For successive residents of the Winter Palace, Romania seemed to have no purpose other than as a marching ground and a supplier of wheat and corn. They assumed it was theirs, if they could ever be bothered to mount a proper invasion. For most Romanians, the notion of joining Russia in the war was repellent, although not half as bad as joining the Hungarians.

On 27 August 1916, Ferdinand made his way to the Crown Council chamber of Cotroceni Palace, ready to announce his decision to the leading politicians of the day. The scene was reminiscent of the one that had faced his uncle, Carol, at the start of the war but since then, some extraordinary territorial promises had been made. In order to drag Romania across the line, the Entente (France, Britain and Russia) had promised land that was beyond the dreams of even the most fanciful nationalist. If Romania were to declare for the Entente, it would receive the forested territory of Bukovina in the far north (a land that was under the control of the Austro-Hungarian Empire), the Banat (another Austro-Hungarian territory to the west) and, crucially, all of Transylvania, including a section inhabited exclusively by Hungarians for which there was no ethnographic justification. This would truly create a Greater Romania.

At 10 a.m. sharp, the shaking Ferdinand entered the room, fighting to be heard above the din of voices. 'Although I am a member of the (German) Hohenzollern family,' he declared, 'I am the king of Romania first, and therefore I have to do what my subjects wish me to do… May Romania conquer her enemies, as I have conquered myself.' Romania, he announced, would side with the Entente. That afternoon, at 5 p.m., he declared war on the Austro-Hungarian Empire. Almost immediately Romanian troops stormed across the border into Transylvania. Caught off guard, the Germans were incensed. Newspapers in Berlin described the Romanians as 'the Latin traitors who were proving their descent from the deported criminals of ancient Rome'.[1] The following day, Germany declared war on Romania.

*

Pouring over the Transylvanian border, the Romanian 1st Army was astonished at the lack of resistance they encountered and found themselves advancing at an exhilarating fifteen miles a day. At the top of the Vulcan Pass, they met and defeated a small Hungarian coal-mining battalion. Further west, the Romanian 2nd Army advanced through the Red Tower Pass almost unhampered, sweeping towards the important cities of Sibiu, Făgăraş and Braşov – places from where Dracula had once launched his invasions of Wallachia. There was jubilation in Bucharest. Photographs of towns and monuments from the Roman era were splashed across the daily papers to prove they were now back in Romanian hands. When soldiers arrived in Romanian-speaking towns, crowds rushed to greet them as they would a liberating army, offering plum brandy, blankets and food.

After two weeks, the Romanian advance paused. Troops set up camp amongst the pine forests of their newly reclaimed mountainsides. The idea was to consolidate their gains and decide which chunk of Transylvania to chew off next. The enemy was still largely absent. Romania had been particularly concerned about the possibility of encountering German soldiers – stronger, more organized, and better trained than the Hungarians – but it seemed they were engaged in combat many miles to the north, against the Russians. As much as they could, the Romanian army began to settle and rest. Soldiers smoked and drank, and waited for orders.

But in their eagerness to take Transylvania, Romania's military commanders had taken their eyes off the country's southern border, where the Bulgarians had decided to fight with the Central Powers. At that very moment, a celebrated German officer, together with a sizeable army, was making his way discreetly southwards, via Serbia, to link up with the Bulgarians and to take command of a multinational task force.

August Von Mackensen was a military phenomenon. At sixty-six years old, with a chess player's brain and athlete's body, the irrepressible field marshal had lost none of his appetite for war. Back home in Germany, he was rarely out of the papers, posing in an oversize Hussar's hat that was emblazoned with a skull-and-crossbones. Such was his celebrity that he attracted a string of young female admirers and was currently married to a woman thirty-six years his junior. Mackensen's arrival in northern Bulgaria was part of a clever German strategy. As he waited astride his favourite white horse, he received a message from the German Command that he could attack. At the same time, 400 miles to the north-west in Transylvania, his German compatriots were hiding in the mountains, preparing for their first assault. Romania was about to be hit from the north and south simultaneously.

Moving steadily along the south bank of the Danube,

through the area of Dobruja so recently acquired by Romania, Mackensen's first target was the allegedly unbreachable fort town of Turtucaia. He attacked on 2 September 1916, making this the opening battle of the Central Powers' offensive against Romania. The fighting lasted four days, at the end of which 7,500 Romanian soldiers were dead and another 25,000 had surrendered. The field marshal's men camped that night beside the Danube and then rode on eastwards, deeper into Romanian territory, towards the country's most important port city of Constanța.

The Romanians were in disarray, trying to fight on two fronts at the same time. The Russians had promised to send a backup army of 300,000 troops to help in case of such an attack, but Queen Marie had been right to question the Czar's commitment to his unloved neighbour – he had sent just a fraction of that, around 50,000 men, and some were POWs with little enthusiasm for battle. Romania fought hard on both fronts but was overstretched and suffered terrible casualties. The country had effectively been abandoned by its allies. France and Britain were both too far away, fighting on the Western Front, and unable to offer any meaningful support. The Russian army, meanwhile, was suffering its own shortages in the face of sustained German attacks, and was stretched to breaking point along the thousand-mile Eastern Front. Left to fend for itself, Romania had just three months' supply of ammunition. Its hospitals were out of medicine, and there were so few doctors to treat the war-wounded that untrained peasant women had been brought in to stitch wounds.

In Bucharest, Queen Marie embarked on a spirit-raising tour of military compounds and hospitals as German Taube warplanes passed overhead. Zeppelins did their work at night, high and silent, tipping twenty bombs at a time onto sleeping homes. The capital's inhabitants hid in alleyways and cellars. In the evenings, Marie decamped to a modest cottage in the grounds of Prince Știrbey's estate, located in woodland outside Bucharest and well-hidden from aerial attack. The whole family relocated with her

– she had six children by then – and even Ferdinand was grateful to accept Ştirbey's hospitality. They lived a relatively spartan life, full of long winter walks and frugal home cooking.

Ferdinand left early each morning for army HQ and stayed away for days on end. For Marie, the king's absences were something of a relief, allowing her to set her own itinerary of hospital visits and meetings with foreign diplomats, occasions that she used to press for more military assistance and supplies. She also continued writing assertive letters to her royal cousins. We can imagine her on one of those bleak autumn nights, beside a flickering kerosene lamp, favourite Ottoman shawl drawn around her legs, a wood burner breathing blue smoke into the air. To her cousin Nick holed up in the Alexander Palace outside St Petersburg, she wrote: 'Unless we are helped *at once,* it may be too late.' But Tsar Nicholas II was struggling to control his own crumbling empire. 1917 was approaching. Revolution was in the air.

*

Britain's Lieutenant-Colonel John Norton-Griffiths would have driven his Rolls-Royce all the way to Romania had the army of the Central Powers not lain in his path. Instead, he had taken the long route, by train, via Norway, Finland and down into Russia before arriving on the far side of the Eastern Front during the third week of November 1916. From Bucharest he drove a borrowed car sixty miles north-west to Dracula's old capital city, Târgovişte, which was located close to the oil fields.

Norton-Griffiths did not have much time. Inside his attaché case were maps showing the locations of rigs and infrastructure across the country. Millions of tonnes of oil lay in shallow deposits at the foot of the Carpathian Mountains. These were the richest fields in Europe outside of Russia, and of huge strategic importance in what was to become the world's first mechanized war. Most countries had deposits in reserve but would be unable to fight for long without replenishing them. Britain and its allies could rely on imported crude from the United States but for Germany, with its rapidly expanding air force, supplies were problematic. The Central Powers had been purchasing Romanian oil for years and had been relying on a continued supply once they secured the country as an ally. When that failed to happen, the Germans diverted huge military effort into taking Romania's oil by force. As Griffiths settled down for the night in a chilly Târgovişte hotel room, German troops were advancing fast over the Carpathians.

Early the following day, a row of nervous-looking Romanian officials sat in front of the British officer as he spread his technical drawings across the table. The Romanian delegation suggested they present their case first. They understood, of course, that Romanian oil was the best hope for Germany and Austro-Hungary, and that it was imperative that the fields did not fall into enemy hands. They had a tentative plan to prevent that from happening: dig long trenches, drain the oil from the sites, set fire to it and then plug the wells. Griffiths listened in disbelief. Romania had fifty refineries and two thousand wells. The operation they were describing might take years to complete. He had a different plan – 'total and radical destruction' of all Romania's oil fields, whether the Romanians agreed or not.

As the German army stormed down the south-eastern flanks of the Carpathians onto the plains below, the oil fields in their sights, Field Marshal August von Mackensen and his troops were busy constructing a pontoon bridge to cross the Danube in the south. It was just a matter of time before they reached Bucharest.

On the evening of 25 November 1916, Queen Marie boarded a train out of the capital, accompanied by four of her children. Her youngest, three-year-old Mircea, had died of typhoid fever just three weeks before, and had been buried in the grounds of her beloved Cotroceni Palace. Marie had left a note for her gardener, written in German: 'I do not know who will occupy this house, this house which I loved – I only ask you not to remove the flowers from the small tomb.' Hurrying her family onto the train, she took a last look at Bucharest. The carriage was packed with trunks of clothes and crates of food. 'Endless, endless luggage,' she wrote. '... I do not know where we are going.' Beside her was Prince Ştirbey's wife, Nadeja, and her children. The train pulled out of Gara de Nord, heading away from the advancing enemy towards Romania's eastern region of Moldova and the Russian border.

Two days later, 27 November, John Norton-Griffiths and his small team arrived at the Romanian Consolidated Oilfields in Târgovişte, just ahead of the invading German army. The fourteen-acre site contained dozens of buildings, machine plants and storage reservoirs containing 35,000 tonnes of oil. Norton-Griffiths' team set to work straight away, digging knee-deep trenches into which they planned to release the reserves and ignite the entire facility. A second team, armed with sledge hammers and spades, smashed pipework, machinery and electrical circuitry, and dropped wrenches, screws and iron bars into the wells in order to jam the equipment. The sun had just set when the large pipes were severed and thousands of tonnes of oil began flooding the trenches. Norton-Griffiths was about to strike a match when a Romanian messenger ran over with an order from the local military commander to stop. 'No heed was paid to these orders', reported Griffiths proudly, 'and before we could be stopped the refinery was ablaze.'

Flames soared fifty metres into the night sky, scattering burning ash across Târgovişte and the surrounding countryside. Inhabitants locked themselves in their homes. The explosions went on for days. That night, the city's orange glow could be seen by advancing German troops.

Norton-Griffiths and his team continued eastwards, stopping at every oil refinery marked on the map. Roads were becoming impassable with refugees and retreating Romanian soldiers. The German army was just one day behind, and closing. At each site, Norton-Griffiths and his men smashed wells and severed pipes, jetting thousands of tonnes of oil into machinery and infrastructure and setting everything ablaze. They encountered fierce protests from Romanian officials. Sometimes there were fights and attempted arrests. But Norton-Griffiths pressed on, determined that the Germans would not get their hands on Romanian oil. He wrote a colourful account of explosions and near fatalities for officials back in London:

At the Vega refinery, one 50,000 ton reservoir was virtually lifted in the air and simultaneously the half-ton plates were scattered far beyond and around the officers working.

Captain Masterson and others barely escaped being crushed and burnt. An officer of the British Mission was literally blown out of the main exit into the open with his clothes partially alight. The spectacular sight was remarkable and the heavy volume of smoke which stretched for some 100 kilometers or more, must have considerably inconvenienced the enemy on the windward side.[2]

On 2 December, as the German army advanced to within five miles of Romania's capital, the people of Bucharest began a chaotic evacuation. Queues of horses and traps, along with what seemed like every car in Romania, snaked eastwards out of town. At one point, German planes appeared and strafed the sitting targets. The idea of having to flee the capital had not seemed at all likely the previous week, and people had had little time to pack. They took with them just clothes and a few valuables, and left the rest to the Germans. Evacuation was so unexpected that one British diplomat burned all his government papers in the consulate's backyard before running to the station, only to find that 30,000 others had got there before him. Desperate crowds were already spilling onto the tracks.

At the same time, in a private rail shed just beyond Gara de Nord, a consignment of secure crates was being loaded onto a different train, this one under armed guard. Inside were thousands of oil paintings, religious icons and priceless antiques, removed from royal palaces and the homes of boyars for safe-keeping. One carriage contained 120 tons of gold bars. Romania's entire treasury was on the move. Following behind were King Ferdinand and Prince Ştirbey, fleeing the capital just ahead of the advancing German cavalry.

The very next morning, a priest was passing by one of Romania's most important oil cities, Ploieşti, when he glanced up and witnessed a near-Biblical scene. 'Giant clouds of black smoke twist and bend like nervous dragons,' he wrote, 'tongues of fire are rising to hundreds of metres high. It is like the burning of Sodom and Gomorrah over which God has brought down fire from heaven. You have the impression that the world is over. It is an apocalyptic sight, pure and simple.'[3]

Somewhere inside the inferno was John Norton-Griffiths, ensuring 'complete destruction' of Romania's oil industry. The Germans arrived just hours behind him.

A week later, on 6 December 1916, a German officer with a skull-and-crossbones emblazoned on his Hussar's hat rode into Bucharest. There was patchy grey snow in the capital and fog hung in the air. The streets were almost deserted. Field Marshal Mackensen was followed by a long line of German cavalry. It was late afternoon but the hour hardly mattered. Bucharest had run out of time.

*

Ten miles from the Russian border was the grand old city of Iaşi (pronounced 'Yashi'), a place of soaring baroque architecture, stunning boyar mansions, avant-garde theatres, artists' studios, galleries and an ancient university. Situated in the eastern region of Moldova, it was Romania's second largest city, a bustling, cosmopolitan hub whose proximity to Russia was both a blessing and a curse. Iași had come under attack from Imperial troops in the seventeenth century and was always vulnerable to lightning Russian incursions. But as German, Austro-Hungarian and Bulgarian soldiers poured into Romania at the end of 1916, it seemed like the safest place to be. The entire machinery of the Romanian government decamped to Iași, huddled in the protective shadow of their Russian ally, from where they continued to wage war against the Central Powers.

By the first week of January 1917, the streets of this great city were awash with a quarter of a million refugees from all over Romania. Abandoned vehicles clogged the streets. Disorientated crowds milled around in the snow. Accommodation was nearly impossible to find. The rich had taken all the houses and single rooms were at a premium. Multiple families squeezed into any shelter they could find. Many slept on the freezing streets, building makeshift tents from blankets and clothes. Within a week, food was scarce. The city's famous Copou Park became a campsite. At night, gangs roamed the wooded areas, felling trees for fuel. At one stage, the French ambassador apologized to the Romanian authorities after discovering his own officials were sourcing the consulate's firewood from the park's ancient woodland. The Romanians told him not to worry. Most of the exiled government had been reduced to doing the same.

The German line swept eastwards almost as fast as their horses could gallop, chasing what was left of Romania into an ever-tightening pocket of land. People abandoned their homes in town after town and began following their government and royal family east. Four million of them were soon on the road, half Romania's population. The Russian Czar suggested they should take refuge behind his borders before the whole country was gone, but Queen Marie refused. The humiliation of surrendering her entire territory to the Germans would be too much to bear. She and Ferdinand insisted on staying in Iași but the territory kept shrinking. The battle lines finally stabilised in the second week of January 1917, and by that time the Central Powers occupied seventy per cent of the country. Around the perimeter of this pitiful rump – containing scattered rural villages on the plains around Iași – Romanian and Russian soldiers joined forces and began to dig themselves in.

Marie spent the first two weeks of her exile living in the railway carriage in which she had arrived. When she was joined by Ferdinand, the royal couple moved into the former nineteenth-century palace of Alexandru Ioan Cuza (founder of the United Principalities), a fussy manor house in the centre of town. Ferdinand had brought with him the couple's eldest son, Carol, whose presence worried Marie. Although she doted on her tall, overly groomed son, she felt it was important that he was seen at the frontline fighting for his country. Now aged twenty-four, Carol had turned into a languorous playboy with a passion for luxury motorcars and dancing. There were rumours he had already fathered two illegitimate children with a teenager. His father had sent him away for military training to instil some discipline but Carol had returned with a nasty streak of aloofness. Marie pressed Ferdinand to take the young man with him while inspecting the trenches but Ferdinand preferred not to have the capricious Carol near him. Left to his own devices in Iași, Carol managed to hire a chauffeur and a car, and installed himself in what must have been the only drinking den left open in the city.

For everyone else, conditions in Iași were worsening. In mid-January, incoming Russian troops had brought with them lice infected with typhus fever. The disease spread quickly through a population already ill with hunger and cold. By February it had become an epidemic, spreading not just through the streets but the trenches as well, claiming the lives of 350,000 Romanians – more than the country lost in fighting.

Russian soldiers who were sharing the city seemed to fare better. They had arrived in Iași before the mass evacuation of

Bucharest and had taken all the plum buildings, some of which they had converted into hospitals. The Russians had better food and more medicines than the Romanians and kept it all to themselves. Officers, in particular, seemed to be in rude health. They had brought with them herds of cows and pigs, as well as supplies of grain and fuel, achieving something like self-sufficiency. Russian imperial commanders were driven to the front by chauffeurs in limousines, with maids carrying picnic baskets of fine foods and champagne. Their mistresses would travel with them, often disguised as nurses or even nuns. Meanwhile, the lower orders shared cheap vodka in the stinking trenches. It was no surprise that Bolshevik leaflets had found their way to the Romanian front from Petrograd. So too had groups of politicized young men preaching revolution. Their message resonated deeply with hungry Russian soldiers defending a foreign border far from home.

There was, though, one small moment of celebration amid the squalor and the death. Marie and Ferdinand had decided to keep parliament functioning and to continue bestowing honours in order to retain a semblance of normality. One of the first to be recognized was a dishevelled Englishman, who rode into Iaşi from behind enemy lines, wearing scorched clothes and wreathed in the smell of oil. John Norton-Griffiths had caused so much damage to Romania's oil fields that the occupying German army were left without meaningful supplies for at least a year. Although many Romanians had objected to his actions, Queen Marie awarded him the Star of Romania, the highest accolade available to a foreigner.

In the meantime, all Romania's gold and royal treasures were sent to Moscow for safe-keeping in the Kremlin. With the Russian revolution just around the corner, they would never be seen again.

*

Dressed in the simple white habit of a nursing sister, Marie toured the field hospitals just behind the lines in February 1917, distributing Orthodox crosses and cigarettes to the wounded and the diseased. She impressed with the same selflessness she had shown in the cholera camps of the Danube, refusing to wear face masks or plastic gloves, while feeding spoonfuls of jam and sweet marmalade into the mouths of the sick – a gesture for which she often received a hug and a kiss. When one alarmed lady-in-waiting urged Marie to comply with the rules, she was withering in her response. 'I really can't ask them to kiss Indian rubber!' she sniffed. Images of Marie kneeling in the mud and the gloom, holding the emaciated hands of soldiers who were able to smile in their final moments were flashed around the world, appearing in European and American newspapers where she was referred to as 'the plucky queen'. But it was the stories she heard about the Russian troops that concerned her.

The Romanian wounded described to Marie how their supposed allies had downed their weapons and refused to fight. Some had pulled themselves up out of the trenches and wandered off in groups, crossing no man's land and waving white flags. They had made contact with the German and Austro-Hungarian enemy and explained that they did not want to fight. Their quarrel, said the rebelling Russians, was not with their fellow working men but with Europe's imperialist leaders. Some spent days in the company of the enemy, sharing cigarettes and brandy, and passing on intelligence about Entente positions.

Then, on 22 February 1917, Marie returned, cold and exhausted, from the field hospitals to her temporary palace in Iaşi to learn of historic developments. There had been a mutiny against her cousin Nick in Petrograd. A quarter-of-a-million starving people were on the streets, demanding an end to the war and the resignation of the Czar. Imperial troops had responded by firing indiscriminately on the crowds, at which point the protests had grown in scale and intensity. Marie listened anxiously to her radio for news. Ten days later, she learned that Nicholas, the man whose coronation she had attended as a spirited twenty-one-year-old in 1896, had been forced to abdicate and replaced by a provisional government. Marie was horrified and anxious about the consequences – for Romania and for her own royal line. Her cousin's empire, it seemed, was disintegrating. If Russia were to pull out of the war, where would that leave Romania? When Ferdinand heard the news, he was overcome. 'What misfortune, what misfortune,' he sobbed. 'It is dreadful, what are we going to do?'[4]

As news of events in Petrograd spread through the trenches, Russian soldiers began rebelling. Refusing to take orders from their 'imperialist' officers, more of them wandered over the front to fraternize with the enemy. In Iași itself, mobs of deserting Russian soldiers descended on the prison where a group of Romanian socialist intellectuals had been held as punishment for their opposition to the war. On 1 May 1917, the Russians sprang them from jail and a jubilant crowd conveyed them to a mass Bolshevik rally in Copou Park. In front of 15,000 people, the ringleaders announced that their soldiers would continue to support their Romanian brothers in the war but only if the Romanians overthrew their own feudal royal family.

The highest-profile escapee that day was an elegant young physician and lawyer from a land-owning family in Dobruja, who had become the spiritual leader of Romania's underground Left. Christian Rakovsky was a close friend and collaborator of Leon Trotsky, the two having met as journalists during the Balkan Wars, bonding over vodka and their passion for Marxist literature. Now the newly freed Rakovsky was invited onto stage amidst cheers and red flags. He congratulated the Russians on their successful revolution but said that Romania was not yet ready to overthrow its monarchy. The crowd applauded anyway, thinking him a typically cautious intellectual but a revolutionary nonetheless. Rakovsky was hoisted onto their shoulders and carried aloft, before being spirited across the border to the Russian city of Odessa, where Romanian socialists were organizing what amounted to a government-in-exile. That afternoon, a small crowd gathered outside Marie and Ferdinand's temporary palace, chanting for revolution and threatening to drag the royal couple off to prison.

In the summer, cornflowers and poppies filled the war-scarred meadows along the length of the Romanian front. With the warm weather came a sense of rejuvenation among the troops. A French military commander had spent several months vigorously rebuilding their morale and their fire-power and, despite straitened circumstances, spirits were high. There was relatively good news, too, from the Russian side. Against expectations, the Russian army had not entirely disintegrated. Most men were still at their posts, though distracted by events back home, and waiting for orders from Moscow's provisional government. During June and July, a young Romanian lieutenant-colonel devised a detailed plan to counter-attack the seemingly impregnable German line.

His name was Ion Antonescu, a quiet, almost monastic, thirty-five-year-old who was chief of staff to the famed Romanian commander, General Constantin Prezan. The young Antonescu was not loved – he was too self-assured and puritanical for most people's liking – but he was a clever tactician and a fierce patriot who commanded the respect of his men. With his wiry red hair and his indefatigable fighting spirit, Antonescu was known as 'Red Dog'. Later, he would become one of Romania's most controversial leaders, heading a fascist-style government and befriending Adolf Hitler.

For now, though, in July 1917, Antonescu was living in spartan conditions at Army Headquarters in Iaşi, a bright star among jaded generals. He took the view that there was no better way of dampening revolutionary fervour than sending men into battle. His superiors agreed and it was decided that Romania and Russia would launch an attack against the German 9th

Army in July. It would take place 120 miles south of Iași, near to
Mărăști, a one-road village with a pretty Orthodox church and
rose-coloured cottages. The plan was to encircle and destroy the
enemy, puncturing a hole in the Eastern Front and showing the
Germans that the Romanians were still full of fight.

A massive artillery bombardment announced the launch of
the famous battle on 22 July 1917, with Romanian and Russian
troops sweeping through the wrecked German defences,
supported overhead by Allied warplanes. Charging through
clouds of mustard gas, ground troops broke through the German
line and advanced an astonishing seventeen miles, resulting in
the liberation of 500 square miles of Romanian territory. It was
the fastest advance of any Allied action in the European theatre
of war in 1917. But all the hard work had been done by the
Romanians. The Russians behaved in a manner that would go
down in Romanian history as a reason never to trust them again.

At the height of the attack, a unit of Russian soldiers could
be heard shouting out warm greetings to their 'brothers' on the
other side in the German trenches. Thousands of Russians leapt
from the trenches and fled, leaving their astonished Romanian
colleagues to plug the gaps in the line. As they ran, the Russians
uprooted telephone lines and blocked bridges so that no more
'imperialist' Romanian troops could make their way to the front.
The hills and forests behind the fighting became a kind of bandit
country, where Russian fugitives camped out and organized
Bolshevik meetings.

The situation became even more tumultuous following
developments in Russia in the autumn of 1917, when Petrograd
Bolsheviks seized the Winter Palace on 25 October and Lenin
and Trotsky took control. News of the Russian Revolution was
greeted by anarchy among Russian soldiers on the Romanian
front. In the trenches, mobs turned on their officers and beat
them. The soldiers of Regiment 119 stormed their officers' mess,
overturning tables, smashing equipment and forcing their leaders

to jump out of the windows and flee. One commanding officer, a General Zuborov, spent five hours negotiating with his men and thought he had persuaded them to see sense. As he tried to leave, they grabbed him and beat him to death. Anarchy spread into the Romanian countryside, with gangs of Russians terrorizing towns and villages, setting fire to property, stealing anything they could find and raping young women. The Romanian army was left with little choice but to take the extraordinary action of turning on its own allies, surrounding units of Bolshevized Russian soldiers at gunpoint and forcing them to disarm.

With Russia descending into civil war, the nascent Soviet state ended its involvement in the First World War in December 1917, negotiating a formal and costly settlement with the Central Powers in the Treaty of Brest-Litovsk. Romania was left in a desperate situation. Abandoned by its closest geographical ally and surrounded by German and Austro-Hungarian forces, it had no choice but to surrender, and sue for peace. The consequences would be catastrophic. The Central Powers could impose any territorial price they chose.

Romania would have to surrender its coastal region of Dobruja – the territory triumphantly seized from Bulgaria just four years earlier. Romania's oil would become the property of an Austro-German company, not just until the end of the war but supposedly for the next ninety years. Most painful of all, the Hungarians would be handed back the talismanic region of Transylvania. There was one glimmer of hope, however – the Romanians would be granted the previously Russian-held territory of Bessarabia, a long, finger-shaped strip of land east of Iași, where ethnic Romanians were in the majority. It would become a useful buffer state between the Central Powers and the Russians along the length of Romania's eastern flank. In the meantime, Romania would be run by a German army of occupation.

Marie would have none of it. She announced she would rather die than be governed by Germans, and threatened to march into

Russia to round up an army of 'still faithful' Cossacks, who would return with her to force the Central Powers out of Romania. Marie's officials gently reminded her that Russia was no longer an ally of any sort and that a growing number of Romanian socialists were gathering there, in the port city of Odessa, proclaiming themselves Bolsheviks and trying to foment a revolution in their homeland. Led by Trotsky's friend, the urbane physician-lawyer Christian Rakovsky, these Romanian revolutionaries were already a belligerent force, kidnapping Romanian officials who had fled to Russia for safety. If Marie so much as put a foot over the border, there was a danger she might follow them into Odessa's cellars. It was Trotsky who now announced that all Romanian gold and treasure sent to the Kremlin for safe-keeping would be appropriated by 'the people'.

In the spring of 1918, Marie organized one last banquet to bid farewell to Entente officials, all of whom had been ordered out of the territory by the occupying Germans. Dressed in a blue gown with cream satin sash, gold and silver medals on her chest, and a peacock feather in her tiara, Marie kissed each of them on the cheeks as they departed. One French official, General Berthelot, tried to give a speech of thanks but broke down in tears. A representative of the American Red Cross fell at Marie's feet and kissed the hem of her dress.

Before she left Iași by train, surrounded by trunks and ladies-in-waiting, on 9 March 1918, Marie wrote one final telegram to her cousin George, king of England. 'It is not peace,' she said, 'it is foreign occupation, it is living death, it is strangulation.' And with that, she withdrew to a small house in the remote Moldovan village of Cotofanesti, where she lived among the gypsies and the peasant farmers, grooming her beloved horses and sleeping beneath the stars.

But what of her delinquent son, Carol? After spending the war intoxicated among the boyar party-set of Iași, the young, uniformed heir to the throne had taken advantage of his country's withdrawal from fighting, making an impromptu attempt to cross the border into Russia on 31 August 1918 – with a girl at his side. Their chauffeur was stopped by a German patrol, who recognized Carol as the heir to the Romanian throne and saw no problem in allowing him out of the country. One less royal would make the German job of converting Romania into a republic a little easier.

The girl accompanying Carol that evening was a well-connected general's daughter by the name of Zizi Lambrino, beautiful, bright and so besotted by the Prince that she was able to forgive him his already-notorious wandering eye. That night, Carol and Zizi discreetly checked in at the Bristol Hotel in Odessa. Days later they were standing before a priest in the city's near-empty Orthodox Cathedral, exchanging rings and placing garlands on each other's heads. Twenty-year-old Zizi had just become the future queen of Romania. The panicking Carol agreed that he should tell his parents about the marriage as soon as possible. But not just yet. He wasn't in the mood.

Marie and Ferdinand were informed by the delighted German occupiers, who read the news on a telegraph from a spy who had been watching Zizi and Carol since the moment they left Romania. The full magnitude of their son's actions took a few moments to sink in. Carol was a soldier in the Romanian army and, even under occupation, needed to ask his commanding officer for permission to leave his post. He had not done so. Technically that was desertion, a serious offence. More troubling was the fact that Carol had married a commoner. The Romanian constitution, written at the time the country had become a monarchy, specified that the crown prince must only marry into royal blood. By failing to do so, Carol had effectively just abandoned his title and could not become king.

Marie rushed off to Odessa, risking being trapped by Romanian Bolsheviks, and found Carol in his hotel room, full of incoherent excuses. He told her that his intention on leaving the country had been to make his way to the Western Front to fight alongside the French. Zizi had come along for the ride. And the marriage? Well, he loved the woman and it had been a spontaneous thing. Marie was touched by his impulsiveness and embraced her weeping son. She reassured him that, after the war, he could re-join his bride but, in the meantime, he had an appointment back home with his less sentimental father.

In occupied Bucharest, a distraught Carol was called to his father's office where he was warned that desertion carried a maximum sentence of death. It was a criminal offence and one that must attract punishment. With a book of military law in his hand, and surrounded by lawyers and aides, Ferdinand himself pronounced sentence upon his son. He would be jailed for two and a half months, and with that Carol was led away, weeping, to serve his sentence at the mountain monastery of Horaitza in the depths of the wild forests to the east of Baltatesti. Of course, imprisonment was really just an excuse to keep him away from Zizi, in the hope that the relationship would fade. In the meantime, Ferdinand consulted lawyers to try to engineer an annulment of Carol's marriage.

That autumn, the queen visited her eldest son in his simple, ecclesiastical cell and took with her books and a pet dog to keep him company. She found him despondent, yet uncompromising in his love for Zizi. He was 'howling', she reported back to Ferdinand, and she had cried along with him, mortified that she had been involved in such 'a cruel and sickening victory'.

The following January, with Carol out of custody but closely monitored, his young wife was rushed to hospital in Bucharest. She had been pregnant at the time of their marriage. Carol knew but had told no one. Zizi gave birth to a baby boy but the palace forbade the father from attending her bedside. Immediately after Zizi was discharged, Ferdinand's aides swung into action, forcing the young mother to move to Paris with the child, where she was promised maintenance payments for the rest of her life if she kept quiet. Ferdinand finally managed to annul his son's marriage in August 1919 but even then, Carol's ardour was not dampened. Distraught and cursing his father, the Prince ran back to Zizi, and renounced the throne.

He ricocheted back and forth between Zizi and his mother for much of 1919 but his father's aides knew Carol's weakness and exploited it mercilessly. They arranged a series of balls, where they placed an assortment of Bucharest's most beautiful women in his sights – a campaign that eventually corroded his loyalty to Zizi and saw him reinstated as Crown Prince.[5]

*

Entente victory in the First World War, secured on 11 November 1918, was greeted with weary relief in occupied Romania but no celebration. As German officials left Bucharest, they looted everything they could find. Livestock and grain were loaded onto trains. Hundreds of factories were stripped of machinery and produce. Private homes were robbed of gold, silver, artworks, everything right down to table linen and crockery. Even the rail network was stolen, with 1,150 locomotives and carriages spirited across the border into Hungary. While London and Paris celebrated the armistice with street parties, Bucharest's shell-shocked inhabitants found themselves wandering around the ruins, scavenging and dressed in rags. With the country's gold now in the hands of the Bolsheviks, Romania's politicians had no money with which to start rebuilding. All eyes turned to Paris and the redrawing of Europe's borders, scheduled for the following year, a process during which Romania might at least win back some pride.

In January 1919, the streets of the French capital were filled with cheering crowds as leaders from around the world arrived to divide the spoils of war. Four power blocks had ceased to be: the German Empire, the Russian Empire, the Austro-Hungarian Empire and the Ottoman Empire. Never had Europe seen such profound political change in such a short space of time.

Equipped with just notepads and pencils, the most important statesmen of the age were ushered into the Quai d'Orsay's famously ornate Clock Room. Here, the continent's future would be decided according to new liberal attitudes towards ethnicity and religion, and a more equitable balance between large and small states. Most left their military uniforms at the door but the seating plan, around the horseshoe table, was still all about military status. At the top end were the French, British and American delegates, with lesser countries positioned further away from the action. Romania's prime minister, the elegant but prickly Ion Brătianu, was incensed to find himself sitting between Poland and Siam. When called upon to make his case for Romanian territorial gains, Brătianu delivered a long-winded and ill-judged speech, in which he railed against the Entente for failing to come to Romania's aid.

Britain and America listened bemused to the unknown parvenu who spoke with such ponderous self-importance. He argued that Romania should receive all the land they had been promised and ought to be treated as if the country had fought with the others to the bitter end. It was not Romania's fault, said Brătianu, that they had been forced to surrender, but that of France and Britain for abandoning the Eastern Front. Brătianu addressed the room about arcane Roman history and the country's ancient territorial rights to Transylvania. At one point, the British prime minister, David Lloyd George, leaned across to a colleague and murmured, 'Where the hell is that place (Transylvania) that Romania is so anxious to get?' One can only assume Lloyd George had not read Bram Stoker's book.

Within days, it became clear to the rest of the Romanian delegation that Brătianu had become a liability. They needed an individual of more refined rhetorical powers, someone who understood Western sensibilities and who might penetrate the cabal of the Great Powers by sheer force of personality.

Queen Marie arrived in Paris on an overcast morning in

March 1919, descending from the train into a riot of flashbulbs and fresh spring bouquets. Quickly engulfed by crowds of fashionable young French women who had seen her picture in magazines, Marie was in her element. One female reporter, caught in the melee, declared herself so overcome by 'the glow in Marie's imperious yet soft eyes' that she was unable to speak. At least twenty journalists followed her to the Paris Ritz and camped outside.

Marie had taken a twenty-room suite, quite against the austere mood of the occasion, particularly as the French prime minister – and president of the Conference – Georges Clemenceau was living alone in a simple flat across the river. Known as 'The Tiger' for his love of war and uncompromising personality (he had loathed the Romanian prime minister, Brătianu), it was he who Marie would need to convince of Romania's case.

When Clemenceau first saw Marie arriving in her limousine, he came bouncing down the steps of the Quai d'Orsay to escort her into his private office. The Frenchman was a throwback to a different age, where armies never surrendered and a nation must suffer in order to raise itself to the civilized heights of France. Such was his hatred of Germany that he is said to have wept with anger when he heard that the Kaiser had agreed an armistice. Romania's capitulation to the enemy was, in Clemenceau's view of the world, inexcusable. He told Marie that he was dumbfounded by her country's actions and needed an explanation as to why they tried to settle their own peace with 'the Boches'. Marie listened and smiled disarmingly. 'Yes,' she said, 'we were encircled by our enemy and our Allies as well… we were tracked like game.' The queen then began explaining her country's Roman roots and the bases of its claims to significant territories around central and eastern Europe.

'How much of that do you want?' asked Clemenceau.

'Nearly all of it,' responded Marie with a mischievous smile.

'What?' gasped the French prime minister. 'Your Majesty

desires the whole of the Banat [a contested region located on Romania's western flank] as far as the Tisza River? – but that is the lion's share!'

Unperturbed, Marie nodded slowly. 'Yes,' she said, 'that is why I have come to see his first cousin, the Tiger!'

Marie's rounds of informal meetings and flirtatious chats ended up bending the arc of history. Followed everywhere she went by admirers and journalists, she represented a refreshing blast of Balkan air into the fusty old order. When the announcement of territorial awards was made in the series of treaties that followed the Paris Peace Conference in 1920, it was nothing short of sensational for Romania. Bucharest would receive all of Transylvania, nearly all of Bukovina, Bessarabia, the southern Dobruja and two-thirds of the Banat. Overnight, Romanian territory would more than double in size. So too would its population, from 8 million to 16 million. Having almost disappeared at the hands of the Germans, it was now the fifth largest country in Europe.

This was the birth of Greater Romania – what Romanians call 'România dodoloața' – 'plump Romania'. It was the moment that nationalists had dreamed of for generations, brought about, largely, by their British queen, and finally fusing together Romanian-speaking regions that had been prised apart by invasion, forced assimilation, treaties and war. But such lightning expansion heralded unforeseen challenges. The country would also inherit hundreds of thousands of Slavs, Magyars, Saxons, Jews and Muslims, the people who co-inhabited these territories and who viewed the government in Bucharest as a hostile agent. Their worries were not without foundation. Romania would have to accommodate them all.[6]

CHAPTER FOUR

Take this stake in your left hand, ready to place the point over the heart, and the hammer in your right. Then when we begin our prayer for the dead, I shall read him, I have here the book, and others shall follow, strike in God's name, that so all may be well with the dead that we love and that the Un-Dead pass away.

Dracula (Dr Seward's Diary), Bram Stoker

At ninety-three years old, George Cuşa is a rare survivor. He talks with the slow purpose and subdued tone of another age, when Romanian politics was violent and polarized, and any misjudged word or deed might cost a life. He speaks of 'underground resistance movements', 're-education programmes', 'preliminary selection for labour camps', words that sound incongruous on a spring afternoon by the sea in Constanţa. He uses the word 'liquidation' often.

Cuşa tells me he doesn't want to cry. He is erudite, erect, sharp-featured with a hawkish nose and pale green eyes, but telling his story will take him back to a time that sounds more fifteenth-century Dracula than twentieth-century Europe, and he is worried he might break down. This solemn gentleman is one of just three survivors of a grotesque human experiment, one so depraved that Aleksandr Solzhenitsyn called it 'the most terrible act of barbarism in the contemporary world'.

Its purpose was to change Cuşa's political views by causing

such trauma to his mind that he would become docile and pliant, and cause no further trouble to the communist authorities. Before we begin, he rises slowly and pads off down the stone hallway, whispering gently to his ailing wife in the next-door room. He returns with a single photograph, inspects it for a moment and then slides it across the table. It bears the image of a young man – handsome, intense, hair swept back like that of a polar explorer. The man is in his thirties, dressed in traditional Romanian costume, a fur-trimmed waistcoat and woollen blazer of the sort favoured by peasants, but his features are pale, chiselled, aristocratic. 'This is where it starts,' says Cuşa, 'this was the man I admired.' He pours himself a glass of water from a plastic bottle, and sips. 'I was only thirteen when I read about him', says Cuşa, 'but I knew I wanted to be one of his followers, a Legionary.' He studies the image, and shakes his head wistfully.

The man in the photograph is Corneliu Zelea Codreanu, a young intellectual and activist who became one of Romania's most alluring political figures between the wars, known to his many followers as *Căpitanul*, or the Captain. Codreanu is often depicted as a religious icon, with a golden halo around his head and a wooden crucifix in his hand. In his marriage photographs, he and his wife, Elena, look like children of the night, with intense, haunted eyes, folk costumes, and cascading glass beads. If you look closely at their fairy crowns, in the centre of each appears to be a swastika.

Codreanu's story begins in the eastern city of Iaşi, shortly after the creation of Greater Romania in 1920 when, all along this border close to revolutionary Russia, the Bolshevik spell had captured people's hearts like nowhere else in the country. The southern quarter of Iaşi, a bleak industrial landscape of half-abandoned factories and soot-stained workshops, had been where defecting Russian troops assembled at the war's end, before joining their comrades after the October Revolution. It was here they mingled freely with locals, and where their ideas began to spread.

As Iași tried to rebuild itself, in the autumn of 1920 there was a communist-inspired demonstration almost every week, with red cotton flags hoisted over the grim rail yards of Nicolina. For Romanian soldiers who had recently returned from the front (Romania carried on fighting in Hungary until the spring of 1920), there seemed little to celebrate. Uninterested in their newly expanded borders, they arrived back to a city plagued by hunger, unpaid wages, and limited infrastructure. It seemed to them that, in return for the sacrifice of so many (600,000 Romanians had died in the war, 8 per cent of the population) nothing had changed. Over the border, they heard that their Russian counterparts were running their own factories and their own regional committees. The bourgeois imperialists had been defeated. The Czar and his family were dead, executed by the Bolsheviks in the basement of Ipatiev House in Yekaterinburg. But the returning Romanians found the old order intact, the king and queen still in the palace.

In mid-October, 5,000 Romanian socialists filled Iași's Union Square, singing the 'Internationale', just as twenty-year-old Corneliu Codreanu arrived to begin studying law at the city's ancient and prestigious university. An enthusiastic nationalist, Codreanu was appalled by what he saw and could only assume that the marchers were sponsored by Moscow, as part of an attempt to try to take over Romania. He searched the university's bars and clubs for people who might take on these Bolshevik sympathizers, but could find no one willing. Horrified by their lack of patriotism, he set off around the city to try to find like-minded individuals, and eventually came upon a group of right-wing locals who held regular weekly meetings in a local church hall.

Their leader was a local tradesman called Constantin Pancu, a thick-necked plumber who believed all communists should be 'knocked out' and that Jews were 'incomers' from Russia who were, without exception, Bolsheviks. Pancu was already something of a local celebrity, having stepped forward at a travelling circus to fight the resident strongman, and won. His subsequent status as charismatic brawler and unyielding patriot attracted a keen following among the local thugs and racists of Iași, and when Pancu clambered onto stage, they realized they had a natural orator in their midst. Codreanu had never met anyone like him. As a privileged student from the wine-making region of Huși, the young scholar marvelled at how a man with no education could have formed such coherent and well-informed views.

From then on, Pancu and Codreanu became firm friends and, when the communists began organizing their winter marches, the pair raised a unit of local patriots and royalists to try to stop them. The men and women who turned up that day to support Pancu and Codreanu were not just the usual band of misfits and malcontents, but educated professionals from all sectors of society. There were trainee priests, academics, lawyers, accountants, and local businessmen. They met at a hall with intended symbolic significance – it was named after their beloved Queen Marie's deceased baby, Prince Mircea – where attendees sang rousing marching hymns and waved the Romanian tricolour. Then they set off to ambush the communists at Union Square. As they rounded the corner, a column of police officers blocked their way. Codreanu and his comrades responded with exaggerated courtesy. Of course they would retreat. They wanted no trouble. They marched instead to Iași's railway station, where they commandeered a train to the sooty rail sheds of Nicolina to confront the communists in their headquarters.[1]

Holding a Romanian tricolour between his teeth, Codreanu scrambled up a rusting fire escape to a rooftop and began tearing down red flags. Encouraging cheers rang out in the yard below but a crowd of communists had also gathered, and the two groups began squaring up. Codreanu shouted antagonistic slogans and then clambered down into what he described as 'an infernal racket', where he was scooped up by the imposing Pancu and manoeuvred through the crowd. The young scholar had every right to be terrified. He wrote later that he was expecting 'the whizz of a bullet' at any moment, but the communists surprised him. 'For about ten yards we walked in tomb-like silence through their midst,' he said. There was no violence. Codreanu was allowed to pass right through. It was, of course, down to the presence of the burly Pancu, but Codreanu believed he had personally repulsed the mob by using his own mystical powers. It is worth noting that, had there been trouble, the trainee lawyer had a more vulgarly material deterrent in his coat pocket. He was now in the habit of carrying a gun.

For Codreanu and his band of nationalists, the creation of Greater Romania had not been a gift from the Allies at the end of the war; it had never been theirs to give in the first place. The dramatic expansion of the country was merely the rectification of long-standing territorial injustices. After 2,000 years of heroic struggle, the Romanians had finally retrieved what had always been theirs. The problem for Codreanu and other nationalists was that all those neighbouring countries who had lost land in the Paris Conference now wanted it back. Wails of irredentism replaced the cries of war and became the dominant theme of international affairs throughout the following decade. Hungary wanted Transylvania; Bulgaria, the Dobruja; Russia, the restoration of Bessarabia and Northern Bukovina. Repelling the threat of invasion became the glue that bound Codreanu and his associates together. This was a form of 'siege nationalism' and the greater the perceived threat, the stronger they became.

It followed, therefore, that the only men and women who could be trusted to protect the nation were pure-blooded Romanians, people whose ancestral bones were scattered in the earth and whose heritage was undiluted by foreign (and therefore, Jewish) blood. Romania's very soil was Christian and holy. Its people were born of it and buried beneath it. The soil tilled by peasants on the Dobruja steppes, the delta's loamy fields, the cracked plains of sunflowers in the south – all were enriched by Romania's war dead, the men who had protected this land from invading armies down the centuries. Codreanu spent his weekends collecting soil from hallowed turf, from Roman ruins and ancient battlefields. He would pray over it and then place the dirt into a leather pouch that he would wear around his neck. He distributed similar lucky charms to his friends and supporters, and these tokens soon became part of the ultra-nationalists' tradition.

Codreanu was starting to tap into a current of xenophobia fuelled by the fear of losing any part of the Romanian homeland. Several of his lecturers recommended books about 'scientific racism', made fashionable by the French writer Arthur de Gobineau, the man who developed the theory of an Aryan master race. Chief among Gobineau's followers at the University of Iași was its professor of law, Alexandru C. Cuza, a priggish intellectual snob who strode the corridors – his pomaded moustache pointing upwards like antlers – pursued by a gaggle of excited, right-wing students. Cuza had set up a xenophobic political party before the war, the Democratic Nationalist Party, and had done so with the help of the famous anti-Semitic historian, Nicolae Iorga. The two had arrived at their ultra-nationalist positions via different routes. The bearded Iorga had seen it as a way of protecting the peasants and preserving their ancient way of life. He still believed Jews were responsible for the extortionate land rents that had precipitated the Peasant Revolt, and viewed himself as an earthy, agrarian traditionalist. Cuza, on the other hand, believed that a worldwide, communist conspiracy of Jews (Judeo-Bolshevism) was trying to take over Europe, led, in the main, by Trotsky, and that they had to be stopped in order to protect Romania's ruling elite.

The Jewish population of Iași in the 1920s was around fifty per cent. It was no mystery how this had come about. Russia's anti-Semitic laws had, for decades, barred Jews from living anywhere other than specially demarcated regions to the extreme west of the country – the so-called Pale of Settlement. The effect was to squeeze them right up against Romania's border, particularly in

Ukraine and Bessarabia. Faced with such a bleak existence, many had melted across the border into Iași.

The university responded to its growing ethnic mix by calling an end to the annual Orthodox service in 1920, the ceremony that traditionally heralded the start of an academic year. Codreanu was appalled by such a clumsy attempt to appease the incomers. A keen admirer of the old Crusaders, and in particular Vlad III Dracula, he believed all institutions must insist on Christian values as a way of protecting Romanian purity. The abandoning of the annual service was irreligious and unpatriotic, and was, for Codreanu, indisputable evidence of a Jewish take-over of the university's board. On the day the event was supposed to have taken place, Codreanu and a friend arrived early at the university's main buildings and barricaded themselves inside. On the door they left a hand-written note: 'I bring to the attention of the students as well as the professors that this university is going to open only after the traditional religious service.'

Within half an hour, 300 students were pushing to get inside. A mathematics professor waded to the front. 'Move,' he bellowed through the door. Codreanu shouted back: 'You swore on the cross when you joined this university... now you want to help the Jews tear down the churches.' The crowd swelled to a thousand. One final surge and they were through, spilling into the lobby where they set upon Codreanu with sticks and fists. A few days later, news of Codreanu's stand against the authorities had spread and, for the first time, the modest beginnings of a political movement began to take root. At the end of the week, a crowd of Codreanu sympathizers raced through the university corridors shouting anti-Jewish slogans. Scuffles broke out in lecture rooms, as Jews were separated from the rest and beaten. Violence escalated to such a pitch that, by Friday afternoon, a new note had been pinned to the front door. It came from the Dean's office. 'The rectorate has decided that this university will be closed until Wednesday,' it read, 'when it will open with a religious service.' Codreanu had won the day. Resisting the abolition of his university's Christian service was his first political success.

If Codreanu had been asked to create a fictional character embodying all the evils of Bolshevism in a single person – one to put the fear of God into the founders of Greater Romania – he might have conjured a figure something like that of Ana Rabinsohn. The gifted child of Orthodox Jewish parents from the eastern region of Moldova, not far from the Russian border, Rabinsohn did not seem to have a Romanian bone in her ill-fed body. Her family had moved to Bucharest and taken residence in a small apartment in a predominately Jewish quarter of the capital before the war, when Rabinsohn was just ten years old. Since Jews were no longer allowed to trade with anyone but other Jews, the area around Unirii Square in the east of the city had become something like a ghetto. Her father was a ritual butcher, selling morsels of kosher chicken to other poor and disenfranchised Jewish families who barely left the neighbourhood, entertaining themselves at the Jewish theatre, praying at the Holy Union Temple, and sending their offspring to local Jewish schools. It was a claustrophobic environment, where children were warned not to venture beyond their own streets.

Fourteen-year-old Ana had returned home one afternoon in a state of such anxiety that her father could not coax a word from her mouth. The only sounds the girl made were gasps and clicks, a Morse code of trauma. She remained silent for a week. When she finally spoke, she described how she had been walking home from school and had seen a Jewish man set upon and beaten unconscious. It was 1907, the time of the Peasant Revolt, and the first evidence, for Ana, that she did not belong.

The experience of being an outsider helped her develop into a steely young woman, who would sweep back her mop of jet-black hair and challenge anyone who disagreed with her socialist politics. Despite her diminutive size and her refined manners, she was both verbally and physically imperious, and soon made a name for herself in the small, male-dominated world of left-wing activism, where marches often came under attack from ultra-nationalists.

In her early twenties, Ana found herself a job teaching at a Jewish school but soon got into trouble for singing revolutionary ballads to ten-year-olds, and was dismissed. Then, in the summer of 1915, just before Romania's entry into the war, she had walked into the Socialist Club at 12 Sfântul Ionica Street in Bucharest and registered as a member of the Social Democratic Party of Romania (PSDR) – the principal party of the Left. The physician-lawyer, Christian Rakovksy, was also a member, and the two got to know each other well, working on campaigns to stop the 'imperialist warmongers' leading Europe into conflict. When Romania joined the Entente, the government had accused the pacifist Social Democrats of indirectly supporting the Central Powers by their refusal to fight, and banned them. At that point, the movement had gone underground.

For Ana, secrecy was part of the allure. She began working as a clandestine agent, running notes between prisons where PSDR members were being held. Then, when she was twenty-five years old, she joined a secret volunteer unit that organized Jewish self-protection against pogroms. As the only woman involved, she toured the Jewish quarter with groups of physically intimidating men who would regularly get into fights with the local anti-Semites. But with Bucharest under German occupation, Ana made plans to go to university abroad, finally leaving for Switzerland in September 1919, to take up a medical course in Geneva. Two years later, she returned to Romania, refreshed, even more politicized and with a husband at her side – an intense, wealthy, Jewish socialist called Marcel Pauker.

Pauker was three years Ana's junior, with a wild beard, penetrating dark eyes and an easiness of manner born of a privileged upbringing. He had developed a finger-jabbing militancy in his teens, confidently taking on the old guard of the movement and accusing them of moderation and cowardice. They were, he argued, nothing but social democrats, a fact that was undeniable since that had been the name of the party until the war. Since then, it had been re-launched as the Socialist Party but its restless activists were divided as to the way forward. As Bolshevist ideas began to infiltrate from Moscow, the party faced an inevitable split. On one side were the centrist, democratic *Minimalists*, on the other, the revolutionary-minded *Maximalists*. Marcel and Ana were enthusiastic members of the latter.

The couple spent their first days back home introducing each other to their respective families, who were eager to see photographs from their quiet, secular wedding ceremony in Geneva. Marcel delighted in introducing his wife with special emphasis on her new surname. 'Ana *Pauker* will tell you our view,' he would say. 'Ana *Pauker* speaks like a true Marxist.' The couple were inseparable, and would soon become the most famous communists in Romania.

But rediscovering the post-war streets of Bucharest during those summer weeks of 1921 required that the newly-weds move around with caution. A new organization had taken root amid the chaos of rebuilding the country, one that wanted to push aside the two fusty old parties of the past (Liberals and Conservatives) and replace them with a new one that was fiercely anti-communist. The People's Party (PP) was a right-wing, populist mirror-ball of a movement that reflected back at Romanians whatever they wanted to see. It was simultaneously both liberal and fascist. It supported the monarchy, but it was also republican. It was a proud supporter of Greater Romania but suspicious about the ethnic baggage that the new regions brought with them. The whole spinning artifice was held together by the magnetism of its leader, Marshal Alexandru Averescu, a war hero who had put down the Peasant Revolt of 1907 and who still believed Jewish landlords were solely responsible for the exploitation of Romanian peasants. Wiry and energetic, with pointed ears, flashing black eyes and a grinning moustache, Averescu managed to capture the mood of the nation. Communists were the enemy, they agreed, and to a lesser extent, Jews – although Averescu changed his message depending on who he was talking to, even managing to lure some Jews into joining the party.

In comparison with the slowly emerging popularity of Corneliu Codreanu and his ultra-nationalists in Iași, the right-wing People's Party was huge in scale and apparently moderate and civilized in its behaviour. There were no guns and no organized violence. All its high-profile leaders were war heroes, which gave the impression that even the army supported it. The party's racism was never openly acknowledged but disguised as a noble concern for holding the country together in the face of sudden ethnic diversity. So, when the newly acquired regions began pushing for their own assemblies, it was with regret that the People's Party politely opposed the idea.

These were politically disorientating times, with polarizing forces leading to the creation of a plethora of tiny political parties, most of which appealed to narrow sets of interests. Averescu's populism seemed to offer the potential to heal and bring disparate groups together. He stormed to power in the spring elections of 1920, taking more than half the seats in parliament and creating something like a personality cult, with supporters wearing badges of his face – an image that soon came to adorn flags, stamps and billboards. It was an early warning to old-school politicians that coherent policies hardly mattered. No sooner was Averescu in power than his more racist inclinations came to the fore. In the new regions, the teaching of indigenous languages was banned. There was a clampdown on regional political parties, while Averescu's supporters were given free rein to launch violent attacks against those they deemed 'unpatriotic' – a term that meant anyone who was not Christian and pure-blood Romanian. The smaller parties watched and learned. These were the policies that seemed guaranteed to win popularity.

Averescu set about destroying the communist movement with equal alacrity, despite the fact that their formal organization – the Socialist Party – had only 2,000 members, of whom many were still social democrats. In May 1920, Averescu's troops stormed the Socialist Party headquarters in Bucharest, rounding up the leaders and throwing them in jail. During the process, several were beaten, one so badly that he died. The remnants of the movement went underground once more, and in July that year its leaders sent a secret delegation to Moscow in the hope of receiving guidance and support from their spiritual masters. Led by the Maximalist Gheorghe Cristescu, a bourgeois businessman whose ownership of a bedding company had earned him the nickname 'The Blanket-Maker', the Romanian group travelled to the Russian capital to attend the 2nd World Congress of the Communist International (Comintern). There was much delight when they were greeted in the Kremlin by their old comrade, the physician-lawyer Christian Rakovsky, who had not been seen since the start of the war when he was jailed and taken to Iași. Rakovsky ushered them straight into a meeting with Lenin.

The issue was this, they were told: the Romanian Socialist Party must declare itself communist right away and sign up to Lenin's '21 Conditions', a list of non-negotiable regulations for all aspiring national Communist Parties.[2] The list included a promise to 'methodically' and 'pitilessly' cleanse the Party of anyone considered moderate or petit-bourgeois; to give unconditional support to the Soviet Republic; and to accept Moscow's line in the making of all decisions. That first clause would have meant the 'pitiless' removal of Cristescu himself, as punishment for his ownership of a blanket factory. The visiting delegation asked for time to think, nodded thanks to Rakovsky and left on the next train for Bucharest.

Within days, they called a debate of the membership to put Lenin's conditions to a vote. The Minimalists were deeply opposed. They argued that the movement's future was as a democratic party fielding candidates in elections, and explained that they felt uneasy about relinquishing decision-making to Moscow. As they tried to speak, Maximalists constantly interjected, jeering and hurling insults. 'You are nothing but liberals,' they scoffed, 'you are in the wrong party!' When the vote was finally called, there was no doubt which way it would go. The Maximalists won with a large and boisterous majority. They renamed themselves the Socialist-Communist Party of Romania and, soon afterwards, shortened it to the Romanian Communist Party (RCP). The Minimalists resigned en masse.

The following afternoon, at 3 p.m. on 12 May 1921, Marshal Averescu's army again raided the Party's offices. This time, there were no half-measures. Everyone they found was arrested and bundled onto army buses. Others were picked up at their homes. That day 271 people ended up in jail, almost the entire party apparatus. The charge was simple: treason – they had all declared loyalty to a foreign power.

It was in the aftermath of these mass jailings that newly-weds Marcel and Ana Pauker had arrived back in Bucharest in August 1921. They stood in the near-empty Party building on Sfântul Ionica Street, surveying the raided filing cabinets and broken furniture, and asked a few timid volunteers for a list of who was left. It was short. A couple of middle-ranking officials were holed up at secret addresses, the rest were trying to run the Party from their cells. The Paukers' unexpected arrival provided an opportunity. They were bumped up the queue into two senior roles that would not have been available to them during the normal course of events. Marcel became a member of the provisional leadership at the age of just twenty-four, while Ana became Secretary of the Central Commission of Women.[3] They had to tread carefully, though. Averescu's men were still out on the streets trying to mop up any stragglers. In the meantime, there was a sensational trial for the government to organize.

Two hundred and seventy-one members of Romania's new

Communist Party stood charged with a long list of crimes, including collaboration with the enemy, terrorism, instigation to riot, and crimes against state security. Dishevelled and ill-fed after eight months of harsh treatment, they were brought to a specially adapted courtroom on Dealul Spirii, a windy hill in Bucharest beside the old senate building, on 23 January 1922.

The scene in court was chaotic. Never had so many accused appeared in a single trial. They sat on windowsills and stairways, squatted in corridors and in gangways. Leading the defence was the dandyish, Paris-educated Dem Dobrescu, a man whose tailored suits and puffed silk handkerchiefs recalled the Côte d'Azur rather than a grimy criminal court. Dobrescu was head of the Bucharest Bar and more experienced than the panel of judges. His tactic was to call a succession of superstar witnesses, who would emphasize the democratic right of everyone to join the political party of their choice. 'Ladies and gentleman, Nicolae Iorga,' announced Dobrescu with theatrical relish, as the country's best-known historian took the stand. The appearance of the co-founder of the anti-Semitic Democratic Nationalist Party was nothing less than a sensation. A virulent critic of communism, Iorga might have been expected to call for the lot of them to be jailed, but he announced that freedom of speech was sacred and was a measure of Romania's democratic maturity.

'Ladies and gentleman, the next witness for the defence, Marshal Alexandru Averescu…' The appearance of the leader of the People's Party drew even louder gasps. Serving as prime minister until just a month before the trial, it was Averescu who had been responsible for their arrests in the first place. His appearance for the defence seemed bizarre. But Averescu was playing a malevolent personal game. A rival had ousted him from government and Averescu saw this as an opportunity to derail his popularity by helping to inflict a humiliating defeat in a high-profile trial. He used the same arguments as Iorga. The communists were entitled to their views, he said, so long as there was no public unrest.

By the end, the defence had called 600 witnesses to the prosecution's 300, in a trial that held the attention of the country for four months. The verdicts took a week to read out. All but thirty-one of the defendants were convicted and sentenced to between one and ten years' hard labour. But, after an appeal for clemency to King Ferdinand, all but forty-eight were released. The trial had been a pointless spectacle that exposed Romania's lack of democratic sophistication to the world. But it had set a precedent for something else. The nation's politicians had realized they could remove hundreds of activists from circulation for months on end, with little public disquiet. It hardly mattered whether they were guilty or not, no one really cared. The false criminalization of opponents fitted well with Romania's Byzantine political heritage of plotting and deceit. Coming, as it did, at the foundation of the new democratic state, it set the tone for what was to come.

This was the political landscape of the new Romania shortly after it emerged from the war; a hugely popular right-wing party in control, a tiny handful of communists to its left, and a small but growing group of ultra-nationalists around Corneliu Codreanu to its right. As it turned out, Prime Minister Averescu and his men had targeted the wrong side to evict from the political scene. The communists had posed no serious threat to either his or Romania's stability – their numbers were far too small and their closeness to Moscow far too unpopular. Codreanu's outfit, on the other hand, was growing astonishingly fast over on the other side of the country in Iaşi.

At the University of Iaşi, Jews often wore kippahs (caps) to lectures. Nothing could have been more 'ostentatious' as far as Corneliu Codreanu and his followers were concerned. They viewed it as evidence of Bolshevism and decided such provocative displays of ethnicity needed to be punished. Caps were grabbed from heads, taken into Union Square and burned. Fights broke out as students tried to block their Jewish colleagues from entering lectures. All of this had become familiar in the corridors of the University of Iași, but by 1923 the violence took an unexpected turn. Previously respected members of the university's academic staff began to join in. A brilliant chemistry scholar, Professor Corneliu Șumuleanu, waited for Jews to be attacked in his lectures and then waded through the mob to deliver blows to his own Jewish students.

At the start of the year, Romania was under pressure from the rest of Europe to incorporate the Minorities Clause into its constitution – a guarantee of equal rights for all ethnicities living in the country. The Paris Conference had made the clause a condition of the country being awarded its territorial enlargement. But now that it was about to be enshrined in law, some Romanians had begun arguing that the country was better off small and pure and unequal, rather than Great and cosmopolitan and equal.

Among them was the curmudgeonly Professor Cuza. He told his students that the Minorities Clause was not about 'equal rights' at all, but about allowing Jews to tighten their grip on Romania. Codreanu agreed and started publishing pamphlets to let his colleagues know what trouble lay ahead. '50, 60, 70 per cent' of the university were Jews, he said. It therefore followed that 'tomorrow we will logically have 50, 60, 70 per cent Jewish leaders for Romanian people.'[4]

At that point, several of the university's professors began arguing for a different approach to equality. Equality for non-Jews. They wanted something called a *numerus clausus*, a quota that would limit student intake to the percentage of Jews in the wider population. With that figure standing at about four per cent, it would entail the expulsion of many hundreds of Jewish students from Iași. The campaign had no real chance of success but was more of a provocation to make Jewish students feel uneasy, and hopefully to inspire violence. In the meantime,

Codreanu, who was by this time barely a student at all but a full-time activist, managed to win one or two racist concessions from the university's board. For a start, Jewish medical students would be barred from using Christian cadavers for their studies. They would need to find their own supply of Jewish dead.

By now, the rather aloof, unreadable Codreanu had acquired a surprisingly dedicated following among his colleagues. His popularity did not arise from his oratory (he was a guarded, cautious speaker), nor his ability to make friends (most found him moody and unpredictable) but from a mysterious inner strength and conviction that seemed to touch everyone he came across. With few words, Codreanu could hold a room. There was a rare energy behind his green eyes, a mystical, magnetic power that seemed to come from beyond the material world. He did not drink, he prayed often, he preached that only pain and suffering would win the holy war for a pure, uncontaminated Greater Romania – the land their ancestors had demanded. He was the solemn voice of history, the successor to ancient nationalist heroes like Vlad III Dracula.

At the end of February 1923, Professor Cuza invited Codreanu around for tea. Not many students knew it, but he was actually Codreanu's godfather and a long-time friend of his father, Ion Zelea Codreanu, a militant nationalist and former member of parliament. Codreanu Snr was invited to supper too. As the evening wore on, cake, tea and Moldovan wine were produced, and more guests arrived including Professor Şumuleanu, the chemistry lecturer who beat his Jewish students. Conversation turned to a mass rally they were organizing for the spring. Their movement was becoming popular, they agreed, and they should give it a name. Someone suggested the National Defence Party. Cuza shook his head. It sounded too formal, too establishment. This was a protest movement that planned to exist outside the formal political structure. The word *League* seemed preferable. They also needed to emphasize that Christian Orthodoxy lay at its roots. What about, suggested Cuza, the League of Christian National Defence (LANC)? The guests nodded. The name of the new movement was settled.

It was up to Codreanu to begin preparing the League's formal inauguration, rallying supporters from Romania's four universities with a promise that a new and violent movement was to be launched to take on communists and Jews. On the evening of 3 March 1923, he collected yards of cotton, which he made into black flags and laid on his bedroom floor. In the centre of each, he painted a white circle, inside of which he drew a symbol he had learned about during a trip to Berlin the previous autumn. Someone had told him about a little-known anti-Semitic activist called Adolf Hitler who had taken charge of the small ultra-nationalist Nazi Party. Codreanu is said to have been intrigued. When he was shown the swastika symbol, he decided it would be ideal for his own movement. He painted it into the middle of each of the flags and had them carried to Iași's ancient Orthodox Cathedral, where they were unveiled before a congregation of thousands and blessed by a priest. It was Codreanu who had insisted that the League be sanctified by the Church. Later that day, at the university's amphitheatre, the leaders of the new movement were announced. The president would be Professor Cuza. The organizing committee was to include the violent Professor Șumuleanu and Codreanu's father. Codreanu himself, still only twenty-three years old, was put in charge of the student wing. But there was already tension.

Codreanu thought that Cuza was strangely opposed to violence. No sooner was the inauguration over than the dapper professor was down at the opera or composing clever articles for magazines. Codreanu wanted his members on the streets. That autumn, the League's frustrated student leader retreated to his favourite hideaway, a hermitage on the high slopes of the Rarau Mountain, a landscape of craggy peaks in the wilderness of Bukovina. He took with him a young activist called Ion Moța, the son of an Orthodox priest who had been banned from every university in Romania. Moța had become Codreanu's most loyal follower. A trouble-magnet with a fascination for martyrdom, it would not be long before he was pledging his life to the League.

The two youths hiked together in silence and then came to a stop somewhere above the clouds. The previous week they had tried to meet with the prime minister, Ion Brătianu, to persuade him that the *numerus clausus* should be adopted in law to rid the universities of Jews. It was quite remarkable that Brătianu had agreed to speak to them at all. But the conversation had been brief. Brătianu had said he did not support the idea and the two young men were moved on by officials. Now, they felt irrationally humiliated that they could not spend longer explaining their reasoning. The pair's mood was black. It was then that they hatched a violent plan, not just to rid the country of its leading Jews but to kill their apologists too, men like Prime Minister Brătianu.

The following week, on Monday, 8 October 1923, Codreanu and his inner circle gathered in the home of a friend in Bucharest, wearing collars and ties, and sitting formally around the dining table. Their friend's mother was in the kitchen, cooking supper. The students chatted and drank wine. Earlier, each of them had written to their families, bidding them farewell. The letters had been left with friends to deliver after the night's planned violence. Hidden among their belongings were two Browning pistols.

At 9 p.m., as they hugged and exchanged oaths of loyalty to the League, they heard a noise outside. Moments later, uniformed police officers charged into the room. There was no time to hide. On the table was a highly incriminating document – a hit-list of targets that Codreanu and the others intended to assassinate with those Browning pistols. Among the names was Brătianu, as well as Romania's foreign minister and several high-profile politicians.[5]

CHAPTER FIVE

During the night Nosferatu clutches his victim and sucks their blood like a gruesome life-saving drink. Beware, so that his shadow cannot burden your sleep with horrible nightmares.

Nosferatu (1922), Henrik Galeen

Along a narrow street in Germany wandered a furtive, hunched figure who appeared to be a long way from home. It was twilight on a grey afternoon in the city of Lübeck on the Baltic coast. There were specks of snow in the air and the stranger was in a hurry to get out of the cold. His head was completely bald, his fingers long and claw-like, his face deathly pale and his ears appeared to be pointed like those of a wolf. Of indeterminate age, he was wearing a long military tunic rather than his customary black cape, and taking exaggerated strides as he approached a crumbling thirteenth-century building by the quayside. He stopped for a moment and glanced over his shoulder with a melodramatic pause. As his eyes caught a ray of fading sunlight, it seemed his pupils were completely white. The man's name was Max Schreck, he was a famous German actor, and the part he was playing was that of a vampire called Count Orlok.

Filming has taken place over the winter of 1921 in various atmospheric, ancient German towns for the silent movie, *Nosferatu*. It is the story of a young estate agent called Thomas Hutter who has been sent by stagecoach to visit a new client in a remote, mountaintop castle in Transylvania. Hutter is welcomed inside by the mysterious Count Orlok, only to cut his finger while eating his dinner. Orlok asks politely if he might suck the blood from Hutter's wound, and the terrified visitor gradually realizes he is in the home of the undead. Trapped in the castle, he peers out of the window, only to see the Count climbing into a coffin. Orlok, we learn, is allergic to sunlight and ends up on a voyage in a schooner, hidden of course, in a casket.

When Bram Stoker's widow, Florence, heard about the film, she sued. Stoker's *Dracula* novel had done moderately well in Britain and America but was far from a commercial hit. In fact, it had earned the author so little money that in the final years of his life, he had to petition for a compassionate grant from the Royal Literary Fund. Stoker died in London in 1912, at the age of 64, not quite penniless, but not far off. The following year, Florence was so hard up that she took the notes and outlines of his novel to Sotheby's and sold them for just over £2. After that, all went quiet on the Dracula front. The war began and the book was in danger of being forgotten.

It was only when Florence was sent a flyer from the launch night of *Nosferatu; A Symphony of Horror*, by the German director Friedrich Murnau – an event held at the ballroom of the Berlin Zoo in 1922 – that she realized the *Dracula* plot had been copied. A lengthy legal battle followed, which Florence eventually won, forcing the makers of *Nosferatu* to destroy every print of their film (although some did survive). Paradoxically, it was the attendant publicity that brought renewed attention to *Dracula*. Interest began to surge and Florence sold the rights to a childhood friend, the actor and writer, Hamilton Deane, who adapted the book into a hugely successful, and much re-imagined, stage production in 1924. Deane completely transformed Dracula's characteristics, changing Stoker's 'tall old man, clean shaven save for a long white moustache' into a louche, purring, lounge-lizard, dressed in high collars, black cape, white tie, with almost lacquered jet-black hair. None of that was in Stoker's imagining of the Transylvanian count but it became the image that stuck. Deane's Dracula was the one who stalked the set of the famous 1931 Hollywood adaptation, in which he was played by Bela Lugosi – the film that made Dracula into the world's most recognizable Gothic-horror icon.

In Romania at the time, neither the book nor the film was widely known. Many people simply failed to make the connection between their national hero, known to everyone as *Vlad Țepeș* – Vlad the Impaler – and Dracula. Familiarity with the latter sobriquet was limited to the educated elite, who found the re-imagining of their hero, the prince who famously defeated the Ottoman army, an insult to his memory. The rest of the population – the few who knew anything of Stoker's work at all – recognized their landscapes and their folklore, but were mystified that stories told to them since the cradle about vampires and the living-dead could cause such a global stir.

Crown Prince Carol was certainly oblivious to the fuss about Western portrayals of his notorious princely predecessor when his parents began preparing him for the role of king in the early 1920s. His louche personality had convinced Marie and Ferdinand that they needed to bring their son into line and invest in him a sense of responsibility. Their first attempt involved leaving the twenty-six-year-old in charge of the country while they were on official business in Transylvania. They suggested he might organize a formal reception for their return but Carol was so alarmed by the prospect, he threw himself off his horse in an attempt to injure himself and avoid any official appointments. Ferdinand tried again, in 1919, asking Carol to serve on a trade mission to the Far East. Carol shot himself in the leg rather than undertake the journey, an act that even his doting mother struggled to forgive. 'For the first time,' she wrote in her diary, 'I nearly hated my son.'[1] Although the leg wound would heal, Carol's mental health issues were more challenging. Marie decided that a long break in the sun was in order, and with the doctor's blessing sent him off on a world tour in 1920.

Carol returned, tanned, healthy and displaying near tantric calm. Memories of Zizi Lambrino seemed to have subsided. He was even in the mood to speak civilly to his siblings, who he usually treated imperiously or ignored altogether. When Carol was on his way back through Europe, he heard that his little sister, Elisabeth, was getting married, and changed his plans so that he could join the wedding party.

Elisabeth was a rather dowdy twenty-five-year-old, introverted, socially awkward, with none of the intellectual sparkle of her mother. Marie had wanted to marry her off quickly and an unexpected solution had arrived in the shape of Crown Prince George of Greece, a dull but brave soldier, who was also Elisabeth's second cousin. They were to be married in February 1921 and the announcement was to be celebrated with picnics and festivities along the train route between Switzerland (where the Greek monarchy was in exile) and Romania. The two royal families had disembarked in the magical mountain resort of Sinaia, where they entertained the Greeks on the sweeping lawns of their fairy-tale summer house, Peleş Castle, playing games and hunting brown bears. Carol's arrival was unexpected, as no one had known where to send his invitation, but Marie was delighted to see him in such rude health.

On a bracing country walk the following day, Carol accompanied the groom's younger sister, Princess Helen, up hillsides and through valleys, talking animatedly about his trip. The British-educated princess was tall, fine-boned, elegant and reserved. She had rarely encountered such exuberance, certainly not from a young royal so determined to please. Carol spoke with no one else. Within hours he had fallen in love. Before the end of the trip, he had proposed.

The impulsiveness was reminiscent of his marriage to Zizi but this time Marie was unreservedly delighted. Helen was not only a princess but exuded a chilly air of conformity and protocol that would have tamed a pack of wolves. When Marie's dangerously spirited friends pointed out the Princess's dreariness, she was untroubled. Nothing mattered, she said, other than Carol's happiness, and his final cutting of ties with Zizi Lambrino. Of course, it had crossed the queen's mind that she could finally hand responsibility for her wayward son to someone else.

There were two royal weddings in Marie's household that spring of 1921. Princess Elisabeth and Prince George were married in a sombre Orthodox ceremony in Bucharest, before being whisked off back to Athens to witness Carol's marriage to Helen. These were the happiest of times for Marie. She had rid herself of a dowdy daughter and secured the next generation of royal leadership for her adopted country.

There was more delight when, nine months later, Carol's dynastic obligations were fulfilled with the birth of a baby boy. They named him Michael, a prince who would be second in line to the Romanian throne. The young family moved into a villa on Boulevard Kisselev, a grand tree-lined avenue in central Bucharest near a lake studded with islands and fairy-lit cafes. Carol employed Harrods of London to redecorate the house. He ordered English wallpaper, Ottoman rugs, French chandeliers and a team of craftsmen from all over Europe. Still nursing painful memories of his own upbringing by nannies and his sexually abusive tutor, Carol endeavoured to do things differently. He fed and walked the baby himself and the young royals became the very picture of modern domesticity.

Soon, however, the routine became burdensome. Cooped up in such a claustrophobic environment, Carol lashed out at Helen, refusing to help her with chores and storming off into town to visit old drinking haunts. By February 1922, Helen was so exhausted with her husband's capricious moods that she asked Marie and Ferdinand for permission to take a holiday with the baby, and sought refuge in the calm of the Greek royal palace in Athens. Four months later, she was still there and Carol had found a new source of entertainment.

The lightning-rod for his affections this time was a divorcee and notorious social-climber by the name of Elena Lupescu. Carol had attended a charity ball to which Lupescu had wangled herself an invitation with the express purpose of meeting the Crown Prince. She had even managed to engineer a seat right in front of him, where she spent the evening playing elaborately with her flaming red hair and coquettishly sipping her wine. Carol noticed her but wisely stayed away. On the second occasion, he was less resolute. Lupescu arrived at a dance dressed in a dazzling virginal white gown, feline green eyes heavy with mascara. She was more self-assured, sashaying around the room with champagne in her hand, devouring canapés while exhaling cigarette smoke down her nose. She danced provocatively with Carol and, at the end of the night, he offered to drive her home. Summoning all her fake virtue, Lupescu smiled apologetically. 'What would the neighbours think if they saw me returning in your Highness's car?' she pleaded. At the next party, there were no more games. Lupescu happily followed Carol into his Rolls-Royce and was driven to his empty villa.

Elena Lupescu was not one of Carol's typical conquests. She was plump, plain-faced, lower-middle-class and walked with swaying and notoriously full hips. She was also Jewish, presenting a challenge for the royalist and fanatically anti-Semitic followers of Corneliu Codreanu, a man who was by now in one of Bucharest's most notorious jails awaiting trial for plotting to kill several high-ranking Jewish politicians.

*

Văcărești Prison was a dank old fort, full of passageways and dungeons, whose centrepiece was a Byzantine Orthodox church incongruously located on a well-kept lawn right in the middle of the complex. Half of the building was occupied by prisoners

– most of them political – and half by monks, who used it as a monastery. When Codreanu and his co-conspirators arrived in the summer of 1923, they were less concerned with the conditions of their confinement than the fact that they suspected a traitor in their midst. Why else would the police have raided their dinner party with such exquisite timing?

Codreanu had been detained for just a matter of days when he looked down into a prison courtyard and saw his father being led away in a work-gang, still dressed in full national costume. As a former member of parliament, it was not long before Codreanu Snr was able to secure certain privileges, including the right to pray in the monks' Orthodox Church, a place he was soon visiting freely along with his son. It was here, in this dark, holy place, that an important chapter of the Codreanu myth was born.

On the left-hand door to the altar was an unusual six-foot-tall icon that caught Codreanu's eye. Exquisitely painted in oil and covered in decades of waxy dust, it depicted St Michael, leader of God's heavenly army, with golden wings sprouting from his shoulders, waving the silver sword with which he had just despatched Satan. In the dim candlelight, surrounded by chanting monks, Codreanu is said to have had a revelation. St Michael seemed to come to life before his eyes. It was a sign, believed Codreanu, that he had been chosen to lead the Holy War against the forces that were trying to destroy Greater Romania. From that moment, he pledged to create his own brotherhood, to fight for 'national renewal'. Before he could begin though, there was the small matter of a trial that might land him in prison for twenty years.

When the day arrived, in January 1924, Codreanu and the other plotters were escorted to the prison office in order to be processed before leaving for court. Standing beside him was his most trusted follower, Ion Moța. Behind Moța came a pale, nervy young man called Ion Vemichescu. The others had been suspicious of Vemichescu from the start, believing he might have been the one who tipped off the police. Codreanu and Moța had had words with him, and believed that his body-language suggested guilt. Now, as they waited for the prison bus, Moța strode over to Vemichescu and marched him into a vestibule. Moments later, gunshots exploded in the confined space.

As Vemichescu's barely breathing body was loaded into an ambulance, his former comrades whistled fighting songs from cells in the basement of the courthouse. Using a smuggled pistol from a prison visitor, Moța had exacted revenge on behalf of the group. It was part of their ethos. Any dishonesty or disloyalty, even in the absence of meaningful evidence, would be dealt with harshly.

Nevertheless, the trial proceeded as planned and a crowd of supporters gathered in the streets outside. It was significant because this was the first time that Codreanu had attracted attention outside of Iași. News about the trial had been the talk of Bucharest, and sympathetic newspapers had questioned why young, patriotic men were being prosecuted for taking on Jews and Bolsheviks, when the nation should be thanking them for trying to protect Greater Romania.

The prosecutor was a Mr Racoviceanu. 'Were there guns in the house?' he asked.

'Yes,' replied each defendant in turn.

Had they drawn up a list of individuals they planned to assassinate?

'Yes.'

Did they want to see these men dead?

Yes, of course. That is why the names were on the list.

Honesty, even at extreme personal cost, was a core value of the movement. There are no records of what Codreanu said when he took the stand but we do know he was fond of a quote that he attributed to Romania's national poet to justify his anti-Semitism: 'By what labour or sacrifices have [the Jews] won for themselves the right to aspire to equality with the Romanian people? Was it they who fought the Turks, Tartars, Poles and Hungarians?... Was it through their efforts that the fame of this country spread, that this language was disinterred from the veilings of the past? Was it through one of them that the Romanian people won its right to sunlight?'

When Codreanu's own advocate, Professor Paulescu, rose before the court, his clients had effectively already accepted their guilt. There was just one narrow avenue of argument left to explore. There was no date, pointed out Paulescu, on which the so-called conspirators were going to commit the crime. How could it be a conspiracy if no one had talked about timings? Wasn't this just a gang of hot-headed students talking nonsense after a few drinks?

The trial continued into the night, with the jury finally retiring at 5 a.m. the next day. Verdicts arrived an hour and half later. The first Codreanu knew of it was from the sound of cheering in the public gallery. All five men had been acquitted and were released to scenes of wild jubilation. Codreanu returned briefly to Văcărești Prison to collect his belongings. Among them was a gift from a fellow prisoner: a six-foot-high replica of the icon of Archangel Michael.

In reflective, rather than celebratory mood, Codreanu chose not to take part in the violent demonstrations about the Minorities Clause that were spreading across Iași. Instead, he retreated to the countryside to experiment with a life of self-reliance and prayer. His followers soon joined him, as he had hoped, and in the summer of 1924, he gathered them for an important announcement. The event was to take place in the rather unpromising surroundings of a broken-down shed at the bottom of an old lady's garden. He had chosen the location carefully, as a symbol of the pure and simple life they must embrace to become members of his new organization.

'There is no-one here to help us,' explained Codreanu, 'just God.' He told them that they must drop their sense of entitlement. Some were so privileged, he said, that they had forgotten what it was like to even carry a bag down the street. Now was the time to get their hands dirty. They were required, said Codreanu, to build a new nation, 'brick by brick'. They needed to become workers, not thinkers, to pray often, and to use their minds only for the study of the *Book of Revelation*. At the end of the meeting, Codreanu announced the new movement would be called *Fratia de Cruce* – the Brotherhood of the Cross. Its members would be Legionaries and would be divided into what Codreanu called 'nests', groups of six men (and occasionally women) who would live together like a family. They would work beside one another, pray together and fight together. Their spiritual guide would be, of course, Codreanu, but their leader was to be the wild, but clever, Ion Moța – who was soon to be acquitted of shooting his former colleague in the prison waiting room at Văcărești. Before the Legionaries left that night, on 6 May 1924, they swore on the Bible to sacrifice their lives for the movement and for Corneliu Codreanu.

Over the following days, they set up a sort of utopian camp in a place called Ungheni on the banks of the Prut River, where they seeded carrots, potatoes and marrows. It was a lifestyle that would become a trademark of Codreanu's various movements: communal work camps with shared living quarters where young men and women worked to the rhythm of fighting songs.

Later, these communes would expand into networks, attracting thousands of residents, including visitors from abroad. The largest would be situated beside the spectacular white beaches of Eforie, near Constanța, and named after the wife of King Carol I: the Carmen Sylva Camp. It would include schoolrooms where homeless and destitute children were bussed in for free tuition, along with restaurants, a theatre and an infirmary for the poor. In the summer, children were shown how to grow maize and oats, while in the evenings, visitors would arrive from miles around for fund-raising events that featured choral recitals and folk dancing.[2] The Carmen Sylva Camp was more than just a commune, it was a philanthropic holiday destination for the poor and a propaganda centre for Codreanu.

On 8 May 1924, Codreanu and fifty of his comrades rose early at the Ungheni camp, pulled on their boots and overalls, and lined up ready to sow tomatoes. Suddenly, dozens of armed soldiers began storming the premises. According to Codreanu's testimony, they were accompanied by forty police officers, 'revolvers at the ready, shouting and swearing'. Their leader was the local police prefect, a Mr D. Manciu.[3] Codreanu tells us that Manciu and others pushed him to the ground and placed three revolvers against his temple. Codreanu is then said to have received a punch to the head from Manciu. It was the cue for other police to join in. As Codreanu was beaten, one of them apparently whispered in his ear: 'Before evening, we will kill you, you will not live to chase out the Jews.'[4] Then Codreanu and the others were marched away to the nearest police station, flanked by 200 gendarmes.

Universul (8 June 1924)

STUDENTS WERE BEATEN BY THE POLICE PREFECT HIMSELF

We imagine Mr. Manciu, the prefect of the Iaşi police, as being like one of the most notorious policemen of the last century, exemplified by violence and brutality.

...Mr. Manciu, who as a student must have studied penal law, personally beat the students, tortured them, and covered them with blood. But, what if the beaten students are not guilty of any of the absurdities of which they are accused? Then what? Should he in turn be thrashed?

Universul (9 June 1924)

IAŞI UNDER THE TERROR OF THE POLICE PREFECT

Transported to the police dungeons, students were subjected to the most terrifying tortures. Some of them were hung head down, beaten on the soles of their feet with the ox sinew. The student Corneliu Codreanu was bound, then slapped and tortured by the police prefect himself. His health was shaken. The other arrested students show serious body lesions. Three hundred students have reported the above-mentioned facts to the general prosecutor demanding that the medical examiner look into the condition of their tortured colleagues.[5]

Codreanu was indeed beaten, and was kept in custody for two days, a period he spent bitterly totting up the 'shame', 'humiliation' and 'torment' heaped upon him by Prefect Manciu. It was left to Codreanu's old mentor, Professor Cuza, to find an imagined Jewish conspiracy behind the arrests.

Unirea (1 June 1924; by Professor A. C. Cuza)

...This provocation is the more undignified and the more irritating because at the same time policeman Manciu frequents the meetings of the Jewish association 'Macabi' and ostentatiously leads these sport-minded Macabees in excursions, behind their white and blue flag.
...we demand that the superior authorities intervene in order to put an end to an undignified and dangerous state of affairs, that neither Iași nor Christian students can tolerate any longer.[6]

Thursday, 23 October 1924 was a piercingly cold morning at the Court House of District 11 in the city of Iași. Codreanu was attending, not as the accused this time but as a lawyer. The arrests in the tomato fields had blown over, for the moment at least, and now he was representing a young student who claimed, like dozens of others, to have been beaten by Prefect Manciu. The courtroom was busy. Gowned advocates flapped in and out.

Codreanu sat down at the front to wait for his case to be called. Suddenly, a door flew open and a gang of men ran into the room. It was Manciu with a team of twenty police officers, shouting and pointing at Codreanu. They launched themselves at him, wresting him to the ground and piling on top. Several lawyers yelled for calm. Then there was the crack of a pistol. In the melee, Codreanu had drawn a handgun and fired, in full view of the judge and several astonished lawyers. He aimed 'at no-one', he said later. But the recipient of his first bullet was dead. It just happened to be Prefect Manciu.

*

While outrages perpetrated by Codreanu and the far-right were justified daily by newspapers up and down the land, even a peep from Romania's nascent Communist Party was met with the equivalent of a call to arms. Communists were fair game. They should be beaten on the streets. Their disloyalty to Greater Romania was a plot conceived by Moscow's Bolsheviks and spread by fanatics. Always, the word communist was interchangeable with Jew. Romanians were bombarded with conspiracy theories about Judeo-Bolshevism. It suited the siege mentality and isolationism to be always on the look-out for culprits. Trotsky was proof enough that Jews had taken over Russia. And his Romanian counterpart, Ana Pauker, was proof they were trying to do the same in Bucharest.

In fact, Pauker was not the instinctive communist she was made out to be. Just like several of her comrades, she had joined the old Social Democratic Party of Romania because it was the only anti-war party in the country. At the time, she had shown no interest in the economics of Marxism. Indeed, several young communists were said to have been horrified when they learned about collectivization and the abolition of private property. Their interest was in a broader set of liberal values that were not represented by the traditional, corrupt Romanian two-party system. They were excited by the notion of a new beginning for all of Europe, with a more equitable distribution of land and an end to imperialism. And it was hardly surprising that many of them were Jews, the group that had been treated so appallingly for generations and denied a voice.

As the Social Democrats became the Socialists, which in turn became the Romanian Communist Party (RCP), its young, impressionable members travelled leftwards with it, seeing the Party as the only platform that might bring radical and lasting change. But both Ana and Marcel Pauker recognized a problem early on. The Party could never be popular as long as Moscow insisted on a dominant role. The achievement of Greater Romania was just too precious, too steeped in blood and history, to accept subservience to Russia.

They made their feelings known, as did several others in the higher echelons of the Party in Bucharest. Moscow delivered a stern rebuke. The Politburo stepped in and dismissed the RCP's first General Secretary, Gheorghe 'The Blanket-Maker' Cristescu, for his apparent Romanian nationalism, replacing him with a tame Austro-Hungarian carpenter named Elek Köblös, who despised the Romanians for taking Transylvania during the war. Moscow then insisted that RCP congresses should be held outside the country, an order that was put into force from 1922 onwards. Even the Party's internal documents were sometimes written in Russian. A clear and cynical takeover of the RCP was well underway through the early 1920s.

The Party was systematically stripped of its Romanian identity, so much so that the Romanian government had every justification in believing it was being run as a front for foreign elements intent on fomenting a coup. With Russia's heavily guiding hand, Romanians were regularly expelled from its ranks, and in particular, from its leadership. By the 1930s, Hungarians made up 26 per cent of the Party, Russians 10 per cent and Bulgarians 10 per cent.[7] The Romanian government was sufficiently concerned as early as 1923 to step in, and ban the RCP.

Ana Pauker was one of those arrested. The thirty-one-year-old, who had just lost her first baby to dysentery in the couple's small, neglected apartment (Ana had been too busy with party work to concentrate fully on childcare) was taken to Văcăreşti prison, shortly after Codreanu and his co-conspirators had left. Communist prisoners were held in a separate wing from the ultra-nationalists and despite their relatively small membership (still just 300 members), the clampdown was so comprehensive that it was they who occupied the most space.

Ana was soon interrogated by an early incarnation of Romania's secret police, known as the Siguranţa. The questioning took place in windowless rooms, and was carried out by anonymous men. They wanted the names of Communist Party members and Bolshevik spies. The RCP had direct links with Moscow, they reminded her. She must know who was responsible for organizing its anti-Romanian strategy. Pauker was a resilient interviewee. They tied her arms to the back of her chair and continued to demand answers. When she refused, they beat her.

After several months in custody, Pauker still had no date for trial, nor, in true Kafkaesque form, had she any inkling of the charges against her. It was during this period, when young RCP women were gathered in the same cells, that their antipathy towards the Romanian government inevitably hardened. At the same time, they were treated as heroes by Moscow. Letters of encouragement were smuggled into the jail and the women became a tough, independent group, looking to Russian comrades for their political nourishment. They went on hunger strike, refusing to eat for fourteen days. Finally, the prison authorities agreed that three of the women would be released. It is said that as the doors of their cells were opened, only Pauker emerged. The rest were so badly beaten and racked with hunger that they could not walk.

*

London, 27 November 1925. A thin layer of snow had formed on the shoulders of the sentries around Buckingham Palace. Crowds waited – ten-deep, drenched and cold – as a coffin was borne by gun-carriage to Westminster Abbey through streets of rutted snow. The funeral of Queen Alexandra, wife of King Edward VII and sister-in-law of Romania's Queen Marie, had brought representatives from all Europe's royal houses into foggy London, including the tall, ungainly figure of Crown Prince Carol of Romania.

Huddled in a long military coat, his riding boots soaked up to his shins in snow, he walked just behind the British royals, a mark of the closeness between the two families. But aside from the funeral, and a few strained days with distant aunts and uncles, Carol had another anxiety playing on his mind.

On the Friday after the funeral, he was supposed to be picking up his younger sister Princess Ileana, who was attending school in London, so that he could accompany her back to Bucharest for the Christmas holidays. But Carol never turned up. Instead, he phoned Ileana in a panic and told her that he was needed urgently in Paris. The following day, Carol did indeed travel to the French capital but not for any official engagement. Rather, he climbed from the train into the arms of Elena Lupescu. The couple then switched platforms and boarded another train bound for Milan, where they checked in at the luxurious Hotel de Ville. Carol signed his name in the visitors' book. His lover did the same. She wrote 'Princess Lupescu'.

Once inside their suite, Carol sat down and composed a lengthy letter to his mother. He declared that he was sick of being misunderstood, misjudged and persecuted. He was 'a victim', he said, and had suffered years of 'condescension'. After listing pages of petty grievances, he told his mother that she would never see him again. He was to disappear forever with his darling Lupescu. It went without saying, he was renouncing the throne.

There was a curious response in Romania. Marie had been

so effective in keeping her son's behaviour out of the headlines in recent years that, having thought little of him until this moment, people suddenly felt a great sense of loss. A small group of 'Carlists' emerged, who began campaigning for the Prince's return. They knew little of his politics because he did not have any. He was vaguely anti-Semitic, like much of Romania's ruling class, but the parties of the right were unhappy with him because he was now dating 'that Jewess'. Carol's only notable opinion was his dislike for the grandest statesman in the land, the five-time Liberal prime minister, Ion Brătianu.

The sixty-one-year-old had been a member of parliament almost from the formation of the Kingdom, and had been involved in every decision of significance ever since, being viewed as the eyes and ears of the king. Every new prime minister of whatever persuasion had to consult Brătianu, just to ensure that the king was content. Many politicians were wary of Brătianu (whose National Liberal Party represented the nobility and industrialists) but no one dared take him on – not even the king himself. That is how Carol's loathing of the old man had begun. The king's decision-making role had diminished in direct proportion to Brătianu's rise. For the timid, weak-willed Ferdinand it had been a blessing to pass responsibility to someone else. But for Carol it represented an erosion of the royal prerogative. None of that really mattered since Carol had run away but it was enough for a small clique to coalesce around their idealized image of the missing Crown Prince, and begin to form an anti-Brătianu faction that was ready to swing into action as soon as Carol returned.

In the meantime, Marie's spies had discovered where Carol was staying and managed to get a letter to him, summoning him back to Romania. The Prince responded by return of post. 'One should find a way', he wrote, 'of declaring that I have been killed in a motor accident... Say drowned in the Lago Maggiore... I'll know how to disappear without leaving a trace.'[8]

Astonishingly, the Romanian public took the view that Carol had been forced out of the country, for daring to speak out against the prime minister. There was even talk that the king was involved along with Marie, conspiring to expel their eldest son at Brătianu's request. Pressure built during the spring of 1926 for the prime minister to resign, and he did so. But, as a measure of just how corrupt and self-serving Romanian politics had become, he was invited to select his own successor. In truth, there was only one man for the job: the popular, centrist politician Iuliu Maniu, a scrupulously honest former lawyer from Transylvania who campaigned on an anti-corruption ticket. A rather dour, bookish Christian, Maniu was a man of honour who promised a moral revolution in public life and would soon launch a new and highly successful agrarian party – the National Peasants' Party. But his honesty was a problem for Brătianu. He threatened the deal-making that had oiled the wheels of Romanian politics for decades. Instead, Brătianu chose the eminently biddable and narcissistic General Averescu, the near-dictatorial leader of the People's Party who, by this time, was being compared to Mussolini. The two made a deal. Averescu would have Brătianu's support so long as he promised to stand down whenever the elder statesman required him to do so.

The king and Brătianu were juggling their own hand-picked placemen to lead an unchanging right-wing government, and had been for years. Next up as prime minister was Queen Marie's lover, the dashing aristocrat, Barbu Ştirbey. It had become a farce. All incumbents were desperate to block the rise of Iuliu Maniu and his left-leaning National Peasants. Maniu and his followers had an idea. In order to break the impasse, they demanded not just the demise of Brătianu but a new king as well – with Carol their potential solution. They set about finding him and persuading him to return to Romania.

In the summer of 1926, their campaign acquired an added urgency. King Ferdinand became seriously ill with cancer. If

Carol failed to reverse his renunciation of the throne, the crown would skip a generation, leaving the country with four-year-old Prince Michael as king. At the same time as these political manoeuvrings were taking place, the nation became gripped by the murder trial of Corneliu Codreanu, spiritual leader of The Brotherhood of the Cross.

It was supposed to happen in Iași, the city where the killing of Police Prefect Manciu had taken place. But the Romanian government was uneasy. Iași was Codreanu's stronghold, a hotspot of ultra-nationalism that might place pressure on the courts to free him. Instead, the trial was moved to the Liberal heartland of Focșani on the shores of the Milcov River, in the hope that a jury might be less inclined to sympathize with the defendant. Endless publicity around the case had given a further boost to Codreanu's profile. The offices of the criminal tribunal in Focșani were inundated with letters from legal scholars and high-profile advocates wishing to represent him.

The longer the delay in bringing him to court, the more support for the mystic anti-Semite seemed to grow. One local newspaper published a series of romantic poems about Codreanu and his love for Greater Romania, after which dozens of schoolgirls began sending him food parcels and offering to mend his clothes. The authorities responded by moving the trial again, this time to the far south-west of the country – the Danubian city of Turnu Severin – where they hoped Codreanu's popularity had not yet reached. But his Legionaries arranged for trainloads of supporters from across the country, who swept through the streets handing out propaganda and delivering speeches. Codreanu's good looks and Christian puritanism attracted the attention of schoolgirls once again. By the time his prison bus arrived in the city, a group of teenage admirers had congregated outside the gates, cheering Codreanu as he was driven inside.[9]

By the time of the trial, on 20 May 1925, the number of lawyers wishing to represent him had reached a staggering 19,300. This was no longer about the shooting of a police officer. Professor Cuza's campaign of disinformation about Manciu had worked. People believed he was a secret Jewish conspirator. The trial was now characterized as a battle for Romania's independence against the Jewish Bolsheviks who were trying to seize control of the country on behalf of Moscow.

The event was held in the city's vast, neo-classical National Theatre, with an auditorium that could hold a thousand people. Thousands more waited outside, carrying portraits of Codreanu and quoting extracts from his self-published prison diaries. Alongside him in the dock would be four of his closest aides – the same ones who had been cleared the year before over conspiracy to assassinate Jewish politicians. There was no new evidence against them but the government viewed this as an opportunity to jail the ruling body of Legionaries, and stop their growing popularity.

This time, the defence team was led by none other than Professor Cuza himself, along with a dozen juniors including the Jew-beating chemistry teacher, Professor Şumuleanu. The defendants took their seats on the other side of the stage. Rather than focus on the shooting, Codreanu's legal team were keen to explore the background of the deceased.

Had Manciu not been responsible for regular beatings in Iaşi? Did this not amount to a campaign of violence and torture against the university's humble students? At one point, Codreanu rose to his feet and asked to take over the cross-examination of police officer Vasiliu Spanchiu himself.

'Are you not the one who struck me in the face with your fist, in the tomato garden?' shouted Codreanu across the stage.

'I am not,' responded Spanchiu.

'Are you not the one who dipped the students' heads into pails of water whilst they had the soles of their feet whipped?'

'I was not there at the time,' said Spanchiu. 'I was downtown.'

Members of the audience shook their heads in disbelief. One

man leapt onto stage, grabbed hold of Spanchiu and carried him out of the auditorium, before ejecting him from the building. On his return, the audience member announced that if a police officer from Turnu Severin had tortured youths as they had in Iași, the townspeople would have lynched him. For the next six days, prosecution witnesses hardly dared leave the building.

The list of defence witnesses was extensive: military officers from the Iași School of Infantry who had witnessed Manciu's beatings; a priest from Bucharest; a naval captain; and the leader of the Christian merchants of Iași. Codreanu's own evidence was brief. 'Gentlemen of the jury,' he said, 'everything we have fought for was out of faith and love for our country and for the Romanian people. We assume the obligation to fight to the end. This is my last word.'

With that, the defendants were marched off stage into a converted dressing room. Within minutes there was what Codreanu described as 'thunderous applause'. The verdicts were in. Audience members ran into the dressing room, and hoisted the defendants onto their shoulders, carrying them back into the auditorium to enjoy the applause. The bench, behind which the jury was sitting, was strewn with bouquets of roses and Orthodox crosses. On the lapel of each juror had been pinned a Romanian tri-colour, emblazoned with a swastika, in gratitude for their verdicts of not guilty on all charges.

The train carrying Codreanu back to Iași stopped at every station and was mobbed by crowds of well-wishers with flowers. At Focșani, supporters waited until 3 a.m. for a glimpse of the leader of the Legionaries. Dressed in a woollen waistcoat and billowing white cotton shirt, he leaned out of the carriage window to thank them for their support. Beside him stood his doting fiancée, Elena Ilinoiu. The two would soon be married in Focșani in a ceremony that would attract a reported 80,000 people. (Elena Ilinoiu would outlive her husband by more than half a century, dying in 1994 at the age of 91.) So popular did

Codreanu become in the city that mothers queued around the block for the privilege of having him invested as godfather to their children.

When his train passed through the city of Buzau, a police report said that Codreanu was 'lifted and carried on the arms of university and high school students, making a grandiose parade and shouting "Down with the Yids"', the grim results of which were bloodied and wounded Jews left lying in the side streets.[10]

*

At 10 a.m. one Sunday morning in 1927, Codreanu and twenty-eight friends marched in two columns along the streets of Iaşi to the church of St Spiridon, dressed in traditional Romanian costume with swastikas pinned to their chests. After prayers, they sang fighting songs and gathered at Codreanu's rooms at 20 Florilor Street, where a solemn ceremony would take place. One of their group produced an envelope of soil collected from the tomb of Michael the Brave, the national hero who had briefly unified Wallachia, Moldavia and Transylvania in 1600. Another submitted a sachet from the victorious battlegrounds of Stephen the Great, the Moldavian prince who fought the Ottomans in the fifteenth century beside Vlad Dracula. The soil was mixed, blessed and poured carefully into pouches. Codreanu had recently fallen out with his mentor, Professor Cuza, over the issue of violence. Cuza wanted the ultra-nationalists to be less militant. Codreanu wanted them to be a band of *haiduci* – the romantic term for outlaws. The two men had agreed to go their separate ways. Freed from Cuza's control and no longer satisfied with the Brotherhood of the Cross, an organization that had been subservient to Cuza's own movement, Codreanu was about to set up his most popular militant group – one whose influence would change the course of Romanian history and politics.

He tied a pouch of sacred Romanian soil around his neck and

named the new organization after the icon at Văcărești prison – it would be called the Legion of the Archangel Michael.

At the same time, in the mountain resort of Sinaia, a tent had been erected on the lawn of the king's summer palace. Ferdinand lay dying. It was easier for him to breathe outside under canvas than in the stifling heat of the house. Marie had been sleeping on a sofa just inside the terrace doors, so that she could keep an eye on the tent and listen for any changes in his breathing. At midnight on 19 July 1927, Ferdinand tried to lift himself out of bed. A doctor was called and he administered an injection but the king could not settle. 'I am so tired,' he said, and Marie bent down and took him in her arms. They remained that way while the doctor went to fetch the rest of the family – all of them except for Carol, who was in exile in France. Marie held her husband's head against her shoulder so that he could breathe more easily. But the children arrived too late. 'His head fell against my shoulder,' she wrote in her diary, 'his already cold hands became limp... it was over – he was no more tired, but at rest.' Ferdinand's successor would be a six-year-old boy.

CHAPTER SIX

The Country, the Captain
And the Archangel from heaven.
Death, only death, Legionary
It is the most precious wedding of weddings
For the Holy Cross, for the country
We will defeat the forests and make the mountains obey
There is no prison that can scare us
No pain, no enemy storm
If we all fall, and are struck in the head
Death is dear to us for the Captain!

The Anthem of the Holy Legionary Youth

Shortly after the creation of the Legion of the Archangel Michael, the Captain (*Căpitanul*) – Corneliu Codreanu – posed for a rare photograph along with his five most trusted lieutenants. The image depicts them in formal pose, sitting like a group of Romantic poets in what appears to be the drawing room of a large house. The Captain is in the front row, green eyes fixed challengingly on the lens. He is all raffish hair and high cheek bones, a Caesar dressed in hand-embroidered waistcoat and high, frilly collar. 'Looking at him, you felt dazed,' wrote one of his (male) Legionaries. 'What was most impressive… was his physical appearance. Nobody could pass near him without noticing it, without being attracted by his looks, without asking who he was… This young man seemed a God descended among mortals… It could be said that he was a synthesis between the beauty of the northern type, and the ideal of beauty of Ancient Greece…'[1] Drawing him as a symbol that bestrode Romania's history like a Colossus, from its heroic roots to the modern day, was a favourite pastime of Codreanu's followers. This particularly effusive description came from a young Legionary called Horia Sima, a school teacher who would later develop close links with Adolf Hitler and contend for the leadership of the movement itself.

On the back row in the photograph, behind the Captain, is Corneliu Georgescu, clean-shaven, boyish, a pharmacy student who had been Codreanu's co-accused in both trials and would later become a government minister. To Georgescu's left is Tudose Popescu, a priest's son, theology student and 'handsome fighter', who had been with Codreanu from the start. He wore shoulder-length black hair and a Mexican-bandit's moustache. Beside him is Ion Moța, the shooter of their former comrade at the prison in Văcărești. Also a priest's son, Moța was ferociously intelligent, wilder even than those around him, all of whom viewed the Legion as a death cult to which they would inevitably one day give their lives. Moța was the Legion's second-in-command, and its strategist. On the front row is Radu Mironovici, a fellow Iași student and Codreanu's first follower. He would later become head of police for Romania's wartime fascist government, before eventually retiring to a monastery. In the middle of the front row is the Captain himself and, finally, to his left, a student lawyer called Ilie Gârneață, who is dressed like a romantic outlaw, a *haiduc*, and would take part in many violent anti-Semitic campaigns and later flee to Hitler's Germany.

These were the founders of the Legion of the Archangel Michael, the six men who would become known as the *Văcăreșteni*, because of their time spent in the prison of the same name. Later, they would change their title to the Knights of the

Annunciation, in keeping with the movement's deep religious roots. Captured on celluloid at the very turning point of their lives, they have a small-town innocence about them, a folksy simplicity. But there is also a chilling intensity to the picture, an absolute self-belief. These educated, self-righteous young men would become assassins, shooting with one hand while clutching the Bible in the other. They would kill and be killed according to their own mystic code. Their influence would touch every person in Romania. They would be raised on shoulders and cheered in the streets, they would make killing and violence an honourable and godly pursuit. And they would become the most popular political movement in the land.

Over the months that followed, Moța began referring to his friend in increasingly messianic terms. 'Nobody but God inspires him because He is sent by God,' he said of the Captain. Codreanu lived in monkish isolation, rising before dawn to pray and practise yoga. He ate little, other than peasants' cheese and home-baked bread. He had no need of possessions and walked tirelessly between rural villages, preaching anti Semitism and self sufficiency, while urging youths to become 'New Men' – an ideal he described as 'a man with heroic qualities, a giant of our history to do battle and win over all the enemies of our Fatherland, a battle that, once won, would extend to defeating evil itself'.

The Legion, said Codreanu, was more of a school and an army than a political party. The Romanian nation had no need of great politicians, but of a great educator and leader who would defeat the powers of evil and 'crush the clique of evil-doers', by which he meant Jews. He slept in hay barns or in open countryside, hitching lifts and sometimes borrowing a horse. The people saw his simple resilience and they admired him. His patriotism drove men to tears. Women knelt and touched his feet. They wrote battle songs about him, rousing marching tunes with symbolism derived, they believed, from ancient Dacia and the monotheism of the region's pre-Christian tribes, who had stood alone in worshipping one

God when all those around them had worshipped many. Even then, before Christ, the people of this land had felt themselves to be special, defending their territory from besieging heathen enemies. They believed that God had invested his spirit in the Dacian water, the sun, the trees and the stars, and that their souls were immortal. When Christianity came along, their single God fused neatly with the new religion, so that they believed it had been the natural predecessor, almost as if Christianity had always been present between the Danube and the Carpathians and they were waiting for the rest of the world to catch up. And so, this romantic imagery was written into the Legion's anthems. They synthesized nature with the ancient spirit of Romania and, in turn, with Codreanu himself, who was compared with Archangel Michael and raised to the status of a saint whose followers would sacrifice themselves for his divine beauty.

'As in the solar system,' Codreanu told his followers, 'each planetary body is in orbit, where it moves around a greater power of attraction, so the people, especially in the field of political action, gravitate around certain powers of attraction... It is a kind of magnetic power, and if someone does not have it, he cannot lead.'² It stood to reason that the Captain, the most magnetic body in the Romanian solar system, did not need confirmation in his role from anything so earthly and trivial as an election.

Still based in Iaşi, the Legion decided that the death of King Ferdinand in August 1927 was an opportunity to remind Romanians of the importance of their monarchy and the necessity for patriotic pride. The Legion still had only a thousand official members and needed to capitalize on the surge in popularity that had followed the Turnu Severin murder trial. It was decided, therefore, that Ion Moța should write a rousing obituary of the king, as the central feature of a new magazine to be called *Pământul Strămoşesc – The Ancestral Earth*. The monthly publication would include articles about the wild Carpathian countryside as well as bitter fulminations against Jews.

Since none of the Legion's leaders had much money, they borrowed printing equipment from the vestry of Ion Moța's father, and typewriters from the university. Then they got to work. On the front cover of the inaugural issue was a picture of the icon of St Michael that Codreanu had worshipped in jail. Above it, on the masthead, was a swastika. Beneath was a map of Romania covered in black spots. Around certain cities were whole clusters of them. These were pictorial representations of places deemed to have too many Jews.[3]

As readership of the magazine grew, its most interesting pages were the readers' letters. Alongside humdrum advice on how to grow carrots and drive livestock to market came insights into the minds of apparently law-abiding, educated Romanians. 'I say: onward, always forward, you, the new men,' wrote a colonel in the Romanian army. 'Long live the troop of Michael the Archangel. May the band of the wicked be swallowed by Beelzebub's darkness. St Michael the Archangel will have to strike unhesitatingly and mercilessly.' An attorney from Galați wrote: 'The bright sun of the swastika has not failed us this time... it gave us its beneficent light for our salvation... From now on the Romanian soul is again warmed by the faith that this Holy movement shall not perish.'[4] Soon, thousands of membership applications arrived at Legionary headquarters in Iași, and the movement began devising initiation tests to make sure it only recruited the fittest and the brightest.

*

Locals must have thought it a curious sight, fifty or so young men rising at dawn, wrapping themselves against the bitter cold and marching resolutely out of town into the woods and fields. The young Legionaries waded through rivers, shot rabbits and birds, and then returned for breakfast and prayers. It was January 1929 and the Captain had invited leaders from each 'nest' to the Legion's first National Assembly at a large town house in Iași.

The lakes around the city had been transformed into bustling skating rinks, where peasant stalls sold hot wine and bowls of cow belly soup, and the Legionaries, in their traditional Romanian clothing, were warmly welcomed.

The villa was owned by a retired army officer, General Ion Tarnoschi, who had been highly decorated in the war. At seventy-eight years old, he apologized to Codreanu for not being able to take part in the ceremonies himself but watched with pride as several young novices were granted full Legionary status, having passed their initiation tests. They had proved their worthiness in long forest walks and tests on the Bible. Reports had been written about their behaviour in work camps, their spirit of self-sacrifice and preparedness to help others; a characteristic referred to as 'white, bloodless martyrdom', as opposed to the 'red' variety that would come later.

Although most recruits were in their mid-twenties, there were pre-graduation sections too. Fourteen-year-old boys could be admitted into 'The Little Brothers of the Cross', while women and girls were encouraged into a group called 'The Citadels'. On the night of that first set of graduations in Iaşi, the retired general watched as Codreanu summoned his 'New Men' one by one, blessing them with ancient oaths and prayers in a ceremony intentionally reminiscent of the 'Order of the Dragon' and the oaths taken by Dracula's father in the fifteenth century. At the end, Codreanu turned to the old soldier, Tarnoschi, and presented him with a pouch of earth imbued with 'the blood of your own soldiers and officers', which he hung around the general's neck. He had been initiated into the Legion of the Archangel Michael despite his age, said Codreanu. Overwhelmed, Tarnoschi turned to the audience, face glowing, and burst into tears.

*

At the time of King Ferdinand's death, Prince Carol was unable to enter Romania, having been banned ever since his renunciation of the throne. Only a vote of parliament could allow him back.

Despondent at being kept away from his own father's funeral, he had commemorated the day with a rather showy appearance at the Romanian church in the Latin Quarter of Paris, wearing a top hat, a Prince Albert coat and a chest full of jangling medals. Exile had not provided the panacea that Carol had hoped for. He'd imagined his new life as sunshine and holidays, without the constant worry of regal responsibility. But losing his status overnight and descending into the anonymity of a Parisian suburb had focused his mind on his own irrelevance. He and Elena Lupescu had fallen into a humdrum existence in the leafy commune of Neuilly, west of the French capital. Their house was modest, by royal standards, with inexpensive furniture, simple décor and just a few paintings. Visitors noticed there were no family photographs to be seen. Carol's routine involved a daily lie-in, followed by tennis at the local club, a book in the afternoon – usually about military history – a walk with the dogs, and then a gin and tonic plus occasional games of bridge in the evenings. Elena was constantly anxious that the Romanian secret services might assassinate her for having shaken the country's monarchy so severely. She shopped for food herself, rather than relying on the two servants, concerned that they might be spies intent on lacing her caviar with poison.[5]

Carol's loneliness had been exacerbated by the cruel instructions of the Romanian prime minister that forbade Queen Marie from visiting her son. In fact, Marie had continued writing secret letters to Carol, and had once bumped into him while passing through Paris en route to the USA. She'd arrived at Gare du Nord, only to see a pale young man running towards her along the platform, armed with a bunch of flowers. It was Carol, breathless and emotional, and she had instinctively opened her arms to embrace him. At that precise moment, a press photographer appeared from the shadows and snapped a picture that was splashed in Romanian newspapers the next day.

Critics of Carol interpreted the photograph as evidence of

a plot to rehabilitate the Prince and install him on the throne. Whilst he was in exile in Paris, his six-year-old son, Michael, had been made king of Romania. Michael was looked after by his recently returned mother, Helen (now Queen Mother of Romania), along with Queen Marie, who was held in the highest esteem and was now seen as the nation's spiritual guide and the true monarch of Greater Romania. Obviously, little Michael could hardly make decisions for himself, let alone the whole country, and so a Regency Council was appointed, consisting of three men hand-picked by Ferdinand's most trusted prime minister, Ion Brătianu. One was the head of the Romanian Orthodox Church, the silver-bearded Patriarch, Miron Cristea, who showed little interest in the job and spent his time trying to devise ways of making money. Then came Carol's younger brother, the Old Etonian Prince Nicholas, a budding aviator who would rush into council meetings still dressed in flying suit and goggles. Finally, there was Judge Buzdugan, a bright and able lawyer who did whatever Brătianu demanded. Unfortunately, Brătianu died unexpectedly at the end of November 1927, leaving the Regency Council rudderless. When Carol heard the news, sitting in his modest drawing room in France, he felt the irresistible tug of the throne once more. Rumours reached Bucharest that he was trying to organize a coup.

The plan was hatched in France but launched from the unlikely environs of a rural estate in the countryside of southern England, owned by a millionaire Romanian exile called Barbu Ionescu. Carol and Lupescu flew into London in the spring of 1928, accompanied by a small group of co-conspirators: Lupescu's father, Nicolae; her brother, Constantin; and Carol's loyal secretary, the unctuous Constantin 'Puiu' Dumitrescu. Arriving in the first week of May, they knew the trip would be impossible to arrange discreetly, and so Carol announced his arrival to the press with an ostentatious visit to the West End, appearing in a limousine and allowing himself to be photographed for the newspapers. Revelling in the public attention after so many months of enforced anonymity, he even granted interviews to journalists. 'Oh no, I am not incognito,' he told them. 'Why play that comedy when I am known everywhere?'

But as he was gallivanting around town, ostensibly taking in the sights, his aides were visiting some unlikely places. They had contacted a small London printing shop and ordered thousands of flyers to be printed discreetly in Romanian. The message written upon each read: 'The government of duplicity, of intrigue, of tyranny, has to be removed'. After the death of Brătianu, the old grandee's brother had been appointed prime minister, a nepotistic move that excited allegations of corruption from beyond the grave. 'As the eldest son of King Ferdinand,' continued the leaflet, 'having been exiled because of malicious people and misfortune, I appeal to you all to come and join me... I want to return and lead Romania to its proper place in the world, and continue the work of our two former Kings.' The flyers were stacked into bundles, placed in a van and driven out to the Surrey estate. Arrangements were made for the hire of two private planes.

In the early morning of 6 May, Carol's party drove to Croydon airport and parked near the runway. The planes' propellers were already turning. Crates of leaflets were loaded through the freight doors at the rear, destined for a dramatic airdrop over the ancient Transylvanian city of Alba Iulia. But as Carol approached the plane steps, police officers ran over and surrounded him. As they led Carol away, accompanied by officials from the Home Office, he demanded to know who was behind the sting. It came from the highest authority in the land, they told him, '... because of the friendly relations between Great Britain and Romania'. Carol was allowed to return that night to his friend's Surrey estate but the next day the Prince's humiliation was complete. The British Home Secretary, William Joynson-Hicks, told the House of Commons that the Romanian coup-plotter had been expelled from the country.[6]

At Cotroceni Palace in Bucharest, Queen Marie was overcome with embarrassment. She wrote a letter to Buckingham Palace apologizing, and then had an aide travel to Paris to confront Carol face to face. Carol is said to have responded 'rudely' and 'foaming at the mouth'. He wrote a wild letter to his mother, warning her: 'My time will come, and on that day there will be many who will be sad that they did not see the reality as it really was.'[7] All the Prince's menace was now spent on trying to undermine his own mother, who, he concluded, was solely responsible for blocking his route to the throne (a throne that he had legally renounced on two occasions). From Paris, he and Lupescu unleashed a bitter campaign to try to chip away at Marie's saintly image. Lupescu's contribution was a bizarre autobiography in which she re-cast herself as a woman of noble birth who had been around royalty all her life, and who had been disappointed by all the rumours about Queen Marie's love affairs. It was a low blow from one who was herself so lacking in virtue.

But despite that, Carol retained many influential supporters back home. Among them, the unlikely figure of Iuliu Maniu, the priestly, anti-corruption politician who had been Prime Minister Brătianu's nemesis. Maniu's representatives had travelled secretly back and forth to Paris for months, trying to negotiate Carol's return. With Brătianu dead, the main obstacle was gone. Of course, Maniu was quietly repulsed by Carol's lifestyle but he believed in redemption, and in the institution of the Romanian monarchy, and viewed Carol as his best hope of modernizing the country.

In the event, Maniu won the 1928 election without Carol's help in a huge swing against the establishment Liberals. His National Peasants' Party (PNȚ), a left-leaning movement that championed the rights of peasant farmers, was progressive and inclusive, and its landslide victory (it secured 79.2 per cent of the vote) illustrated that, at this point in history, the vast majority of Romanians were not anti-Semitic or fascistic in outlook. In fact,

Professor Cuza's far-right National Christian Defence League – whose campaign symbol was the Romanian flag emblazoned with the swastika – had stood in the same election and managed to attract just 1.2 per cent of the vote. With Maniu's peasants occupying almost every seat in parliament, he was under no pressure to make difficult decisions that might undermine his soaring popularity. And yet he decided that now would be a good time to invite Prince Carol back to Bucharest.

Maniu's aides contacted Carol in France, and offered him a deal. He could return home if he were to abide by three strict conditions. The first was that he must promise to rule only as part of the Regency, not as sole ruler (his son Michael would remain titular king). Second, he must break with Lupescu and leave her behind in France. Third, he must reconcile with his wife, Princess Helen. The real question was, whatever he agreed, could anyone really trust him to keep his word?

*

49 Leningradsky Prospekt in Moscow was a pink neo-classical building, decorated with muted columns and restrained stone murals that depicted great books of learning, alongside Communist Party motifs. This was the International Lenin School, where future party leaders from around the world were trained. Inside were lecture halls, a library and film theatres. Many of the young men and women hurrying up the steps in the late 1920s were on the run from regimes that had outlawed communist movements, and had arrived in Moscow under assumed names.

Among them was Ana Pauker – also known as Comrade Marie. After her release from prison, Pauker had been provided with a fake ID by party officials in Bucharest and then smuggled herself across the country's eastern border. Her first application to the Lenin School had failed. The entry requirements of communism's most prestigious school were notoriously strict, requiring applicants to be members of the Central Committee in their home country, or to have been a Party leader for at least four years. Ana did not have the necessary connections to circumvent the rules but managed to gain entry as a lowly auditor, a role in which she impressed her teachers so much that they offered her a place on the faculty's most prestigious course. She learned military science and Marxian economics. But she also learned the skills of a revolutionary operative – public mobilization, espionage, sabotage and the use of explosives.

On the same course were several men (they were all men, apart from Ana) who would become the most well-known communist leaders of the era. Sharing a lecture room with her in the winter of 1928/9 was an eighteen-year-old German called Erich Honecker (cover name: Fritz Malter), who would later become the hard-line communist leader of East Germany. Also present was a professional revolutionary from the old Austro-Hungarian empire called Josip Tito, the future communist president of Yugoslavia.

The emphasis for all Ana's generation of students was on undercover work and fomenting revolution across Europe. Ana was despatched as Comrade Marie first to France and then to the Volga German Soviet Socialist Republic, to assist in 'correcting the mistakes' of collectivization.[8] As a young Socialist back in Romania, she had been opposed to Moscow's heavy-handed intrusion into the affairs of communist parties outside Russia but the brutal smothering of the movement in Romania had forced her to reconsider.

Joseph Stalin was now installed in the Kremlin and had been running the Soviet Union since the death of Lenin in 1924. He soon took an interest in the indefatigable young woman from Romania who might one day be General Secretary in Bucharest. With his quiet intervention, Ana was able to skip her final year at the Lenin School and was named as advisor to the Comintern's (Communist International) Latin secretariat, responsible for the Communist Parties of Spain, France, Portugal and Italy, a hugely influential job. Any of her misgivings about Moscow had evaporated. Ana was now a faithful Stalinist.

Her husband, Marcel, meanwhile, was anything but. He had spoken out strongly against Stalin's desire to take back a prized piece of the Greater Romanian jigsaw: Bessarabia, the territory occupied by Romania during the war, and later confirmed as Romania's in the Treaty of Paris. Stalin did not recognize Bessarabia as Romanian and was constantly threatening to incorporate it into the Soviet Union, an issue that had divided what was left of the underground Romanian Communist Party. Always outspoken, Marcel Pauker came to Moscow to see his wife and clashed with one of Stalin's aides about the issue. As a result, he slid rapidly out of favour and by 1930 he was ordered to leave Moscow, to be sent into internal exile in Siberia. The same fate soon befell the spiritual leader of the Romanian Communists, Christian Rakovsky, who, as Trotsky's personal friend and supporter, was fortunate to have got away with his life.

Ana Pauker hardly seemed to care about her husband's exile. She was too focused on her own career and knew that any perceived contamination from a sceptic such as Marcel might cause problems. Working undercover in France, she had an affair with her Stalinist boss, Eugen Fried, and gave birth to a baby girl. Pauker's apparently flint-hearted abandonment of her husband is often cited as evidence of her cruelty and lack of compassion, but Marcel was also having affairs. More difficult to excuse was Ana's abandonment of the couple's two children – Vlad, aged five, and Tatiana, aged two – whom she left at a children's home run by the Communist International.

Her clandestine work around Europe had been building to one purpose. Ana believed the time was fast approaching when she could smuggle herself back into Romania and put her Lenin School training into effect. She would rally together her old colleagues in Bucharest, and start tipping the country towards revolution. Meanwhile, seismic political changes of another sort were already taking place.

On a thundery June night in 1930, a small group gathered at the edge of a runway in Bucharest to wait for the arrival of a biplane flying in from across the still-snowy peaks of the Carpathians to the north-west. The young pilot, Marcel Lallouette, had been hired for his daring antics, which included breaking speed records above the French countryside, but he had never dealt with weather like this. The mountains had been buffeted by storms all day. Huge black clouds towered above Bucharest. By 10 p.m., the solemn greeting party at Băneasa airport had given up hope. They switched off the landing lights and summoned their limousines. Then one of the guests heard the noise of an engine high above the clouds. Moments later, a plane dipped from the night sky, circled the airport and landed smoothly on the flooded tarmac. Sitting behind the pilot in the two-man cabin was a helmeted figure who eased back the glass canopy and clambered down the ladder. With a scarf still wrapped around his face, Prince Carol ducked inside a waiting car and was whisked off to Cotroceni Palace, where his brother Nicholas was waiting.

Just after 5 a.m. the following morning, Prince Carol met with his sponsor, Prime Minister Maniu. All seemed well. Carol had not slept but was excited to be back in his country. Maniu reiterated the conditions of his return to Bucharest, Carol accepted and the two men shook hands jovially.

Hardly had Maniu returned to his office than a note arrived. It was from two of his officials who had visited Prince Carol later that same morning and had rather alarming news to report. Carol had told them he intended to become king of Romania straight away. Maniu assumed there must have been a misunderstanding. He jumped in a car and headed back to Cotroceni, where he found Carol in his office. It was true, said the Prince; he had taken a quick reading of public opinion that morning and concluded that the people wanted him as king.

Maniu called an emergency cabinet meeting to stop Carol from assuming control. But half way through, about thirty of Maniu's own MPs entered, uninvited, and announced that they agreed with Carol: he should be installed as monarch as soon as possible. By lunchtime, crowds started to gather on the streets. Military bands were quickly organized and were soon marching along Calea Victoriei. A carnival atmosphere descended over all of Bucharest. Iuliu Maniu was so furious with Carol's deceit that he resigned that same afternoon. Just two days later, in bright summer sunshine, Carol was driven in a golden horse-drawn carriage through the streets of Bucharest, smiling broadly and waving to the crowds. He was back, and he was king. The ovation that greeted his oath in Parliament lasted a thunderous fifteen minutes.

In the days that followed, the new king began using his royal prerogative to appoint loyal followers as senior government aides. These were men with no political background, friends and 'business associates' who promised unstinting loyalty to Carol. They had no official positions but because of their status as his intimates, began to run entire government departments. Known as Carol's 'camarilla', they executed whatever laws he requested. Among the group's members was a corrupt arms-dealer called Nicolae Malaxa, who was a business partner of Hitler's close associate Hermann Goering, as well as several anti-Semitic academics and a few supporters of a new movement becoming increasingly popular across the country – the League of the Archangel Michael. This was their first taste of power.

When Marie returned to Bucharest after a trip abroad, she was appalled by her son's behaviour. Carol had hoped that her attitude would soon change as she came to recognize his suitability for the role, but the usually forgiving Marie remained cold and distant. Carol was indignant. He began portraying himself as a martyr forced to return to his frigid, unsympathetic wife for the good of the country. He created a new medal, La Décoration de la Souffrance (The Order of Suffering), for citizens who had triumphed over similar miseries, and then commissioned a set of stamps and coins depicting himself wearing a crown of thorns.

He treated his mother like an enemy agent, banning her aides from visiting her in Cotroceni Palace, and having spies follow her around taking notes of her conversations. Previously loved by everyone, Marie was forced to stay in her rooms, cut off from anyone with influence. Carol even slashed her monthly allowance in an attempt to stifle her movements.

At least, it seemed, he'd stuck to the other two conditions of his agreement with Maniu. Lupescu had been left behind in France, and Carol seemed to be making a go of it with his former wife, Helen, speaking with her civilly and sometimes staying in the same house. Maniu was told that Carol was trying his best and that he should take pity on the confused king. He grudgingly agreed, and re-instated himself as prime minister. Maniu's first task was to put pressure on the Orthodox Church to annul Carol's divorce, putting this dark episode behind him and saving the reputation of the Romanian monarch. All seemed to be going well until Carol's personal secretary, Puiu Dumitrescu, noticed something strange happening in the royal kitchens.

The king, Dumitrescu realized, was eating twice as much as usual. He challenged the royal chef, who confirmed that Carol was regularly ordering for two. Deepening his suspicions were the strange goings-on at the usually deserted Foisor hunting lodge in the mountains behind Peleş Castle. There were rumours of lights being switched on and cars coming and going in the middle of the night.

In late November 1930, it became scandalously apparent that Elena Lupescu was back in town. Maniu responded with puritanical outrage, resigning once again. Carol, on the other hand, seemed relieved that the whole thing was finally out in the open. He escorted Lupescu to Bucharest, installed her in an official residence and gave her a position in his influential *camarilla.* Taking full advantage of his royal prerogative, he began sacking ministers and replacing them with friends. Anyone who questioned his decisions was immediately dismissed. Carol invited the ageing historian Nicolae Iorga to become prime minister in the spring of 1931, putting him in charge of a cabinet of experts. The experiment failed.

Carol's grenade-throwing style of politics meant that Romania had six prime ministerial changes in the space of just eighteen months from the summer of 1932 until the end of 1933. The queen watched with dismay. Her stipend cut to the point where she could no longer travel, she was a virtual prisoner in the palace. 'At times I wonder if he is completely sane,' she wrote. 'It's amazing how fast he has destroyed all the popularity he had nine months ago. What curse has been placed on this poor boy? Why does he always botch things up?... It is tragic to see all those who once believed in him, who considered him a victim, to see the truth, which his father and I had known all along.'[9]

Amid Carol's terrifying unpredictability, there was one political movement that had secured his unwavering support. Corneliu Codreanu's Legion of the Archangel Michael appealed to the king's irreverence, his patriotism and his growing right-wing tendencies. The movement had created its own paramilitary wing in 1930, known as the Iron Guard, a title that would soon take over from the Legion as the new and menacing name for the whole movement. Support for the Iron Guard increased as a result of the Carol-inspired chaos in parliament, attracting democrats who had lost faith in the system's ability to deliver order and stability. More Romanians joined up when the global depression of the early 1930s began to bite, leading to a collapse in world grain prices. Romania was still primarily an agricultural economy and plunging prices for corn and wheat meant peasants could no longer pay their landlords. Many moved to cities to find work, adding to the rising unemployment and poverty. Distrust of government accelerated further when

Europe suffered a financial crisis in 1931 and the flow of foreign capital into Romania dried up.

On the look-out for populist solutions, men and women of all political hues became attracted to the slash-and-burn politics of the Iron Guard, from aristocrats who formerly supported the Liberal Party to the young trouble-makers of the Vlad Țepeș (Dracula) League. King Carol's affection for the Guard was more than just gratitude for their loyalty while he was in France. He fancied he saw something of himself in the enigmatic young fascist Codreanu, and decided to help the movement grow. In 1930, the king began giving financial donations to turn the Guard into an electoral force.

With the boost in campaign funds, along with the Guard's internal re-organization brought about by the recruitment of professional politicians and strategists, Codreanu was eventually persuaded to stand for parliament in the summer of 1931. He was put forward as the Guard's candidate in a by-election for the fiercely Orthodox county seat of Neamt, not far from Iași. Typically, Codreanu campaigned on foot and on horseback, dressed in peasant clothes. Arriving unannounced in market squares, he would ask locals to kneel and pray, and speak to them in mystical terms unlike any politician they had heard before. In the mornings he would rise early and ring the church bells. Contesting the seat against the National Peasants' Party and the Liberals, he was thought to have little chance of victory. But in a sensational count on 31 August, Corneliu Codreanu was announced the winner. The fascist Iron Guard would have a seat in Romania's parliament.

But the formality of the chamber did not suit him. Codreanu was not used to being challenged, or talking to anyone who might disagree with him. Nor was he used to debating issues of uninspiring public policy, such as tram budgets, sewage transportation and mine safety. Indeed, the Iron Guard still had no concrete policies, just a general philosophy that could not easily be applied to real-world problems. He was a poor speaker who easily lost his train of thought and was mocked by other members. He did, however, come into his own when attacking corruption and explaining the Guard's position on law and order. To much derision and laughter, he accused other deputies in the chamber of fraud and embezzlement and called for the death penalty for abuse of government funds.[10] These were the issues that brought him to the attention of a wider, supportive audience. Typically for Codreanu, even in parliament, violence was never far away. Hidden in his jacket pocket at all times was a loaded pistol. His closest lieutenants were always similarly armed, and while Codreanu was trying to find his feet in parliament, they were in training for the movement's first high-profile assassination.

It was 1933 and Carol's chaotic rule had left parliament fractured, and the country without a prime minister. He turned to the suave, civic-minded Ion Duca, the new leader of the National Liberal Party (and creator of Romania's scout movement) to step in temporarily, in the run-up to the national elections of December that year. Duca was only needed for six weeks, just a caretaking job to make sure there was no violence. He reluctantly agreed and identified the Iron Guard as the main threat.

After seeing Legionaries marching around town in paramilitary uniforms, Duca asked Carol to sign a decree making the movement illegal. Carol refused, explaining to his prime minister that such a move might attract 'serious reprisals'.[11] Dismayed by the king's lack of cooperation, Duca decided to take matters into his own hands. He signed the decree himself and launched a fierce crackdown on Codreanu's movement, arresting 18,000 people during a spree of violence that ended with eight deaths.

It was the last thing Carol needed during the winter holidays, and on 29 December he summoned Duca to his mountain retreat, Peleş Castle, where he was preparing to celebrate New Year. The meeting lasted a couple of hours, after which Duca made his way to the pretty, old-fashioned railway station at the foot of the mountain in Sinaia. It was 10 p.m. There was a blizzard and Duca sheltered beneath a wooden canopy with a small party of local officials. As he bid them farewell, four volleys of gunfire rang out around the empty platforms. Duca was shot in the base of the skull, the first Romanian prime minister to be assassinated.

CHAPTER SEVEN

I dream of vengeance, black as the grave
Your sword of blood, steaming from the enemy,
and on top of the hydra which billows by the wind
Your dream of proud, succeeding glory
What they say of the world, coloured flags,
That which are the people, grand and Romanian,
When he strikes, sacrificing his naive flame
Sweet Romania, this I wish for you.

'What I Wish For You, Sweet Romania!' (1867),
Mihai Eminescu

The young assassins fleeing through the forest that night were members of an elite unit of Legionaries known as the Nicadors, a three-man team that had travelled from Bucharest earlier in the day under orders from Codreanu. Their leader was a business student called Niki Constantinescu, another bright, promising undergraduate who had been drawn to the Guard's fascist mysticism as a panacea for all his country's woes. It was Constantinescu who fired the fatal shots. Accompanying him were Ion Caranica and Doru Belimace, who had acted as spotters, hiding near the ticket office and signalling the best moment to strike. Both men were Aromanians – an ancient Balkan ethnic group who considered themselves descendants of

Roman legionaries, and viewed Greater Romania as their sacred homeland. They had formed the Nicadors as a legionary death squad, to kill anyone opposing the Iron Guard, while hoping to achieve martyrdom for themselves.

Plenty of other legionary recruits were eager to make the ultimate sacrifice on behalf of Codreanu, forming assassination squads with historically inspired names such as the Avengers and the Decemviri – a ten-man brigade named after the law-makers of the Roman Republic. A rare insight into members' lives at that time comes courtesy of a priest called Father Ion Dumitrescu-Borsa, a keen memoirist who was sent to look after the Nicadors prior to their hit. It was the summer of 1933 and they had been campaigning on behalf of the Iron Guard in the western city of Resita. As the Nicadors left town, they and some junior Legionaries picked up a few local girls. Father Borsa was asked to drive them to the forest, where they leapt out of the van and scattered, in couples, into the trees. He and the Nicadors' leader, Constantinescu, were left alone. 'We will wait here an hour,' reassured Constantinescu, 'and they will have finished.' Later that evening, the men emerged amid 'farewell whispers, kisses, tears, and prolonged hugs'.[1] The girls were so reluctant to let them go that they lay across the bonnet of the vehicle, and Father Borsa had to pull them off. Membership of a legionary death squad had an attractive cachet, as if they were ancient crusaders and these final carnal pleasures were their right.

The etiquette of killing was set out in chilling terms. They were told to enjoy pulling the trigger because this was the ultimate achievement of a Legionary. They should smile and remain at the scene. When police arrived, they should politely greet them and deny nothing. But in the panic of killing the prime minister, Constantinescu and the others had bolted. They were caught in the woods the following morning and taken to a police station, by which time they had recovered their composure and seemed relaxed and in good spirits. Constantinescu admitted the murder but explained calmly that Prime Minister Duca had committed the bigger sin, repressing a religious organization (the Iron Guard) and imposing a violent clampdown that had led to eight deaths.

At the military courtroom a few weeks later, the Nicadors arrived dressed in smart black suits, fine silk ties and cufflinks. Pushed into the dock beside them was Corneliu Codreanu, charged with conspiracy to murder on the grounds that everything the Guard did must have been sanctioned by him. The panel of judges were all ex-military men, former soldiers who had fought in the war for the creation of Greater Romania and who admired anyone trying to protect their legacy. They quickly cleared Codreanu of any involvement in Duca's death, but the confessions of the Nicadors were impossible to ignore. All three were sentenced to hard labour for life.

Despite the murder of his prime minister, Carol's admiration for the Iron Guard was undimmed. Indeed, he was impressed by their code of honour and their uncompromising view that Romania's weak politicians needed to be swept away and replaced with an authoritarian leader. Carol looked north to Hitler's Germany and west to Mussolini's Italy, and saw two leaders who were taking a firm, absolutist grip over their countries to create powerful, industrially advanced, patriotic and militaristic states. Romania's corrupt politicians, it seemed to him, were irresolute and self-serving, and the system was paralyzed from top to bottom with bureaucracy. The country was still in the grip of the Great Depression and every week there were strikes, with protestors on the streets. Duca's complaint that the Iron Guard was stirring trouble seemed to Carol wide of the mark. In fact, the Guard were the best enforcers of discipline. If Carol could have joined them, he would have. However, he could not countenance the idea of being a member of a party that was led by someone other than himself. So, he decided to set up his own.

Carol's creation was called the Romanian Front (FR) and was launched in 1935 as a near carbon copy of the Iron Guard.

The only missing element was Codreanu and his mysticism. The Front devised its own form of *numerus clausus* to limit the number of Jews in public posts. Aggressively anti-communist, it wanted an end to elections and parliamentary politics and the introduction of a 'supreme leader'. The similarities with Codreanu's movement did not end there. The Front created youth groups with titles such as 'The Country's Sentry', 'The Romanian Falcons' and 'The Romanian Archers'. Uniformed children as young as seven years old were invited to join and would go on patriotic retreats to the countryside. Carol appointed himself as their commander-in-chief.

But the king felt he could not openly lead the Romanian Front himself. He needed a frontman and that job went to an eccentric former prime minister, Alexandru Vaida-Voevod. As an ethnic Romanian from Transylvania, Vaida-Voevod had been instrumental in helping Queen Marie negotiate the inclusion of his home territory in Greater Romania at the Paris Peace Conference, but his politics vacillated wildly. Vaida-Voevod was a leader of the anti-fascist National Peasants' Party until he received a call from Carol, inviting him to lead the 'moderately fascist' Romanian Front. Many respectable colleagues joined him, and soon he was saluted in the street by black-shirted men bellowing *'Hurrah for Vaida'*, with arms outstretched in fascist salutes.

Vaida-Voevod's defection to another party, and indeed ideology, was part of a huge recalibration of Romanian politics during the mid-1930s. The old National Liberal Party split over whether or not to support Carol and his far-right views. Its replacement as the dominant force in Romanian politics, the National Peasants' Party, split along similar lines. So too did Averescu's People's Party. These were the giants of the Romanian political system, shattering into dozens of fragments, each defined by their allegiance to the king and his *camarilla*, or simply by their efforts to curry royal favour. And as the king swung his wrecking-ball at every traditional party in sight, he pointed at their disintegration as evidence that the country needed an authoritarian leader to stop the slide into political and economic chaos.

Peasants still represented around 80 per cent of the population. They were Romania's economic and cultural backbone and, with Carol's encouragement, they sought refuge from the Great Depression in extremist politics. They might well have chosen the communists under different circumstances – anything that might lead to radical change – but the Romanian Communist Party (RCP) was banned and, anyway, their pro-Moscow stance was extremely unpopular, particularly with the generation who had witnessed how the Bolsheviks had behaved in Romanian trenches during the war. Instead, peasants protested by joining the various parties of the far-right.

Those pastures were becoming crowded indeed. Professor Cuza was back on the scene, peddling his 'scientific racism' to a new generation. He joined forces with another ultra-nationalist who had skipped from one political home to another, a moderately successful Romanian poet called Octavian Goga – an intense man with strange unblinking eyes who was shamelessly sycophantic towards the king. Goga was uncompromisingly anti-Semitic, and the dispossessed peasants loved him. 'There is only one final solution to the Jewish problem,' he told reporters, 'the collection of all Jews in a region which is still uninhabited, and the foundation there of a Jewish nation... the further away the better.'[2] Together, Goga and Professor Cuza created the National Christian Party, which was launched just four months after Carol's Romanian Front and branded itself with a red swastika.

None of these new creations of the far-right could compete with the undisputed original. By 1936, Codreanu's Iron Guard had acquired a membership of 250,000. Its Legionaries took to the streets in uniforms of green shirts, black military-style trousers and leather boots. Green became their defining colour. It was said to represent renewal. They paraded green-tinted portraits of Codreanu and green flags emblazoned with both swastikas and Orthodox crosses. Codreanu inspected his Nazi-saluting troops outside their Green House headquarters, wearing a long fur coat and fedora hat. When they marched through central Bucharest, it was a terrifying sight for those Jews who had strayed into their path. The Guard stamped the ground as hard as they could and organized themselves into strange formations so that from above they looked like a series of arrows passing down the streets.

In order to compete with them, the newly formed party of Goga and Professor Cuza adopted similar militaristic paraphernalia. The National Christian Party dressed in blue shirts and black trousers, carrying blue flags emblazoned with red swastikas. They were known as the Lăncieri and could raise a crowd of 100,000 in Bucharest alone. There was no real difference in politics between the Iron Guard and the Lăncieri, but Codreanu's men claimed to have Christian Orthodoxy at the heart of their philosophy. Nevertheless, if they met in the street, Green Shirts and Blue Shirts would invariably end up in a fight.

Carol's far-right party could simply not compete. In a huff, he withdrew his support from Codreanu and began backing anyone who would undermine the Iron Guard. That included a former close aide to Codreanu, Mihai Stelescu, who had fallen out with the Captain and left the Guard to set up his own far-right movement, known as the White Eagles, a party that Carol began to fund purely to annoy Codreanu.

Stelescu's defection from the Guard was toxic. He set up his own magazine and wrote highly critical stories about Codreanu, mocking his unease at speaking in parliament, and alleging that he had indulged in sexual relations with the nuns of Agapia Monastery in Moldova. For good measure, he also threw in an accusation that Codreanu was no lionhearted crusader, but a coward who had run away from a fight with the police.[3] It was reckless stuff, and Codreanu responded as he inevitably would, by calling a meeting of elite Legionaries and sentencing Stelescu to death.

In July 1936, Stelescu was taken to a Bucharest hospital to have his appendix removed. While recovering, he heard a commotion in the corridor outside his room. Suddenly the door flew open and ten Legionaries marched in. Most of them he recognized. They were a group of theology students, with senior positions in the Romanian Christian Student Association. They were also members of an Iron Guard death squad. These were the Decemviri. They drew guns from beneath their coats and shot their old friend with several dozen rounds of ammunition. Once they had finished, they put their guns down and took axes out of their bags. They then chopped Stelescu into steak-size pieces.

Even when news of such atrocities reached the press, they seemed to have little effect on the Iron Guard's popularity, a fact that further annoyed the king. He became obsessed with bringing Codreanu down but was too afraid of a public backlash. Instead, the king focused his resentment on his own family.

Largely confined to her quarters in Cotroceni palace, Marie had been reduced to the ghostly pallor of an apparition. She spent her days writing children's fairy tales and reading her diaries. The high point of her week was riding her beloved horse among the chestnut trees of the palace gardens. On the rare occasions that Carol allowed her to leave the country, he blocked her money and Marie found herself begging accommodation from friends. He took great satisfaction in banishing her lover, Barbu Știrbey, from Romania and shutting down his business empire, viewing it as revenge for the treatment he had received during his own love affairs. When Carol heard that Marie had ignored his orders and visited Știrbey in Switzerland, he told her that such disobedience was a declaration of war. There were even rumours that the king sent an assassination squad to try to kill Ştirbey while he was travelling on the Orient Express.

Painfully aware that his mother still enjoyed a great deal of public affection, Carol grudgingly allowed her to attend official events but ensured she was kept in the background at all times. At Independence Day celebrations in Bucharest in 1936, Marie sat near the back of the stage and described her son's arrival 'on a huge white horse with the attitude of Kaiser Bill... surrounded by brilliant uniforms and busy sycophants'. His autocratic behaviour combined with his fragile mental health, she told her diary, was a dangerously combustible mix. Her son, she said, was 'dancing on a volcano'.[4]

Carol displayed similarly ugly behaviour towards the rest of his family. He banished his former wife, Helen, from the country, allowing her to visit just twice a year to see their son, Michael. He expelled his young sister, Ileana, as punishment for marrying an Austrian and decreed that she could not return without his permission. His most deranged behaviour, though, was reserved for his younger brother, the Old Etonian, Nicholas. Just like Carol, Nicholas had fallen in love with a divorcee commoner who he was prevented from marrying by the constitution. Carol told him to ignore the law and marry in secret, but when Nicholas followed his brother's advice, Carol stripped him of his military rank, drummed him out of the royal family and then had him arrested and exiled.

As the far-right fought among themselves for supremacy during the hot summer of 1936, Stalin's favourite Romanian communist, Ana Pauker, had already slipped back into the country to try to rebuild the country's tiny underground movement. She stayed on friends' floors and moved around by cover of night. But secrecy for such a well-known political figure required absolute discretion from everyone she met, and the RCP was known to be riddled with government spies. On the night of 12 July 1935, Pauker was leaving a clandestine meeting of the RCP secretariat when a unit of security police (the Siguranța) confronted her. Pauker tried to run but one of the officers opened fire. The bullet passed through her left leg and became lodged in her right, bringing the forty-three-year-old crashing to the ground. Instead of rushing her to hospital, the police took Pauker to Siguranța headquarters. Bleeding profusely, she was hauled before Police Inspector Turcu, who told her: 'The agent who shot you was an idiot for not shooting you through the heart… if you fall into my hands again I will shoot to kill.'[5]

Eleven months later she was driven in a prison van to the city of Craiova, 140 miles west of Bucharest, and from there to a sleepy village in the countryside, where her trial would take place in a converted hall. Attempts to hold it in Bucharest had failed after three days of anti-fascist protests had blocked the court entrance. The authorities chose the new location because of the absence of communist sympathizers, and the increased likelihood therefore of securing a conviction.

Pauker was accused, along with eighteen others, of spying on behalf of Moscow. Each day, the defendants were marched into the courtroom in shackles, the women chained in groups of three, the men chained separately. It was the news event of the year and the hall had been adapted accordingly, with a makeshift stage for a panel of judges and rows of seats for the lawyers. The defence team of twenty-four advocates occupied the first two rows and included lawyers flown in from abroad. The main seating area was strictly reserved for soldiers, Siguranța agents and dozens of Lăncieri fascists dressed in their customary blue shirts with swastikas, who cast a cloud of simmering violence over proceedings.

The Lăncieri acted as self-appointed court security. When one of Pauker's lawyers refused to adhere to the judges' instructions to sit down, dozens of them tried to wrestle him out of court. The defence team formed a protective ring around him but soldiers backed up the Lăncieri, making stabbing gestures with their bayonets. Finally, the offending advocate was shuffled outside for his own safety, prompting Pauker to shout that the trial was unfair since her legal team was facing intimidation. At that point, the soldiers turned on all eighteen defendants. There was 'a stampede towards them; the accused were hit from all sides and dragged out by their arms and legs as they defiantly resisted,' wrote a journalist present on the day. 'Two of them fainted and were carried out by the others. Ana Pauker was handcuffed.'[6] In a further incident, a soldier tried to strike Pauker with his bayonet but another defendant blocked the blow.

The intimidatory conduct of the Lăncieri continued throughout the trial, with successive defence lawyers being shouted down for their 'communist sympathies' and expelled from the hall (the allegations were largely correct; one of the defence lawyers, Ion Gheorghe Maurer, was a revolutionary who would later become prime minister under Nicolae Ceauşescu). It was Ana herself who led much of the forensic questioning of witnesses, demonstrating a passion and erudition that surpassed that of her legal team. The problem was, of course, that she *was* an agent of the Communist International in Moscow and *was* actively working against the Bucharest government.

In the end, she was convicted and sentenced to ten years' hard labour. The press coverage of Pauker's trial ensured she became the symbol of Romania's communist movement, drawing more recruits into its clandestine network. But the real propaganda victory belonged to the far-right, who portrayed Pauker's Bolshevik plot as evidence that only they could be trusted to protect the nation against a 'Jewish-communist conspiracy'. Carol and his henchmen greeted the verdict as justification for an escalating programme of anti-Semitism, waging war against the democratic ('Jewish-owned') press and imposing further restrictions on Jewish employment.

*

The summer of 1936, and the trial of Ana Pauker, was to become the defining moment for the growth of the far-right in Romania and soon another important character stepped from the shadows. The accomplished military officer, General Ion Antonescu, had been impressed by the activities of the Iron Guard and was trying to make a move into the political sphere. We last met Antonescu during the First World War, when he helped strategize the famous Romanian victory over the Germans at the Battle of Mărăști. After the war, he was rewarded with military attaché positions in London, Brussels and – after a struggle – Paris. The French initially rejected him, describing Antonescu as: 'Brutal, duplicitous, very vain, with a ferocious will to succeed... these are, together with extreme xenophobia, the striking characteristics of this strange figure.'[7]

On his return to Bucharest, Antonescu was made chief of staff of the Romanian army, where his 'strangeness' won him few friends. Viewed as arrogant and self-absorbed, he did, however, impress with his work ethic and his strict moral discipline. Antonescu was a puritanical Christian who was sickened by corruption in public life and, hardly surprisingly, found the king's behaviour reprehensible. He was always cold and uncommunicative in Carol's presence but Carol hardly seemed to notice, awarding Antonescu the highest military role in the state and welcoming him into his inner circle. If Carol imagined Antonescu could be bought, he was very much mistaken. The General used his new job to launch an investigation into government corruption, during which he uncovered a multi-million-dollar fraud involving an arms contract that implicated not only the king and his mistress, but dozens of ministers and high-ranking soldiers. Carol was speechless with fury, and sacked Antonescu immediately.[8]

Since then, Antonescu had been skulking around looking for gainful employment. He lived in a pretty villa with his socialite wife, Maria, in the city of Pitești, from where he observed the rise of the Iron Guard and Carol's frustrated attempts to undermine it. Whilst in Carol's employment, Antonescu had commissioned a report into the activities of Corneliu Codreanu to assess his influence upon the armed forces. He'd concluded that Codreanu was something of a braggart, but nothing for the government to worry about. He did, however, find common ground in Codreanu's suspicion of Jews. Now unemployed and smarting at Carol's treatment of him, Antonescu found the Guard an alluring prospect. He called Codreanu and invited him around for tea. 'With all my achievements and symbols of rank,' he is said to have exclaimed on meeting Codreanu for the first time, 'I cry out today: Long live the Captain!'

Later, in the winter of 1936, the two met again, at a skiing event in the fashionable Carpathian resort of Predeal. Photographed against a backdrop of snow-covered pines, the General wore a military-style jacket and black tie as if he were attending a formal ball, while Codreanu relaxed in sports gear. They wanted the king to know that they were meeting and that an historic political deal was on the table; the tough, establishment soldier who might take the army with him, and the popular mystic with a ready-made party for the General to join. There is no doubt that Carol would have been alarmed.

Antonescu did not commit himself, however. He wanted to keep his options open, in the full knowledge that a powerful and well-connected figure such as himself could take his pick of far-right parties. He had lunch, too, with the poet and joint leader of the National Christian Party, Octavian Goga, a man with whom he had more in common than Codreanu. The pair bonded over a mutual passion for classical music and their rejection (at that time) of violence, but they could not agree on King Carol. Goga wanted to maintain him on the throne. Antonescu despised him and wanted him out.

For the rest of that crucial autumn of 1936, the Iron Guard were in the ascendant and their popularity was about to soar once again, this time due to an extraordinary endorsement from the powerful Orthodox Church.

*

A mortuary train crept through the snow-covered forests of Bukovina in January 1937, before crossing the border into Romania and stopping at the first provincial station it came to. On the platform waited a delegation of seventy Legionaries in full uniform, along with a local priest who said prayers as the train drew to a halt. On board were two simple coffins that had travelled all the way from the battlefields of the Spanish Civil War. They contained the remains of two of the Iron Guard's most famous Legionaries, killed while fighting for Franco at the Battle of Majadahonda. One was called Vasile Marin, the other was Codreanu's fanatical deputy and best friend, Ion Moța.

When the train reached the next station, Lujeni, dozens of school children gathered. There were legionary songs and fascist salutes. The coffins of Moța and Marin were carried through the streets, accompanied by eight priests.

As news of the train's progress spread through Transylvania and Moldova the religious ceremonies became increasingly grand. By the time the coffins arrived in the city of Roman, a bishop had been called to conduct ceremonies, along with fifteen priests and a large choir. At the ceremony in the small town of Burdujeni, it was noted that the clergy exchanged their normally black attire for white vestments – clothing usually reserved for an Easter service or the canonization of a saint.[9] The bodies then passed through the Transylvanian city of Sibiu, where Bishop Vasile Stan told the large crowd of mourners that the two Legionaries were examples to everyone. 'We would be reckless and foolish,' he declared, 'if we did not follow them.'

The funeral train finally reached Bucharest on 11 February 1937, where the coffins were transferred to the Church of St Ilie to lie in state beneath a golden chandelier. The final ceremony was attended by four bishops, 400 priests and a congregation that spilled onto the road outside. 'We pray for the souls of the heroes Moța and Marin,' one of the bishops announced above the sobs, 'who fell in battle against Bolshevism for the Cross.' As the sun set that day, the coffins were transported on a gun-carriage through crowds of mourners, who showered the caskets with flowers and raised their arms in Nazi-style salutes. Marching just behind his lost comrades was the unmistakable figure of Corneliu Codreanu, dressed in a long, black leather coat and followed by diplomats from far-right regimes in Nazi Germany, Spain, Portugal and Italy.

Carol watched from his palace window and realized the futility of his fight with the Guard's leader. Soon after, he called Codreanu to a meeting and made an extraordinary proposal. He, the king, now wished to become leader of the Iron Guard himself. Codreanu would be compensated, of course. He would be awarded the title of Minister President of a new fascist government. So, what of it? Was it a deal? The Captain thought for a moment, and said 'No!'

The Romanian national elections of 20 December 1937 promised to be the most violent and unpredictable in the country's history. As people queued to vote, Green Shirts and Blue Shirts fought running battles on the streets. In the cities of Orhei and Târgu Mureș, more than 300 people were arrested and four killed. Never had the far-right stood a better chance of taking power. Even the normally anti-democratic Codreanu sensed the possibility of an upset and changed the name of the Iron Guard to the more voter-friendly 'Everything for the Country Party', just for the duration of the election. Although a plethora of small parties were standing, the real contenders were the National Liberals (centre-right and currently in government), the National Peasants' Party (centrist) and the two fascist movements, Codreanu's and the blue-shirted troops of Octavian Goga and Professor Cuza.

After the vote, journalists hung around outside the offices of the Electoral Commission in Bucharest, only to see the lights switched off and officers leave for the night without declaring a winner. It was unprecedented. We only know what actually happened thanks to diary entries from a well-connected politician called Constantin Argetoianu. At 6 a.m. the following morning, he received a call from a friend at the ministry who told him the result of the count. The Liberals had won, with 32 per cent, but were some way short of the 40 per cent required to form a government. Codreanu's party had achieved a staggering 22 per cent in its first proper outing as a political party, making it the second largest party in the country. It was conceivable that Codreanu might organize a ruling coalition.

The following day, still no result had been announced. Then, on 22 December, an announcement was finally made. The Liberals had won, but their result had been massaged upwards by 4 per cent, while Codreanu was now in third place, having been deprived of 6 per cent of his vote. 'They are false,' wrote Argetoianu in his diary – the percentages had been manipulated for all parties.[10] The Liberals still fell short of the 40 per cent needed but their main reason for fixing the result was not to ensure a Liberal victory, but to manufacture a resounding Codreanu defeat. In the event, the public saw through the sham, and realized that history had been made.

Law-abiding people took to the streets to sing and dance. Fascist banners were unfurled in provincial towns. 'The sympathy which the Legionary movement enjoys', wrote Argetoianu, 'is thanks to nothing other than a reaction against the dishonest and corrupt government, from top to bottom, under which we live. The man most cursed is not [Liberal Prime Minister] Tătărescu, but the king.'[11]

And now it was for the king to decide who would become prime minister. He knew the public wanted a change, and began looking down the table of results. In fourth place, behind Codreanu's Legionaries, was the 'moderately fascist' National

Christian Party, led by Octavian Goga. The anti-Semitic poet was a great friend and supporter of the king, and Codreanu's most bitter rival. He had scored just 9 per cent of the vote. As far as Carol was concerned, he was perfect for the job.

Within forty-eight hours of Goga becoming prime minister, two of the biggest Jewish-owned newspapers in Romania were shut down. The Bucharest Bar suspended the licenses of 1,540 Jewish lawyers. The right to sell liquor or tobacco was suspended for Jewish shopkeepers.[12] A week later, Goga withdrew citizenship from all 225,222 naturalized Romanian Jews. Violence followed, with pogroms unleashed in the Jewish quarter of Bucharest.

There was fighting, too, between rival fascist groups, with Codreanu's Green Shirts furious at being outmanoeuvred by Goga. Two Legionaries were killed and fifty-two wounded. Uncommitted people hardly dared leave their homes. It was all playing into King Carol's hands. He had proved that the parliamentary system could not work, and that Romania needed an authoritarian leader, in the mould of Hitler or Mussolini. On 10 February 1938, Carol forced Goga to resign, dissolving parliament and putting himself in charge, as Romania's royal dictator.

*

Marie watched events unfold from her sick bed. The previous spring, her health had suddenly deteriorated, leaving the sixty-one-year-old with massive internal bleeding. Court doctors diagnosed cirrhosis of the liver, despite the fact that she rarely touched alcohol. In the hope of finding transformative air in the mountains, Marie went to live in Bran Castle, the ancient fortress from where Vlad Dracula's soldiers had once watched the border for invading Ottoman troops. Her condition continued to deteriorate and so she was moved again, to her seaside villa beside the Black Sea in Dobruja, then to a sanatorium in Italy, then to a clinic in Germany. Her treatment was disorganized and half-hearted, and two of Carol's sisters later wrote that the king had not been 'particularly interested in prolonging his mother's life'.[13]

Marie's last letter to her exiled lover, Barbu Ştirbey, had to be smuggled out of the country in the hands of a Viennese doctor to avoid Carol's spies. 'So much unsaid,' she wrote, 'which would so lighten my heart to say: all my longing, all my sadness, all the dear memories which flood into my heart... The woods with the little yellow crocuses, the smell of the oaks when we rode through the same woods in early summer – and oh! so many, many things which are gone... God bless you and keep you safe.'[14]

On 18 July 1938, she lay on her bed, staring at the door in Sinaia's Pelişor Castle, hoping for the arrival of her favourite daughter, Ileana. But Carol had failed to call her. Marie asked for the Lord's Prayer to be recited in English, and then whispered to Carol that he should be 'a just and strong monarch', before lapsing into a coma. She died just after 5 p.m. that same day.

She had requested that no one wear black for her funeral, rather her favourite colour, mauve. Bucharest was decorated with lavender-coloured flags and bunting. Crowds dressed in mauve capes and waved mauve handkerchiefs. The coffin of the English princess who had arrived by train into that snowy land four decades earlier, left in bright sunshine, with the crowd whispering her name. *Mama Regina*, they repeated again and again as Marie made her final journey. *Mama Regina*.

CHAPTER EIGHT

I hope you have not been leading a double life, pretending to be
wicked and being good all the time. That would be hypocrisy.
The Importance of Being Earnest, Oscar Wilde

After his coup, King Carol's days were spent taking part in over-
elaborate military parades, usually dressed in his beloved self-
styled uniforms of candy-coloured blue and gold braid with a
chest of saucer-sized medals. He extended his palace to spectacular
proportions, building an extra wing with ornate ceilings and
marble floors. Sometimes he ate in the fine banqueting rooms
beneath glittering chandeliers, but he preferred taking meals at
Elena Lupescu's modest villa in Avenue Vulpache, where they
dined in her kitchen, often feeding morsels from the table to her
pet dogs.

Carol grew more suspicious of politicians and relied heavily
on his *camarilla*, in particular Lupescu, who took an increasingly
prominent role in decision-making. In her shadow emerged
another opportunist peddler of banal advice and gossip, Lupescu's
former chauffeur, Ernest Urdărianu. While driving Lupescu
around town, he had impressed with his reflections on business
and the royal court, and the king's mistress was keen that he was
given more influence. Carol obliged, making Urdărianu minister
of the court and the king's representative in government. Rarely
away from Carol's side, the obsequious Urdărianu was soon

using his royal connections to strike illicit business deals, while jealously blocking anyone else's access to the monarch. Urdărianu quickly adopted the tone and unshakeable self-confidence of an old boyar. 'Madam Lupescu controls the king,' he bragged to one acquaintance, 'but I control Madam Lupescu, so I control Romania.'[1]

These three people – Carol, Lupescu and her former driver – ruled the country according to their own whims and petty desires throughout the late 1930s. While the rest of Romania struggled to recover from the Depression, it is estimated that Carol and Lupescu spirited away between $40 million and $50 million into Swiss bank accounts. Aware that other European leaders might view a royal dictatorship with suspicion, Carol installed a frontman as prime minister and referred to the assorted corrupt businessmen in his *camarilla* as 'a government of national unity'. The frontman was Miron Cristea, the Patriarch of the Romanian Orthodox Church (the organization that had already shown its true colours at the extravagant funeral of Moța and Marin). Cristea was an enthusiastic womanizer with far-right views. In his first official statement, he announced that he would pursue '… the departure from the country of foreign elements who, recently established in the country, damage and weaken our Romanian ethnic national character' and offered to cooperate with 'other states… that have an excess of Jewish population.'[2]

There were 728,000 Jews in Romania at the start of the 1930s but during all of this, Carol gave no apparent thought to the fact that his own mistress was Jewish. Without his protection, the fact that Lupescu's family had converted to Christianity would have counted for little. She would have been barred from most professions, forced to prove her suitability for citizenship and would have risked a beating in the pogroms that were taking place in several Romanian cities. Carol did not rescind the oppressive anti-Jewish laws imposed by Goga's short-lived leadership and, indeed, looked to extend them. The far-right had affixed Jews so firmly to Bolshevism and, therefore, to the destruction of Greater Romania, that to tolerate them was tantamount to treachery. With the head of the Church, as well as the king, intent on driving Jews out, anti-Semitism became the pre-occupation of much of the country.

At the same time, Carol could not get over his bitter obsession with the popularity of Corneliu Codreanu. Reports reached the palace of Codreanu's spontaneous appearances in rural villages, dressed in virginal white on the back of a horse. People would greet him with fascist salutes, before gathering around him in prayer. One young villager called Nicholas Nagy-Talavera wrote about his impressions when the Captain arrived at his town square in the Apuseni mountains: 'There was suddenly a hush… A tall, darkly handsome man, dressed in the white costume of a Romanian peasant, rode into the yard on a white horse. He halted close to me… his childlike, sincere smile radiated over the miserable crowd and he seemed to be with it, yet mysteriously apart… He was part of the forest, of the mountains, of the storms on the snow-covered peaks of the Carpathians… He had no need to speak, his silence was eloquent.'[3]

By 1937, fascist leaders in Germany and Italy were viewing Codreanu as a likely ally, much more so than the unpredictable and embarrassingly needy Carol. Codreanu had no official status but his command of large swathes of the peasant population meant that he might take the country at any moment. Hitler was already providing the Iron Guard with money and weapons on a small scale. Then, on 12 March 1938, the German 8th Army crossed the border into a largely welcoming Austria. In May the same year, the Führer declared his intention to destroy Czechoslovakia. As war in Europe looked more likely by the day, King Carol was in danger of Codreanu siding publicly with Hitler, a move that might lead to the offer of German troops to help the Captain launch a coup.

Frightened and humiliated, Carol employed the Iron Guard's fiercest critic to help stamp them out once and for all.

That man was the monocle-wearing Armand Călinescu, a brilliant economist who had been lured to the far-right by Goga, under whom he had served as interior minister. Călinescu had spent much of the election campaign arresting Legionaries and shutting down their printing presses, and had become as obsessed about eradicating the movement as Carol. Rather oddly, his journey from moderate politician to rabid Carolist had been accompanied by a change in attire. Gone were the suits and ties, to be replaced with all manner of elaborate military uniforms. His favourite was one of pure ivory-white, with giant batwing lapels and an array of tight leather straps. He and Carol could not understand why others did not share their militaristic sartorial passion, and made uniforms compulsory for the leaders of all government bodies. Even members of the Royal Academy were instructed to buy them, an order that the historian, Nicolae Iorga, mercilessly lampooned. He announced that he would only conform if he was allowed to wear a speared helmet, upon which he could impale Călinescu.

Călinescu set to work on his master plan for destroying the Legionaries in the spring of 1938. He began with police raids on private addresses. In Bucharest, 150 Legionaries were dragged from their homes and jailed without charge. On the coast, in Constanța, 538 homes were raided in a single night. Particularly repellent to Călinescu was the way in which the Iron Guard helped impoverished peasants with their funeral costs by erecting Orthodox crosses for free. Each was inscribed with Legionary motifs, as if the dead were supporting Codreanu from beyond the grave. 'The Iron Guard is not a movement of [public] opinion', said Călinescu, 'but rather an association of assassins and foul profaners of tombs.' He had all the crosses uprooted and destroyed.

Next, Călinescu proposed jailing Codreanu himself. Even

Carol was hesitant. Inevitably, there would be street protests and violence. Remember what had happened to Prime Minister Duca when he tried to take them on? But Călinescu insisted. 'If we act with kid gloves,' he told Carol, 'our authority will be weakened.' Still, everyone agreed that they needed a pretext, some plausible criminal charge for which they might arrest him. It was Călinescu's task to contrive one.

Gradually, an improbable plan began to take shape. Earlier that year, the anti-Semitic historian Nicolae Iorga had fallen out with his old friend Codreanu. The pair had argued over the unlikely issue of Legionary-owned restaurants, eateries set up by Codreanu – in summer camps and several cities – to raise funds for the Iron Guard. Iorga told Codreanu it was a risky business, investing the movement's money in such unpredictable ventures, and had been proved right when King Carol banned the Iron Guard, shutting down all its restaurants and leaving Codreanu with large debts. Of course, Iorga had been instrumental in the evolution of Romania's far-right ever since the Peasants' Revolt thirty years earlier and, as one of the spiritual fathers of the movement, felt he was within his rights to publicly criticize Codreanu for such a costly financial error. In response, Codreanu wrote a firm but restrained riposte to Iorga, one that was published in the papers. 'You are unfair,' he wrote. 'You are, in spirit, dishonest.' It was a trifling insult, by any measure, but in Călinescu's frantic imagination, there appeared an opportunity.

Iorga was now employed as a Royal Councillor – an aide to the king. To allege he was anything less than scrupulously honest wasn't just damaging to him, but to his position. More than that, to the king's governance. Corneliu Codreanu, he announced, must be arrested for criminal libel.

At a cabinet meeting of 28 March 1938, a vote was held on whether it was a satisfactory charge. Everyone in the room nodded their assent, apart from one. The newly appointed minister of defence was the puritanical General Ion Antonescu – Codreanu's friend and ski-partner – who had taken the job grudgingly and still loathed the king. He announced angrily that such trumped-up charges were an abuse of power and resigned on the spot. The rest shrugged their shoulders and carried on. The next day, Codreanu was charged with 'defamation of a public official'. The problem was, the leader of the Iron Guard had vanished.

Codreanu was hiding out in the dimly lit vestry of a Bucharest church, living off rations of cheese and eggs supplied by the priest. Alongside him was a pudgy-faced academic called Constantin Papanace, head of the Macedonian Legionary movement and sometime aide to the Captain. He was outlining Codreanu's diminishing options. First, they should consider a coup. They had enough supporters, said Papanace, but the cost of failure would be high. Codreanu shook his head. The idea of regicide, he said, was 'foreign' to the movement's spirit. What about fleeing abroad, Papanace suggested? Rome for instance, where Mussolini promised a warm welcome? No, said Codreanu, he would prefer martyrdom to fleeing his homeland. He should stay, he concluded, and take whatever Carol threw at him.

The two men put on their hats and coats, and tried to leave the church discreetly but Codreanu was recognized. 'The crowd on the stairs and in the market raised a forest of arms to the sky,' wrote Papanace, 'as if it was following a spontaneous command coming from the depths of their hearts... I have rarely felt so much collective spiritual vibration as in that moment. Could that crowd, made up of Legionaries and "unknown sympathizers" have had the intuition that it was the last salute they would give to their adored Captain?'[4]

As news of his whereabouts spread, Codreanu was arrested. Now that the authorities had him under their control, they needed to make sure he never got out. The problem was that defamation was hardly worth twenty years in jail. The public would not stand for it. But a fortunate piece of incriminating evidence turned up in the meantime that would prove far more damaging.

The defamation trial was hurried through, with Codreanu sentenced to six months' imprisonment. While he was in jail, a letter had been found in one of his coats that was being repaired by a tailor in Bucharest. It was a letter intended for Hitler, congratulating him on his annexation of Austria and predicting an imminent coup in Romania that would transform the country into a Nazi state.[5] As a result, Codreanu faced charges that carried a substantial jail sentence – high treason and complicity with foreign organizations.

The military courtroom into which Codreanu was led, in May 1938, was an altogether more business-like setting than the converted theatres and provincial town halls of his legendary acquittals. Soldiers stood at the door wearing immaculate blue tunics and armed with bayonets. A stern-looking military judge sat behind a desk covered in legal documents. Codreanu was no longer the Captain but Prisoner Codreanu, granted the right to wear a sombre suit and a quiet cotton tie. Journalists noticed the dark circles beneath his eyes.

His chief counsel was relying on two star witnesses. First was the former National Peasants' leader, Iuliu Maniu, Romania's principal upholder of democratic propriety and a Christian centrist whose word carried much weight amongst Romania's educated classes. Most people would not have realized that Maniu and Codreanu knew each other quite well and had even struck a secret pact in the 1937 election, agreeing not to criticize each other but to aim their joint fire at the corrupt Liberal Party. Maniu was appalled by Codreanu's anti-Semitism but that was not the issue here. They shared a faith and an aversion to corruption.

When called to the witness stand, Maniu philosophized that a nation could not exist without a solid basis of Christian morality, and said that this was a quality he had found in Codreanu. He and the Captain, he explained, had met on several occasions and had discussed politics and morality. No such negotiations, said

Maniu, would have taken place if for one moment he suspected Codreanu of planning a coup.

The next witness caused even more of a stir. Into the court marched General Ion Antonescu, the king's former defence minister who had resigned over the plan to prosecute Codreanu in the first place. Saluted by the sentries, he took his seat in the witness stand, nodding at familiar faces and smiling at the journalists.

'Would you', asked Codreanu's advocate, 'consider Corneliu Codreanu a traitor?' The general puffed out his chest and marched across the courtroom towards the accused. He then shook Codreanu by the hand. The two men stood there for a moment in front of a transfixed courtroom. 'Would General Antonescu give his hand to a traitor?' boomed the most well-known soldier in Romania (he often talked about himself in the third person) and then returned to his seat.

It was headline-grabbing stuff but the judge was unimpressed. He wanted to explore more broadly the murderous nature of the Iron Guard. Codreanu was asked to explain why the assassins of Prime Minister Duca, and those who had chopped up their former colleague Stilescu in his hospital bed, had been promoted in the organization's hierarchy. Wasn't this, asked the chief prosecutor, evidence of incitement to violence? Codreanu's response came close to self-deification. He had promoted them for their sacrifice, he said, and was merely offering prisoners comfort, just like Christ had advised his disciples.[6]

On 27 May 1938, the military judge ordered Codreanu to stand. By this time, the Captain was pale and drawn and seemed to have aged a decade. There were no chanting crowds or supporters wearing swastika badges, just a room full of sombre legal personnel and international journalists. With little drama, the judge read out the verdict. Guilty on all charges. Codreanu was sentenced to ten years' hard labour (the same fate as Ana Pauker) and led to a waiting prison van.

During most of the trial, King Carol had been confined to bed with flu. On hearing the verdict, he was in celebratory mood and arranged a holiday for himself and Elena Lupescu on his newly purchased royal yacht, the *Nahlin*. The 300-foot super cruiser, moored on the Black Sea, had already been dubbed 'the royal love boat' after Edward VIII and Mrs Simpson used it to escape the paparazzi following the British monarch's abdication. Carol revelled in its royal notoriety. Whilst he enjoyed the bar and the gymnasium, Lupescu wafted around in sunglasses and gown, instructing the crew how best to prepare the king's favourite cocktails. They sailed south to Istanbul for a lengthy recuperation, Carol reflecting that his most dangerous rival was now out of the picture but unsure how Hitler might respond to the loss of his Romanian protégé.

*

The threat of war in Europe was about to open the same old territorial wounds that had afflicted Romania since its creation. Competing claims for various parts of the country had never gone away, and Carol would inevitably be judged by his ability to keep hold of both Transylvania and Bessarabia. Losing either would be a disaster of historic significance.

Hungary and Germany posed the greatest threat, with both intent on avenging the territorial losses imposed on them after the First World War. Hungary was still simmering over the loss of Transylvania, and considered a war in Europe an opportunity to take the region back. All Budapest needed was a nod from its ally, Hitler, and its troops would pour across the border into the mountain passes, and begin the bloodiest of battles. They would follow it up with German-backed campaigns to retrieve lost land in Czechoslovakia and Yugoslavia too.

These three militarily vulnerable countries – Romania, Czechoslovakia and Yugoslavia – decided that the best hope of preserving their borders was to join together in a mutual defence pact known as the Little Entente. But the Little Entente needed a big brother, and France agreed to underwrite the whole scheme, promising to gallop to the defence of each should Hitler, or any of his allied countries, decide to invade. The three felt they could sleep more easily at night with Paris watching their back.

It was with absolute horror, therefore, that on 30 September 1938 Carol discovered that France had allowed Hitler to march right into Czechoslovakia and annexe the Sudetenland. The French had promised to protect Czechoslovakia, just as they had promised to protect Romania, and yet Édouard Daladier – France's prime minister – had just signed the notorious Munich Agreement with Hitler, Mussolini and Neville Chamberlain, gifting the territory to the Führer. If they had failed one member of the Little Entente at the first time of asking, what hope for Romania? Carol needed to find other backers.

The Romanian king's naval destroyer emerged from thick fog into Dover's docks in November 1938, guided by pier bells and ghostly tugs. Beside him on deck stood his son, Prince Michael, and his minister of court – the former chauffeur, Urdărianu. The last time Carol had set foot in Britain was during his ill-fated attempt to organize a coup in Romania. Now he was met with the full pomp of the British state. A military guard played the Romanian national anthem before Carol was driven in an open-top carriage through the drizzle to Buckingham Palace to meet King George and Prime Minister Neville Chamberlain.

Carol wanted a £30 million loan and guarantees of protection against German and Hungarian aggression in the event of war. Chamberlain was bemused by the appearance of the desperate Romanian monarch, with his endless concerns about Transylvania. Hadn't he heard the news? Britain and France had just signed the Munich Agreement with Hitler precisely to avoid war! Chamberlain had stood at the foot of the plane steps and waved the famous peace agreement. War had been averted. Chamberlain recommended that the Romanian king stop worrying and sent him politely on his way, without the loan or an agreement on defence.

Carol decided to change tack, and in November headed for the snow-capped peaks of the Bavarian Alps and Hitler's Eagle's Nest retreat, the Berghof. If he could persuade the Führer to keep Hungarian hands off Transylvania, he would not need the protection of Britain or France. Carol's strongest bargaining chip was Romanian oil. Hitler had only the synthetic variety and knew that any sustained military campaign in Europe would require Romanian supplies, either by agreement or by force. The trick for Carol was to ensure it was the former and that, in return, Hitler would guarantee his borders.

Carol tried his best to appear confident and statesmanlike, but made a significant blunder. He offered Hitler an increase in oil, but then added that he must continue selling to Britain and France too, because he intended to stay neutral in any war. Hitler was cross, and thought Carol's negotiating tactics naïve. Nevertheless, he told the Romanian monarch not to worry about an invasion from Hungary, saying that he had warned Budapest for years that they must be reasonable with their revisionist demands, particularly in respect of Transylvania. The two men parted with a handshake. But a casual remark at the end of the conversation darkened Carol's mood. Hitler expressed his admiration for Romania's Iron Guard, and in particular Corneliu Codreanu. The Führer said that the young Legionary's views were very much those of Nazi Germany and that one day Codreanu would make an excellent prime minister. The comment played on Carol's mind during the long train ride home. Even with Codreanu in jail, he realized, his own royal dictatorship was still not safe.

The night after the king's return, Codreanu was summoned from his cell at Doftana Prison, south of Bucharest, and led downstairs into the prison yard where he was surprised to find several of his old colleagues already gathered. Niki Constantinescu, leader of the Nicadors, greeted him warmly, as did the other two members of that first death squad. It was five years since their assassination of Prime Minister Duca, and the harsh prison routine had hollowed their cheeks and reduced their frames. Next in line was Ion Caratănase and the nine members of the Decemviri who had shot and dismembered Stilescu. They too embraced Codreanu. Then they stood waiting in the moonlit prison yard, smoking and chatting, and wondering why they had been called together in the middle of the night.

Eventually, a unit of prison guards arrived and escorted the men to two waiting police vans. As they clambered inside, each prisoner was instructed to kneel on the floor while their hands were bound to the seats. They were then driven out of the prison northwards, through the streets of Bucharest, past the airport and on to the long straight road that leads to Ploiești. After an hour or so, the vans pulled off the main road, down a rough track through the forest and into an area known as Tâncăbești, close to where Dracula is said to be buried at Snagov. Another car was waiting for them, driven by an army officer called Major Dinulescu. He flashed a torch three times to indicate his presence.

The door beside Codreanu was flung open to reveal the silhouette of a guard. The Captain was on all fours and still tied to the seats. He struggled to turn around. 'Comrade,' he said, 'please allow me to talk to my Comrades.' The guard paused for a moment. Major Dinulescu told him to get a move on. Someone went to fetch a length of rope.

When they returned, they came at Codreanu from behind, slipping the rope around his neck, pulling his head sharply back against the seat and strangling him. It was a violent death, the screams of his thirteen comrades coming from all directions. The fourteen Legionaries were killed simultaneously.

On the way back into Bucharest, the guards blacked out their windows in case anyone saw the piles of bodies. They took the dead Legionaries to Jilava Prison, where a trench had been dug. Each of the men was removed and laid out face-down on the dirt.

Then an officer walked along the line and shot them, to make it look like they had been killed during an attempted escape. The bodies were then rolled into the pit and the guards got to work with spades.

It was 30 November 1938. The trees were leafless, the air filled with thin rain. In the city, lights were coming on and telephone calls were made. King Carol was notified of the previous night's events before breakfast. The news reports praised the 'brave' guards who had stopped the Legionaries from escaping. Immediately, Carol was under suspicion. To lose his most feared opponent, along with thirteen other leading Legionaries, in one night of murderous activity seemed far too convenient. In Germany, Hitler revoked the ceremonial medals he had awarded Carol during his trip to the Berghof and made it clear that he held him responsible for the Captain's death. The Führer told an Italian delegation that Carol 'would have to pay dearly for the murder of Codreanu who, on his mother's side, was of German blood'.[7]

Meanwhile, Hitler's designs on Europe continued apace. By March 1939, Nazi troops had marched into Prague, further dismembering Czechoslovakia. At the same time, a Nazi envoy arrived in Bucharest to explain to Carol that Germany required a monopoly over all Romanian exports – wheat, corn and, most importantly, oil. The beleaguered Carol had little choice but to accept. In the vain hope that Germany would protect his borders from Hungary, he agreed that they could have almost all of Romania's agriculture and oil. *Time Magazine* was so appalled by Carol's behaviour that it declared Romania had made itself a German dependency. 'In no instance of modern times has one state made such humiliating, far-reaching economic concessions to another,' said the magazine.

When London and Paris saw what Hitler had done, they quickly made a counter-offer. In April 1939, the two countries promised to protect Romania's independence (though not its integrity) against any German-backed takeover. It was an act entirely atypical of Britain's foreign policy, which considered East Central Europe a distant and unimportant region. France, on the other hand, had had a long and fruitful relationship with Bucharest, and it was Paris that carried out all the diplomatic heavy-lifting, persuading London to sign the Anglo-French Guarantee as a show of solidarity against Hitler.

Carol could, of course, accept both deals, and indeed, he did. It was part of Romania's eternal balancing act between regional superpowers. Choosing sides had to be avoided at all costs. If he chose Hitler, for example, he might well protect Transylvania but would inevitably place other territories at risk. The Russians, for instance, might punish him by marching into Bessarabia – a territory they still considered theirs. If, though, he backed Russia, the Germans would undoubtedly respond by encouraging Hungary to storm into Transylvania. Carol was in trouble whichever way he turned. Being trapped in the middle was the curse that every leader of Romania had wrestled with since the medieval period. For Dracula, the choice had been between the Ottoman Empire and the Hungarians. Now it was Hitler's Germany or Stalin's Soviet Union. Carol was best served by a continuing tension between the two. So long as they remained equal and opposite forces, they effectively cancelled each other out and Bucharest could be spared a terrible choice.

On 23 August 1939, a German Focke-Wulf Condor touched down in Moscow, a small metal door opened at its rear and out stepped the German foreign minister, Joachim von Ribbentrop. As he descended onto the tarmac, a Soviet band struck up 'Deutschland, Deutschland über Alles' – 'Germany, Germany above all'. The welcoming delegation led him past a Soviet flag propped against a Nazi swastika to a line of waiting limousines. Ribbentrop was driven straight to Red Square to meet with the new Soviet foreign minister, Vyacheslav Molotov.

The first that most Romanians knew of the Molotov-Ribbentrop

Pact was from the newspapers the following day. 'Guided by the desire to strengthen the cause of peace between Germany and the Soviet Republics', read the statement, 'and based on the fundamental stipulations of the Neutrality Agreement concluded in April 1926, the German Government and Soviet Union have come to the following agreement...' There followed seven articles spelling out a treaty of non-aggression between the two. It was sensational news. Hitler and Stalin would work out their respective zones of interest, while agreeing not to compete militarily. For Bucharest, the budding new friendship spelled disaster. The Germans and the Russians might agree to take whatever territory they desired from Romania, without risking recrimination from the other. And indeed, that was the case. The Molotov-Ribbentrop Pact contained a secret protocol that included not only the division of Poland but also an agreement between the two countries that Stalin could seize Bessarabia from Romania. That night, Carol wrote in his diary: 'Everything is black!... black! Completely black!' A week later, Germany invaded Poland.

*

The Iron Guard was in chaos. Instead of entering the Second World War with a leader who was close to Hitler, the movement was descending into factionalism. Rivals were lining up to inherit Codreanu's crown. The first was his father, Ion Zelea Codreanu, who was touring the country with a group of heavies, telling crowds that he had Codreanu's blessing. Second was a small ultra-religious group that idolized the deceased Spanish Civil War heroes Moța and Marin, and who had not yet chosen their candidate. Third was a schoolteacher from the provinces called Horia Sima. The thirty-one-year-old had been a member of the Iron Guard since the early days and had described Codreanu as 'a God descended among mortals', but none of Codreanu's mystical powers had rubbed off onto Sima. A short, puny man with twitching, rodent-like features, Sima tried to make up for his lack of star quality by outdoing the others in his use of violence against Jews. But Codreanu's closest followers were sceptical about him, and with good reason. Before Codreanu died, he had drawn up a list of worthy successors. Thirteen people were ranked in order of preference. Sima came in at number thirteen.

The young teacher began adopting the clothing, hairstyle and mannerisms of Codreanu. During public meetings, he would throw back his head and pout his lips. While delivering speeches he would lapse into what was supposed to be contemplative silence. His followers began talking about his 'grace' and his 'teachings', in pseudo-religious terms. But all this was unconvincing. Sima was a man defined by what he wasn't. He wasn't Corneliu Codreanu, but his whole life would be spent trying to emulate him.

The other candidates fell away one by one. Codreanu's father was drunken and violent, and set up his own small breakaway faction. The ultra-Christian faction, inspired by memories of Moța and Marin, wanted to abandon politics altogether and retire to a monastery. That left Horia Sima. He pronounced himself leader of the Iron Guard and began to organize a spectacular campaign of terrorism from his headquarters in Nazi Berlin, where he and his followers had fled in order to escape a blanket clampdown on the Iron Guard.

Meanwhile, in Bucharest, King Carol was busy rewarding his uniform-loving interior minister, Armand Călinescu, for his role in the capture and eventual murder of Codreanu. Călinescu – known as the Black Monocle – was promoted to prime minister and marked the occasion by joining with Carol to create yet another right-wing political party in the hope of dislodging some of the remaining supporters of the Iron Guard. It was to be called the Front of National Renaissance (FRN) and immediately began indulging in the kind of fascistic theatrics that Carol loved. Senior members wore compulsory navy and white uniforms, plumed hats and brightly coloured medals. They marched in formation, while supporters raised their arms in the now very familiar fascist salutes. Carol banned all other political parties, making the FRN the first monopoly party in Romanian history. Călinescu even began to borrow the language of Codreanu. The FRN, he said, was 'mainly a spiritual movement... [giving] life a sense of moral value'. The voting age was dramatically raised to thirty years old in an attempt to disenfranchise young Legionaries, and the unemployed had no vote at all.

Even far-right veterans mocked their newly attired colleagues in the FRN. They were 'white elephants' engaged in 'operetta fascism', said one. Iuliu Maniu said the party had taken the wrong name. It should not have been the Front of National Renaissance, but the Front of National Disgrace.[8]

A month after the start of the war, on 21 September 1939, with Romania still maintaining its neutrality, Prime Minister Călinescu was being driven through Bucharest in his limousine near the pretty Dâmbovița Bridge. It was 2 p.m. on a Thursday and the road was busy with lunchtime traffic. As they came around a corner, they saw a peasant's hay barrow blocking the road and Călinescu's driver tried to reverse. It was too late. Another car rammed him from behind. Before he could accelerate out of danger, two more vehicles pulled up, one on either side, and a group of young men surrounded the limousine. Without a word, they drew pistols and began firing into the rear seat. Călinescu was hit eleven times and died in his favourite ivory white uniform.

The six assassins – all Legionaries and medical students – decided to follow an old death squad tradition. They drove to a local radio station, which they took over at gunpoint, and introduced themselves on air as the 'Brigade of the Knights of Death'. Each calmly confessed to the shooting and said it was in revenge for the murder of Corneliu Codreanu. They then sat back and waited for the police to arrive.

The following night was a busy one in downtown Bucharest. Crowds emerged from the National Theatre having watched

Oscar Wilde's *The Importance of Being Earnest*, performed by the Dublin Gate theatre company. Outside, powerful arc lights had been switched on above a nearby square. It was 10 p.m. and passers-by pushed up against a cordon of military officers to see what was happening. In the centre stood six dazed young men, among them 26-year-old Miti Dumitrescu – leader of the 'Brigade of the Knights of Death' – dressed in a smart wool suit. The crowd looked on uneasily and saw a unit of young soldiers appear with machine guns. The six students were all tied to a plank of wood. They knew what was coming but the audience was still trying to make sense of it all. The unit of soldiers knelt and calmly mounted their guns on triangular stands. Some in the audience began to cry. The burst of gunfire sent nesting birds screeching into the night sky.

Diners at the Athénée Palace Hotel spoke in horrified whispers about how they had seen the soldiers spitting and stamping on the corpses. No one was allowed to move the dead Legionaries. Their bodies were left in the square for a week, as a lesson to everyone. Residing at the hotel at the time was a renowned American journalist, Countess Rosie Waldeck, who was reporting on the opening months of the war. She fell into a conversation about the executions with a Romanian aristocrat in the hotel bar. 'Leaving them with their brains hanging out,' he told her, 'like calves' brains at the butcher's' was not an ideal scenario. It showed that Carol had lost control of the country.[9] Whatever one thought of the Iron Guard, he continued, it was 'unsound' to machine-gun one's own citizens in front of crowds of theatre-goers. Not only that, Hitler would be watching and Carol would have to pay a heavy price.

In the meantime, a group of fanatical Legionaries had decided that the spirit of Codreanu might continue to lead them, if they could just dig his body out of the ground.

CHAPTER NINE

Our native soil draws all of us, I know not by what sweetness, and never allows us to forget.

The Poems of Exile, Ovid

If you walk around the headland of the Black Sea port of Constanța on a misty autumn night, between the empty boardwalk and the gently curling waves, you will see a startling architectural apparition looming from the shadows: Romania's finest piece of architecture, a crumbling, barnacle-encrusted pavilion that looks like it was built in ancient Rome. Resplendent with stone motifs of grapes and vines, tulip-shaped towers and peacock-fan widows, the derelict structure is now inhabited by a single security guard who warms himself by an electric fire. But when the Constanța Casino was first constructed in 1880, more than a decade before Queen Marie arrived in Romania, it quickly became the most fashionable destination on the Black Sea coast, a place where Europe's wealthy elite gathered for cocktails and beach games, while horses and carriages awaited beneath the fairy lights on the promenade.

The spot has a mystical significance for Romanians because it was here that the poet Ovid was exiled after being banished from Rome by Emperor Augustus in 8 AD, as punishment for mocking the Emperor's moral reforms. The city was called Tomis at the time and Ovid thought it a rough and unwelcoming place

– a remote community right on the edge of the civilized world. He sat despairingly on the shore, staring out across the Black Sea, dreaming of the honey-coloured steps of the Forum and the bustling civic centre of Rome. Nevertheless, exile was considered a soft punishment, reserved for those whose execution might inflame the masses and detract from the Emperor's popularity. It was always preferable to keep such a person alive and out of sight, so that they might return if circumstances were to change. The Emperor would then be viewed as a merciful leader.

King Carol had not left himself that option with Corneliu Codreanu. But he had used the same reasoning as Augustus when he exiled Codreanu's old friend, the army general – and increasingly popular right-wing politician – Ion Antonescu. The dedicated anti-corruptionist was still not a member of any political movement but after his theatrical appearance at Codreanu's trial, many old Iron Guardists viewed him as a natural successor to the Captain, certainly in preference to the sneering, sinister Horia Sima. Antonescu also attracted support from men and women who disliked the king.

As a result, Carol had exiled the general to Romania's eastern region of Bessarabia in September 1939 and put him in charge of the Third Army Corps, to defend the territory that Stalin was almost certainly planning to invade. Antonescu took residence in the regional capital, Chișinău, where he received regular updates on the German and Russian invasion of Poland as he prepared his Romanian troops for war. In the meantime, Carol hoped that the death of Corneliu Codreanu had brought an end to the constant and often violent pressure from the Iron Guard for Romania to side with Hitler. Carol still favoured making an alliance with Romania's spiritual mentors, the French, but knew that neutrality was still the country's best bet of surviving the war in one piece.

*

On a wild and rainy night in May 1940, two young Legionaries were sheltering in a barn on the border between Yugoslavia and Romania, listening out for the footsteps of gendarmes through the storm. The farmer's wife brought them straw and warm blankets, and apologized for the discomfort. Yugoslav government agents, she said, were everywhere in the woods and would almost certainly search the house. Her husband, Neagu, was a member of the Legionary underground and helped Nazi-supporting Legionaries into Romania across a patch of wild and remote border.

As Neagu entered the barn to meet his new charges, he was dumbfounded. Sitting among the cattle in filthy rags appeared to be Corneliu Codreanu. The lookalike drew his fingers proudly through his hair as if to acknowledge the resemblance and explained that he was Horia Sima, the new leader of the Iron Guard, on his way from Berlin to Bucharest with a colleague, Nicolae Petrascu. The two men were on a mission, he said, and needed to be cautious. Sima was wanted by the Romanian authorities, and had a price of 3 million lei on his head.

As Neagu prepared to escort them the ten miles to the border, Sima heard the voice of a gendarme outside the barn. 'Where are the people who came to you tonight?' the officer shouted through the rain to Neagu's wife. She feigned innocence. 'I have seen no people here,' she bellowed back. It was a signal for the two Legionaries to take flight. They ran out of the rear exit of the barn and fled across ditches and fields, but the gendarmes spotted them and gave chase, firing guns into the darkness. After a couple of minutes, Petrascu gave himself up, providing enough distraction in the process to allow Sima to escape into the night.

In the early hours, the Iron Guard leader crossed into Romania and arrived at a small Roma Gypsy village called Clopodia, where the appearance of a limping and exhausted stranger aroused the pity of a family who offered to take him in for the night. The menfolk of Clopodia were less inclined to charity than their wives, and one of them contacted a group of Romanian soldiers who were garrisoned nearby.

Just after dawn, Sima heard whispers outside. The door was thrown open and three soldiers marched in. 'Who are you?' the first asked. Sima had to think quickly. 'Constantin Popescu,' he said, 'a local man who has lost his way.' The lieutenant produced a picture from his pocket and held it up to the suspect's face. It was a photograph of a class of children from Lugoj High School in Romania's Banat region, taken a few years previously. In the centre of the front row was their philosophy teacher, Horia Sima. The gendarmes grabbed him.

Three days later, Sima was back in Bucharest but instead of being taken straight to Jilava Prison, he found himself in a quiet office with soft furnishings, pot plants and a large, important-looking desk. It was 22 May 1940, the shackles had been removed from his ankles, the bruises on his face were fading and it seemed he was being treated as a guest. The building he was sitting in belonged to the General Inspectorate of Gendarmes on Bonaparte Road, and the first man who came into the room to see him that day was Romania's new interior minister, Mihail Ghelmegeanu, who had replaced the assassinated Călinescu.

'Don't think I am afraid of you,' the minister began. He was circling Sima's chair, gesturing and shouting.

'But Minister,' Sima protested, 'none of my Legionaries are tracking you.'

Ghelmegeanu wanted to know why, if that were the case, Sima was back in Romania at all. Sima said his purpose was not murder, but persuasion. He wanted to change the king's foreign policy – his reliance on France and Britain for protection – to ensure Romania joined with Hitler and the Axis powers before it was too late.

'How did you intend to stop the continuation of our current foreign relations?' inquired the minister.

Sima paused for a moment. 'By any means,' he said.

'Really, by killing the king?' replied the minister.

'I said by any means,' said Sima, 'revolution... attack... if that is the only way.'

There was silence, during which Sima sensed he was being invited to elaborate. 'I thought there was not a moment to lose,' he recorded later in his memoirs. 'Even from Berlin I saw that Romania would be sacrificed and torn apart by its neighbours.' He told Ghelmegeanu: 'A change of traditional allies is needed immediately... just see what is happening on the French front.'

At that very moment, 1,500 miles away, the invading German army was sweeping through the French countryside with such rapidity that Hitler was afraid they were moving too fast. They were already at the Channel, with British forces evacuating out of Dunkirk in a flotilla of small craft. The French response had been ponderous and sluggish, and already Paris looked likely to fall to Hitler. In Bucharest, the news of impending French capitulation was greeted with particular horror. In the Athénée Palace Hotel, American journalist Countess Rosie Waldeck summed up the mood:

To the Romanians, England, the Empire, the Anglo-Saxon way of life, were admirable but something as exotic and far away as the Chinese civilization of the 16th century. In spite of its failings during the previous twenty years, France was the dominating force in Romania and the liberal order ruled only through the medium of France... Nowhere in these parts of the world was England real enough to be accepted as a dominating force. This was why, tonight, after the fall of Paris, the English were already licked in Romania, though they did not acknowledge it. It was not so much that the defeat of France confirmed the notion of the supposed invincibility of the German army, but more that the fall of France robbed the English of their Viceroy in Romania. This Viceroy was France.

With Carol's favoured French alliance now impossible, Sima's interrogation took an unexpected turn.

'What kind of connections do you have in Germany?' asked Ghelmegeanu.

'Our Comrades have managed to enter the highest spheres of government and Party,' replied Sima. 'Father Dumitrescu [the priest who had looked after the Nicadors on their final night of passion in the woods] has connections in the Gestapo.'[1]

Soon after, Sima was whisked off by men in dark glasses and handed over to the notoriously violent General Mihail Moruzov, founder of the Romanian Secret Intelligence Service. Moruzov had been in charge of tracking down and killing Legionaries on behalf of the government, and would ordinarily have done the same to Sima. But he was under instruction from Carol to treat the leader of the Iron Guard in a civilized fashion and assess whether he might be of any value. According to Sima's account, Moruzov offered an unexpected invitation. 'We want the Legionaries to help us, or at least not create any obstacles, to approach [Hitler] and the Axis… we call on your patriotism to collaborate with us to ease the external situation of Romania.'[2]

Next, Sima was invited to meetings with politicians, generals and royal aides where he was asked to address Prime Minster Gheorghe Tătărescu. He repeated his insistence that Romania must align with Hitler. He was then taken from his prison cell to a luxurious villa in the centre of Bucharest, where a table had been set with silver cutlery and fine French wines. The disorientated Sima walked in to find half a dozen top brass from the Romanian military, who offered him the place of honour at the top of the table. Over canapés and caviar, they told the head of the Iron Guard that they wanted to discuss the formation of yet another new political party. This one had Carol's blessing and would merge all the king's supporters with Sima's remaining Legionaries to form a single patriotic movement to lead the country forward. Carol's 'Renaissance Front' would be abolished and replaced with something called 'The Party of the Nation', in which Sima would play a leading role. The hosts explained that they had Carol's authority to form the party there and then. They just needed Sima's agreement. He nodded his assent and, with the wine finished, was driven back to spend his final night in a cell.

From the moment of its inception, the Party of the Nation (PN) was the younger sibling of Hitler's Nazi Party. Members goose-stepped around in elaborate uniforms, greeting each other with fascist salutes. It became a criminal offence to criticize the movement publicly or to deface any of its literature. Under the PN, anti-Semitic legislation was taken to a new level. There were segregation laws aimed at keeping Jews from public places such as government buildings and galleries. Jews were prevented from Romanianizing their names, which many had done to try to hide their heritage – including the family of Elena Lupescu, who had originally been called Wolff (the Romanian word for wolf is 'lup', hence Lupescu). Jews were barred from marrying Christians and, no matter how long their family had lived in the country, could never acquire the status 'Romanian by blood', a term that was written on the official papers of all non-Jews.

The policies of hate and discrimination were designed to flatter Hitler into keeping Hungarian hands off Transylvania. One last gift to the Führer was the inclusion in cabinet of his unofficial Romanian representative; Horia Sima was made minister for arts and culture. But even as Carol desperately tried to win back the respect he had lost with Hitler after Codreanu's murder, the situation on his eastern border began to take a dramatic turn.

At the Romanian mission in Moscow, ambassador Gheorghe Davidescu had just finished his supper and was preparing for bed on 26 June 1940 when he received a telephone call from Stalin's foreign minister, Vyacheslav Molotov, requiring the Romanian's immediate presence. Davidescu protested that the hour was late and suggested that they talk in the morning. No, said Molotov, the issue was of such pressing importance that they needed to discuss it now. Then he put down the phone.

Arriving at the Kremlin, Davidescu was shown into a high-ceilinged stateroom, where Molotov greeted him briskly and handed him a type-written message. The note was just a few paragraphs long and written in heavy black ink. It demanded the immediate 'return' of Bessarabia to the Soviet Union, as well as the surrender of the neighbouring Romanian region of Northern Bukovina – a beautiful land of beech trees and wooded valleys between Romania and Ukraine. Bukovina had never belonged to the Soviet Union but Stalin regarded it as 'interest' on the 'twenty years' loan' of Bessarabia, and wanted the two returned simultaneously. Of course, they were both integral parts of Greater Romania, without which the dream achieved at the end of the First World War would be shattered. It was no coincidence that the Soviet ultimatum had come just four days after the fall of France – and the loss, therefore, of Romania's best guarantor of its borders.

Davidescu re-read the ultimatum with alarm. Attached was a tiny map showing the disputed territories marked in blunt red pencil, as if applied by a child. The line was so thick, it covered seven miles on the ground, obscuring entire towns and villages. Davidescu was unsure what Stalin wanted and what he was allowing Romania to keep. There was no time to delay, announced Molotov. Bucharest must respond within twenty-four hours. If they failed, Stalin's army would march in and take both territories, killing many Romanians in the process.

Davidescu arrived back at the Romanian mission at midnight, with the intention of telegramming the ultimatum to Bucharest immediately. But the telephone lines were down and nothing could be sent until 2 a.m. He attached a note demanding that King Carol be woken immediately and informed, but further technical problems delayed the message by another four hours. The full text only arrived in Bucharest at 6 a.m. on 27 June.

At midday, several ministerial limousines pulled up outside Carol's palace, carrying the historian Nicolae Iorga, Professor Cuza (now a member of the Crown Council) and former Prime Minister Iuliu Maniu, along with other leading politicians of the day. They were ushered upstairs into the grand conference room and informed of the ultimatum. Options were limited, they agreed. They could either surrender to Moscow's demands and hand over Bessarabia and Northern Bukovina, thus sacrificing everything for which their ancestors had fought, or they could refuse and fight the Soviet army – a contest Romania would almost inevitably lose.

Their first tactic was for Carol to send an urgent telegram to Hitler, in which he asked the Führer to intervene on his behalf and call off Stalin. Hitler's reply came back within the hour. 'In order to avoid war between Romania and the Soviet Union,' it read, 'we can only advise that the Romanian government yield to the Soviet government demands.' Carol was numb with anger and left the conference room in silence. Of course, at that point, he still had no idea that Hitler had formally recognized the Soviet claim to Bessarabia in the secret annex of the Molotov-Ribbentrop Pact.

With Carol sulking in his rooms, ministers began a series of calls to try to whip up some international outrage and apply pressure on Moscow. They called Rome, Belgrade and Athens, but all responded in the same manner: conceding to Moscow was the only option. At 2 p.m., Nicholae Iorga rose to speak. He counselled for Romania to stand up to Stalin, to fight as their ancestors had done and never surrender. The rest looked at each other in disbelief. If Stalin was forced to fight, he would not stop with Bessarabia, they said, but would continue marching westward all the way through to Bucharest. Romania would cease to exist.

Ministers decided to write a polite telegram to Moscow, asking for a little more time to consider, and suggesting that they all try to get around a negotiating table as soon as possible and sort the whole thing out. Moscow shot back that they needed an answer by the end of the day, and added a further ultimatum: all Romanian troops must be evacuated from Bessarabia within four days.

At 6 p.m. that evening, with just six hours to go until Stalin's deadline, an immaculately dressed military officer arrived at Carol's palace and demanded to be allowed into the meeting of the Crown Council. General Ion Antonescu had left Bessarabia that morning and managed to reach Bucharest in near record time. He had a hand-written note to deliver to Carol. In it, he demanded a leading role in the decision-making and said his invaluable advice would only be given if Carol agreed to dismiss his *camarilla*. 'The men and system must be changed immediately,' wrote Antonescu. 'If your majesty does not turn his ear to the suffering of the people in this last hour, total collapse, irreparable collapse… will follow… Listen to me, at least in this hour, Majesty.'[3] It was with some irony, then, that when Antonescu was finally admitted into the palace, he was stopped by Elena Lupescu's former driver, and now senior member of the *camarilla*, Ernest Urdărianu, who grilled him as to the precise nature of his business with the king, and then refused him entry. Antonescu was so enraged, he lunged at Urdărianu, brawling with the startled parvenu until palace guards intervened. The General was sent away, fuming, and was not allowed in.

At the moment the deadline passed, at midnight on 27 June, Carol could not be found. Then, at 2 a.m. a junior foreign minister received a call summoning him to the king's study. When he entered, he found Carol sitting in a huddle with his former prime minister, Constantin Argetoianu, the current prime minister, Gheorghe Tătărescu, and former driver, Ernest Urdărianu. With tears running down his face, Carol was lighting one cigarette after another, throwing each away after a couple of puffs and lighting a new one. Argetoianu, a sombre, battle-hardened veteran, leaned forward in his chair and said quietly to the king that they had no choice. The majority of the Crown Council had voted for surrender. With a final sob, Carol nodded. The Soviets, he agreed, could have Bessarabia and Northern Bukovina. The evacuation would begin the following morning.[4]

It was a Monday and a young Romanian woman called Victoria Angelescu was in the Bessarabian capital, Chișinău, unaware that Soviet troops were pouring across the border. Victoria was visiting her aunt and uncle, and had done each summer for as long as she could remember. Born in the year that Bessarabia became a Romanian possession, she was now twenty-two years old and had spent her precious holiday lolling on the crimson Turkish carpet in her uncle's study, book suspended over her face, shutters thrown open, the scent of linden trees in her nostrils. For Victoria, Chișinău, and her uncle's book shelves, were a magical place. When she was younger, she had read *One Thousand and One Nights* lying on the same rug, and imagined it was a flying carpet.

On 28 June 1940, Victoria was finishing breakfast with her aunt when the classical music on the radio station was interrupted by a solemn voice. Communiqué No 25 of the General Staff of the Romanian Army announced that all Romanian troops had to leave the region, and that Bessarabia would be handed to the Soviet army by 1400 hours that very day. There were 1.6 million Romanians in the territory – more than half the population – living in an area of land the size of Denmark.

Neighbours rushed into the streets. Had they heard the news? Was it true? How could they pack a lifetime of possessions in five hours? Columns of Romanian refugees began making their way towards the railway station, carrying suitcases stuffed with jewellery and family heirlooms. Disorientated pensioners stood at the roadside yelling for help. By midday the first Soviet tanks began rumbling through the streets of Chișinău, past the pretty theatre and the once bustling market place.

Not everyone fled. There were Russians in those towns who had got along with their Romanian neighbours for years, and now embraced the invading Soviet troops while watching old friends being evicted from their homes. Some Russian-speakers chanted thanks to the 'liberators' and planted red flags in their gardens. A few became unexpectedly hostile, ripping the epaulets off departing Romanian soldiers and beating them. The Romanians did not fight back. They had been instructed to take the blows and walk away. Any resistance at such a volatile moment might trigger a marauding take-over, rather than a supposedly organized handover of power.

In the home of Victoria Angelescu's aunt, pandemonium broke out. 'The books,' shouted her uncle, 'pack the books'. Ancient Latin texts, beautifully-bound Greek poems, Transylvanian fairy tales, all were scooped from the shelves. 'Keep this one... and this.' Her uncle's attempts at triage were failing. There were only four suitcases and a couple of wooden boxes. Then they heard the sound of approaching boots, and three Soviet soldiers stamped across the Turkish rug.

'We are going,' said Victoria's uncle, 'we are leaving in minutes... but please, give us time.' A Soviet soldier picked up a book from the shelves and pretended to leaf through it, with a look of mock studiousness. There was near silence in the house. Just the distant sound of car horns. The soldier turned his back to the room and thrust his groin towards the shelves. He stood with his legs apart. It was the smell that Victoria registered first. Cow sheds. Rotting fruit. Ammonia. The soldier swung his hips from side to side, spraying as many books as he could reach. Then he drained the rest of his bladder onto the Turkish carpet.

The heat outdoors was almost overwhelming. The Angelescu family paused in the pretty front garden to divide the suitcases between the three of them. Victoria's uncle panicked for a moment, thinking he had forgotten to lock the door, then he realized, with a slump of his shoulders, that it no longer mattered.

That afternoon, they made it to the train station and Victoria's last glimpse of Chişinău was a street filled with marching communists waving red flags. Behind them, plumes of smoke rose from Romanian army headquarters. As her train passed over the Prut River and back into Romanian territory, she saw troops being led to the edge of the water, stripped naked and ordered to swim back home. Victoria Angelescu would later become my grandmother-in-law, and would never overcome her distrust and revulsion of Russians, which originated that day in Chişinău in the summer of 1940.

But while civilians got out alive, many Romanian soldiers did not. Some felt so humiliated by the loss of Greater Romania that they shot themselves. Others were beaten to death and shot by rampaging Soviet troops.[5] The next day's Romanian newspapers blamed the Jews. It was inconceivable to many Romanians that anyone else would have welcomed the Soviet takeover. They were communists and Jews – one and the same. King Carol reflected the views of the nation when he wrote in his diary:

> … the behaviour of the population of Bessarabia, especially that of the Jews, leaves much to be desired… The columns of refugees and trains were attacked by communist hordes which delayed even more the opportunity – ridiculously short as it was – for evacuation.[6]

A journalist on the last train out of Chişinău wrote that 'Jewish communists began their wicked deeds against Holy sites' and went on to accuse Jews of setting fire to Orthodox churches. 'The Jews of Bessarabia', reported another newspaper, had been 'cossetted for so long at the generous breast of the [Romanian] people' and yet this was how they repaid the kindness. In their field reports, some Romanian army officers spoke only of 'Jewish abuse' without mentioning the communists at all.

In Bucharest, events were moving quickly. With Bessarabia

now lost and Carol's preferred Western ally, France, defeated by the Germans on 22 June 1940, he was running out of options. There was every possibility that Stalin would not stop at Bessarabia, so Carol needed urgent protection. It was not going to come from the British, and the French were defeated, and so, on 5 July 1940, Carol threw his lot in with the only European power that might halt both Stalin and the revisionist-minded Hungarians who could smell Transylvanian blood – Hitler's Germany.

Carol cast away the now meaningless Anglo-French Guarantee and expelled British technicians from the oil fields around Ploieşti. At the same time, he invited a huge German mission into Bucharest to start training Romanian troops. The Germans mocked the king behind his back for his desperate aping of Hitler, exemplified by his creation of an ersatz Nazi party. They were under no illusion that Carol's apparent love for Nazi Germany stemmed from any genuine ideological common ground, but entirely out of self-preservation. 'The ruthlessness with which he is now treating the British', said one German Special Representative, 'shows how he would be treating us if we had lost [in France].'[7] Likewise, Hitler had no love for Carol. He was in it for the oil.

So where was General Antonescu in all of this? He had stormed away from the king's palace after the fight with Ernest Urdărianu but was still viewed as the best hope of protecting what was left of Greater Romania. Carol knew it, and also realized that Antonescu's popularity, if allowed to grow unfettered, might well spell his own demise. The question was whether the king would put his pride to one side and invite his old adversary back into government, so that the whole country might benefit from his undoubted military brilliance. The answer came on 9 July 1940, when Carol had his security officers raid Antonescu's home and drag him off to jail.

It was a terrible error of judgement, showing to everyone just how much Carol feared his own military leader. With the king's recent track record of murdering opponents, there was a possibility no one would see Antonescu again. The General's supporters were so concerned that they wrote to the German mission in Bucharest to intercede, prompting the Reich's Special Representative for Economic Problems in Romania to write to Carol's gatekeeper, Ernest Urdărianu, warning that the 'accidental death' of Antonescu would make a 'very bad impression in German quarters'.[8]

In fact, despite the German's eagerness to protect Antonescu, there was no evidence that the General supported Hitler. He was a natural ally of France, where he had lived and met his wife, and had reproached both London and Paris for their willingness to concede to Hitler in the Munich Agreement. Nevertheless, he was seen by the Germans as a more likely candidate for meaningful alliance than Carol, and certainly a more able one.

The list of Carol's insults to Hitler was growing. First Codreanu and then the jailing of Antonescu. In response to this, and buoyed by the fact that Carol had lost his French protection, the Führer made a proposal that he knew would make Carol's position as royal dictator untenable. Germany, he said, would protect Romania from further incursions if Carol were to settle his outstanding territorial disputes with both Hungary and Bulgaria first. In other words, Romania would have to surrender large swathes of Transylvania to Hungary and much of the seaside territory of Dobruja to Bulgaria. It would signal a near complete reversal of Romanian gains made by Queen Marie in the Paris Peace Conference, the dismemberment of Greater Romania and a catastrophic collapse in public support for the king.

Carol clung onto a sliver of hope. When Hitler spoke of settling 'outstanding territorial disputes', there was no concrete evidence of precisely where the borders of Transylvania should lie. All disputes needed to be resolved according to interpretations of history that went as far back as Vlad Dracula and Stephen the Great. It was, therefore, with some relief that

Carol learned that a commission would be set up to adjudicate. Much would depend on the identity of the adjudicators, and Carol was hoping for some neutral European diplomats with expertise in such things. But when he heard who Hitler was proposing, his heart sank.

Arbitration would be overseen by Germany's foreign minister, Joachim von Ribbentrop, and Benito Mussolini's son-in-law, the corrupt philanderer Count Galeazzo Ciano, whose interest in Romanian affairs was nil. The two men met in Vienna, drinking, smoking cigars and exchanging gossip, before finally getting down to business. Von Ribbentrop summoned the Romanian delegate, foreign minister and financial backer of the Iron Guard, Mihail Manoilescu. In Ciano's diaries, he mocks the Romanian for not 'knowing what to do or what to say' and appearing 'terrified for his country and for himself'. Manoilescu, he said, nodded meekly to all suggestions but explained that the surrender of large parts of Transylvania was a steep price to pay for German protection during the war.

The next day, 30 August 1940, all sides met at Vienna's spectacular Belvedere Hotel to hear the result of what became known as the Second Vienna Award. A map was produced by the Germans and laid across the table. When the Hungarians saw how much territory they had been granted, they could hardly contain their joy. Then there was a loud thud from the other side of the room, as Romania's Manoilescu fainted onto the table. Doctors were called. Camphorated oil was administered. Eventually the shaken Manoilescu came round but, Ciano said, he 'showed the shock very much indeed'.[9]

Romania would have to surrender forty per cent of Transylvania, the entire northern section, with a population of 2.6 million people – around half of whom were ethnic Romanians.[10] By this time Carol had surrendered one third of his Kingdom and one third of his population, with three million ethnic Romanians now adrift behind new frontiers. Economically, the losses were crippling; 37 per cent of Romania's arable land had gone, 44 per cent of its forests, 37 per cent of its vineyards and 86 per cent of its soya crop.

The country watched with dismay as tens of thousands of Romanian refugees began pouring out of Russian-held Bessarabia and Hungarian-held northern Transylvania. As people reflected on the loss of their French allies, the endemic corruption of Carol's *camarilla* and the murder of Codreanu and his Legionary elite, they decided that they had had enough. The Iron Guard suddenly spotted their chance of seizing power, and encouraged their supporters onto the streets. Huge protests took place in Bucharest and other major cities. Crowds gathered outside Carol's palace chanting, 'We don't want to cede Transylvania… Give us Transylvania back.' Some protestors wept with anguish, while others threw stones and yelled at Carol's troops.

Later that evening, the crowd parted to allow through a limousine, inside of which was a face so popular that they broke into cheers. General Ion Antonescu had been freed from jail by Iuliu Maniu and was on his way to the royal palace. Even Carol could see that the country was slipping from his grasp and had been persuaded that Antonescu's appointment as prime minister might be his last chance of survival. This time, Ernest Urdărianu did not block his path and the General was escorted upstairs into the presence of the king.

The typically bullish Antonescu began by announcing that he would only accept the role of prime minister if he were given full powers to run the country, not to serve as some kind of military window-dressing behind which Carol would continue as if nothing had changed. The king was astonished. What Antonescu was describing sounded like abdication in all but name, he said, and he could not accept. 'Traitor!' he yelled at Antonescu, or so the story goes (we only have Antonescu's account), at which point Antonescu apparently rose calmly from his chair and shot back: 'So far, Your Majesty, only one of us two has committed high treason.'[11]

At 10 p.m. on 3 September 1940, just after Antonescu's limousine had left the palace, there was the sound of gunfire in the square. Legionaries were firing at Carol's living quarters.

On 5 September, Antonescu headed back to the palace, where he found Carol's attitude had softened significantly. He would like to remain on the throne, he said, but only in a ceremonial capacity. It was important that Romania had a king and if he kept out of politics and stuck to awarding medals and the like, he was sure the country would wish to keep him. In the meantime, with tears in his eyes, he agreed to hand power to Antonescu.

The General was not satisfied. He left and put word out to Codreanu's old Legionary units, who came marching in their thousands to Palace Square, firing pistols and chanting: 'Give us the king... Don't let him leave the country with his money... Don't let him get out with Lupescu.'[12] When Antonescu judged that the king was sufficiently terrified, he returned to the palace once again, this time wearing full military uniform. He informed Carol that he had tried hard to form a government, with Carol as a ceremonial king, but that all political parties had refused. 'Everyone is demanding Your Majesty's abdication,' said Antonescu. Carol, agitated and chain-smoking, was clearly distracted by the cries of the Legionaries outside. Antonescu shook his head apologetically. The Legionaries were so angry, he said, that they might start a civil war. He turned to Carol once more and told him he had until 4 a.m. to abdicate. With that, he marched from the room.

'Abdication Friday rose gloriously over Bucharest,' wrote American journalist Countess Rosie Waldeck, who had been observing events from the Athénée Palace Hotel across the road. 'The sky was very blue and the air had the dry cool quality of air in the high mountains... when the crowds began to gather on the square, I could see the first green shirts of the Iron Guard.'

They marched in long columns throwing fascist salutes, joined by priests in black cassocks and white-robed nuns. Youngsters paraded in green shirts too, garments that must have been hidden in cupboards and drawers for years, since anything but the king's uniforms had been outlawed. Shortly after 10 a.m., the first verses of 'Capitano' could be heard echoing around the boulevards of downtown Bucharest – the anthem to their murdered Captain. Royal sentries had been replaced by green-shirted Legionaries, as had the soldiers around the edge of the square. The king had abdicated at 6 a.m. His challenge now was to escape the country without being shot.

On the evening of 7 September 1940, a small group of photographers and press men gathered on the platform at the tiny station of Lugano in Switzerland. The first train to arrive was occupied by an Italian military protection team, guns at the ready, binoculars peering through the windows. A few minutes later, huge plumes of smoke could be seen from the trees at the foot of the valley. The unmistakable blue-and-gold trim of the Orient Express emerged into the gentle sunshine, pulling behind it all eleven carriages of Carol's escape train. The former king was travelling with Elena Lupescu, Ernest Urdărianu, a personal valet, several servants and hundreds of pieces of luggage, including famous paintings by El Greco (such as the 'Adoration of the Shepherds') and several crates of gold. When the train crossed the Romanian border earlier that day, a unit of Legionaries had opened fire, hoping to stop the theft of millions of dollars of state property. It is said that Carol threw himself on top of Lupescu to protect her. Less generous reports suggest he threw himself into the train's tin bath. Now, as the bullet-ridden carriages drew into the station with a great hiss of steam, journalists crowded around the steps. Moments later, Carol appeared, waving and wearing a wide grin.

CHAPTER TEN

Dudard: I suppose I might as well tell you... it's really rather funny... the fact is, he turned into a rhinoceros.

Berenger: A rhinoceros! Mr Papillon a rhinoceros, I can't believe it! I don't think it's funny at all! Why didn't you tell me before?

Rhinoceros (1959), Eugene Ionesco

On a train speeding north from the coast was a golden receptacle, polished sunshine bright, with a texture so deep and honeyed it seemed you could dip your fingers through its sides. It was a tiny casket, no bigger than an owl's coffin but assigned a detail of soldiers as if it contained Romania's national treasure. And in a way it did. Beneath the sealed golden lid, embossed with Orthodox crosses and the names of Romania's provinces, was a human heart. It had spent the last two years at a royal seaside villa in southern Dobruja, but with the region now surrendered to Bulgaria, 100,000 Romanians were fleeing north and the heart had joined the exodus.

The organ once beat inside the chest of Queen Marie and was removed from her corpse before burial as if she were some ancient saintly relic. Its transportation from her favourite summer residence in the Black Sea resort of Balcic to Bucharest was arranged by General Antonescu, in the hope that he might harness some of Marie's mystical allure and help bring the nation together. In the capital, a formal reception was held, with Marie's heart borne aloft by soldiers, draped with a Romanian flag and blessed by priests. Afterwards, it was transported to Bran Castle in the Carpathians – the old watchtower of Vlad Dracula, where it was encased in a marble sarcophagus.[1]

Antonescu was trying to salvage his country's beloved royal heritage after Carol's years of vandalism. He had also sent aides to Greece in order to coax back the former monarch's estranged wife, Princess Helen. She was offered the title Queen Mother of Romania, and returned to Bucharest a week after the coup, stepping off the train into the stiff embrace of her nineteen-year-old son Michael, before offering her gloved hand to a beaming Antonescu. They paraded through streets filled with joyful crowds, the two royals sitting demurely in an open-topped limousine, Antonescu standing erect and proud in the car behind. Although the General was Romania's new leader, he wanted Michael to have the ceremonial powers that he had refused to grant his father a week before.

As Helen and Michael returned to the royal palace, the gates closed firmly behind them and Antonescu was content not to hear a peep from them again, until they were required for the handing out of medals. Eschewing the offer of a villa for himself and his wife, the famously spartan Antonescu lived in the Presidency further down the street, where he slept and ate in a small room beside his study, almost as if he were living in a theatre of war. He refused to employ chefs, preferring the home cooking that his wife brought him on a tray, as he struggled to form a stable government.

His first problem was how to accommodate the powerful, and demanding, Legionaries of the Iron Guard. In the build-up to the coup, their leader Horia Sima had fled to Transylvania fearing arrest and execution for his involvement in the protests that eventually unseated Carol. In doing so, he had lost the respect of many mainstream Legionaries, who turned to Antonescu for leadership instead. In fact, Antonescu had never been a member of the Iron Guard, but merely an acquaintance of Codreanu and a supporter of elements of their right-wing ideology; he was a fanatical patriot, like them, but he was opposed to their violence against Jews.

Antonescu had never tested his popularity in an election. He was not a politician, but a soldier who viewed Romanian politics as an extension of military strategizing; a way of protecting Greater Romania. Even in the hours after forcing Carol to flee, he had tried to take a back-seat role, contacting the old Peasants' Party leader, Iuliu Maniu, and telling him: 'You wanted the abdication of the king, here, now take the leadership of the state.' Maniu refused and, reluctantly, the General placed himself in the maelstrom of national politics.

The Legionaries of the Iron Guard had, doubtlessly, played a key role in Carol's overthrow and now they wanted their reward: cabinet positions, of course, but also revenge against anyone perceived to have wronged them in the past. They were in control now and they wanted blood. 'I am not one of you,' Antonescu said to them carefully in a radio broadcast, 'but I understand your explosion of joy... I have suffered terribly with you and for you... I wanted what you wanted, my thoughts were your thoughts. I wanted Greater Romania to be a Great Romania.' He paused, and changed tone, trying to appeal to their reason. 'I have put all this behind me,' he said solemnly. 'You should do the same. We cannot build with revenge, but with labour, not with disorder, but with order.'[2]

The Green Shirts of the Iron Guard paraded through Bucharest in their tens of thousands, chanting eulogies to their deceased Captain and cheering the 'Guardist' revolution. Queues of armed men snaked around the Legionary Green House headquarters to become members. Some carried photographs of Legionary martyrs, others wore swastikas on their green lapels. Membership lists were so overwhelmed that thousands were sent home disappointed. It was the first week of the new Romania, 7 September 1940, and the excitement was intense. But on the periphery of the celebrations, groups of green-shirted young men were peeling off the main boulevards to hunt for Jews.

It was only after Carol had fled the capital that Horia Sima dared return, claiming back his leadership of the Iron Guard and insisting on a senior cabinet post. He petitioned strongly for the job of interior minister, which would have put him in charge of justice, policing and score-settling. But Antonescu considered the role far too sensitive for such a violently unstable man. He knew Sima to be a narcissist and incurable plotter who would try to launch a coup against him the moment he had a chance. Instead, he made Sima his deputy prime minister, so that he could keep an eye on him.

A week later, on 14 September, King Michael appeared on the balcony of the royal palace, above ecstatic green-shirted crowds. Ministers had been chosen, government departments prepared – the revolution was officially inaugurated. Michael announced that Romania would become a *National Legionary State*, dominated by the Guard but not quite under its control. The real power would lie with General Antonescu, the *Conducător*, the man with the army behind him, a counterbalance to the youthful excesses of the Codreanu faithful. The Guard were, by and large, content. They were the heroes of the hour. They were the only legal party. They had the backing of Nazi Germany. And it was Antonescu, they believed, who would have to conform to their wishes.

The two weeks that followed were dominated by mass open-air religious ceremonies and Legionary rallies, organized so that the Guard could experience the exuberance of a revolution without indulging their hunger for violence. As in most revolutions, the true believers desired blood, to chase their enemies through the streets, subject them to kangaroo trials and summary justice. Only then could things calm down. But the Legionaries were deprived of all this. It had been a bloodless revolution carried out by men sitting in armchairs in a distant wood-panelled study. Even the chief offender, Carol, had survived unscathed. So, the crowds were offered parades in place of sanguinary vengeance. In one, Romanian Legionaries were joined by uniformed SS paramilitaries, Italian Blackshirts, Spanish Falangists and even emissaries from the Japanese Emperor. It became a giant fascist rally.

Among the crowds were the families of famous Legionary martyrs: Codreanu's wife and his mother, their faces invisible behind heavy widow's weeds; relatives of the Decemviri and Nicadors; mothers of assassins and bombers; all followed by humble priests praying and blessing and wafting trails of rose-scented incense through the streets. A makeshift stage was constructed in a Bucharest square that was later renamed Square of 6th September to commemorate the great day. From behind a screen adorned with willows and autumnal flowers emerged General Antonescu, wearing a green shirt for the first time, in honour of his new government colleagues. He smiled awkwardly and threw a couple of hesitant fascist salutes. Then came Horia Sima, imperious and haughty. These were his people, this, his world. The two men held hands and stood motionless, staring into each other's eyes as the crowd cheered. Behind them, at the rear of the stage, hung a giant woodblock image of Corneliu Codreanu, his chiselled features cut from bolts of lightning. No one was more present at these Guardist rallies than the dead.

At the end of the week of marches, the Legionaries were still not ready to return to their jobs and families. Off they went into town, hunting for former government officials, police officers and spies. There was a modicum of order at the beginning, with suspects hauled in front of inquiries and military committees. First up was Carol's spy chief, Mihail Moruzov, followed by his prime minister, Gheorghe Argeșanu, then the former justice minister, Victor Iamandi. All were carted off to the notorious

Jilava Prison and detained indefinitely without trial. Particular attention was paid to anyone involved in the death of Codreanu. A legionary informant disappeared from his home one night, as did the staff sergeant who placed the rope around the Captain's neck.

The homes of the wealthy and corrupt were next. Former government officials were forced to account for jewels, works of art, hoarded gold and income going back ten years. Without receipts or explanations as to the source of their wealth, their property was confiscated by young men in green shirts. Members of Carol's *camarilla* had their villas cleaned out almost overnight. Special relish was reserved for the home of Elena Lupescu, on Avenue Vulpache, which was opened to the public as the ultimate example of the *camarilla*'s corruption. Young Green Shirts acted as guides, showing curious visitors Lupescu's 'priceless' silks, lace's and brocades, and her 'unique perfumes and soaps'. They pointed to the floor where a heap of empty jewel cases lay, bearing the imprints of pearls, diamonds and necklaces that had been scooped up in a hurry when Lupescu fled – 'the jewels which Carol bought with the tears and the sweat of the Romanian people for Elena Lupescu' intoned a guide. Some visitors sighed wistfully, saying that they should have killed off 'the Jewess' when they had the chance.

Within two weeks of the declaration of the National Legionary State, a series of draconian anti-Semitic laws were passed. They were meticulously recorded by a Romanian Jewish lawyer, Matatias Carp, in what he called 'The Black Book of the Suffering of Romanian Jews'. Writing in plain, dispassionate language, he recorded every law enacted during Antonescu's rule, along with statements and testimonies from the victims, as well as horrific photographs.

Under Law No. 3361, Green Shirts were allowed to take over any Jewish company 'whenever considered necessary, without any justification'. Calling themselves 'Romanianization Commissars', they took over businesses worth millions of lei, putting themselves in charge and sometimes taking on the former Jewish owners as low-paid assistants. Carp listed hundreds of examples of businesses being seized. Typical were those in Petrosani, where all Jewish merchants were summoned and told they must sell their shops within two days. After the deadline passed, gangs of Legionaries simply took them over.

Under Law No. 3789, Jewish physicians were banned from treating any patients other than Jews and forced to wear badges bearing the words 'Jewish Doctor'.[3] Law No. 3487 stated that Jewish lawyers still working at the Bar would no longer be able to carry out legal services of any nature. Some of the laws were ruinous to Jewish lives, others tacitly allowed violence. Some were remarkable simply for their pettiness. Law No. 3627 stipulated that 'Breeding farms of travelling pigeons are authorized only for ethnic Romanian citizens'.[4]

The new laws represented Antonescu's attempts to pacify the Guard, but the movement was a broad church that defied any normal governance. At its less toxic margins were normal folk who had become infected by the patriotic romance of it all, while at its core were deeply anti-Semitic and heavily armed zealots who were growing more and more impatient by the day. Under their restless glare, Antonescu had two priorities. The first was to impose order on the streets. The second was to secure Romania's borders against any further incursions. He decided both could be achieved through a single controversial invitation.

Antonescu made a call to Hitler, asking for a German military mission and, on 13 October 1940, thousands of soldiers from Nazi Germany began arriving in Bucharest. They took over hotels and public buildings and were soon shopping along Calea Victoriei in their fur-lined coats with lacquered-red lapels. Ostensibly their purpose was to train the country's ill-equipped armed forces but, in reality, Antonescu wanted them to police the city streets as well. Within days, the Germans had decided to make the most of Romania's unexpected hospitality, with several units of soldiers travelling up to Ploieşti and Romania's oil fields, where they built air defences and watchtowers, and effectively took over the running of Antonescu's most precious resource.

Soon the German military mission expanded to include an army mission, naval mission and air force mission, each controlled by their service headquarters in Berlin. The number of political staff at the German embassy quickly expanded too. This was a military occupation in all but name. But if Horia Sima and his Legionaries thought that the Nazi presence would help them overthrow Antonescu and impose a fully Nazi-sponsored government in Bucharest, they were mistaken. The Germans had no interest in interfering in Romania's domestic politics. They were determined not to play nursemaid to the fledgling Romanian fascist revolution. Hitler cared little who actually ran the country, whether it was Antonescu or Sima or anyone else – he just required peace and quiet so that there would be no disruption to the Reich's crucial supply of oil.

*

By the autumn of 1940, Ana Pauker was being held at a remote, crumbling prison outside the eastern Romanian city of Râmnicu Sărat. She was four years into her ten-year sentence and was part of a group known as the 'Women's Collective of Anti-fascist Prisoners', comprising around a hundred communists. Most were university graduates and professionals and, although the regime was strict, they held political meetings in jail and were allowed to receive deliveries of newspapers and letters. All of them realized that the dawning of the National Legionary State meant that their lives could now be at risk.

Although Pauker was their leader, she was not treated well by her comrades at Râmnicu Sărat. The women had received notification from Moscow in 1938 that Marcel Pauker had been arrested and executed in Stalin's Great Purge over allegations that he was a Romanian spy. It was devastating news for Ana but the other women wanted an explanation from her as to why she had been married to a traitor. A meeting was called. Everyone spoke, all of them equally indignant and appalled by Pauker's alleged failures. 'Look,' said one, Liuba Chişinevschi, 'I criticize Ana that, being the wife of Marcel Pauker, she did not warn the Party that he was an agent provocateur.' Ana sat in the middle of them, agonizing. 'I am now wracking my brain', she said, 'to find something, a sign of any kind, that would have led me to believe that he was an enemy of the people... I'm not placing any doubt on the Party's decision; the Party knows better than I. But I did not see anything; and as much as I search my soul, my recollections, my memory, I don't find anything that could prove such a thing.'⁵ The women were unconvinced and sent a note to Moscow describing her response to the questioning. It said, simply, that she had refused to denounce her husband, even in death.

A month after the fascist revolution, in October 1940, a column of buses and cars arrived outside Râmnicu Sărat jail. Pauker and the others heard the stamping of boots, whistles and slamming doors. Then they saw men in green shirts flashing by their peepholes. An army of Legionaries had arrived on a so-called pilgrimage to the jail in which they had once been held. There were 2,000 of them in all, running excitedly along the corridors. 'Pauker?' they shouted. 'Where is Ana Pauker?'

First, they found twenty-three-year-old Vilma Kajesco, a young firebrand who had been convicted at the same trial as Pauker. She recoiled in terror as a Legionary burst into her cell, but instead of drawing a pistol, he produced a camera and began taking photographs of the hovel, explaining that this was where he himself had spent five years of his life. 'You should know', she related to an interviewer many years later, 'that to my surprise they did not behave badly at all. On the contrary, they were quite nice.'⁶

Moments later, another Legionary peered through her peephole and asked excitedly, 'Were you a communist?'

'I was, I am, and always will be,' responded Kajesco, to which the Legionary retorted 'Bravo...'

When they finally tracked down Pauker, they pushed inside her cell and to her astonishment tried to engage in polite political debate, referring to her respectfully as 'the Captain of the Communists'. There is no record of what they discussed but they were civilized and courteous, and no doubt curious to finally come face to face with the woman who was supposedly their deadly enemy.

Once the Legionary marches had abated in Bucharest, General Antonescu set off for Berlin and his first meeting with Hitler, in the New Reich Chancellery on 20 November 1940. The two men settled on a silk sofa in the Führer's vast new study, beside a large wooden globe where they could survey the whole European continent. An open fire blazed in the handsome marble hearth. Hitler's aides handed paperwork to Antonescu, which he read under the shade of a Japanese lamp. Far from being overawed by the Führer, Antonescu spoke uninterrupted for two hours. It was unprecedented for anyone to upstage the Führer but Hitler sat and listened. Antonescu's monologue, delivered entirely in French, was translated into German by Hitler's interpreter, Paul Schmidt. The General explained, in passionate terms, that Romania insisted on the return of northern Transylvania. He spoke of nationalism, the Romanian spirit, the economy and military cooperation. Hitler was impressed by the sheer determination and intellectual clarity of his earnest and articulate guest. It was a welcome change from the smug ramblings of Mussolini. The Romanian had dignity and class, and Hitler was engrossed. This was a man whom he could trust. As the photographer snapped away, the two new partners stood beside a polished wooden table on which sat a pre-prepared agreement. It was a copy of the Tripartite Pact – signed by Germany, Italy and Japan a month before – and Antonescu added his signature to it as Hitler watched. Romania was now an Axis power, albeit an unequal partner. In return, Hitler said he would support Romania 'in every way'. But no sooner had Antonescu returned home, than a new, macabre crisis engulfed Romania.

The scene was Jilava Prison in southern Bucharest, and the grave of Corneliu Codreanu. A team of Legionaries had erected a drill the height of a house and used it to puncture through the concrete seal protecting the mass grave. Dressed in long winter coats, the men then worked carefully with picks and spades, digging gingerly downwards into the loose earth, before lowering a step ladder inside the hole.

This was an official team of Legionary diggers, hired by the state to exhume Codreanu's body. They were restricted to the area around the hole and not allowed inside the jail itself, which now housed several hundred high-worth prisoners, including cabinet ministers from Carol's regime. On day two of the dig, they found a corner of clothing and then a bleached human bone that they removed with the care of archaeologists. The artefacts were placed tenderly on blankets and in trays to be analysed later in a laboratory. These were the mortal remains of the Nicadors and the Decemviri, but even to the diggers' untrained eyes, they knew they had still not found Codreanu.

Then, on the night of 26 November 1940, with the exhumation still underway, news reached the Legionaries that their services were no longer required. Antonescu had decided that the work was too politically and emotionally charged, and should be carried out by non-Legionaries, a group of soldiers in fact. The Legionaries were incensed, believing that they had been deprived of their most holy task – the resurrection of their prophet. They threw down their spades and broke into Jilava Prison intent on revenge against Carol's former ministers and officials.

Forcing the keys from a guard, they entered the long, dimly lit tunnels that many of them knew well from their own time behind bars. There were metal cell doors to either side, each with a rectangular hole to check up on the prisoners. The Legionaries spread out, running along the network of passageways and peering into every cell for recognizable faces. One of the first they saw was the former prime minister, Gheorghe Argeşanu, standing terrified inside a whitewashed dungeon. They unlocked the door, levelled their rifles and shot him several times. Next was the former justice minister, Victor Iamandi, responsible for so many Legionaries being detained and beaten. They shot him dead and moved on. Most of the high-value prisoners were in the same wing of the jail, making the job easier. When they found the former head of Carol's secret police, Mihail Moruzov, they cheered with delight before killing him. From cell to cell they went, shooting military chiefs, gendarmes, the men who had taken the Captain to the woods. In the end, the frenzied Legionaries just wanted to empty their guns and shot anyone unlucky enough to be housed on that wing of the prison. When they had finished, the bodies of sixty-four political prisoners lay in the blood-drenched corridors and cells of Jilava.

The retribution against old Carolists did not end there. The following afternoon, the polymath historian Nicolae Iorga was putting the finishing touches to his latest book, *Istoriologia umană – Human Historiology* – a study of the methods of historians, at his villa in the mountain resort of Sinaia. An earthquake had forced him out of his home in Bucharest and the cool alpine air seemed the best tonic for a writer with a deadline. Iorga was once the political hero of Codreanu, in the early days, when the Legionary leader was still a student in Iaşi. Gradually, with age, his anti-Semitism had mellowed and now, at the age of sixty-nine, he had given up politics to concentrate entirely on academic work. But Iorga had played a crucial role in Codreanu's demise. It was his allegation of criminal slander that had been Carol's excuse to arrest the Legionary leader in the first place, and the Iron Guard would never forget his betrayal. Over recent months he had received dozens of death threats and had been cautious at all times when walking in public. Now, at work in his discreet villa, he heard the footsteps of several men coming up the path. It is not known whether the Legionaries broke down the door or whether Iorga invited them inside, but soon afterwards the historian was in one of their vehicles, being driven southwards towards Ploiești. The car pulled into an area of forest near a small rural village called Strejnicu. Iorga was ordered out of the vehicle. It is said the Legionaries surrounded him, grabbed his beard, and swung him around until it had torn from his face. Then they shot him several times and left his crumpled, bleeding corpse among the trees.

Antonescu was horrified by the murder of one of Romania's greatest writers and historians and tried to resign from his post, only to be talked around by the German minister in Bucharest, who needed the General with his stability and common sense at the helm. But each night there was a reminder of just how sinisterly violent the Guardist revolution had become. At the top of Calea Victoriei, young Green Shirts gathered on motorbikes, dressed in leather jackets with high fur caps, roaring off into the moonlight to raid Jewish homes. Two hundred squads were established, creating a kind of paramilitary police force, supposedly searching for hidden money. But really, they were just looters and terrorists. The sight of them bulleting through the streets in packs became a regular feature of Bucharest life. So too did the macabre pomp of huge and extravagant Legionary funerals, and the exhumation of murdered Legionaries who had been denied a proper burial by previous regimes.

*

On a bitingly cold Saturday in November 1940, green flags fluttered from lampposts all the way along Boulevard Elisabeta, while huge woodcut portraits of Corneliu Codreanu had been hung from public buildings. The Captain's remains had been carefully extracted from the pit at Jilava Prison and were in a worse state than expected. After being strangled and then shot, it seemed that Corneliu Codreanu had still posed a potential threat to Carol's officials. They had been so worried that the truth about his murder might come out (specifically, the fact that there had been no attempted escape) that they had dug him up once again and tried to dissolve his remains in acid. They reinterred what was left and that is what had ended up in the coffin for his funeral on 30 November. His casket, along with those of the thirteen Nicadors and Decemviri, was carried down the steps of the little church of Ilie Gorgani at 8.30 that morning, through a corridor of saluting arms and into a swirling crowd of mourners.

Behind the caskets walked the relatives of the fourteen dead, followed by King Michael dressed in a gold-coloured uniform, then General Antonescu and Horia Sima walking side-by-side in green shirts. Special representatives had flown in from other fascist parties around the world. Representing Germany was Baldur von Schirach, head of the Hitler Youth, and Ernst Bohle, the English-born leader of the Foreign Organizations of the Nazi Party. There were delegates too from Italy and Japan. Marching behind them, in arrow formations, were thousands of green-shirted Legionaries. The procession weaved through saluting crowds to the outskirts of town, and the Legionary's Green House headquarters. There, the coffins were lined up on the ground, accompanied by litanies and clouds of incense. As they were lowered into the earth, Sima stood alone on a small mound above the other mourners, as if hoping to receive Codreanu's rising soul. It was only after eight hours that the freezing crowds were finally allowed to disperse. Antonescu was driven back to his small apartment in the government buildings. It was the last time he would wear a green shirt, and the last time he would be seen in public with Horia Sima.

While the Legionaries were indulging in their macabre funeral rituals, Romania's tiny Communist Party was organizing itself behind prison walls. By 1940, there were still just a thousand communists in the entire country and, paradoxically, the safest place for them to be was in the specialist political jails where they were allowed to mix freely. Ana Pauker and her women's collective had been transferred to one such jail, Caransebeş in the far west of the country, a place that had become a hub for the movement's future leaders.

While walking through the prison one day, she was introduced to a burly railway worker who had become a famous trade unionist in the rail yards of Dej, and who had been renamed after the municipality in honour of his work. Gheorghe Gheorghiu-Dej was a lolloping forty-year-old with hands clenched in permanent clubs. His expression was solemn beyond his years, his hair prematurely receding, his jet-black eyebrows expressing his mood. Gheorghiu-Dej's background could not have been more different from that of the bourgeois Pauker. Leaving school at the age of eleven, he had worked in a series of filthy factories and rail yards, witnessing first-hand the deprivation of low-paid workers before teaching himself about Marxism. He had been rewarded for his diligence by election to the Romanian Communist Party's Central Committee and was then crowned leader of the Party's so-called prison faction, the largest bloc of communists in the country.

Pauker's encounter with Gheorghiu-Dej was like an anthropologist stumbling upon a lost Amazonian tribe. Everything she knew about the working classes was from books. She could tell you what Gheorghiu-Dej ate, how he slept, where he lived; she even knew how his life could be improved but she did not *know* Gheorghiu-Dej or any of his kind.

After that brief meeting, Ana Pauker and Gheorghe Gheorghiu-Dej would not meet again until the communists were on the cusp of taking over Romania. Gheorghiu-Dej was soon transferred to Doftana Prison, in the countryside north of Ploieşti, which became the principal jail for male communist prisoners. It was in Doftana that the whole future hierarchy of the Romanian Communist Party began taking shape – men like Soviet agents Emil Bodnăraş and Gheorghe Pintilie, and the veteran communist intellectual Vasile Luca. They had a lackey in prison, a young hooligan who brought them food packages and ran messages. His name was Nicolae Ceauşescu, a twenty-two-year-old trainee cobbler who was regularly in trouble for fighting and delivering communist leaflets. Some of his fellow inmates thought him 'weird' and said they avoided him because he was 'such a bore with absolutely no sense of humour'.[7] In the presence of big men like Gheorghiu-Dej, Ceauşescu remained largely silent and deferential. He avoided speaking whenever possible because of a stutter so severe it made his legs shake. But he also possessed a powerful memory and instinctive intelligence and sat among the future leaders listening to everything they said, and slowly learning.

As for Pauker, soon after the encounter with Gheorghiu-Dej she became part of a prisoner exchange with Moscow. Despite her husband's miserable death as an enemy of the people, Stalin wanted her back and on 7 May 1941 she was driven across the border to freedom in the Soviet Union.

*

Snow has a special smell in Bucharest, of strong chilled tea and wood-burning stoves, and in the winter of 1941, the capital was covered in an aromatic grey rug. Antonescu was having trouble with his deputy, Horia Sima, and a hard core of Guardists who were behaving like bandits. Antonescu was trying to run the country through discipline and order, while Sima and his colleagues were off around town robbing and beating Jews. To sack Sima was impossible without provoking an uprising from his most violent followers. But neither could he continue to work with him. By December they were no longer on speaking terms, and an arbitrator was required.

On 14 January, a private plane flew into snowy Bucharest, a big four-engine Focke-Wulf Fw 200 Condor, gunmetal-grey with a large swastika on its tail. This was one of the most prestigious aircraft in Germany: Hitler's chosen personal transport. Antonescu climbed on board, accompanied by the German ambassador Wilhelm Fabricius. Horia Sima had been invited to travel with them but he'd refused to sit on the same plane as Antonescu.

Later that afternoon, the party arrived at Hitler's Eagle's Nest retreat. Antonescu spoke freely about Sima's behaviour. He outlined how the Guardist leader had tried to impose his revolution too quickly, how the expropriation of Jewish property was undisciplined and designed to line the pockets of Guardist leaders, how Guardist-run government departments were in a state of chaos and how the goodwill of the Romanian people was evaporating. His tone was measured, his choice of words scrupulously fair. Antonescu was anxious not to exaggerate but equally careful not to underplay the seriousness of Romania's predicament. The Führer was just as careful in his response. He said that Antonescu was the only person in Romania who could cope with any situation, and that he accorded greater importance to his relations with the General than he did with the Iron Guard.[8] He did, however, caution that it was impossible to govern Romania without them and suggested that ultimately Antonescu might have to become leader of the movement, not just the country. Buoyed by Hitler's words of encouragement, Antonescu returned to Bucharest knowing he had the likely backing of Germany when the critical moment arrived.

It did so on 19 January 1941, when a German officer, Major Doering, was murdered outside his headquarters at the Hotel Ambassador in Bucharest. At first, no one knew who was responsible. But Antonescu saw an opportunity. He realized he had an excuse to dismiss his Guardist minister of the interior, General Constantin Petrovicescu, for failing to protect the 'brave Germans' in Bucharest. Petrovicescu was the second most senior Guardist in government, after Sima himself. The next casualty was the Guardist head of the national police – also sacked for his alleged ineptitude in allowing Bucharest to become lawless. Then, in quick succession, came the dismissals of the Guardist chief of the Bucharest police and the Guardist chief of the Siguranța (Security Police). Antonescu had managed to wipe out the entire upper echelon of the movement's law-and-order officials in one fell swoop. Sima saw this for what it was, an attempt to neuter the Guard.

He ordered two of his sacked officials to barricade themselves inside Siguranța headquarters, along with fifty Green Shirts who positioned themselves on the roof, pointing their rifles onto the streets below. It was a move intended to provoke Antonescu to send in his army, for what Sima hoped would escalate into a violent coup. The events that followed were to become known as the 'Legionary Rebellion'.

The next day, the Romanian-Jewish novelist and playwright Mihail Sebastian was sitting in his apartment near the Calea Victoriei when he heard gangs of Legionaries massing beneath his window. 'We want a Legionary government,' they shouted – by which they meant a government without Antonescu. By lunchtime, 5,000 Green Shirts had gathered on the main boulevard leading to Palace Square. When Sebastian switched on his radio to find out what was going on, the airwaves had been taken over by Legionaries demanding 'the replacement of all Masons and Yid-sympathizers in government'. They included Antonescu in that category because his stepmother was Jewish, and so was his wife's former husband.

Mihail Sebastian phoned his mother because he was worried about her safety. The telephone lines were down. The Legionaries had taken over the exchange. The next day, 22 January, Legionaries on motorbikes and in cars moved into the Jewish quarter of Bucharest. They entered Jewish shops and announced that they were from the Legionary Working Group Corps – a fascist association of workers – and that there were trucks waiting outside. Jews were forced into the back of the vehicles and driven to a dozen locations around Bucharest, including Legionary-run police stations, a town hall, the Green House HQ and even the Malbim Synagogue at 4 Bravilor Avenue, which they had taken over the previous night.

The account of one family, out of many hundreds, will suffice. It is based on details from Matatias Carp's *Black Book*.

Rabbi Zvi Hersh Guttman was not yet fifty, but his beard was tinged with grey and the pouches under his eyes no longer disappeared with a good night's sleep. He was at home with his two sons, Jacob and Joseph, when a truck pulled up at 6 a.m. Jacob, the younger of the two, was a lawyer. There is no record of the occupation of Joseph, but the two helped their father into the truck and then climbed up behind him. They were driven to 37 Călăraşi Avenue, the Legionary Working Group Corps headquarters, where 200 Jews had already been detained, their watches and wallets removed. The men were made to run up and down stairs lined by Legionaries armed with clubs and metal bars. The beatings went on all day and through the night. When someone asked for water, the Legionaries went over to Rabbi Guttman, wiped the blood from his body with a cloth and wrung it into a bucket of water, which they then offered as refreshment.[9]

The following morning, a column of trucks arrived at Călăraşi Avenue and drove the Jews to a forest near Jilava Prison. There was snow on the ground (we know this from photographs taken on the day). The trees were young and leafless. There was nowhere to hide. The truck pulled up on the edge of the forest and already the occupants could hear gunfire. Rabi Guttman reached over and held on to the hands of his two adult sons, one on each side. The continued to hold hands as they were ordered out of the vehicle and told to lie face down in the snow. The gunfire began moments later.

When it stopped, Rabi Guttman realized he had somehow

avoided the bullets. He lay as still as he could, holding on to the hands of his two sons, waiting for the Legionaries to climb into their trucks and leave. As the noise of the engines faded, he squeezed Jacob and Joseph's hands tightly and realized they were both dead. Clambering to his feet, Guttman surveyed the scene. There were more than a hundred bodies scattered through the trees. He was the only survivor.

Guttman set off back down the road but he was intercepted by two German soldiers. The German army had been ordered not to take part in the Legionary Rebellion and to remain neutral at all times. They took pity on Guttman and gave him a lift to Jilava town hall, where a group of sympathetic gendarmes agreed to take the Rabbi back to the woods to bless the bodies of Jacob and Joseph.

When they arrived at the scene of the massacre, they discovered that the corpses of all the men and women had been stripped. Shoes, clothing, identification papers, everything was gone. Some had had their mouths smashed to remove golden fillings. Among the dead, Guttman found the naked bodies of Jacob and Joseph, and asked to borrow a pen from one of the gendarmes. He knelt beside his sons and wrote their names in black ink on their bodies – the only memento he could give to them. Then he left. Public records show that Rabbi Guttman eventually fled Romania for Israel shortly after the war, where he died in Tel Aviv in 1973.

The pogroms of the Legionary Rebellion spilled into every street in the Jewish quarter of Bucharest. At the Jewish abattoir, Legionaries rounded up victims and speared them on meat hooks in the freezer, leaving them to hang with their entrails wrapped around their necks. Among them was a five-year-old girl. Synagogues were burnt to the ground, husbands were forced to watch their wives and daughters being raped, before being shot themselves. Witnesses described a young green-shirted boy on the Calea Victoriei 'emptying his gun at passers-by and laughing as if the detonation and the sight of the men toppling gave him exquisite joy'.[10]

The Iron Guard controlled the radio stations, the telephone exchange and several blocks in the city centre. For the first two days, General Antonescu was reluctant to intervene, unsure whether an assault against the Legionaries of the Iron Guard might ignite an even graver civil conflict. But by the third day, 23 January 1941, he had had enough and sent in the tanks.

The Legionaries fought back with suicidal resolve. They fired upon the tanks from city-centre buildings and when they ran out of ammunition, doused themselves and their positions in fuel, going out in a blaze of martyrdom. Others ran into a hail of machine-gun fire. In the end, it was the German special representative, Hermann Neubacher, who contacted Horia Sima and told him to withdraw, promising safe passage to Germany. The National Legionary State was over.

Horia Sima was hidden in the back of Neubacher's car and driven first to Sofia in Bulgaria, and then placed in an army lorry and driven a thousand miles north to Nazi Germany. Over the following months, hundreds more exiled Guardists arrived in Berlin and were allowed to live freely under Hitler's rule, kept safe as a warning to Antonescu. If he failed to perform to the Führer's liking, a German-sponsored regime was ready and waiting to take over.

Now General Antonescu was in sole charge of the country. Nine thousand Guardists implicated in the attempted coup were arrested. Five thousand firearms, including rifles and machine-guns, were found in their homes. This had been the only self-grown fascist state in Europe, outside of Germany and Italy, and the only one toppled during German domination of continental Europe. Antonescu appointed a new cabinet, formed almost entirely of his old friends from the military. In the circumstances, with Romanians exhausted and the economy near breakdown, even the democratic parties gave the new militaristic government their backing.

In his first address to his new cabinet, Antonescu announced: 'I am, by fate, a dictator, because I cannot return to the old constitution nor to parliament. Nor to anything...' On 11 June 1941, he flew to Munich for a private audience with Hitler. The following morning, he was invited into the Führer's study and informed of Operation Barbarossa. Germany and its allies were about to invade the Soviet Union with three and a half million military personnel and 600,000 motor vehicles, making it the largest invasion force in the history of warfare. It was a mark of the high esteem in which Antonescu was held that he was the first non-German to be told of the plan. The General declared his enthusiastic approval.

CHAPTER ELEVEN

There was earth inside of them,
and they dug.

They dug and they dug,
day and night they dug. And they did not praise God,
who, so they heard, wanted all of this,
who, so they heard, knew all of this.

'There Was Earth', Paul Celan

Islands of foliage floated along the Danube's lower reaches that late spring of 1941; tangled rings of willow, bindweed and white lilies, drifting to the sea like so many fallen wreaths. It was after midnight when the first silhouettes of boats passed by, long and narrow, waves curling from their bows, gun-barrels thick as oaks. The Romanian Danube flotilla was patrolling the great Prut River, the waterway that demarcated the continuous 500-mile border between Romania and Russian-held Bessarabia. On the Romanian side of the river, a long line of men slipped through the tall grass, rifles at port, faces blackened with clay. They were German and Romanian soldiers, thousands of them, joining together for the first time and preparing for an invasion in the coming dawn.

There had been no formal declaration of war against the Soviet Union. Antonescu did not even bother to inform King Michael about his decision to join Operation Barbarossa, the largest military confrontation in history. But in the early hours of 22 June 1941, Axis troops from Nazi Germany and Romania stormed the 2,000-mile Soviet border from the Arctic Circle to the Black Sea – 3.5 million soldiers pouring across in tanks and armoured vehicles, supported by 4,000 aircraft. Romanian troops fought on the southern third of the front – under the command of Hitler's Army Group South – supplying an invasion force of 680,000 soldiers, an army second in size only to that of Germany. Whilst Hitler's troops were aiming to conquer the entire western Soviet Union and seize the precious oil reserves of the Caucasus, Romania's ambition was rather different. Antonescu wanted to recapture Bessarabia and Northern Bukovina from Stalin, and every step his soldiers took across the Prut River was the start of the resurrection of Greater Romania.

The beautiful, historic city of Iaşi, home to Queen Marie and King Ferdinand during the German occupation of the First World War, was immediately vulnerable to a Soviet counter-attack. Sitting just ten miles inside the Romanian border, it was an organizational hub for both Romanian and German soldiers on their way to the front, and Stalin's forces launched an aerial bombardment on 24 June, just two days after the start of Operation Barbarossa. Damage was minimal but rumours spread quickly that Jewish inhabitants of the city had used radios and flashlights to signal to the Soviet bombers and indicate where to attack. With its strong Legionary tradition, Iaşi provided fertile ground for anti-Semitic paranoia and soon every Jew in the city was under suspicion.

Romanian soldiers, many of whom were active Legionaries, began house-to-house searches, looking for Jews who might be hiding torches or even pieces of red cloth that were supposedly waved at the Soviet planes. The Dorobanţi 13th Regiment arrested three Jewish suspects on their first day of inquiries and took them to divisional headquarters for interrogation. Having found no evidence against them, officers released them into the hands of Sergeant Mircea Manoliu – an uncompromising

Legionary, who was concerned, or so he claimed, that the Jews now knew the location of divisional headquarters. Instead of freeing them, he took them to his garrison's rifle range, ordered them out of the vehicle and shot at them. One of the three managed to run to safety, another was seriously injured and the third was killed.

That same day, a group of five Jews was instructed to sweep divisional headquarters for unexploded bombs and to mark any devices they discovered with white paint. But the regimental commander accused them of painting signals for Soviet aircraft and placed them in the hands of Sergeant Manoliu again. He drove them to the same rifle range and had them shot. The future of the Iași Jews had become horribly interwoven with something entirely out of their hands: the Soviet bombing raids. Every bombardment led to anti-Semitic recriminations. Then, on 28 June, there was a huge phosphorescent flash in the night sky, which the terrified citizens of Iași concluded had been a flare intended to light the way for Soviet parachutists who were now roaming the city as spies.

General Antonescu was on his private train, *Patria*, travelling eastwards towards the battlefront when he heard the news. He was informed that communist agents had been parachuted into the city to sabotage the war effort. Antonescu's response was severe. A message was sent to the Iași divisional headquarters: 'General Antonescu orders that all Jewish-communists in Iași, and all those found with red flags and firearms, are to be executed tonight.'

At the same time as the phosphorescent flash, reports came in to the police station in Iași that gunfire could be heard across the city, and that 'it probably came from communists and Yids'.[1] Although a Romanian column had come under fire that night, there were no casualties. Nevertheless, German command reported to their Romanian counterparts that they had suffered 'about twenty dead or wounded', and at that point, German officers took off into the city to round up thousands of Jews

– men, women and children – who were marched in columns to the police station. En route, several of them were murdered.

On the approach road to the police station, German and Romanian soldiers, along with some civilians, formed a corridor and as Jews were marched through, they spat, jeered and threw stones. Some Jews were struck with metal bars. Once through the corridor, they were funnelled into a large plot of rough ground, the size of a football pitch, with old car parts and office waste stacked in corners, the perimeter sealed off by high stone walls. Many injured and dying Jews were already lying in the shadows, and by late that evening there were around 4,500 of them crammed inside this walled compound.

The next day, at 2 p.m., a unit of soldiers arrived in the yard, set up their machine guns and opened fire randomly into the assembled crowd. When they ran out of ammunition, they calmly reloaded and began again. The shooting continued until 6 p.m. that evening. Several hundred Jews were killed. The fact that it happened is not disputed, but there are disagreements over the identities of the killers. Some say they were German soldiers, others say a combination of Germans and Romanians. Whatever the truth, we know that one of Romania's most distinguished commanders, General Stavrescu, of the 14th Infantry Division, arrived at the yard in the middle of the massacre and tried to persuade the Germans to stop. The fact that it continued suggests the majority were German, and that any Romanians involved were ignoring Stavrescu's orders.

The sound of gunfire from inside the police yard provoked shooting outside too. Armed Legionaries set off into town, dragging Jews from their homes and killing them. That night there was said to be so much blood on the streets of Iaşi that dogs were drinking it from puddles. There are no official figures for the numbers of dead but in the police yard alone it was said to be around 2,000.

Two days later, survivors of the massacre at the police station

– around 2,500 of them – were led in columns down to Iași train station, where metal-roofed cattle trains were heating up like ovens in the afternoon sun. Several tried to make a run for it, only to be gunned down by German troops. The rest were packed inside the carriages and the doors slammed shut. Around the top of each carriage was a narrow opening, which served as a ventilator when the trains were carrying livestock. Romanian soldiers nailed them shut with planks of wood and then waved the carriages on their way. The first of two trains rolled out of Iași station just after 3.30 p.m. on 30 June 1941, disappearing into the heat haze of the wheat fields beyond.

With no space to sit, the Jews stood braced against each other, swaying to the uncertain rhythm of the train. After seventeen hours, they had covered a distance of just 40 kilometres, little more than an amble in the sun. There were conflicting orders as to where to take them next and as officials squabbled, temperatures continued to rise. By the second afternoon, the human cargo was drinking urine to stay alive.

The first train came to a stop at a tiny rural station called Târgu Frumos, where peasant farmers wandered over the tracks, selling fruit and plum brandy. A lorry-load of gendarmes arrived from Iași and ordered the wagons to be opened. Among the spectators that day was the town's mayor. 'We tried to get the bodies out with the help of those still alive,' he told a war crimes tribunal later, 'but this was impossible because of their weak condition and because of the stench from the bodies… When we tried to give water to [those in] the first wagons… we were prevented by German and Romanian soldiers who were in the station in large numbers, but after about an hour we succeeded in giving the water. This was because of a moving scene when a man in one of the wagons on the fourth siding tied together strips torn from his dirty shirt and dangled them from the wagon into a puddle from which he sucked the water.'[2] The wagons stood in the baking heat for two hours, doors open, corpses scattered on the grass. More and more locals arrived to see what was going on. Few tried to help. Some of the Jews asked for the doors to be shut because they were being hit by stones thrown by soldiers.

When the train arrived at the rural community of Mircești the following day, another 300 corpses were offloaded. It moved on to the town of Roman on 3 July, where it was waved through because of the stench. At several stations thereafter, more corpses were pulled from the carriages, including at the oil city of Ploiești. No one in authority had issued orders as to where the trains should be going next.

A full six days after leaving Iași, the first train eventually arrived at an internment camp in the far south-east of Romania, Călărași, on the banks of the Danube. The few remaining survivors were unloaded and given bread and water. The second train was close behind after following a similarly tortuous route. But once in Călărași, the authorities seemed unsure how to proceed. Seven weeks after their arrival, and without any explanation, all the survivors were released and told to go home.

The human toll in the Iași pogrom and the 'death trains' that followed was in excess of 4,000 people. Some historians put the total as high as 12,000.[3] It had been planned by the Romanian Secret Service, whose operatives had passed on information about the location of Jewish homes to the Romanian and German military in Iași to make the hunt more efficient, egged on by the rhetoric and orders of General Antonescu.

*

To understand the sickening momentum of the impending Romanian Holocaust, one needs to know the geography, defined by three great parallel rivers. First, the mighty Prut, just ten miles east of Iași, forming the border between Romania and Bessarabia. The Prut has already witnessed Antonescu's troops cross its fast-flowing currents on day one of Operation Barbarossa, pouring into the contested region of Bessarabia and Northern Bukovina, a landscape of flat prairies, windmills and dirt roads.

The next river to the east is the Dniester, looping across the landscape in a serpentine tumult, broad and metallic, with currents too challenging for even the strongest of swimmers. Across the other side are the vast steppes of the Soviet Socialist Republic of Ukraine, and Stalin's breadbasket painted in golden barley and sun-ripe corn. Eastwards again and, after sixty miles, we come to the deep, dark waters of the Southern Bug, draining the fields and forests of the southern steppes into the Black Sea.

These three rivers, the Prut, Dniester, and the Southern Bug, will mark the inexorable advance of the fighting front, and witness the atrocities that are perpetrated in its wake.

The war effort, meanwhile, was going well for the invaders. In a little over three weeks, Romanian and German troops had driven the Red Army back an astonishing 150 miles across Bessarabia and Northern Bukovina, to the second of the great rivers, the Dniester. In so doing, Antonescu had regained two prized territories. Governors were appointed to administer each region, taking charge of more than two million new citizens almost overnight, a bewildered mix of ethnicities, languages, and religions, who had only just re-adjusted to Soviet rule and were now expected to act as loyal Romanian citizens. Many were Jews. Now they were in the hands of anxious, inexperienced troops who had fallen for their own regime's propaganda. The Jews, the Romanians believed, were the same ones who had applauded the invasion of Bessarabia by the Red Army the year before, tearing epaulets from Romanian soldiers and throwing roses at Stalin's tanks.

Ruth Glasberg had just celebrated her eleventh birthday when the Romanian army blasted their way into her home town, Cernăuți (Chernivtsi), the capital of Northern Bukovina. Her family was Jewish but they were also proudly Romanian, and the arrival of Romanian troops felt like a liberation. Life under the Bolsheviks had been tough. Private enterprise was eliminated and Ruth's middle-class parents had been forced to share their apartment with strangers.

As Romanian troops fanned out across the city, they were followed by groups of German soldiers wearing grey-green uniforms unfamiliar to the Glasberg family. They turned out to be Hitler's *Einsatzgruppen* – Nazi paramilitary death squads – who torched the city's Great Synagogue and began randomly shooting Jews in the street. Ruth's family hid in their apartment until the initial killing spree seemed to have died down. They assumed that, once under Romanian rule, the situation would improve. But over the following weeks, the new Romanian authorities issued a barrage of anti-Semitic laws. Ruth and her older brother, Bubi – a classical violinist – were banned from attending school. There were restrictions on employment too. Jews were ordered to wear a yellow Star of David whenever they left the house. We know what happened to Ruth because she and her brother kept notes about their treatment over the coming months, and Ruth later wrote of her experiences in a book, called *Ruth's Journey*.

Within days of the Romanian takeover, the new governors of both Bukovina and Bessarabia decreed that Jewish ghettos should be established in all major cities. The Jews of Cernăuți were given twenty-four hours to collect their belongings and move to a demarcated zone surrounded by barbed wire and sentry posts. It was already overcrowded when Ruth's family arrived, and they were fortunate to find a single room occupied by just three families. Another Jewish family arriving in the ghetto that day were Leo and Fritzi Antschel and their twenty-one-year-old son, Paul, who would later become one of the most revered German-speaking poets of his generation, changing his name to Paul Celan (one of his poems serves as the epigraph for this chapter).

The Jews of Cernăuți were soon ordered into columns and marched out of the ghetto, eastwards, to the rear of the advancing Romanian army. No one was sure of their final destination. Ruth

Glasberg closed her ears to rumours that were too terrifying to contemplate, and tried to convince herself it would be like a holiday. Whilst her family waited for orders to join the march, Paul Celan was engaged in forced labour, clearing rubble from the streets and collecting and destroying Russian literature. As other Jews gradually disappeared from the ghetto, Celan suspected the worst and rushed home one evening to tell his parents they must escape before it was too late. When he arrived on 21 June 1942, he found their hovel already empty. They had been taken from their room by Romanian soldiers, and deported eastwards with the rest of the city's Jews.

Similar scenes were taking place in every recaptured city in Bessarabia and Bukovina. Antonescu's plan was to push the region's 270,000 Jews further and further east, beyond the borders of Greater Romania and eventually into Soviet territory. He called the procedure 'evacuation' but his vice-premier, Mihai Antonescu (no relation), gave a more candid description to the Council of Ministers in Bucharest. 'At the risk of not being understood by some traditionalists,' he said, 'I am for the forced migration of the whole Jewish population in Bessarabia and Bukovina, which must be expelled over the frontier... there is no moment in our history more favourable... for a complete ethnic unshackling, for a national revision and purification of our people... if we have to, we should use the machine-gun.'

During late July 1941, the front settled along the banks of the Dniester. Beyond was Soviet territory proper, land that had never belonged to Romania. Antonescu stared out across this broad, symbolic river, the very edge of all that was, to him, Roman and Latin and pure, and contemplated his next move. From Bucharest, the ageing Iuliu Maniu counselled a halt to the invasion, as did other mainstream politicians. The Germans, they said, must now go it alone. For Romania to proceed would no longer be a war for the retrieval of territory but a war of aggression and conquest. Romania would become an imperialist state.

Antonescu watched his proud troops make camp that night beside the new frontier, repairing their vehicles and greasing their guns. Enormous sacrifices had already been made. Twenty thousand Romanians were dead, wounded or missing. But there was still work to do, the hubristic general decided. The Bolsheviks were on the run but not defeated. Leaving Hitler's 11th Army to fight this ideological crusade alone would be dishonourable. Antonescu could never abandon an ally. Gradually another thought took shape in the General's mind. If Romania battled on beyond the Dniester, maybe Hitler would award him the biggest prize of all: Northern Transylvania, hundreds of miles away, now part of Hungary, but with its majority Romanian population inextricably bound to the nation's fate.

On 3 August, the Romanian 4th Army poured across the Dniester into new territory, moving swiftly towards the next river to the east, the Southern Bug. Hitler was so impressed that he awarded Antonescu the Knight's Cross of the Order of the Iron Cross, the highest military honour available in Nazi Germany, which Antonescu wore proudly around his throat for most of the rest of the war. He also raised himself to the rank of marshal.

'Out, out, you dirty Kikes.' Ruth Glasberg's family had been herded into a cattle train with thousands of other Jews from Cernăuți, and had come to a stop in a desolate rural landscape. Romanian soldiers organized them into a column, with the Glasbergs near the rear, and armed guards on either side. Ruth carried a small brown knapsack made from an old dress of her mother's, while her brother had his violin in a case, and her father a large bag with money and jewellery stitched into the seams. They were marched through newly won territory, eastwards, and after several days came upon a wide brown river, high with recent flooding. Fifty metres across and eddying with fast currents, this was the Dniester, the edge of their homeland. On the banks awaited thousands of Jews. Romanian soldiers pointed towards a

1. Vlad III Dracula, brilliant military strategist, famed impaler and Romanian national hero.

2. The supposed tomb of Vlad III Dracula (right, beneath the chandelier), on the fifteenth-century Island monastery of Snagov, thirty miles north of Bucharest. Killed in battle, his head was cut off and taken to Constantinople.

3. Fairy tale queen: Marie revelled in her image as Europe's last Romantic. 'I rejoice in my own beauty,' she wrote of herself, 'men have taught me to.'

A.S.R. PRINCIPESA MARIA A ROMÂNIEI

4. Marie in her boudoir, where she wrote fairy tales and redesigned the decor in sweeping Baroque-style splendour.

FINE BRITISH SOMME SUCCESS—FALL OF CONSTANZA

The Daily Mirror

CERTIFIED CIRCULATION LARGER THAN THAT OF ANY OTHER DAILY PICTURE PAPER

No. 4,057. Registered at the G.P.O. as a Newspaper. | TUESDAY, OCTOBER 24, 1916 | One Halfpenny.

RUMANIA'S BEAUTIFUL QUEEN TENDING THE WOUNDED: EXCLUSIVE PHOTOGRAPH OF HER MAJESTY AS A NURSE.

The Queen of Rumania is devoting herself entirely to the welfare of the wounded. At the outbreak of war she converted the ground floor of the palace at Bukarest into a hospital, where she works untiringly every day, and this photograph shows her cutting up the dinner of a soldier whose injuries prevent him from using his hands. It was taken by her Majesty's special permission by *The Daily Mirror* staff photographer on the eastern front. Rumania's Flag Day will be on Thursday next.

5. How the *Daily Mirror* reported Queen Marie's new role as field nurse, tending troops during the First World War, an activity which endeared 'Mamma Regina' forever to Romanians.

6. Marie at Bran Castle, where she spent many happy summers.

7. Queen Marie with King Ferdinand I. He was awkward in public and preferred pressing wild flowers to royal banquets. She helped him navigate the monumental decision of who to back in the war.

8. A rare image of Queen Marie with her lover, the dashing prince, Barbu Ştirbey.

9. John Norton-Griffiths ('Hell-fire Jack') before his enthusiastic and near suicidal 'total and radical destruction' of Romania's oil fields.

10. Prince Carol before he was King. Marie loved him dearly, but already he was lurching from scandal to scandal, displaying unmistakable signs of serious mental instability.

11. Child king, Michael I of Romania (second left) on holiday with his mother, Princess Helen, in 1928, and his friend, Prince Philip of Greece (second right) the future Duke of Edinburgh and husband to Queen Elizabeth II of the United Kingdom.

12. Carol and his mistress, Elena (Magda) Lupescu. Gauche, unrefined, and a tireless social climber, Carol gave up the throne for her before becoming Romania's dictator king.

13. 'Looking at him, you felt dazed,' said one Legionary, 'he was a god among mortals.' The photo of Corneliu Codreanu (The Captain) that followers still revere today.

14. Fairy crowns with a Nazi twist; Codreanu and his wife Elena Ilinoiu. Around his neck hangs a pouch of sacred Romanian earth.

15. Codreanu (front, centre) with founding members of the Legion of the Archangel Michael. Behind him (back row, right) is Codreanu's most loyal lieutenant, the wild and highly intelligent Ion Moța.

16. Corneliu Codreanu clambering through bones of Romanian soldiers killed during the First World War. Images of heroic sacrifice were used to inspire Codreanu's ultra-nationalist death squads.

17. A young, defiant Ana Pauker at her trial for being a Soviet spy. Beside her, eighteen co-accused. 'there was a stampede… the accused were hit from all sides.'

18. Carol II trying to make a deal with Hitler, a man he much admired, November 1938. A chill descended when the Führer said he was an admirer of Corneliu Codreanu.

19. General Ion Antonescu shortly after taking sole charge of Romania in 1941. 'I am, by fate, a dictator,' he told his first cabinet.

20. Ion Antonescu, at the inception of the National Legionary State (left, arm raised), with his deputy, Horia Sima, leader of the Iron Guard. The two despised each other.

21. Ion Antonescu (right) greeting Hitler. The Führer preferred Antonescu to Mussolini, and was impressed by his sheer determination and intellectual clarity.

22. A Romanian death train stops to unload Jewish corpses after the Iași pogrom, signaling the start of the Romanian Holocaust, June 1941.

23. Jews being deported eastwards to the Romanian killing fields of Transnistria.

24. A young Nicolae Ceaușescu greeting Red Army troops surging into Bucharest on 30 August 1944.

25. Seventy-five-year-old Iuliu Maniu, leader of the National Peasants' Party, on trial by the communists in November 1947. Inevitably, he was sentenced to life in prison with hard labour.

26. Gheorghiu-Dej with Ana Pauker on a walkabout, 23 August 1951, celebrating the anniversary of the overthrow of Marshal Antonescu, and the start of the communist takeover.

27. Gheorghiu-Dej (third from left) welcoming Nikita Khrushchev (hat in hand) to Romania in June 1960. Behind the scenes, the two bickered like an old married couple.

28. Ceaușescu leaving the famous Ninth Party Congress in Bucharest flanked by Soviet leader Leonid Brezhnev and China's Den Xiaoping, a historic meeting where the forty-eight-year-old Romanian was in his element.

29. Ceaușescu with his wife, Elena, feasting at a villa in the countryside.

30. Ceaușescu's trip to Disneyland, in October 1970, came as he and President Nixon were striking unlikely deals over trade and foreign relations.

31. Ceaușescu with Queen Elizabeth II, June 1978. 'He is as absolute a dictator as can be found in the world today,' advised the British ambassador before the trip.

32. Crowds of protestors take cover behind army tanks as Ceaușescu's loyal Securitate sharpshooters fire on them from buildings across the capital.

33. The last speech, 11am, 21 December 1989, in front of huge crowds in what is now Revolution Square.

34. Crowds gesture to Ceaușescu's escape helicopter as it takes off from the Central Committee Building on 22 December 1989.

35. Nicolae and Elena Ceaușescu facing a kangaroo court. 'You had palaces,' says the prosecutor, 'whilst children cannot even buy plain candy.' Minutes later they were executed in a hail of bullets.

creaking wooden bridge that led to a settlement on the other side called Yampol, situated in what had once been Soviet Ukraine. Ruth and her family waited in the beet fields for their turn to cross the river.

Antonescu's 'evacuation' was not going as well as he had hoped. His Jewish solution required the new territory on the other side of the Dniester to serve as a dumping ground. But, for the moment, it was the Germans not the Romanians who controlled it, and they were unhappy that the Romanians were trying to export their problem without a formal plan. All along the river, the Romanians had been constructing pontoons and herding Jews across. The Germans had been sending them back. On numerous occasions, the Romanians had then waited for cover of night and returned the favour, sending the Jews back once again and then packing up the pontoons before the Germans could respond. The creaking, old bridge into Yampol became the focal point of the disagreement.

In the third week of August, Colonel Otto Ohlendorf, head of the German *Einsatzgruppe D,* 'pruned' his Jewish columns – shooting the old and infirm so as not to slow the rest down – and then sent them over the bridge back to the Romanian side. As the Jews reached no man's land, half way across, the shooting began, with both sides opening fire upon the unwanted traffic. More than a thousand Jews perished that night on a meaningless line in the middle of the Dniester river.[4]

By the end of the summer of 1941, it is estimated that German and Romanian soldiers had shot dead more than 12,000 Jews on the Dniester, and even Himmler's death squads were appalled by the undisciplined methods of Antonescu's men – not on any moral grounds but because they were worried their ally's behaviour and sloppy practices would undermine the prestige of the German army. One *Einsatzgruppen* commander wrote a report to his bosses complaining: 'The Romanians act against the Jew without any idea of a plan. No one would object to the numerous executions of Jews if the technical aspect of their preparation, as well as the manner in which they were carried out, were not wanting. The Romanians leave the executed where they fall, without burial.'⁵ Another German commander called for an intervention against the 'sadistic executions' carried out by the Romanians, and asked if moves could be made to prevent Romanian soldiers looting Jews' belongings.

With the backlog of Jews building up in transit camps and ghettos across Bessarabia and Bukovina, on 19 August 1941 Hitler decided that the best solution was to award Romania the newly conquered territory beyond the Dniester, eastwards all the way to the Southern Bug; in other words, the area of occupied Ukraine into which Romania was driving its Jews. It was an immense slab of land, larger than Belgium and home to 2.5 million people, a place of washed-out skies and primeval forests. But the Romanians would still need to defeat Stalin's Red Army, which continued to hold major cities – including the port of Odessa ('the Marseilles of the Black Sea'), one of the Soviet Union's most treasured maritime assets. The fierce Romanian and German siege of the city, pitting vast numbers of Romanian and German troops against a heavily outnumbered Russian garrison, lasted over two months and ended with at least forty-five thousand dead or missing. The victory was costly for the Romanians, with the loss of 17,700 soldiers, but resulted in the region of Odessa being awarded to Antonescu on 17 October (aside from the rail tracks and port facilities, which would be controlled by Germany). This was imperial conquest at its most exhilarating. The land had never been ruled as a single administrative entity before but it would now be called Transnistria – literally 'Beyond the Dniester' – with Antonescu as its *Conducător*. The fact that fewer than ten per cent of its population were ethnic Romanians hardly mattered. Transnistria's primary purpose was, for the moment at least, not about ethnic cohabitation but to provide a dumping ground for Jews.

Celebrations over victory in Odessa were short lived. The top brass of the Romanian military command were moving into their new offices, near the old People's Commissariat of Internal Affairs (NKVD) in Odessa, when an explosion tore through the building, apparently ignited by a booby-trapped safe in the cellar. The force of the blast was devastating, leaving a huge crater in the centre of town and killing sixty-one military personnel, including the new Romanian military commander of the city, General Ioan Glogojanu. Antonescu's response was monstrous. Instead of consulting with judges and prosecutors and ordering an investigation, he sent Telegram No. 562 to the head of his military office, ordering that:

a) For every Romanian and German officer killed in the explosion, 200 Communists will be executed; for each soldier who died, 100 Communists. The executions will take place on this very day.

b) All Communists in Odessa will be taken hostage, as well as a member of each Jewish family.

Marshal Antonescu's gangs of marauding thugs rampaged around the city, carrying out the order however they saw fit. Later that same day, the deputy commander of Romania's 4th Army, Colonel Stănculescu, ordered 'the elimination of 18,000 Jews in the ghetto, and [the hanging] of at least 100 Jews for each regimental sector'. On the night of 23 October 1941, many hundreds of Jews were hung from lamp posts and trees along Odessa's grand boulevards. Most historians agree that the number of victims was around 5,000. Their bodies were left suspended for days as a grim warning to Antonescu's newly acquired subjects.

The Marshal ordered further reprisals the next day, relayed in Telegram No. 563 through the head of his military office. It stipulated that all Jews not yet executed in accordance with the previous day's telegram must be rounded up and placed inside a building that 'will be mined and detonated' to coincide with the funerals of the Romanian military personnel killed in the explosion. The final item in the telegram left no doubt that Antonescu knew he was committing grave crimes. 'This order will be destroyed after being read,' it said.[6] Later that day, 25,000–30,000 Jews were marched out of Odessa to a nearby village and herded into three long sheds. Slots were cut in the walls so that machine-guns could be poked through. The executions were carried out under the leadership of two Romanian colonels, Nicolae Deleanu and Mihail Niculescu-Coca. After several hours of firing, and with many of the victims still alive, the soldiers sprayed oil over the sheds and set them alight. Jews appeared at the windows, pointing to their heads and hearts indicating where the Romanians should shoot them to put them out of their misery.[7]

Antonescu's anti-Semitism had not, of course, erupted overnight, nor had his merciless punishment of those he perceived as enemy combatants. But it had been invigorated by a new set of circumstances. First was his 'special' relationship with Hitler, and the consequent normalization of a programme of violence towards and extermination of the Jews. Second was the 'evidence' of Judeo-communist involvement in the devastating Odessa bombing – although it was almost certainly carried out by retreating Soviet soldiers. Third, the number of Romanian war casualties was growing daily and Antonescu, again, blamed Judeo-communists. The Marshal was not out of step with Romanian public opinion. Disturbed as some may have been by details of the Odessa killings, most would have considered it reasonable in a time of war. Anti-Semitism had been passed down through the generations, unquestioned, communal, a measure of one's loyalty to the Romanian dream. As it reached its apocalyptic height, some did resist, offering food and clothing to the refugee columns as they walked through their villages, even hiding Jews from the police. But many preferred the comfort of the herd.

'Was that repression severe enough?' asked an impatient Marshal Antonescu at a Council of Ministers meeting after the Odessa massacre. The new Governor of Transnistria, Gheorghe Alexianu, a senior lecturer in public law before the war, looked uncomfortable. 'It was, Marshal,' he confirmed. Antonescu was doubtful. 'What do you understand as "severe enough"?' he demanded. 'You are rather soft on others...' When the governor reassured him that the orders in Odessa had been carried out, Antonescu responded: 'That's how you should act, because I am responsible before the country and history. Let the Jews come from America and hold me responsible!... Don't think they will not exact revenge when they can... [But] I'll finish them first, and I am not doing that for personal reasons, but for the people of this country.'[8]

Two months later, the Marshal was mystified and hurt when Britain declared war on Romania. He was fighting communism on behalf of the civilized world. How could Churchill fail to understand? America was next, declaring war on Romania a week later. It made no sense to Antonescu, who believed he was risking his life to defend Western values: the Church, capitalism, freedom. All this, and his preferred allies in the West wanted to destroy him. 'I am an ally of the Reich against Russia,' he said. 'I am a neutral in the conflict between Great Britain and Germany. I am for America against the Japanese.' It was as if the world needed to readjust itself to accommodate the Marshal's grand plans and complicated loyalties.

In November 1941, snow fell upon Ruth Glasberg's marching column. They had crossed the Dniester at Yampol without incident. A few now dared run into the fields to pull rotting beet from the soil, which they ate raw. Now they were forced to march twenty miles a day eastward. When they stopped for the night, whoever had money or jewellery to pay the Romanian soldiers was allowed to walk into a town, where they could beg for food and lodging, as long as they left a family member behind as collateral. A barter system gripped the column at each village when local peasants arrived with paltry offerings of food in exchange for clothing. A shirt in exchange for an onion. A coat for a loaf of bread. As the weather deteriorated, the poorer were stripped of all but a thin layer of clothes.

At the end of November, the column arrived in Bershad, a rural Transnistrian town of tin-roofs and bonfires. It had once been famous for its Jewish weavers but they were long gone, some having fled during the Soviet retreat, others murdered by the occupying Germans and Romanians. Antonescu's governor had since turned a large part of Bershad into a ghetto. Thousands of Jews were packed inside, prevented from leaving and shot if they dared try. There was no medical assistance, no limit on numbers and no food or water. Bershad was in almost every respect a concentration camp, as were the other 200 Romanian-government camps and ghettos around Transnistria. The only difference was that instead of purpose-built sheds, Jews lived in bombed-out buildings.

This is where the Glasberg family would spend the next few months of their lives, at the height of Romania's Holocaust. There was a hovel in Bershad consisting of three rooms, and the Glasbergs moved into the one at the rear, the least crowded, where fifteen people were already squatting. The only furniture was an old metal crib and a makeshift stove that consisted of two bricks and a wire grate. By this time, Ruth's father, Mendel, had been rendered almost mute with the shock of the journey and the many beatings. He hunched his skeletal frame in the crib, while Ruth's brother, Bubi, went foraging for twigs and broken furniture to burn on the grate. Like his father, Bubi never spoke.

That Christmas of 1941, Ruth was astonished to hear the clanking of sleigh bells outside their hovel. Back in Cernăuți, the sound had been a signal for children to hitch a ride with peasant farmers through the powdery snow. She could hardly believe a similar tradition was alive in the muddy unpaved streets of Bershad. When she ventured out, she found an adapted sleigh pulled by two horses. Stacked in the middle were piles of naked corpses, men, women, children, their limbs dragging in the snow. As the horseman walked through the streets he shouted, 'A meth, A meth'; *a body, a body?* And Jews brought out their dead.

Many died through cold and hunger, others from typhus, which was spreading through the ghettos and the camps. Doctors were only called when there was a possibility the disease might spread to non-Jewish areas of town. But in Bershad, the Glasbergs were fortunate to have a physician in the next-door room. Dr Menschel was facing the same predicament as the rest and had no medicine, but at least he might offer a diagnosis for Ruth's father. The doctor appeared at the door and surveyed Mr Glasberg from a distance. The patient was barely breathing and his body looked as light as the cinders in the grate. 'Mrs Glasberg,' said the doctor, 'what your husband needs is medicine, food, a warm bath and a comfortable bed, none of which I can offer.' And with that he turned and left. In her memoirs, Ruth tells us she felt like hitting him. When her father finally expired a day or two later, there was no mourning, no condolence, not even a kind look from the other squatters. It was as if they were all waiting for the same fate, a peaceful route out.

As the numbers of dead rose that winter, sightings of the sleigh became fewer. The horseman was just too busy to collect from every corner of town, and so Ruth's room gradually turned into a mortuary, corpses stacked like logs waiting for the next collection. By this time, Dr Menschel was allowed out of the ghetto to treat sick Ukrainians in the rest of town, a service for which he was paid in groceries. Every night, after supper, he would give the water in which he had boiled his potatoes to the grateful Glasbergs. They fed small spoonfuls to Bubi, whose eyes had turned glassy and unfocused like those of his father. The water stuck for a moment in Bubi's throat and came back with froth. The next bells they heard were for him.

There was a long line of towns and villages just to the rear of the Romanian front, in what was called the Romanian Transnistria Governate, that had been transformed into ghettos like Bershad. Even remote farming villages became transit camps, or orphans' camps, or labour camps. Places that had once been idyllic peasant communities were now scenes of starvation, with bodies stacked in buildings and on the streets. The pretty farming village of Djurin was now a ghetto containing 4,050 Jews; the wheat-trading town of Balta had 2,723 Jews; the little wine-producing centre of Shargorod, 5,300; the vast urban sprawl of Mogilev, 15,000. Nowhere in Transnistria remained untouched. The parents of the poet Paul Celan were held in a village converted into a labour camp. His father died of typhus, a disease that claimed tens of thousands of lives in Transnistria, while his mother was shot after becoming too exhausted to carry out her back-breaking work. Celan himself was being held in a forced labour camp in Romania when he was informed of his parents' fate.

Years later, after being awarded the Bremen Prize for German Literature, he reflected on his darkest hour. 'Only one thing remained reachable, close and secure amid all losses: language. Yes, language. In spite of everything, it remained secure against loss. But it had to go through its own lack of answers, through terrifying silence, through the thousand darknesses of murderous speech. It went through. It gave me no words for what was happening, but went through it. Went through and could resurface, "enriched" by it all.'

There were no gas chambers. Romania's industrialized killing was different, achieved not in the main through executions, although there were many of those, but by the slow torment of forced deportation, detention, starvation, and disease. Transnistria became Romania's instrument of ethnic cleansing and mass murder. It was not just Jews – there were Roma (Gypsy) deportees too, 25,000 of them who were sent to Transnistria where they were forced to live in pig sties and cattle sheds, and died in horrific conditions.

For Antonescu, it seemed his 'Jewish problem' was being resolved in the eastern areas of Romania, but 300,000 Jews still lived in the Old Kingdom, Romania proper. In Bucharest and Ploieşti, in the southern Transylvanian cities of Braşov and Sibiu, and all across old Wallachia and Moldova, the Jews, although subject to harshly repressive laws, had been largely spared deportation to Transnistria. The further west one went, the safer Jews were from the horror. Antonescu considered these men and women to be less contaminated by Bolshevism. They had not thrown flowers at Stalin's Red Army. Nonetheless, there was a separate plan for them.

It was devised in the offices of a four-storey town house at 116 Kurfürsten Strasse in Berlin, the headquarters of Gestapo department IV B4, a unit of the Reich's Main Security Office that was implementing Hitler's Final Solution. Presided over by Adolf Eichmann, in the summer of 1942 the unit made what it thought was a breakthrough with the Romanian government, with the offer of a new deportation plan. 'Political and technical preparations for a solution to the Jewish question in Romania have been completed,' announced delighted German officials. '… the evacuation transports will be able to roll in a very short time.' The plan was for the Jews of Romania to be loaded onto trains and taken to the district of Lublin in German-occupied Poland, where 'the employable segment will be allocated for labour utilization, while the remainder will be subject to special treatment.'[9] There was no doubt what 'special treatment' meant. The two Antonescus, vice-premier Mihai and the Marshal, both agreed to the plan and it is impossible that they did not know what it implied. Orders were made for the rail cars to be prepared. A provisional date was set, 10 September 1942. Twenty-five thousand Jews were to be in the first consignment, from Arad, Timişoara, and Turda, marking the start of Romania's involvement in Hitler's Final Solution.

But then an unexpected confluence of events caused Antonescu to question his decision. First, the Marshal's personal physician, Dr Stroescu, informed him that he had received a donation of 100 million lei ($3 million) for his Palace of the Handicapped (a hospital for Romanians with disabilities) from wealthy Transylvanian Jews, and recounted the good deeds of many others. Then two Romanian Jewish industrialists donated 4 billion lei ($12 million) to a charity run by Maria Antonescu, the Marshal's wife. Many others who counted themselves friends of Antonescu lobbied him to stop all Jewish deportations, including the head of the Romanian Catholic Church, the head of the Red Cross, liberal politicians such as Iuliu Maniu and Constantin Brătianu, and several foreign envoys. Perhaps most persuasive was Wilhelm Filderman, president of the Jewish Federation in Bucharest, who had attended school with Antonescu and knew him well. He began visiting the Marshal regularly at his presidential offices, giving accounts of fresh atrocities and presenting letters from around the world urging Romania to desist. Significantly, a warning also arrived from the White House, explaining to Antonescu that if the deportation of Jews to Transnistria continued, there would be reprisals against Romanians living in the US.

There was also pressure placed upon King Michael, by his own mother, Helen. It was a disgrace, she said, how the Marshal was treating the Jews and he, Michael, would always be associated with it and remembered through history as 'Michael the Wicked'. If he failed to step in, she said, she would leave the country right away. At the same time, a seismic military event was about to take place that would turn Romania's involvement in the war on its head.

*

A thousand miles from Bucharest, two dogged Romanian armies had made their way through the vast southern Russian steppes to help the Germans fight one of the bloodiest battles in history. It was September 1942 and Romania had committed 225,000 troops to this new offensive. They were in good spirits. The war seemed to be going their way, despite the huge losses they'd suffered. The next phase would be decisive. Over the other side of the Don, hugging the banks of the Volga, lay the city of Stalingrad.

The mission of the Romanian 3rd and 4th Armies was to form a protective corridor through which the German army could stream into Stalingrad from the west. By the time they had taken position, the city was almost surrounded by Axis troops, save for a Red Army bridgehead from the east across the Volga. The initial German assault was swift and savage, with Luftwaffe aircraft dropping 1,000 tonnes of bombs on the city in just forty-eight hours. Even before German troops reached the outskirts, Soviet casualties had reached 200,000, and Stalingrad was locked down with another 400,000 people trapped inside. The Red Army was in desperate retreat. An Axis victory seemed inevitable. But as the weather turned colder over the coming weeks, the Soviets called in almost a million reinforcements from the east, and the German and Romanian divisions ground to a halt amid savage street fighting.

In freezing temperatures of minus 20 degrees, Stalin targeted the weaker Romanian armies to the north and south, easily punching holes through their flanks, which allowed the Red Army to stream in behind them and encircle the Axis armies. Romanian losses in the ensuing fighting were enormous and would change the course of the country's involvement in the war. In total, 158,000 Romanians were killed, wounded or listed as missing, and as the Soviets sealed off the city at Christmas 1942, 12,500 Romanians were among the 300,000 Axis troops trapped inside.

Back in Bucharest, the cattle trains were already supposed to have left, deporting Jews from Romania to Poland for 'special treatment'. But the enormous losses being incurred in Stalingrad gave Antonescu pause for thought. If he ended up on the losing side in the war, his treatment of Jews would doubtlessly be examined by the Allies. There were likely to be war crimes tribunals. With that in mind, he began dragging his feet, something that German officials noticed straight away. They suspected that some senior figures in Romania were starting to consider swapping sides and scoffed at the Marshal's apparent dilemma. Romania, they said, was already too compromised by its part in the extermination of Jews to suddenly side with the Allies. Antonescu ignored them. He announced the postponement of the entire deportation, pretending it was not for political reasons but merely because the winter weather was unsuitable.

Situation reports reached Antonescu each day about the Romanian soldiers trapped in Stalingrad. The promised Luftwaffe airlift of supplies had failed to materialize and soldiers were beginning to starve to death. In plummeting temperatures, Soviet forces were gradually tightening the noose around the quarter of a million Axis troops trying to fight their way out of a shrinking pocket of the city. Eventually, the Germans and Romanians were confined to just a few ruined blocks, reduced to eating rats and drinking melted snow. By the morning of 2 February 1943, ten weeks into the siege, the German commanders were left with no choice but to surrender on behalf of themselves and the Romanians. Out of the ruins emerged just 91,000 soldiers. The rest – 180,000 men – had died from starvation or battle injuries. Romanian survivors numbered fewer than 3,000. As the pitiful remnants of the Romanian 3rd and 4th Armies filed out of the city to be taken prisoner, Antonescu's re-appraisal of his Jewish policy became ever more pressing.

His deputy, Mihai Antonescu, began putting out feelers to the Allies to assess the conditions under which they might accept Romania's surrender. He did so discreetly, through embassies of neutral third countries. Two conclusions emerged from these informal conversations that troubled the Marshal. The first was that Britain and America would insist on 'unconditional surrender', which would almost certainly mean sacrificing some degree of Romanian independence to Stalin – and probably the region of Bessarabia. Secondly, the Allies would indeed seek punishment for crimes perpetrated against the Jews. From that point on, Antonescu was certain he needed to minimize his culpability.

That spring, the Governor of Transnistria received a secret note. It came from the Council of Ministers in Bucharest and stated that certain categories of Jews could be released from camps and ghettos: parents of soldiers killed in battle, retired civil servants, Jews married to Christians, pensioners, all could be freed. They would have to stay in Transnistria, for the moment at least, but the note signalled a marked change in attitude. The categories were gradually extended to include orphans who had lost both parents. The first Ruth Glasberg knew of it was when boxes of clothes and provisions arrived at her orphanage in Bershad.

Over the harsh winter, her mother had finally succumbed to cold and starvation, leaving Ruth to fend for herself. She'd been taken in by a series of local families who required payment from the tiny amount of jewellery and bank notes cut from the seam of her father's bag. When the funds ran out, so too did the generosity. Ruth was eventually taken to an orphanage where children slept ten to a bed, but even the existence of such a place was evidence of a softening of attitude on Antonescu's part.

Over the summer of 1943, the categories of Jews to be repatriated from Transnistria were extended further. Lists of the missing were drawn up and searches began for survivors. The head of the gendarmerie in the ministry of the interior, General Constantin Vasiliu – once a merciless supporter of the Holocaust who had ordered 'cleansing' of the Jews so that 'not a single guilty individual escapes the retribution he deserves' – now began quizzing subordinates as to why they had approved the deportation of 'innocent Jews'. By the autumn, the proposed trains to Poland were suspended indefinitely, while repatriations from Transnistria included almost all categories of those who had been deported.

It was only in the months and years that followed that the full enormity of Romania's Holocaust emerged. More Jews were killed by Romania than any other Axis state, aside from Germany itself. According to the International Commission on the Holocaust in Romania, the number of Romanian and Ukrainian Jews who perished in territories under Romanian control was between 280,000 and 380,000. Between 120,000 and 180,000 of them died as a result of deportation to Transnistria.[10] The Gypsies who died in similar circumstances numbered 11,000. Antonescu's policies were directly responsible for most of the deaths and yet his role is still fiercely debated in Romania today. Supporters point out that, while his policies led to so many deaths, he also 'saved' more than 300,000 Jews by refusing to deport them to Poland. But Antonescu's volte-face had not gone unnoticed in Berlin, and he was about to receive a chilling summons.

*

After Stalingrad, it was clear that the tide of war was turning against the Axis powers and the pressure for Antonescu to surrender to the Allies was building. The usually apolitical King Michael, along with Iuliu Maniu, was leading the lobby for withdrawal. More discreet approaches were made by Romanian officials – including Maniu himself – via third parties to the Allies, asking for at least some territorial guarantees if they were to surrender. It was naïve of Bucharest to imagine the Germans would not hear of these back channels, and on 12 April 1943, Antonescu was summoned to Klessheim Castle, just outside Salzburg, for a meeting with Hitler.

The Führer had a few questions to put to his special friend. German intelligence, he said, had reported that Romanian officials were making approaches, via Madrid, to the Allies. Hitler asked politely if Antonescu would 'analyse' the reports to see if they were true. Antonescu feigned innocence. The entire Romanian nation, he said, supported Hitler, now more than ever. The next day, Hitler called him back in again and raised the question a second time. Antonescu held his nerve. He was 'grateful' they had discussed the matter, he said, but the truth was 'totally the reverse of what Germany knew'.[11]

In fact, after two devastating Allied bombing raids on Bucharest in April 1943, very few ministers had any appetite for remaining in the war. Most of the ardently pro-Hitler faction – those who had been members of the Iron Guard – had been purged by Antonescu during the failed Legionary Rebellion of 1941, and had joined Horia Sima in exile in Berlin. The tens of thousands of rank-and-file Nazi-supporting Legionaries who had regularly paraded on the streets of Bucharest before the war had been young men who'd ended up on the front line and thus seen their numbers hugely depleted.

Any pro-German sentiment left among remaining Legionaries evaporated further when they learned that Hitler was refusing to pay for the oil that Romania was obediently piping out of Ploiești every day. Having failed to conquer the rich Russian oil fields of the Caucasus, Hitler was entirely reliant on Romanian oil and yet he was taking it for free. He was doing the same with wheat and corn too, and the consequence was sky-high inflation. As public opinion turned against the Germans, Antonescu became increasingly isolated in his refusal to accept unconditional surrender, saying that he would need to discuss any withdrawal from the war with Hitler first – as he had given his word that he would remain loyal until the end.

In the meantime, Romania's oil fields around Ploiești became the target of the Allies' most daring bombing raid of the war. Just as Britain's Major John Norton-Griffiths had tried to destroy the country's refineries in the First World War, to stop them falling into German hands, now American B-24 bombers did the same from the air.

Victoria Angelescu, the young woman who would later become my grandmother-in-law, was living in Ploiești at the time and was just on her way to church on Sunday, 1 August 1943, when a deafening shriek pierced the morning sky. A swarm of US planes roared so low across the city that she could see the silhouettes of the pilots in their cockpits. The Americans called it 'a tree-top level' attack, and the noise was so deafening that the residents of Ploieşti instinctively fell to their knees. An astonishing 178 bombers took part in Operation Tidal Wave, unleashing wave upon wave of bombs across the nearby refineries. This was the most heavily fortified Romanian asset, and Romanian and German anti-aircraft guns erupted into action, while hundreds of metal-grey barrage balloons were released into the Sunday morning sky, creating an airborne forest through which the US planes had to navigate. Victoria ran for the safety of her house, terrified at the sight of orange fireballs bursting from the edges of town as oil reserves were ignited. Columns of acrid, black smoke drifted across Ploieşti and the explosions were so powerful that it seemed the whole city was shaking.

Fifty-three US planes were brought down that day, crashing to earth in the countryside around Ploieşti with the loss of 310 US airmen. Ploieşti's oil capacity was badly hit, with 42 per cent of its productivity lost, but the damage turned out to be less serious than that of Major Norton-Griffiths intervention in the First World War. Within weeks, Ploieşti was back up to full capacity.

Nevertheless, Romanian civilians were horrified by the intensity of the attack and the damage to civilian buildings caused by a war that most of them thought no longer worth fighting. Opposition to Romania's continued involvement stiffened when, in the months that followed, a Red Army offensive began to push Romanian troops into reverse, right back across the territory they had seized at the start of the war. By April 1944, they were back to the Dniester River and by August the Soviet line had been pushed all the way to the Prut. Bessarabia and Northern Bukovina had been lost – the very cause of Romania's involvement in the war in the first place. The clamour for Antonescu to surrender took on a new urgency when the Red Army poured across Romania's border into the Old Kingdom itself and looked set to occupy the entire country.

At that point, King Michael, along with a group of high-profile liberal politicians, agreed that the only way to solve the problem of the unyielding Antonescu was by way of a coup. It would happen, they decided, in the refined environs of the royal palace, over lunch. King Michael sent the Marshal an invitation.

CHAPTER TWELVE

One does not inhabit a country; one inhabits a language. That is our country, our fatherland – and no other.

Emil Cioran, Romanian philosopher

It would be a memorable lunch party, with an explosive final course. Set for 1 p.m. on Saturday, 26 August 1944, at the royal palace in Bucharest, the two main guests were Marshal Antonescu and his deputy, Mihai Antonescu, neither of whom had any idea of the event's true purpose. King Michael would host the lunch, along with two elder statesmen, Iuliu Maniu (leader of the National Peasants' Party) and Constantin Brătianu (leader of the National Liberals). Aides and military personnel of all sorts would also be on hand, some lurking in adjoining rooms and some of them armed.

The idea of organizing a coup against Antonescu had taken shape in King Michael's head after the disaster at Stalingrad. He'd wanted Romania out of the war immediately and was infuriated by Antonescu's stubbornness. The king approached Maniu and Brătianu, hoping to prod them into action. But both men urged caution. There were thousands of German soldiers in Bucharest, they reminded the king, and a plot to overthrow Antonescu without detailed planning would be suicidal.

Maniu preferred the diplomatic route; coded conversations and deniability. He was in regular contact with London through a radio operator with the clandestine name of Reginald, exploring the possibility of negotiating an armistice behind Antonescu's back with British help. The sticking point, as ever, was Stalin. Maniu wanted to keep him out of the conversation, certain of his predatory intent towards Bessarabia, but the British were ruthlessly uncooperative. Whenever Maniu contacted them for a secret chat, they shopped him to the Kremlin. 'Negotiate with us all, or negotiate with none,' was the message. Britain would not be unshackled from its allies. The more Maniu tried to cut Stalin out of the deal, the more Moscow seemed to be calling the shots.

Increasingly desperate, Maniu threw caution to the wind and began offering up Antonescu's head, unwisely hinting to the Allies of his plans for a coup. The Allies were unmoved. Maniu upped his bid. What about Antonescu's head and a promise that a future Allied Romania would be governed by a democratic coalition, including representatives from the Romanian Communist Party? And there it was, the game-changer, the most cynical of concessions – the Romanian Communist Party had only 700 members at the time, yet Maniu was happy to include them in government in order to sweeten the deal for Stalin. A British official responded on behalf of the Allies, declaring that the suggestion was 'warmly welcomed'.

In his next ignominious act, Maniu – the man who had once tried to accommodate Codreanu and the Iron Guard in government for the sake of national unity – now inquired of the Soviets who they might like to see in such a coalition. The pool of potential talent was shallow, with most of Romania's communists either in jail or in exile in Moscow. The Soviets shot back the name Lucrețiu Pătrășcanu.

Pătrășcanu was a diffident, intense law professor, a young man who had rebelled against his petty-noble Transylvanian ancestry to join the communists in the romantic haze that followed the October Revolution of 1917. He had been the lead lawyer in Ana

Pauker's trial before being denounced as a communist himself, an incident that had elevated him to RCP legend at the age of just thirty-four. In jail he had cemented his status by forming a close friendship with the rail worker and 'prison faction' leader, Gheorghiu-Dej. Now under house arrest at his family's villa in central Romania, if Moscow's price for peace was Pătrăşcanu in a new government, then Maniu was willing to pay it.

It was an immense risk for Maniu, and more so for the king, to widen the circle of conspirators in a planned coup d'état against Antonescu, to include a little-known communist, but these were desperate times. Pătrăşcanu was summoned to the palace and introduced to the rest of the gang, which consisted of a representative from each democratic party and the king himself, who then set up a series of informal committees that met over tea and sandwiches as if they were organizing a Scouts jamboree rather than a potentially bloody overthrow of a fascist dictator. Pătrăşcanu was accepted without question and was soon drafting legal documents for a post-coup Romania, and even composing the king's speeches.

The conspirators shared a nagging worry though. What would happen if the army sided with the Marshal? How would they secure control of Bucharest? Pătrăşcanu had a solution. He knew a man, a senior communist, who could mobilize small cells of armed workers in the capital. His name was Emil Bodnăraş, a large man of military bearing whose personal history was peppered with mysterious black holes. No one cared. If he could muster a band of guerrilla fighters, he was in. Bodnăraş joined a coup sub-committee and was soon impressing them with his commitment and his grasp of detail. But Bodnăraş was not just a member of the Romanian Communist Party (RCP), he was also a Soviet spy.

Emil Bodnăraş did not have the face for espionage. Once you had witnessed the fierce hawk eyebrows, the boxed-flat nose and the curiously protruding monkey-muzzle, you would never forget it. He had started his career as a Romanian intelligence officer, who had been sent into the Soviet Union in 1931, only to be captured, turned, and recruited by Stalin's NKVD. Then, while travelling undercover to Bulgaria in 1935, he was passing through the Gara de Nord in Bucharest when he was recognized by an old school friend and arrested by the Romanian police. Bodnăraş was charged with spying and jailed for ten years. His journey through the Romanian prison system eventually brought him into contact with the country's top communist leaders at Doftana prison, including Gheorghiu-Dej – and the young lackey, Nicolae Ceauşescu.

There was one final pre-coup meeting, on 21 August 1944, chaired by King Michael. Whilst Bodnăraş prepared and armed his personal militia, Pătrăşcanu attended the event on behalf of the RCP. He arrived clutching his draft proclamation for the king to read after the coup, and then told all those gathered that he thought Iuliu Maniu should be the new government's prime minister. Maniu demurred, knowing that surviving the furious heat of a revolutionary Romania was a young man's game, and suggested instead a government of technicians to handle affairs and await the inevitable arrival of the Red Army. No decision was taken. Instead Maniu and Pătrăşcanu were asked to compose a list of ministerial suggestions and report back. It was an extraordinary promotion for a man who was under house arrest just days before. As the gathering broke up, it was confirmed that the lunch party coup would take place on 26 August, five days hence.

Every detail of the plot had been finalized – the Allies had been notified, the Red Army had synchronized a massive assault on Romania's borders and all that remained was to invite the two Antonescus to lunch. But then word arrived that the Marshal was leaving for the Eastern Front. He might not return for weeks. In a panic, the conspirators tried to re-schedule the meeting for that very afternoon, 23 August.

The Marshal was at home, packing, when a mysterious phone call came through. It was his old friend, historian Gheorghe Brătianu, nephew of the Liberal leader, sounding breathless and unusually insistent. He implored the Marshal to go to the palace for a meeting with the king. At the same time, royal aides hurried around Bucharest trying to round up the conspirators in time for a 3 p.m. encounter. When they arrived at Maniu's home, the place was empty. No one could find him. Brătianu too had mysteriously disappeared. Both men, it seems, were planning on deniability should the coup misfire. The king's men tried to contact Pătrăşcanu that same morning. He would be there, he said, but only after nightfall, when the action was completed. It was going to be a very thinly attended coup.

Vice-premier Mihai Antonescu arrived at the palace at the appointed time. Marshal Antonescu came later that afternoon, flushed and irritable. He launched into a breezy update on the military situation at the border, finishing with an insistence there would be no armistice, at least until he had discussed the matter with Hitler. An exercised King Michael responded that there was no time, the Soviets had already broken into Romania just south of Iaşi and he needed to act now. Would the Marshal stand aside and allow someone else to conduct an armistice? 'Never!' snapped the Marshal, at which point the king rose from his chair and made an excuse to leave the room.

In a huddle outside, he told his aides to prepare for an arrest, and then returned to announce that, in accordance with the wishes of the Romanian people, he was personally taking the country out of the war. Antonescu, almost incandescent with rage, said he never took orders from anyone. At which point Michael announced he should consider himself dismissed and made a signal towards the door. A four-man security team, made up of trusted soldiers, marched in. As they searched Romania's most senior and very overbearing officer for weapons, Antonescu remarked, in the third person as ever: 'General Antonescu does not carry side-arms. His authority does not rest on guns.'[1] He was led from the room shouting: 'Tomorrow I will have you all shot for this.' Mihai Antonescu followed without protest. The two men were taken upstairs and locked inside the palace strong room.

Downstairs, the conspirators now realized that the hasty re-scheduling of the coup had left them without a premier or even a cabinet. The king and his aides began to appoint ministers from the men who happened to be in the room at the time. In the absence of any democratic politicians, he elevated the astonished head of the royal military household, General Constantin Sănătescu, to the prime ministership.

Of the original plotters, it was Pătrășcanu who was first to arrive, as promised, at 8 p.m. He brought with him an agreed speech for the king, and two previously agreed decrees providing for the release of all political prisoners. Noting the chaos in the palace, Pătrășcanu was smart enough to ask if he might take the job of minister of justice. The king considered for a moment. At least Pătrășcanu was a lawyer and must have some modicum of expertise. The rest of the cabinet were just random lackeys and security personnel. He looked at the young communist and nodded his approval, but only for the interim, he said, until things were sorted out. This was a moment that communist historians would later proudly refashion as proof of the Party's decisive role in the coup, and the start of the communist takeover of Romania.

Arriving shortly after Pătrășcanu came Emil Bodnăraș with his motley band of paramilitaries. While everyone else was either hiding or panicking, this group of communists were calmly manoeuvring themselves into positions far exceeding their trifling domestic strength. Bodnăraș was in his element. Only he, of those in the palace that night, knew something of the broader Soviet design for Romania.

Controlling the RCP had been an objective of Moscow for some time but it was faced with three rival groups to choose from. First was the Muscovite faction, made up of Romanian communists who had spent the war years in Russia. Their undisputed leader was Ana Pauker. Second was the prison faction, who had spent the war years in jails and internment camps in Romania. This group was suspicious of what they regarded as the intellectual, bourgeois Muscovites. Their leader was former rail worker Gheorghiu-Dej. The third faction consisted of the tiny number of communists who had managed to avoid arrest in Romania and who had organized the RCP's underground operations. They were grouped around Lucrețiu Pătrășcanu – the man who had just been elevated to justice minister, although their general secretary was a mild-mannered former journalist by the name of Ștefan Foriș.

It had hardly mattered who was leader of the Romanian Communists prior to August 1944 when Romania was still allied with Hitler, but now, with Bucharest surrendering to the Allies, and cabinet positions suddenly available, it was of critical importance to the future direction of both the communist movement and of Romania itself. Soviet spy Bodnăraș was a member of the second faction, allied to Gheorghiu-Dej, and had already made threats of violence to the Party's official general secretary, Foriș, who he regarded as far too moderate to lead a unified RCP and too suspicious of Moscow to be suitable for the job.

Bodnăraș and his paramilitaries were roaming the palace corridors on the night of the coup and had placed themselves in charge of the two detained Antonescus. While the king retired to his study to record his historic speech for radio transmission, Bodnăraș slipped upstairs with the keys to the strong room and opened it to find that the Marshal had already requested a pen and paper to write his will.

Late that evening, radios across Bucharest suddenly crackled into life. 'In this most difficult hour of our history,' began the king, 'I have decided... that there is only one way to save the country from total catastrophe: our withdrawal from the alliance with Axis powers, and the immediate cessation of the war with the United Nations.'

Crowds gathered in Palace Square, shouting 'Long live England!' and 'Long live America'. Union Jacks were unfurled from windows and waved joyfully in the night sky. By themselves in a far corner of the square, a small crowd of communists shouted, 'Long live Stalin'. Few people noticed the cavalcade of armed vehicles leaving the palace that night carrying the two Antonescus through the bombed-out streets of Bucharest to a communist safe house. The two were led inside, the Marshal to a room on the second floor with a washbasin and bed, Mihai Antonescu to a room on the ground floor.

They were woken at dawn by the sound of a sustained aerial attack. It was no longer Allied warplanes overhead but the roar of what remained of the German Luftwaffe. With Romania having swapped sides, it was now in the catastrophic predicament of being at war with Nazi Germany, while 100,000 German troops were stationed inside its own borders. The Luftwaffe struck dozens of civilian buildings, while German ground troops who'd been based in the north of Bucharest around Otopeni began a frantic fight to resist the coup. Romanian soldiers fought them street to street, assisted at 1 a.m. on 26 August by a US bombing raid that helped destroy several German positions around the city. 1,400 Romanian soldiers were killed trying to defend Bucharest.

Fighting continued for a week against German units across Romania, particularly fierce battles taking place around the oil fields of Ploiești where the Germans maintained their largest camps. My future grandmother-in-law now found herself running from the bombs of German planes, when just a year before, she had been running from the huge aerial bombardment of Ploiești by the Allies in Operation Tidal Wave.

During the clear-up of German troops, the Romanians took

an astonishing 56,000 prisoners of war – all of whom were handed over to the Red Army – but suffered losses of 8,500 of their own soldiers. The largest Romanian action was against their former Axis ally, Hungary, with 265,000 Romanian soldiers storming into northern Transylvania, a campaign that took two months and ended with the Romanians occupying the region on behalf of the Allies.

Soviet tanks arrived onto the streets of Bucharest a week after King Michael's coup, drawing crowds of curious, rather than welcoming, Romanians. People were unsure what to think of their traditional enemy in the role of liberating ally. One of the first Red Army units to arrive was from the Second Ukrainian Front, whose leader went straight to Romanian army headquarters to ask for the handover of the Antonescus. The request was greeted with blank stares. They had no idea where the two men were being held. Neither did the office of the minister of the interior, nor the mayor of Bucharest. Presently an odd-looking man arrived, with a squashed nose and wild eyebrows, and introduced himself as Emil Bodnăraş, a member of the central committee of the Romanian Communist Party. He knew where the prisoners were, he said, and led a cavalcade of forty vehicles to the safe house.

That afternoon, Marshal Antonescu and several other high-value Romanian prisoners from the former regime were transferred across the Soviet border, to a castle 40 miles outside Moscow. Each was given a room and permission to exercise in the castle grounds. Antonescu, whose actions in Operation Barbarossa had led to countless thousands of Soviet soldiers' and civilians' deaths, was now in the hands of the very army he had been fighting. While it is said he was treated well by the Russians, on 8 November he tried to hang himself with a noose made from strips torn from his bed sheet.

Whilst Antonescu was placed on suicide watch, Ana Pauker was on a train travelling in the opposite direction. She was on a mission from the Kremlin to take over the tiny Romanian Communist Party and, in time, the country. Arriving in Bucharest on 16 September 1944, Pauker kept a low profile but she was soon to become known among Romanians and the foreign press as the 'Iron Lady of Romania', for her role in organizing demonstrations against the transitional government. Ministers had a less flattering name for her, referring to the Sovietized Pauker as a 'hyena' and a 'foreigner without God or country'.[2]

The first urgent matter for King Michael's new Romania was the signing of an Armistice Agreement with the Allies. Flying out to Moscow to negotiate was the country's new justice minister, the communist Lucreţiu Pătrăşcanu, accompanied by Queen Marie's former lover, Barbu Ştirbey, to represent Romania's democratic parties. But it soon became clear that, although this was an armistice between Romania and the three main Allies, it would be overseen exclusively by Stalin. Not a single request from the Romanian delegation appeared in the final form of the Armistice document, and while they were 'debating' its detail in Moscow, more than a million Soviet troops spilled across the border into Romania, taking control of the entire country. A condition of the Armistice was that the Romanians must support the occupying Red Army and pay war reparations of $300 million in six years. Alarmed at what appeared to be a takeover, the Romanian delegation insisted that a provision be made that all Soviet troops leave the country at the end of the war but the Russians refused, while the Americans and the British stood to one side and gave Stalin free rein.

As defeat of Germany neared, Stalin met with Churchill at his Kremlin apartment in October 1944 to divide up the territorial gains of the Allies. In a whisky-soaked late-night summit, Churchill proposed a 'naughty document' to list their respective interests in the small countries by percentage. 'Might it not be thought cynical if it seemed we'd disposed of these issues, so fateful to millions of people in such an offhand manner?'

remarked a gleeful Churchill, and then went about doing exactly that. Beside the word 'Romania', the British prime minister wrote that he had a '10 per cent' interest; Stalin wrote '90 per cent'.[3]

Of course, Stalin was able to keep Bessarabia and Bukovina, the regions that Bucharest had gone to war in the first place to wrest back from the USSR. The one ray of light was that northern Transylvania would be returned to Romania. The rest of the Armistice Agreement was interpreted by Stalin as permission for him to secure a dominant political and economic interest in all Romania's affairs.

Inside the country, an Allied Control Commission was set up to oversee the imposition of the Armistice but it was entirely dominated by Soviet representatives, and indeed the British and American members were denied permission to travel in the country without Soviet permission. The Romanian Army was pruned to three skeleton divisions, effectively neutering it. The police were scaled back too, placing law and order and the country's security in the hands of the Red Army. Crucially, the Armistice also provided for the banning of all 'fascist type' organizations. In the eyes of the Soviets and their communist friends in Romania, that meant banning almost anything but socialist organizations.

The Romanian Communist Party was starting from a position of such paltry support, they would have had no future without the occupying Red Army. Just as in other East European countries, the communists' tactic was to join a coalition of left-leaning parties – in Romania's case, a group called the National Democratic Front (NDF) – where they could camouflage themselves and begin the process of expansion. The RCP relied on the Red Army as its enforcer and began a process of intimidation against other parties and the population at large. RCP members toured factories instructing staff to vote out their old works committees and replace them with RCP-friendly representatives. If the workers refused, they were threatened with arrest by the

Soviets. At the same time, Emil Bodnăraş and his ragtag militia, known as the Guards of Patriotic Defence, patrolled the streets, imposing RCP-controlled justice.

Romania had high hopes of being offered US and British assistance against Soviet domination in the Yalta Conference, but the vague 'Declaration of Liberated Europe' issued at the end of proceedings on 11 February 1945 proved no obstacle to Stalin.[4] A week later, one of Stalin's favourite henchmen, Andrei Vyshinsky – Molotov's deputy – flew into Bucharest to supervise the formation of a new Romanian government. Vyshinsky was a former star prosecutor at Moscow's show trials, a lawyer who had pioneered a pre-Orwellian belief in 'thoughtcrime', where an actual crime need not have been committed in order for a suspect to be convicted. A Western journalist who witnessed Vyshinsky in court during the Great Purge compared his appearance to 'a prosperous stockbroker accustomed to lunching at Simpson's and playing golf at Sunningdale', but behind the horn-rimmed spectacles, the dapper suits and the manicured grey moustache was a ravenous sadist who took delight in writing diabolical fabrications about leading communists, finishing each with his standard flourish: 'I recommend death by shooting.'[5] Vyshinsky wore the menace of violence like an expensive cologne. Now he arrived in Bucharest to ensure the imposition of Stalin's will, as spiritual head of the body tasked with overseeing the Armistice Agreement – the Soviet High Command.

Within days of his arrival, King Michael summoned Vyshinsky to the palace to ask him to stop trying to communize the country. He reminded the Soviet prosecutor that Romania had not been defeated in war but had overthrown its own fascist dictator and joined the Allies, with whom it had then fought in several campaigns during the final months of the war (including the Iaşi-Kishinev Offensive and the Budapest Offensive). Vyshinsky nodded politely and carried on as before.

The Russian quickly joined forces with the newly arrived Ana

Pauker and Gheorghiu-Dej to enforce the domination of the left-leaning coalition in cabinet, eventually securing a ministerial role for Gheorghiu-Dej himself. Once installed, Gheorghiu-Dej began plotting to undermine every non-communist around him, calling them fascists and enemies of the people, and demanding they were dismissed. The ageing caretaker-prime minister, Nicolae Rădescu, tried to impose order but the communists turned on him too. Rădescu tried to dismiss obstructive communist ministers, such as the NKVD-trained Teohari Georgescu, but Georgescu simply ignored him and remained at his desk taking phone calls as if nothing had happened. Rădescu then tried to ban Bodnăraș's 'Patriotic Guard' but it continued operating as before. Whenever Rădescu attempted to speak in public, Ana Pauker organized groups of jeering communists who shouted 'fascist' and booed him off stage. When he tried to have rebuttals printed in Romania's newspapers, they were blocked by the now communist-controlled print unions.

Pauker and Gheorghiu-Dej were in their element making such mischief. Although bitter rivals for the RCP's leadership, they were happy to cooperate in ousting caretaker prime ministers. Their problem was that the Romanian public would still not stomach an actual communist at the helm, so they would need to find an unprincipled non-communist prepared to do their bidding for them. They chose the leader of the left-wing Ploughman's Front, Petru Groza, a self-made landowner with a passion for dimly lit drinking dens and dirty stories. Clubbable and well-meaning, he was also entirely corruptible, and Pauker knew it.

It was Vyshinsky who went to the palace to inform the king that Petru Groza should be made prime minister. Deploying his usual courtroom doublethink, Stalin's prosecutor argued that Groza represented a more 'democratic' choice, who would help maintain order and ensure that the conditions of the Armistice were met. King Michael asked for time to think, hoping that the British and American representatives on the Allied Control Commission might intervene. The next day, a petulant Vyshinsky returned and snapped to the king that he had until 6 p.m. to choose Groza. When he left, Stalin's emissary slammed the drawing room door behind him so violently that plaster fell from the ceiling. King Michael signed the necessary documents that same day.

And so it was that on 6 March 1945, Romania had its first communist–controlled government, camouflaged in the colours of the coalition National Democratic Front. Romania was a captured state, seized not by a people's uprising or a coup, but by a sly Soviet formula and the overwhelming presence of the Red Army. But the question of who would lead the RCP when it finally broke cover was to be vigorously contested.

That summer, the mild-mannered RCP general secretary, Ștefan Foriș, was ordered to resign from his post. He had little choice. Emil Bodnăraş was holding a gun to his head. Even then, Foriș failed to understand the fierceness of the battle for supremacy within the RCP and assumed it would be alright if he remained an active member. Subsequently, Bodnăraş had him kidnapped by the 'Patriotic Guard', who accused Foriș of being an informant for Marshal Antonescu – an entirely concocted but toxic allegation. The campaign of intimidation against Foriș was an attempt by the prison faction of the RCP (led by Gheorghiu-Dej) to annihilate the tiny domestic faction. Eventually, Foriș realized what was happening, wrote a will, and began making plans to flee the country.

On 9 June 1945, he was shopping for provisions in Bucharest, apparently preparing for his journey, when he was bundled into a car by NKVD agent Gheorghe Pintilie, a prison friend of Gheorghiu-Dej. Foriș was held in cells at the ministry of the interior for several months, his fate ultimately in the hands of Stalin. During his detention, his mother regularly contacted the Patriotic Guard to ask for help in tracing him but was told that they had no record of his arrest. The following spring, Foriş was taken in a car to a grand villa which now served as Communist Party headquarters. He was told to wait at the door of the annex. Pintilie disappeared for a moment along with his chauffeur, and then the pair returned with an iron bar and bludgeoned Foriş to death.

Considered an exemplary execution in the high-Stalinist style, ruthless and improvised, it signalled the start of Romania's purges. The killer, Gheorghe Pintilie, would go on to become the first director of the much-feared Securitate, the communist regime's powerful secret police. One of his co-conspirators in the murder, another Soviet agent called Alexandru Nicolschi, would become the agency's deputy director. Together the two created the apparatus of terror that came to define successive communist dictatorships in Romania.

In the aftermath of Foriş's disappearance, his mother continued appealing for information about her son's whereabouts. Despairing of her persistence, Pintilie told her that her son had been spotted in her home city of Oradea, on the Hungarian border, and that she would be taken by security officials to find him. Madame Foriş was grateful and agreed to go with them. At some point that afternoon she was set upon by Securitate agents, beaten, and a heavy stone tied around her neck. She was then thrown into the deep waters of the Crişul Repede, the broad river that flows through Oradea.

With Foriş out of the way, the competition for leadership of the RCP was between Ana Pauker and Gheorghiu-Dej. When Pauker heard of Foriş's fate she was horrified, protesting that he should have been put on trial. Her response caused concern in Moscow, where the Kremlin was already becoming suspicious that Pauker was a moderate, or as Gheorghiu-Dej called her, 'a liberal democrat'. The evidence for such an allegation seemed to be building. Pauker had already argued for more democratic parties to be involved in the governing coalition. Then she had alarmed both Moscow and her comrades in Bucharest by ordering the release of thousands of jailed Legionaries.

Pauker's plan was to recruit 200,000 of them into the still unpopular RCP, pointing out that many of them were working people who had joined the Iron Guard out of desperation for change. She argued that their revolutionary zeal could easily be harnessed by the communists. At the same time her villa in the Primăverii district – where all the communist nomenklatura were now living – was becoming an informal counselling centre for all manner of former right-wing government ministers and businessmen who would visit Pauker for advice on how to deal with purges and upcoming trials. It was all part of her recruitment drive, but to Gheorghiu-Dej and his stalwart supporters, it was simply more evidence that Pauker was a 'traitor'. Gheorghiu-Dej expressed a desire to see Legionaries 'eradicated like vipers', a position far more in tune with Moscow's position and Stalin's inclinations. Pauker was in danger of being accused by Moscow of the cardinal sin: 'deviation' from official party doctrine.

Her attempts at compromise with Romania's democratic politicians soon triggered the bat-like radar of Vyshinsky, Stalin's demented prosecutor. Assuming that Gheorghiu-Dej might welcome a helping hand in dealing with his rival for the leadership of the RCP, Vyshinsky sidled over to the former rail worker and asked, 'Comrade Gheorghiu-Dej, how does Ana Pauker help you?' Gheorghiu-Dej, by his own account, was taken aback with where the conversation seemed to be heading. 'You can see for yourself how she helps me,' he claims to have replied. Vyshinsky ruminated for a moment, a man at ease with high-stakes coded conversations. 'Would it be better', he smiled, 'if Ana were removed from here?'[6]

The intimidation of Pauker by the Kremlin had actually begun the previous year. A late-night summons to the office of Comrade Stalin was a terrifying moment in the career of any member of the Secretariat of the Romanian Communist Party, particularly those who knew the old man well. It usually came in the form of a crackling telephone call from Molotov or Vyshinsky on Stalin's behalf, inducing a frantic mental revision of every recent utterance in search of some unintended 'deviation' or 'counter-revolutionary' gesture. The normally unflappable Ana Pauker had received such a call in late 1944, just four months after being despatched to Bucharest as Stalin's favourite. She had immediately begun making arrangements to protect herself.

Pauker took with her to Moscow her twenty-three-year-old daughter, Tania, and her chief aide, Ana Toma, who Pauker knew to be a Soviet agent but trusted more than many others in the RCP. When the trio arrived in the snow outside the Central Committee building, Pauker took Toma to one side. 'Look, I am going in that door,' she whispered, gesturing towards a set of marble steps beneath the crenelated burgundy battlements. 'If I come out and go through that other door, everything is fine, and you can take Tania to the museum.' The three stood shivering in the snow for a moment. 'If I don't come out,' Pauker whispered, 'go to the hotel, pack your things, and get away from here as fast as you can.'[7]

Gheorghiu-Dej received a similar summons a few weeks later, in January 1945. Since leaving prison he'd habitually dressed in slippers and an old pullover but was persuaded by his aides to pull on a woollen jacket and tie for the occasion. On his arrival, he was faced with the diminutive Stalin pacing the study 'like a military prosecutor', firing questions while staring menacingly into his eyes. Gheorghiu-Dej spluttered a few responses about following the Soviet model and supporting the Red Army, and a long and uncomfortable silence ensued. It was broken by Stalin, who lowered his voice into a conspiratorial Georgian burr and said: 'Ana [Pauker] is a good reliable comrade but, you see, she is a Jewess of bourgeois origin, and the Party in Romania needs a leader from the ranks of the working class, a true-born Romanian.' With that, Stalin marched over to the bewildered Gheorghiu-Dej, held out his hand and announced: 'I have decided. I wish you every success, Comrade Secretary General!' The lolloping rail worker from Bârlad in Moldova had just been anointed head of the Romanian Communist Party, in preference to Ana Pauker. It was an extraordinary show of faith in a man Stalin barely knew. Gheorghiu-Dej would be the only communist leader in Eastern Europe with no Moscow connection, his elevation made possible by positive appraisals from Soviet spies in Bucharest, and in particular Emil Bodnăraş, the squash-nosed NKVD agent who had been in the royal palace on the night of the coup.

When Pauker heard the news, she responded as she knew she must, writing to her friend Vyacheslav Molotov, the Soviet foreign minister, and conceding that Gheorghiu-Dej was best for the job. Romania was too 'culturally backward', she said, to accept a woman and a Jew as leader. Molotov, who'd witnessed the grizzly denouement of many a Stalinist rivalry, wrote back a single line: 'You're a clever woman.'

*

A week after Hitler's suicide on 30 April 1945, with Germany's unconditional surrender waiting to be signed in Berlin, Marshal and Mihai Antonescu were transferred back to Bucharest and led into a dusty courtroom to stand trial before a People's Court.

Gone were the flamboyant, ruddy-faced, advocate-dandies of old Romania, replaced by a panel of earnest, communist functionaries. The president of the seven 'People's Judges', Alexandru Voitinovici, contrived his own particular menace by hiding behind goggle-sized black sunglasses and placing a carved image of Christ incongruously before him on the table.

Antonescu was charged with 'bringing disaster upon the country' and 'the crime of war', and was cross-examined for two days. He responded fluently with calm military precision, comparing himself with Napoleon and even Russia's Alexander

I. On the persecution and deportation of Jews, he said these were laws imposed by the people and by the Iron Guard. If he had not acted, the people would have robbed and killed even more of them. He reminded the court that he had saved 300,000 Jews from death camps in Nazi-occupied Poland. On the mass killings in Odessa, he said the reprisals were a lawful response to an enemy who had broken the normal rules of war. All these things happened in war, he said. Repressive laws were a function of war.

Antonescu's calm refusal to apologize for fighting the very people who were judging him was viewed as a golden moment of defiance and integrity. 'I declared war against the Soviets,' the Marshal told the court, 'and I continued the war to regain the Romanian provinces of Bessarabia and Bukovina.'[8] Many Romanians watched with admiration. 'They couldn't help but rejoice', wrote one journalist who was present, 'when they saw a Romanian stand under Russian gallows and calmly defy Russia.'

But even as the Marshal finished his two days of evidence, an insistent chant broke out on the road outside. 'Make an end to the trial!' yelled RCP-organized crowds. 'Antonescu should be hanged.' They inevitably had their wish. The execution party made its way through tall grass near to Jilava Prison on 1 June 1945. Marshal Antonescu led the way, stalking determinedly along the path as if he were leading his troops into battle, flanked by a line of nervous-looking young Romanian soldiers. Three hours earlier, he had said goodbye to his wife, Maria, with a huge bunch of red flowers in his cell. He regretted nothing, he told her, he had done his duty for his country, history would judge him. 'Not one tear,' he implored. 'As we are lowered into the earth, me today, and you tomorrow, we will be uplifted, I am sure. It will be the only just reward.'[9]

Four wooden stakes had been erected in a clearing at a place called 'The Valley of the Peach Trees'. The two Antonescus stood side by side, both refusing to wear a blindfold. Further along were

General Constantin Vasiliu (the former head of the gendarmerie in the ministry of the interior) and Gheorghe Alexianu (the former Governor of Transnistria, the crucible of the Romanian Holocaust).

As the execution detail organized themselves, the Marshal gazed into the summer trees and seemed to manage a weak, pensive smile. From the pocket of his double-breasted suit, an extravagant white silk hanky fluttered in the breeze. He made a remark to the cameraman, lost now on silent film, his eyes twinkling with some shared mischief. Then the priests and the ministers and the lawyers and the doctors retreated to one side. A signal was given. Antonescu raised his trilby hat theatrically in the air, before slumping to the ground under a volley of bullets.

The decision to go ahead with Antonescu's execution was taken by one Lucreţiu Pătrăşcanu, the communist who had politely asked the king if he could be minister of justice on the night of the coup. The king and several democratic politicians had favoured clemency for Antonescu, but Pătrăşcanu turned them down. Ultimately, of course, it was Stalin's decision. Now, with the war officially over and the wartime leader dead, Soviet officials and secret agents begun to tear apart the political and cultural institutions of Romania in readiness for a communist takeover. First they would need to prepare the ground, by convincing Romanians that the communists were simply following the people's will.

*

The Romanian bureau chief for the *Christian Science Monitor*, Reuben Markham, was reporting on the country's first post-war election, and decided to do so by accompanying the favourite – Iuliu Maniu's National Peasants' Party (PNT) – on the campaign trail. He got a place on the bus with Maniu's deputy, Ion Mihalache, a former schoolteacher, and set off in March 1946 on what was supposed to be a low-key tour. Speeches in village halls. Suppers with local mayors. Standard election fare. But the innocent, rather bumbling provincial campaign was about to collide with hardcore Bolshevik black ops.

Markham and the PNT delegates arrived at the ancient city of Bacau, near to Iași, late on a March evening in 1946 and checked into a hotel. Mihalache, like any good leader, contacted local PNT activists to invite them to dinner before a speech the following day. They had bad news. Local communists had got wind of the meeting and broken into the PNT's club, smashing furniture and beating up PNT officials. The place was wrecked. Worst of all, the thugs had been assisted by local police.

Mihalache told them to remain calm and insisted he take them all out for dinner at a restaurant near to the hotel. But shortly after arriving, the front window was smashed and a gang of young communists chased them away.[10] Next, they travelled to a PNT congress in the Black Sea port of Constanța. By the summer of 1946, the beautiful resort city – a key strategic base for the Romanian navy – had already taken on the appearance of a Russian stronghold, with Soviet troops in every street and bar. Seafront villas were commandeered by officers of the Russian navy or looted and wrecked. When Markham arrived at the venue, a movie theatre, it had already been smashed to pieces. Two burly men stood in the ruins and introduced themselves as 'Secret Police', while gangs of communist youths burned Peasants' Party literature on bonfires outside.

On the Danubian plain, in the ancient city of Roșiorii de Vede, a PNT congress was interrupted by a man from a neighbouring city repeatedly bellowing 'Long live Stalin'. Markham wrote: 'This exclamation was a favourite device of the communists who want to break up opposition meetings because, if repeated loudly enough, it completely drowns out what the speakers are trying to say... if, on the other hand, the crowd begins to boo the hooligans (for interrupting)... they are immediately accused of insulting the Soviet empire.' When PNT delegates asked the communist intruder in Roșiorii de Vede to leave, he returned with Russian soldiers who stationed themselves at the door of the little movie theatre, drew their firearms and shot volley after volley over the heads of the delegates.

Romania's first post-war election was held in the steel-grey November of 1946, with communist violence at its apogee. As voting booths opened, election observers found ballot boxes already sealed and stuffed with votes. Non-communist officials were soon removed from their polling stations and detained by police.

As in all the worst rigged elections, there was a delay in announcing the results, almost as if the communist-backed Groza government had underestimated how much foul play was required to overturn the will of a nation. They needed more time. Two days. Three days. Five days. Eventually the result was announced to an astonished country on 24 November. Groza and the communists had won by a landslide, achieving almost 70 per cent of the vote. If Emil Bodnăraș had got his way, it would have been higher. He'd argued for 90 per cent but even his most hard-bitten colleagues had recommended something a little more realistic for the doubting Romanian public.

There was a brief but intense international protest. Washington complained of 'manipulations of the electoral register' and 'intimidation through terrorism', London of 'wholesale falsification of results'. Groza and his cronies hardly cared. They had a majority of almost 300 seats in the new parliament. The Liberals and National Peasants had just 36 between them. The communists could do what they liked, against whomever they liked, and all with Soviet backing. Under pressure from Ana Pauker and Gheorghiu-Dej, Prime Minister Groza sacked 70,000 government employees and replaced them with 'honest, democratic and capable elements', by which they meant communists. One of Pauker's most devoted followers from the Moscow faction, Vasile Luca, was made finance minister and deputy prime minister, while for the sake of balance, one of Gheorghiu-Dej's prison faction, Teo Georgescu, was made minister of the interior. Former NKVD spy Emil Bodnăraș was made secretary general to the prime minister.

But Stalin was still unhappy with his Romanian cousins, imagining there might be elements within the RCP who were not sufficiently loyal to Moscow. In February 1947 he summoned Gheorghiu-Dej and Ana Pauker to the Kremlin once again. The pair walked into Stalin's study together to find him smoking at his oak desk, sallow-faced, unshaven, unreadable. The old man, already sixty-nine years old, studied his Romanian guests as they walked across the thick Persian carpet. Molotov was at Stalin's side. There was small talk about the communists' success in the Romanian elections, and then Stalin turned to address Gheorghiu-Dej. Were there any 'divergences', he asked, within the Party leadership? Gheorghiu-Dej, normally a master of self-control, struggled to disguise his discomfort. The only 'serious divergence', he muttered, was with Pătrășcanu, the minister of law, who had been in the royal palace on the night of the coup but was now understood to be bourgeois and a 'Rightist deviationist'. Stalin pressed him further. Was there any truth in the rumour that there was a current of opinion in the Party that believed Ana Pauker and Vasile Luca should not hold leadership positions because they were not of old Romanian stock (Pauker was Jewish, Luca Austro-Hungarian). Gheorghiu-Dej shook his head quickly. He had heard no such rumour. If there were such currents, persisted Stalin, staring unblinkingly at the squirming Gheorghiu-Dej, then the Romanian Communist Party was being 'transformed from a social and class party to a race party'. No, absolutely not, insisted Gheorghiu-Dej, there was no such current. A long, uncomfortable silence followed. Then the matter was closed. All this in front of Pauker, who followed Gheorghiu-Dej out of the meeting and asked, 'What the Hell was all that about?' To which Gheorghiu-Dej shrugged his shoulders uncomfortably, and headed off to find his driver. On their return to Bucharest, the two decided to cease their rivalry and concentrate instead on ending any possibility of a resurgent opposition.

At twilight on 15 July 1947, a line of speeding cars made their way through the parched agricultural landscape thirty miles east of Bucharest to a small rural airport called Tămădău, where they had a rendezvous with two private planes. Behind the wheel of the first car was the deputy leader of the National Peasants' Party, Ion Mihalache. In the next was Nicolae Penescu, the PNT's former interior minister. Then came Nicolae Carandino, a famous PNT-supporting journalist, and his glamorous film star wife, Lilly. Another half-dozen vehicles followed, filled with assorted PNT chiefs and stacked high with suitcases.

The entire leadership of the National Peasants' Party was on the move that morning – except for its leader Iuliu Maniu who had remained behind in Bucharest. The plan was to flee the country before the communists began rounding up opponents and for the PNT to set up a government-in-exile in Turkey. The party had been considering the idea for weeks and then a stranger had appeared out of the blue and offered them a couple of aircraft. It seemed like an opportunity that should not be missed.

The cars swung off the main road and pulled up beside a small airport building where two bi-planes were waiting. They unloaded trunks and cases, Persian carpets and mink coats, jewellery and family heirlooms – everything they needed for years in exile. Then they heard shouting. A dozen armed men were hiding in the planes and the airport buildings, and now ran towards them, pointing pistols and yelling for them to stand still.

The sting had been organized by Gheorghe Pintilie, the NKVD agent who'd bludgeoned to death the former RCP general secretary, Ștefan Foriș. He was refining the skills of agents in Romania's fledgling Securitate and had devised a textbook operation on behalf of the communist-sponsored government. Pintilie had recruited an *agent provocateur* to offer the PNT a plane and lure them into action.

His agents took the would-be passengers to cells at the ministry of the interior and had them charged with treason. They also arrested PNT leader Iuliu Maniu at his home and accused him of being part of the plot. The trial that followed was pure Stalinist theatrics. The entire leadership of the PNT was in the dock and Maniu was accused of leading a conspiracy to overthrow the 'democratic regime'. He was denounced, variously, as a British spy, an American spy, a fascist and a Nazi. At seventy-five years old, he presented as an elegant pensioner who defended himself vigorously in court. But the verdict was agreed long before the trial began. Maniu was sentenced to life in prison with hard labour, a death sentence in all but name. His deputy, Ion Mihalache, received the same.

They were taken to Sighet Prison on the border with Ukraine, a dimly lit warren of damp cells and wire-framed beds, where they were soon joined by the leader of the National Liberals, Constantin Brătianu. Conditions were so harsh that Brătianu committed suicide soon after arriving there. His cousin Gheorghe (who had helped organize the coup against Antonescu) survived two years of beatings and hunger before dying in his cell. Romania's former foreign minister, Mihail Manoilescu, died of heart problems in the same jail in 1951, only to be put on trial again *after* his death and sentenced to a further fifteen years. Iuliu Maniu managed to survive six years in Sighet, reaching eighty years of age before dying on 5 February 1953. His body was thrown into a common grave beneath the prison courtyard.

The only obstacle left between the communists and total control of Romania was King Michael. He was at his mountain retreat in Peleş, preparing for a New Year's Eve party on 30 December 1947, when he received a call from Petru Groza and Gheorghiu-Dej. They told him he was needed in Bucharest immediately. The king returned to find himself presented with an abdication statement, which he was given half an hour to sign. Having ousted Marshal Antonescu, and inadvertently prepared the way for the communists, he was now treated as an enemy of the people. Prime Minister Groza is said to have produced a gun, pointed it at the king and told him that unless he complied, they had 'no choice' but to execute a thousand students held in Romanian prisons. The king said later that he thought it an odd phrase, 'no choice', when the opposite was true, but with Groza and Gheorghiu-Dej pacing the room, he eventually agreed to put pen to paper. That same day, the country officially became a Marxist-Leninist one-party state known as the Romanian People's Republic.

CHAPTER THIRTEEN

But behold, I, among all nations, choose the imagination.

Ilarie Voronca, Romanian/Jewish
avant-garde poet

While the ousting of King Michael was the event that grabbed world headlines, we need to look behind the scenes into the darker recesses of the Romanian Communist Party and its leading personnel if we are to understand the extraordinary events that were about to grip Romania. Everything must be seen within a framework of Moscow-imposed Stalinist dogma, but there was a small coterie of men and, in Romania's case, one uniquely powerful woman, at the very top of the Communist Party whose actions would now shape the lives of millions. It was they who would decide whether to transform Romania into a supine Soviet satellite or pursue some quasi-independent communist path that would place them in enormous personal peril.

Just as in the other Leninist parties of East-Central Europe, those struggling for power in Romania were pre-occupied with one hallucinatory challenge: the detection of 'enemies' within the Party. It was the cultish duty of every devout Stalinist militant to find and expose them. From now on, observes Romanian historian Vladimir Tismaneanu, 'purgers and purged, tormentors and victims, were caught up in an infernal mechanism of continuous, endless liquidation'.[1]

Within hours of the declaration of a Republic, Ana Pauker became Romania's foreign minister, the first woman to hold the post anywhere in the world. She was thus catapulted into the role of international communist superstar, mentioned in the same breath as Rosa Luxemburg and Spain's Dolores 'Las Pasionaria' Ibárruri, neither of whom had managed to get their hands on any actual power. American newspapers competed for exclusive interviews with Romania's most famous revolutionary. *Time Magazine* featured a less than flattering artist's impression of a snarling Pauker on its front page, framed by a golden sickle. The publication's roving reporter described how Pauker 'sped around Bucharest on the front seat of a bullet-proof Cadillac, casually remarking that she preferred the front of the vehicle because shots aimed at a moving car usually hit the rear.'[2] *Life Magazine* published a five-page spread, describing Pauker as looking like 'a wrestler... broad in beam and bust... chunky throughout... washbasin hands'. But despite the crude assault on her appearance, the writer was in awe of Pauker's political achievements. She was 'the most overpowering woman in contemporary Europe', said the magazine, her strategy, 'ruthless, patient and obedient'. It described how she had waited three years 'with all the threads of power in her hands, until the signal flashed from Moscow to take over the foreign ministry', a move which, *Life* noted, signalled Pauker was 'Romania's master'. Omitting any mention of Gheorghiu-Dej, the magazine announced it was Pauker who 'runs the Communist Party, and through it the lives of 16 million Romanians'.[3]

We can only imagine Gheorghiu-Dej's humiliation. He was general secretary of the Party – now renamed the Romanian Workers Party (RWP) – but he was largely unknown. Even when walking down Calea Victoriei, Gheorghiu-Dej was not recognized. Of course, at that moment Party and state were separate. Gheorghiu-Dej was master of the RWP and was also deputy prime minister in the government. Pauker was supposedly his subordinate in both hierarchies, and yet she was the dominant of the two.

Pauker mothered Gheorghiu-Dej like a subversive old hen, admonishing him for his excessive caution and his insistence on getting a good night's sleep before making decisions. She was an instinctive radical, a firework display of big ideas and devil-may-care actions. Gheorghiu-Dej preferred sitting at home, dismantling electrical appliances and putting them back together, with a cup of sweet coffee by his side. When Pauker threw one of her fabulous dinner parties, Gheorghiu-Dej would excuse himself early, leaving the others to joust over interpretations of Marx or recount louche tales of bed-hopping in the Communist Youth. Even Pauker's most ardent critics fell helplessly under her spell. Emil Bodnăraș was Gheorghiu-Dej's most loyal ally but was often coaxed into staying late at Ana's house. Intellectually a cut above the others in the prison faction – he was fluent in German and Russian, and an avid reader – he described glittering scenes of artists, writers and activists coming and going as Ana's sister-in-law 'walked around with bottles of cognac and liquor and got everyone drunk'. Ana would hold court, presenting herself on a level that 'exceeded that of any local cadre', while recounting whisky-soaked evenings with Molotov and Stalin. Gheorghiu-Dej was envious. He still considered Pauker his chief political danger.

Pauker's ebullience and intellectual flair all but silenced the awkward Gheorghiu-Dej in meetings of the powerful, four-person Secretariat that ran the RWP. It was supposed to be a perfectly balanced unit, representing rival groups and ethnicities. From the old prison faction was Gheorghiu-Dej himself and his cell mate, Teohari Georgescu, a former apprentice type-setter who'd left school at the age of eleven. Despite his pock-marked face and premature baldness, Georgescu was viewed as something of a Casanova in the Party, with many female admirers, and prison friends who included Emil Bodnăraș.

From the Muscovite faction was Ana and her most loyal follower, Vasile Luca, a former railway shop steward who'd fled to Moscow in the 1930s, where he'd become an unquestioning

Stalinist. Luca was an Austro-Hungarian by birth, an important detail in a communist movement that was paranoid about 'outsiders' and was lacking in intellectual sophistication. Even Ana secretly described him as 'arrogant' and of 'limited mind'.

Problems began to surface for Gheorghiu-Dej on the Secretariat when his former loyal supporter Georgescu became overwhelmed by Pauker's force of character and switched allegiance. She was, Georgescu decided, 'incapable of making major mistakes'. That meant Ana Pauker had three votes on the Secretariat to Gheorghiu-Dej's one, something that Moscow was concerned about now that Gheorghiu-Dej was their man.

With King Michael out of the country – living first in Italy, then Switzerland and England – and all political parties banned, Romania cemented itself, militarily, into the Soviet bloc by signing a treaty of friendship, cooperation and mutual assistance with Moscow in February 1948. Immediately afterwards, Gheorghiu-Dej unleashed a massive industrialization programme that was entirely unsuitable for Romania's predominantly agrarian economy. A Five Year Plan was launched, in homage to Moscow, and 30 per cent of the country's population was forced to move from agricultural areas to work in towns and cities. Next, the RWP's attention shifted to the legal system.

Lounging behind his desk at the ministry of justice was the Party's most cherished son, Lucrețiu Pătrășcanu. After cheekily asking the king for his post on the night of the palace coup, Pătrășcanu had grown into his role with increasing confidence. He'd purged the ministry of non-communists and in April 1948 began superimposing a near identical copy of the Soviet model onto Romania. He introduced 'people's assessors' to sit beside judges and ensure that decisions were ideologically compliant. He made it easier to secure convictions by giving 'suspicion' more evidential weight than evidence. And, just like his mentors in Moscow, he sanctioned 'confessions' extracted by means of torture. The erosion of the rule of law was now complete.

But Pătrăşcanu's presence was starting to annoy Gheorghiu-Dej. Famous, loved and effortlessly smooth, the minister of law attracted more column inches in the communist-controlled daily papers than anyone except for Pauker. Crowds chanted his name at rallies. When meetings ended, Gheorghiu-Dej would pull on his grey mac and wide-brimmed fedora before heading off home to potter with his radios and toasters, while Pătrăşcanu invited comrades to a local bar, where he'd sit among his shiny-eyed admirers, happily telling them how unimpressed he was with Gheorghiu-Dej and hinting that he intended, one day, to take over the Party leadership. It was not long before reports of his treacherous intent reached the Party's embryonic security apparatus – the Securitate.

Meanwhile, the Sovietization of Romania was continuing apace. In the summer of 1948, the Romanian Orthodox Church was placed in the care of the Gothic-sounding ministry of cults, its hierarchy quickly culled of suspected opponents. The Church's vast estates were seized by the state, along with its gold, diamonds and family heirlooms. By the end of 1948, the Romanian Workers Party had taken over the Church's schools and seminaries and was running them as communist-controlled colleges.

Easter was banned, as was any public celebration of Christmas. There would be no more church weddings, no baptisms. Although religious worship was not outlawed per se, it was discouraged, and soldiers and Party members were instructed not to attend. From now on, instead of marking Christ's birth, Romania would celebrate those of Marx and Stalin. Father Christmas was killed off, and replaced with Father Frost.

Stalin's speeches were translated into Romanian and sold on every street corner, with 13 million copies purchased. At the same time, books considered ideologically unsound were banned. The first list of censored publications was issued in early 1948 and included 7,300 books and magazines. Margaret Mitchell, Graham Greene, Gustave Flaubert, James Joyce – all were seen as Western and decadent. Bram Stoker's *Dracula* was insulting to one of the country's great sons so was also banned, as was all 'vampire literature'. Foreign books were confiscated and burned on the streets, with the exceptions of the Russian greats. Alexander Pushkin, Leo Tolstoy, Anton Chekhov, Fyodor Dostoyevsky were all judged acceptable, while Romania's home-grown writers were not. The nationalist Romantic poet, Mihai Eminescu, was proscribed, as was the historian and anti-Semite, Nicolae Iorga, along with the poets Lucian Blaga, Ion Pillat and Adrian Maniu. In their place, the government promoted obscure, unchallenging writers such as the 'cobbler poet' Theodor Neculuță, who wrote dull little rhymes about love and the countryside. Romania's population was to be starved of the Western canon of high culture, art, satire, and philosophy, and caged inside a drab, hermetically sealed world where every word had to be disinfected by the Directorate of Propaganda and Agitation.[4]

The very language of the country was hijacked. Printing ink was withheld from rightist newspapers as early as the summer of 1944, and by the spring of 1947 non-Marxist publications were banned. The communist daily *Scînteia* (*The Spark*, the same title as Lenin's original underground newspaper *Iskra*) presented news about Party affairs in a baffling Soviet-imported vernacular. Parliament was now the 'Grand National Assembly' or the 'supreme organ of state authority'. There were editorials calling for action against 'counter-revolutionary diversion', 'saboteurs' and 'hostile elements'. People were told to be 'vigilant' at all times and to 'eradicate without mercy... subversive anti-democratic activity'. Bucharest was no longer the 'Little Paris' it had been during the *belle époque*; it was becoming 'Little Moscow'.

The city's streets, too, needed to conform to the new ideology. Statues were toppled. First to go was King Carol I and his mighty bronze steed, pulled down from his stone plinth outside the Royal Palace. Then King Ferdinand disappeared from Calea

Victoriei, then the former Liberal leader, Ion Brătianu. In their place arose icons of the new age: Stalin at the entrance to the newly named 'Stalin Park' and, later, Lenin outside the Party's newspaper office, which itself was built in the style of the Moscow State University.

Thanks to Ana Pauker's invitation to former Legionaries, membership of the RWP grew to more than a million by the end of 1948. But instead of being cause for celebration, the Party was worried that it was being infiltrated by spies and foreigners, and launched a 'verification campaign'. From the winter of 1948, 200,000 'investigators' were employed to pry into the lives of every new recruit. As a result, 192,000 members were expelled, often on the strength of rumour. From then on, membership of the RWP had to be earned. Proof of loyalty was required, by way of recommendation from trusted members, giving rise to a new and privileged class, a class that would protect itself by creating one of the fiercest spying organizations of the Cold War.

*

In the catacombs of the ministry of the interior in Bucharest, an organization was being created that would root out spies, foreigners, heretics and enemies of the people for the next fifty years. Sprouting from the walls were thousands of electrical cables, coded and numbered. Paperwork sat in unsorted heaps on brown-swirl carpet. Men sat hunched over slowly rotating spools of tape the size of bicycle wheels. This was the headquarters of Romania's new secret police, the Securitate. Its role was to 'ensure the security of the Romanian People's Republic against the plotting of internal and external enemies', and by the end of 1951, a staggering 417,000 people were under its surveillance.

The organization's director was the Soviet agent, Gheorghe Pintilie, who we met earlier while he was clubbing to death the Party's former general secretary, Ştefan Foriş. Pintilie possessed a boyish charm, lit by winter-blue eyes and an ambiguous smile.

As a teenager in Imperial Russia, he had fought with the Red Army, displaying a rare ability to administer violence without any apparent emotion. It was a talent that had brought him to the notice of the NKVD, which then despatched him to Romania on sabotage missions during the regime of the Iron Guard. In the end, Pintilie took one risk too many and landed himself in jail beside Gheorghiu-Dej.

Pintilie's blood-soaked journey from boy-soldier in Tiraspol to director of Eastern Europe's most feared secret police force had left him with a serious drink problem. In 1949, Moscow despatched chaperones to Bucharest to try to keep him dry each day until at least early evening. The task was shared with Pintilie's wife, Ana Toma, an NKVD agent who doubled as Ana Pauker's aide. Like Pintilie, Toma's first allegiance was to Moscow.

The unschooled Pintilie was soon exhibiting the kind of megalomania familiar to Stalin's courtiers in the Kremlin. In May 1949, he attended a concert given by the ministry of the interior, most likely performed by the Ciocârlia ensemble that the ministry owned, and which performed imported Soviet rural folkdances and folk music. Attended by the pitiful remnants of Bucharest's concert-going bourgeoisie, these were popular events. But Gheorghe Pintilie was not entertained. He fired off a note to the organizers. 'I order the artists not to be so glum!' he said, 'Why is the symphony orchestra in the pit and not on the stage?' The whole presentation, he said, offended his political sensibilities. 'The orchestra should immediately mount the stage... accordions should be added forthwith... so that vigorous and mobilizing marches can be played.'[5]

Pintilie's Securitate behaved as if it were a foreign intelligence network on Romanian soil. It gathered information on Ana Pauker and Gheorghiu-Dej, and immediately passed any concerns to Stalin. Among its most closely monitored targets was Romania's young minister of law and the would-be leader of the RWP.

On 28 April 1948, Lucreţiu Pătrăşcanu was awoken by a knock

at his front door and confronted by a group of men in cream-coloured raincoats. He was taken to the interior ministry for interrogation, along with his wife and several close associates. Their arrests had been ordered by Gheorghiu-Dej. Just before the interrogations began, on 1 May, Pătrășcanu asked for a pen and paper to be brought to his cell, and wrote a letter to his 'brothers and sisters' in the Secretariat; Gheorghiu-Dej, Pauker, Georgescu and Luca. 'It will soon be twenty-nine years since I joined the Communist Party,' he told them. 'I may often have been wrong, done poor work, and even been guilty of misconduct, but nobody ever questioned my sincerity as a communist, my devotion, my wish, and my efforts to follow our Party line without hesitation.' He finished with a desperate plea that they should spare him 'physical destruction'.[6] Ominously, the letter went unanswered.

Pătrășcanu's interrogation was not in the hands of the Romanians, but the Soviets in the shape of Aleksandr Sakharovsky, an officer of the MGB (the precursor to the KGB), who followed a course of questioning dictated down the line from Moscow. The treatment meted out to Pătrășcanu was rough but he was not tortured. By the winter of 1949 – after a year and half in custody – he was still refusing to confess to the fictitious crimes of which he was accused, and a decision was made to place him in the custody of Emil Bodnăraș's ruthless SSI, the Secret Service of the Council of Ministers.

The very next day, the distinguished former minister of law cut his veins with a razor blade, and then broke the blade into pieces and swallowed the fragments. It was a near miracle that he survived. The interrogators needed him to recover quickly, so they could resume their work.

*

Out in the wheat fields west of Bucharest strutted a little man in a charcoal-grey suit and city shoes. His metallic hair was flattened to his head with sweat and morning dew. In one hand he held a briefcase filled with legal orders, in the other a Russian-made TT semi-automatic pistol. If anyone resisted, he was fully prepared to use it. The newly appointed deputy agriculture minister, Nicolae Ceaușescu, was busy imposing Romanian's Stalinist land reforms on a highly resistant peasantry. It was the summer of 1950 and the whole process of land confiscation had already dragged on for eighteen months.

Ceaușescu was short on patience. As far as he was concerned, many of these people were not genuine peasants but *chiaburi*, the Romanian equivalent of Russian *kulaks*, or 'peasant bourgeoisie', who hired out labour and machinery and owned parcels of land. Ceaușescu considered them as loathsome as aristocrats, and was infuriated when they whined about the absence of compensation. That was the whole point of the reforms. Land was a communal asset and should be owned by the state. Their farms and livestock would be removed by force.

Appointed by his old mentor, Gheorghiu-Dej, and working under the stewardship of the Party's agriculture secretary Ana Pauker (she was still foreign minister, but oversaw agriculture policy on behalf of the RWP at the same time), Ceaușescu knew that the land seizures were his first ministerial test and he was determined to deliver. 80,000 peasants were imprisoned, and displaced families were relocated in special resettlement areas, where they lived in communes.

Gheorghiu-Dej had broken his protégé into public service slowly. First, he had flown Ceaușescu to Moscow for training at the revered Frunze Military Academy, a trip from which the impressionable young communist had returned dressed proudly in the uniform of a major-general. After that, Ceaușescu was placed in charge of educating the Romanian army in the new Marxist-Leninist spirit, a task he carried out with undisguised sanctimony. The young man who had left school at eleven years old was to be an educator on a vast scale. He had no idea of grammar, syntax or punctuation, no knowledge of history, geography, economics or technical sciences. But that was the power of communism. It turned old assumptions on their head. Why shouldn't the uneducated become teachers?

The process of devising an actual programme of military indoctrination had been a little more complicated. Ceaușescu hadn't read Marx's shorter works, let alone *Das Kapital*. In fact, he'd not read a single book until his time in jail. It was in Doftana that he'd taught himself to read, while running messages and food for the future Party leaders. He would sit in the timber yard, take out his copy of Stalin's *Problems of Leninism* and slowly try to make sense of each stone-dry paragraph, reading the same book over and over again until he could memorize entire sections.

After his promotion to the ministry of agriculture, Ceaușescu still tried to avoid writing letters or speeches, embarrassed by his near illiteracy. A side-effect was that he committed everything to memory and gradually became an 'encyclopaedist' on anything from designing tractors to applying manure in farming. He possessed no depth, no historical context, just a bewildering array of Christmas-cracker facts he could use to impress. But his memory would also become a powerful tool for understanding the Party's monolithic structures and its impenetrable procedures, of which he would later become a master.

The collectivization that Ceaușescu helped impose was far from universally popular in the RWP. Ana Pauker was outspoken in her opposition. She had witnessed the disaster of forced collectivization in Russia in 1930 when crop yields had plummeted as a result, and warned that the same would happen in Romania because the country was insufficiently mechanized for a centralized system to work. If Romania wanted bread, she said, the peasants should be left alone to work their plots. But Pauker was, again, overruled by Moscow when the Soviets imposed collectivization on the entire communist bloc in 1948.

Her enemies in the RWP now had more 'proof' of Pauker's lack of revolutionary vigour and 'deviation' from Stalinist ideology.

Meanwhile, Ceaușescu's star was rising. He and his young family moved into the most exclusive neighbourhood in the capital, Primăverii (Springtime), an enclave of wide leafy boulevards by the banks of Lake Floreasca bordering Stalin Park (today, King Michael I Park), an area chosen by Gheorghiu-Dej to house all the leading Party members. The former bourgeois residents were evicted and by the time the Ceaușescus arrived, senior members of the Politburo had already taken most of the best manor houses, erecting walls and fences for privacy and installing militia at the gates. Ceaușescu was left with a modest semi-detached property on a less prestigious road but it suited the young junior minister well. In Primăverii, he could take his obsequiousness to the drawing rooms and garden patios of any minister he chose, even at the weekends, indulging a Machiavellian talent that even his critics reluctantly described as 'genius'.[7]

The height of the fences around the properties of Primăverii was commensurate with party rank. Junior ministers and officials were allowed only waist-height partitions, while inner Politburo members were completely shielded from view. In the summer evenings, Emil Bodnăraș, owner of one of the tallest fences in the neighbourhood, could be seen strolling through Primăverii with his neighbour, Leontin Sălăjan (chief of the general staff), while Ceaușescu, whose fence was low but growing, would pop round for tea with Gheorghiu-Dej, who lived behind the highest fence of all.

The assimilation of an elite lifestyle did not end with bricks and mortar. Ceaușescu's wife, Elena, shopped at Comturist department stores with other Politburo wives, luxury shops reserved exclusively for the nomenklatura, always stocked with foreign foods and quality clothing. During winter, the Party's leading families relocated en masse to the ski resort of Predeal, where they had villas on the exclusive slopes of Cioplea Hill. In summer, they would travel to their coastal residences overlooking the sandy beaches of Constanța County, properties that would remain empty the rest of the year. Every leisure pursuit they had, they indulged together, constantly attended by aides, personal security, drivers and an entourage of family and friends. This was Gheorghiu-Dej's magic circle and Ceaușescu was on the glittering periphery.

Elevated overnight from peasant housing and cramped city blocks, Romania's rulers had no idea how to furnish these vast empty spaces. They positioned faux leather sofas in echoing palatial rooms and tore down traditional tiled stoves, replacing them with cheap Chinese electric fires. Traditional paintings were viewed as decadent and bourgeois, so they bought works from a new breed of Party-sanctioned artist, with titles such as 'Armed Women in the Patriotic Guard', 'The Lupeni Strike' and 'Party Propagandist in a Village'. Swimming pools, Italian marble and gold baths would come later.

Polite social chat among the self-elevated elite did not come easily. Most had little but prison stories to swap. Even those with a rich cultural hinterland, such as Ana Pauker, needed to express themselves with sterilized conformity at all times. At one social get-together, round at Gheorghiu-Dej's place, Ana Pauker, Vasile Luca and the Party's chief propagandist, Iosif Chișinevschi, talked politics for a while and then had no idea what to discuss next. In the end, the most powerful people in the country sat hunched around a small wooden table in silence playing Tabinet, a pensioners' card came.[8]

*

The Danube–Black Sea Canal had been Stalin's suggestion. He had given one of his twinkling grins across the desk to Gheorghiu-Dej in 1948 and suggested that the Romanians needed some heroic monument to illustrate the superhuman strength of the Communist Party, a dam perhaps or an impossibly long suspension bridge. It would rejuvenate the people's spirits, said Stalin, and help them focus on the possibilities of collective endeavour.

He and Gheorghiu-Dej finally hit on the idea of an epic canal that would provide a shortcut from the Danube to the Black Sea, cutting 160 miles off the normal journey, therefore saving two days' sailing on Europe's most commercially important river – something that would help Stalin export his iron ore to central Europe. Tens of thousands of labourers would be required, perhaps for a decade or more, and Gheorghiu-Dej turned to Romania's prison camps for a solution. Thousands of former Legionaries, along with purged army officers and suspected spies, were co-opted within a few months and put to work digging a trench that would be wide enough for oil tankers to pass with ease through the flatlands of eastern Romania. All work was carried out under the punishing regime of guards armed with whips and guns. From 4.30 a.m., armies of forced labourers would be marched to the site of the canal, in what became the Soviet bloc's most notorious post-war symbol of Stalinist repression.

The slightest misplaced word or deed could land someone in a work gang on the canal. Some were sent there as punishment simply for visiting the libraries of the American or British embassies.[9] Prisoners were prevented from changing clothes from the day they were arrested. Everything they wore quickly turned to rags. Shoes, even in the freezing winter months, were a rare commodity. A file was kept on each prisoner that carried a coloured diagonal stripe indicating the severity of the punishment. The worst offenders were forced to dig 4 cubic metres of earth a day, equivalent to 6 tonnes.[10] The only mechanized assistance came in the shape of worn-out drills and wheezing earth-movers imported second-hand from the Soviet Volga–Don Canal.

By the end of 1950, 20,000 forced labourers worked in fourteen camps along the banks of what became known as the 'Death Canal'. They represented just a fraction of the political prisoners kept in Gheorghiu-Dej's seventy-five gulags. These prisons and camps housed upwards of 100,000 inmates, most of them former Legionaries. Across the gulag system, men and women laboured on roads, bridges and tunnels. Many tens of thousands died from exhaustion, disease and beatings. The canal exacted the highest casualty rate of all, with a conservative estimate of 10,000 deaths, most in the first three years of construction – a mortality rate of nine people every day.

Ana Pauker was opposed to the Danube–Black Sea Canal from the start, much to the annoyance of Gheorghiu-Dej, who viewed it as his shot at immortality. The cost was astronomical – $2 billion in today's money – at a time when Romania was desperately trying to meet the targets of its first Five-Year Plan. 'We shouldn't spend such money,' said Pauker, 'we should build residential units instead.' The masses did not have enough cement to build their own houses, she said, but 'millions of tonnes' was being poured into Gheorghiu-Dej's pet project. Later in life, Pauker denied any knowledge of what happened at the canal, saying she only knew what was written in official reports – that it was 'a re-education camp for bourgeois personalities'.[11]

The notion of re-education was not a new one but the Romanian Communists were becoming increasingly interested in whether it could be used to change a person's behaviour and views. Could, for instance, a former Legionary be cured of their right-wing opinions? Was the reprogramming of a human mind even possible? The testimony of George Cuşa, the former Legionary I met in Constanţa in 2019, was enlightening.

In 1948, Cuşa was a student member of an underground organization called 'The Brotherhood of Blood', which trained aspiring Legionaries. Corneliu Codreanu had been murdered ten years before but his cult had survived the sudden Stalinization of Romania. Faced with the prospect of a Jewish woman as foreign secretary, and the wholesale importation of a Soviet-style system, the nationalists of 'The Brotherhood' had, if anything, stiffened their resolve. The risk, though, in a country increasingly controlled by secret police, was huge.

Cuşa was, and still is, fearsomely bright. He was studying veterinary medicine and philosophy at the time, and spent his leisure time singing in the university choir or putting on Molière plays at the student union. On the night of 28 September 1948, he was asleep in his dormitory at Bucharest University when he was awoken by three men. They wore long leather coats with collars turned up and fedora hats. One of them told Cuşa he should bring a blanket with him because 'it might get cold'.

Cuşa was taken to the catacombs of the ministry of the interior and was astonished by the size of the place. He slept that night on a concrete bed and was left in the cell for a week before he was taken upstairs to a small office where he was relieved to see the sky again. There were two interrogators. They did not wait for him to sit down. 'What are you doing here, you bastard?' shouted one. And then the man punched him so hard in the face that he collapsed on the floor. Days later, after several more beatings, he was sentenced to four years in jail.

The first months of his sentence were spent at Jilava, where Codreanu and Antonescu had both been held, but he was then taken to Piteşti Prison on the Argeş River, not far from Dracula's castle. It was 7 March 1950. Cuşa was led through a door into something called 'Room No. 1', a large empty space, windowless and without furniture. It was also known by the inmates as 'Purgatory'. In one corner, huddled together, were a group of forty young men. Cuşa recognized one of them as a friend from high school but his features were distorted. The man's jaw and cheekbones seemed misshapen and parts of his face had turned livid purple. The others carried similar injuries. As Cuşa approached, accompanied by a guard, the whole group cowered in a corner.

Cuşa was then taken before a committee, a panel of young students like himself, in their early twenties, who turned out to be former prisoners. He recognized their leader as Eugen Țurcanu, a volatile young law student who had once been a Legionary himself. Țurcanu was handsome with 'a well-proportioned body that seemed like that of an athlete', but when he got mad 'he destroyed everything in his path'. As Cuşa was marched into the room, an eerily calm Țurcanu asked if he would willingly be re-educated, the first step of which would involve becoming an informant. The word he used was '*turnător*' – a 'snitch'. Cuşa said he would not and a few days later was taken to 'Purgatory'.

At first all seemed quiet. Then an old friend of Cuşa appeared in the room and asked how he was faring. Cuşa was relieved to see a friendly face and was about to respond, when the friend punched him hard in the head. Cuşa fell to the ground and was immediately set upon. The beating was frenzied and inflicted by men Cuşa had once called comrades.

This was the defining characteristic of the programme at Pitești. Inmates were repeatedly tortured by family and friends, and could only avoid further beatings if they became torturers themselves. They must confess to all 'crimes', supply names of offenders and then 'prove' that they had been 'disinfected' by inviting those who they had snitched on into Room No. 1, where they must beat them senseless.

It was this grotesque twist that gave the victims a psychological collapse of such intensity that it was supposed to cleanse the brain of all that had gone before. If the 'reformed' prisoner delivered only a light beating to their former friends, the whole process would begin again. The intensity of the beating supposedly proved the level of 'recovery'.

In their desperation to show they were 'cured', some prisoners beat their friends so badly that they died on the floor of Room No. 1. Some were so traumatized that they killed themselves rather than administer punishment. Many of these young men were the brightest stars of their generation, snuffed out in the name of a demented notion of progress.

Pitești did not just involve a bunch of psychopathic prisoners-turned-torturers. Helping to oversee the experiment were prison guards, doctors, psychiatrists, the prison governor, Securitate officers, and the very senior politicians who visited the prison. Whilst George Cușa was in Pitești, he was taken from his cell one day and saw the solid, bustling figure of a woman he recognized as Ana Pauker. Cușa is one of only three survivors of this barbaric experiment who is still alive. He was spared because his mind was strong but his body was weak. He had a form of leukaemia and kept having to be taken to the hospital wing for treatment. The torturers needed their victims healthy in order for them to focus on the matters in hand.

*

A cavalcade of black limousines drove from the airport in Bucharest to the ministry of the interior in January 1952, carrying a group of Soviet advisors sent by Stalin. Gheorghiu-Dej was in high spirits. The Soviet leader had hinted that Pauker was no longer in favour due to her 'Zionist deviation' (assisting Jews to migrate to Israel), just as Stalin was adopting an increasingly hostile position towards the Jewish state.

It was not just Pauker who Stalin wanted to eliminate but her entire coterie of 'deviationist' ministers, including Vasile Luca, whose Hungarian roots were particularly suspicious to the Soviets, and Teo Georgescu.

The softest target appeared to be Luca, who the Kremlin accused of a brand of deviationism known as 'peasantism' – Marxist-speak for favouring peasants over the industrial working class. The allegation went like this: as finance minister, Luca had made industrial goods cheaper for peasants, while at the same time raising prices for agricultural goods. He had thus favoured small farmers above the workers, a serious offence given that

Marxist-Leninist doctrine held that the working classes were the driving force behind the world revolution.

By way of punishment, Stalin decided to impose a series of strict financial reforms on the Romanians that would place the working class in the driving seat and effectively confiscate the life savings of every peasant in the country. The details of his scheme were arriving in the briefcases of the Soviet delegation in their sleek black limousines. But within days of their arrival, they became distracted by the far more enticing prospect of inflicting a traditional Stalinist purge upon Vasile Luca.

The Soviet team installed themselves in government buildings and compiled a fictional report that accused Luca's office of being riddled with 'enemy activity' and 'sabotage'. In Stalin's heyday, he would have been dragged off to prison there and then, but the Romanian Politburo still preferred the illusion of process and decided that a week-long meeting to decide his fate should suffice.

Just as the inquiry was ending on that Friday afternoon, the die-hard Gheorghiu-Dej supporter, Alexandru Moghioroş, rose to his feet and announced with solemn regret that he believed Luca was indeed guilty of 'peasantist deviation', for which he should be purged. There was a pause. Then murmurings of agreement. Luca grabbed his chest and fainted. He was taken home by ambulance and monitored through the night by a physician.[12] In the event, he was sacked from his post as finance minister but, crucially, was allowed to remain in the Politburo.

Days later, Stalin called. He needed an update on the purge. Gheorghiu-Dej flew to Moscow with his entourage to meet the Soviet leader. It was April 1952. Waiting in Stalin's study were the normal circle of grinning, inebriated faces: Vyacheslav Molotov, Lavrentiy Beria (head of the NKVD and Stalin's purger-in-chief) and Anastas Mikoyan (the vice-premier of the Council of Ministers). Stalin puffed angrily on his pipe and invited the Romanian delegates to sit down. Gheorghiu-Dej drew out a file and began reading in his usual wooden monotone. He could report that Luca had been removed as finance minister, he told Stalin and his circle, and that an investigation had been launched into any further action that might be taken. There was a demonic snort from the Soviet contingent. Gheorghiu-Dej tried to continue. One of the Russian leaders – we don't know who because Gheorghiu-Dej in his account does not identify the heckler[13] – shouted in a pantomime voice: 'Look, they threw out Luca from his post, but left him the Politburo.' The whole room fell to laughing. Stalin interrupted. 'What kind of proletarian are you?' he growled at Gheorghiu-Dej. Molotov was next, pointing at the old railway worker and announcing in a high, lampooning voice: 'Look, he has velvety hands… what a refined and delicate man.'

That same night back in his Moscow hotel, Gheorghiu-Dej was suddenly awoken at 2 a.m. by a phone call. He and his entourage were required for a very late dinner at the Kremlin. When they arrived, Stalin, Molotov and Beria were at the table, drinking Georgian wine and champagne. The astonished Romanians had glasses thrust in their hands and Gheorghiu-Dej was told to sit on Stalin's left. 'Dej,' began Stalin, 'how many times did I tell you to get rid of Ana Pauker, and you didn't understand me?' Gheorghiu-Dej pushed a spoonful of caviar around his plate and said nothing. 'If I were in your place,' admonished Stalin, 'I would have shot her in the head a long time ago.' Gheorghiu-Dej smiled weakly. Pepper vodka followed. As Stalin spooned pickled herring into his mouth and called for brandy, he leaned into Gheorghiu-Dej's ear. 'I was convinced that only proletarian blood flowed through your veins,' he said, 'but now I see it is petit bourgeois blood.'

The next Politburo plenum was organized for 26–27 May 1952 in Bucharest. Pauker was, by her own admission, 'terrified', having discovered that the allegations against Luca were to be ramped up. With Stalin's mockery still hanging in the air, Gheorghiu-Dej and his faction wasted no time in dismissing the former finance minister from the Politburo. By now a physical wreck, Luca was whisked off to the dungeons of the interior ministry where, under interrogation, he sobbingly confessed to the most bizarre sins imaginable and accused Pauker of anything that entered his head.

Then came the case against Teo Georgescu, minister of the interior and vice–premier. Georgescu was fond of dressing like a prize-fighter, in a pimped camel-hair suit and cocked trilby, and counted among his friends some of the most feared communists in the country. The Politburo needed to tread lightly with Georgescu, to avoid causing some unexpected fissure. He was accused of 'lacking militancy against the class enemy' and dismissed from all positions, but Gheorghiu-Dej's 'velvety' hands ensured he was simply assigned to 'working at a lower level', rather than thrown in a dungeon.

Next came Pauker, who the plenum attacked in an 'almost mob-like atmosphere'. She was accused of 'right-wing deviation' for inviting Legionaries into the Party, as well as for having allowed Jewish emigration to Israel. Her friendship with the former justice minister, Lucreţiu Pătrăşcanu – still in custody and undergoing interrogation – was deemed evidence of her lack of 'revolutionary vigilance'. Her loyalty to her dead husband attracted particular opprobrium. She had been offered the chance to denounce Marcel, they said, while in prison in 1938 and had refused.

When the allegations of 'right-wing deviationism' had finished, they threw in some 'left-wing deviationism' for good measure. The detail hardly mattered. Ana was ousted because they wanted her ousted, because if they failed to get her ousted, she might oust them. She was ordered to 'self-criticize', an old Stalinist trope that entailed imagining the worst that could be said about you and then saying it about yourself. Pauker was expelled from the Secretariat and the Politburo but allowed to stay at the foreign office. At the same time a criminal investigation was launched, in which Pauker gamely participated, responding in detail to all manner of written questions. It was to no avail. Early one morning in February 1953, officers from the Securitate arrived at her home, walked into her living room, ordered her to turn around and put a blindfold around her head.

Arrangements began for a spectacular show trial. Pauker, Luca and Georgescu were all set to be despatched in one merciless purge.

*

On Sunday, 1 March 1953, one of Stalin's servants, the short, burly Peter Lozgavech, entered his master's vivid-green dacha at Kuntsevo near Moscow with some trepidation. No one had heard a peep from Stalin all day. The last anyone had seen of him was at 4 a.m. the previous night, ruddy-faced, drunk and jousting with Nikita Khrushchev after another marathon drinking session. It was 10 p.m. when Lozgavech let himself into Stalin's dacha and walked breezily through the lobby, making plenty of noise so as not to be accused of creeping up on the boss. As he turned into the dining room, he was confronted with a terrible sight: Stalin in pyjama bottoms and an undershirt, one of his arms contorted beneath his body, barely conscious and making faint buzzing noises. Lozgavech rushed to the phone and called two colleagues who arrived panting and pale. They helped lift the shaking, soiled Stalin onto a sofa. In the early hours of Monday, Stalin's courtiers began arriving, tiptoeing around his barely animate body, administering sweet tea and jockeying for position. Stalin had suffered a cerebral haemorrhage and died four days later without regaining consciousness.

As Beria, Molotov, Malenkov and Khrushchev lined up for their lethal game of succession, in Romania the news broke like a crash of winter lightning. Party leaders tried to work out the storm's likely path. Gheorghiu-Dej had bound himself firmly to Stalin's side since the start of his premiership. He'd happily pronounced himself the most Stalinist of Stalinists but now, with his chief sponsor dead, Gheorghiu-Dej's own position was in serious jeopardy. Whatever dark processes played out in Moscow would inevitably bleed through to Bucharest. If a Stalinist replacement was found, Gheorghiu-Dej was safe. If it were to be a reformer, he would likely be a casualty of a mirror-image change of direction in Romania.

Within days, Gheorghiu-Dej began receiving phone calls from the Soviet foreign minister, Molotov, demanding the release of his old friend Ana Pauker. Gheorghiu-Dej's instinct was to refuse. But what if Molotov became Stalin's replacement? Gheorghiu-Dej might find himself in mortal danger for having ignored the order. Then again, if he were to release Pauker, only to be faced with a hardliner in the Kremlin, he would be accused of reformism himself and risk the same fate.

Gheorghiu-Dej temporized. He released Pauker immediately but kept her under strict house arrest, while jailing Georgescu for a trifling three years, with the option of extending the sentence later should Moscow desire. Astonishingly, he had the charmless but unthreatening Vasile Luca sentenced to death to give the impression of toughness, but later commuted the sentence to life in prison.

When the reformist Nikita Khrushchev emerged victorious in Moscow on 14 September 1953, Gheorghiu-Dej had to pretend he was delighted and that all the Stalinist stuff had been an act in order to curry favour with his dangerous neighbour. To make the claim appear credible, Gheorghiu-Dej was suddenly expected to announce some great gesture of liberalization. He quickly halted construction of the Danube–Black Sea Canal and shut down the forced labour camps. It was hardly enough. People expected some memorable symbolic act, the rehabilitation of a 'living martyr' perhaps, a Party figure who had been wrongly purged when Romania was under Stalin's spell and who could now be released into the new reformist world.

Pauker was the obvious candidate to free from house arrest but anti-Semitism was rearing its head once again. Just like the Legionaries before them, the communists decided that hatred of Jews could bind the country together in patriotic self-embrace. Jews trying to emigrate to the newly created Israel were accused of being pro-American and pro-imperialist and were prevented from leaving the country. The ban was only lifted when Israel agreed to pay hard currency in exchange for refugees. In addition, all Jewish organizations in Romania were banned. The rehabilitation of Pauker, therefore, would not have been universally welcomed.

Attention turned instead to the former justice minister, Lucrețiu Pătrășcanu, arrested and detained five years previously, and still under investigation. The problem for Gheorghiu-Dej was that the popular and relatively liberal-minded Pătrășcanu posed a genuine threat to his leadership, should he be freed. Instead, in a fit of pique, Gheorghiu-Dej phoned his new minster of state security, Alexandru Drăghici, and ordered that Pătrășcanu be put on trial for his life.

Drăghici was a sinister ex-railway worker who had two 'qualifications' for the security job. Firstly, he'd shared a cell with Gheorghiu-Dej. Secondly, he'd convinced Gheorghiu-Dej that he was a witch-hunter extraordinaire – that he could identify and purge 'enemies' with almost supernatural prowess. Having cut his teeth on the liquidation of anti-communist students, Drăghici was now put to work on Pătrășcanu.

The charges against the former minister of law were to be heard before a military tribunal in April 1954. They ran to thirty-six pages, and included allegations of spying for Britain, America and for Antonescu's secret police. The hearing was reminiscent of a Stalinist show-trial in terms of procedure, but held *in camera* to avoid potential embarrassment by the articulate Pătrășcanu, who was likely to put up a fight and draw Gheorghiu-Dej's circle into an unnecessarily messy debacle.

For the first two days, Pătrășcanu sat silently in the dock, refusing to answer questions, but when a parade of his former

RWP comrades were ushered into the court room, all testifying solemnly that their former poster-boy was a heretic and informant, he struggled to remain calm. Pătrășcanu finally erupted when the prosecution called King Carol's bourgeois former prime minister, Gheorghe Tătărescu, from his prison cell. Pătrășcanu leapt to his feet, shouting that if such 'scum of history' has to 'prove that I am not a communist, it is only proof of the low level of the RWP'.

In the end, the verdict was decided not in court but by a unanimous vote of the Romanian Politburo, and telephoned through to the judge. Pătrășcanu, the early hero of the communist movement, their first minister and one of the organizers of the coup against Antonescu, was hauled off to Jilava Prison, and executed by firing squad at 3 a.m. on 17 April 1954.[14]

Gheorghiu-Dej was so elated that his Pătrășcanu problem was finally resolved, he rewarded the hard-line Alexandru Drăghici with a position on the all-powerful Central Committee. At the same time, he elevated an avowedly Stalinist friend of his as a candidate member of the same body – thirty-year-old Nicolae Ceaușescu. But retaining a Stalinist grip on the country while pretending to be reform-minded was about to become a lot more challenging.

On 25 February 1956, the new Soviet leader, Nikita Khrushchev, delivered his epoch-changing speech to the 20th Congress of the Communist Party of the Soviet Union, repudiating Stalin's cult of personality and denouncing his purges. In doing so, he destroyed the image of his predecessor as an infallible leader and began reverting the country to an idealized Leninist model. This was to be an era of liberal reform that would become known as 'the Khrushchev thaw', and the satellite states were expected to follow suit. It looked like the end for ageing Stalinist dictators.

In April, Bulgaria's Marxist-Leninist dinosaur, Valko Chervenkov, resigned his post. Poland's hardliner Edward Ochab was next, but only after the threat of Soviet military intervention. In June, Hungary's Mátyás Rákosi was forced to flee to the Kirghiz

Soviet Socialist Republic and the Hungarian public then took to the streets to demand the removal of all Soviet troops. The bloody uprising that followed tested the limits of what Moscow would allow. Khrushchev might be a reformer but he was not going to let Hungary detach itself from the mother ship. On 4 November 1956, he sent a huge invasion force into Budapest and wrested back control, killing 2,500 Hungarians in the process. He then installed a puppet government that suppressed all opposition.

Gheorghiu-Dej watched nervously from Bucharest. Khrushchev wanted his satellite states de-Stalinized but he did not want them de-Sovietized – in other words, moderate liberalization while remaining firmly in Moscow's orbit. Gheorghiu-Dej wanted the opposite. He wanted to remain ruler of a Stalinist state, while shaking off Moscow altogether. It would require all the former rail worker's cunning to survive unscathed.

Gheorghiu-Dej had already begun the pretence of a de-Stalinization programme, in order to keep Khrushchev off his back. He pointed, preposterously, to the purging of Pauker, Luca, and Georgescu as evidence that the old guard was being swept aside. Of course, Gheorghiu-Dej had actually purged them for being reformists. His aim was to quietly de-Sovietize Romania while clinging on to the Stalinist model, right beneath the nose of Khrushchev.

Whenever the two leaders met, they bickered like husband and wife. Gheorghiu-Dej thought Khrushchev high-handed, short-tempered and too unstable to be in charge of nuclear weapons – a worry that Gheorghiu-Dej believed was proved well-founded later during the 1962 Cuban Missile Crisis. Khrushchev thought Gheorghiu-Dej dull, guarded, tortoise-like and the product of a second-rate country. When Gheorghiu-Dej invited Khrushchev to Bucharest in 1957, he had him driven through regimented crowds to drink in the fake admiration. That evening, at a welcome dinner, the boorish Khrushchev upbraided Gheorghiu-Dej for his alleged policy of slaughtering pigs at just

25 kg, something that was deemed wasteful when a pig could be expected to grow to 100 kg.[15]

'Perhaps', shot back Gheorghiu-Dej, 'you are thinking of our policy on sucklings, not pigs.'

Hunched over his salty pig, Khrushchev snapped back, 'No.'

Gheorghiu-Dej went on to explain, with faux bemusement, that Khrushchev clearly knew little about modern farming techniques and that the Romanian policy was to kill pigs at 100 kg. The bickering continued through the meal, with each man determined to have the last word. When Khrushchev arrived back at his hotel, he phoned Gheorghiu-Dej and admitted that he was mistaken about the figure of 25 kg but that he was still broadly right because he had just found out Romanian pigs were being slaughtered at a below-ideal 50 kg.

The next day the two men travelled by train to the port of Constanța without exchanging a single word. When they arrived, they began quarrelling over the best way to sow maize. It was out of this niggling contrarianism that Gheorghiu-Dej conceived an idea. If the Soviet leader instinctively disagreed with everything he said, why not pretend the last thing he wanted, ever, was a break from Moscow? In newspaper articles and public pronouncements, Gheorghiu-Dej began pushing a hard line, praising the presence of Soviet troops in Romania and insisting that they should stay for 'as long as NATO existed'. It turned out to be a clever piece of reverse-psychology.

On 17 April 1958, Khrushchev informed Gheorghiu-Dej that he was planning to withdraw Soviet troops because he trusted Romania to stay close to the Soviet Union. Gheorghiu-Dej, who could imagine no greater pleasure than seeing the back of the Soviets, played it cool and waited six days before replying, saying that he reluctantly accepted Khrushchev's decision. The Soviet leader then notified Bucharest that Soviet advisors would also be withdrawn. It was more than Gheorghiu-Dej could ever have dreamed of, but he did not reply in the affirmative for two weeks.

As the final Soviet representatives left for Moscow, Gheorghiu-Dej had them presented with a leather-bound photo album of the Romanian Army, collections of military songs, postcards, cigarettes and bottles of plum brandy.[16]

With the Soviet overseers gone, Gheorghiu-Dej set to work ridding the country of any visible connections with Moscow and creating a home-grown totalitarian state. Statues of Stalin were torn down and framed portraits of Romania's nine Politburo members began appearing around the country – in public buildings, shops and city squares. Ceaușescu was the youngest, having been elevated to the nine-man committee in 1954 at the age of just thirty-six.

By 1961, we find Ceaușescu wandering the mortuary-white corridors of the Politburo from sunrise until sunset, overseeing the arid regulations of the Party apparatus, indulging his passion for secrecy and intrigue, and ingratiating himself more deeply with Gheorghiu-Dej. His role was still ostensibly that of 'fixer', just as it had been in Doftana Prison all those years before, although now with a title – Secretary in Charge of Party Organization and Apparatus, a role ideally suited to Ceaușescu's fondness for obscure and recondite Party rules. By mastering them, quietly and with fierce commitment, he was cleverly placing himself in a position of power. The oracle of such labyrinthine structures and countless committees was consulted by everyone on how the Party functioned. Still very much in Gheorghiu-Dej's political shadow, Ceaușescu was invited onto the stage at the Central Committee plenum of 1961, an event that Gheorghiu-Dej later described as 'the most beautiful plenum ever held'.[17]

We can imagine a mumbling Ceaușescu trying to swallow his stammer for the duration. He would have prepared every aspect of his presentation: the scrawled words from which he would not deviate, the tone, the manner, the absence of facial expression – all, almost certainly, practised in front of a mirror. He spoke in a coarse rural monotone, leaving long awkward pauses during which his eyes darted anxiously around the room. The subject was the 'rightist deviationist' Pauker, her dead husband and her whole despicable bourgeois clan. Gheorghiu-Dej was delighted. Afterwards he reached for his highest words of praise. Ceauşescu, he smiled, had said 'some very nice things'.

It had become de rigueur to attack Pauker since her release from Malmezon Prison in March 1953. At first, she had been placed under a loose form of house arrest in Bucharest, where she was watched day and night by her housekeeper and chauffeur, who were both employees of the Securitate. She then moved in with her daughter, Tatiana, and son Vlad, and earned a small salary translating for a local publishing house. Several more rounds of investigation and interrogation came and went. One day, when her interlocutors ran out of ammunition, they accused Pauker of being a 'Soviet informer', a charge that could have been levelled against almost all her comrades, including some of those involved in her interrogation.

Pauker became a pariah, barely leaving her home and reduced in physical bearing after a diagnosis of breast cancer. Her comrades deserted her overnight, no one daring to risk a fall from grace by association with her. There was, however, one moving show of affection for 'the iron lady' in defiance of the Party's edict. In 1955, Pauker accompanied her family to a performance at Bucharest's opera house. The hall was said to be full of her former comrades, none of whom exchanged a word with her. But as she left, the crowd of Party functionaries formed a corridor for her to walk along and stood 'almost at attention' as she passed by.[18]

In the late 1950s Pauker's cancer returned. She died, without ever having regained favour, on 3 June 1960.

*

Throughout the early 1960s, while pretending to be Khrushchev's number-one ally, Romania continued to pursue a uniquely independent course among the satellite states. Gheorghiu-Dej cleverly tapped into years of pent-up Romanian nationalism and anti-Semitism, re-shaping it as support for a form of national communism that celebrated Romanian history and culture, and rehabilitating previously banned nationalist figures. The long-dead, far-right historian Nicolae Iorga – former mentor of Corneliu Codreanu – was brought in from the cold and celebrated as an 'anti-fascist'. Even Marshal Antonescu had a renaissance of sorts, no longer viewed as a fascist but as admirably patriotic. Anti-Semitism was framed as a healthy distrust of foreigners and proof of pure Romanian heritage. In truth, it had never really gone away.

Gheorghiu-Dej completed Romania's Stalinist-style collectivization of agriculture and continued investing most of Romania's budget in heavy industry. When Khrushchev insisted that Romania use its vast cereal acreage to become the bread-basket of the communist bloc, Gheorghiu-Dej waved him away, saying that Romania would not be bossed around any longer by Moscow. The relationship was reaching its inevitable, chilly end.

With the Soviet Union at arm's length, Gheorghiu-Dej became more confident about following his own instincts. In 1963 he began trading with the West, sending officials to the United States and France. At home, he relaxed some of his more repressive policies, releasing thousands of political prisoners. But his autocratic tendencies were never far away. When his younger daughter, Tanti, fell in love with a 'bourgeois singer', Gheorghiu-Dej had the Securitate interrogate and beat the man. The couple ignored her father's wishes and eloped but Tanti finally gave way to Gheorghiu-Dej's threats, leaving the singer and marrying a sculptor and actor, whose working-class roots her father found less offensive.

Dej's glamorous older daughter, Vasilica, an actress who Romanians described as 'nu e talentata, dar e tare-n tată' – 'untalented but strong-in-father' – took a young divorcee doctor as her lover. Gheorghiu-Dej disapproved and had the unfortunate fellow jailed for five years, a sentence he did not survive. He could, on the other hand, be lavish with public money and patronage, particularly where family were concerned. He built two palatial homes in Primăverii for his daughters, and made Vasilica's first husband a minister of trade, while the second became a deputy prime minister. Watching all this unfold was the young Nicolae Ceaușescu.

Then, one February morning in 1965, Ceaușescu walked into a Politburo meeting, sat down, arranged his files on the table and calmly announced that Gheorghiu-Dej was about to die.

CHAPTER FOURTEEN

Still earth shall only earth remain,
Let luck its course unfold,
And I in my own kingdom reign,
Immutable and cold.

'Luceafărul' (1883), Mihai Eminescu

'Pāsārica' they called her, 'Little Bird', as she grew up in the tiny village of Petrești in Dâmbovița County. Elena Petrescu spent her solitary teenage years clambering up the church tower to watch the starlings. If she was lucky, she might spot a steppe eagle circling like a glider against the burning afternoon sun. During harvest time she would wander into the fields to watch squirrels and pheasants scrambling from her father's horse-drawn plough. Elena had little interest in school. Her teachers were exasperated by her slow progress. At the age of fourteen, she failed almost every academic subject, passing only singing, gymnastics and needlework. They told her to stay down a year. Elena refused. Instead, she left for Bucharest, where she stayed with her brother, Gheorghe, whose friends called him 'Cap de Lemn' – literally 'wooden head', on account of his less than sparkling intellect.[1]

Gheorghe had attended meetings of the Young Communist League (YCL) in the 1930s and Elena had tagged along, not for the politics but for the boys. At the time, she worked in a two-room apartment in a low-rent area of town. The establishment served as a black-market pill factory, stealing the formulas for patented slimming tablets and vitamins and producing copies at a knock-down price. Each day, she was greeted by the smells of rosehips and oranges from the milling machine. Elena liked the look of the bottles and the pretty-coloured powders. Chemistry, she thought, might offer her a future.

In the summer of 1939, the YCL held a picnic and a small fair that included a light-hearted fund-raising competition. Each girl was allotted a number and the one who inspired the greatest number of ticket purchases would be named 'Queen of the Ball'. Elena – pallid, uncommunicative and plain – seemed out of contention but a twenty-one-year-old called Nicolae Ceauşescu was in attendance and became smitten. Just out of prison for 'distribution of communist propaganda', Ceauşescu was already known as something of a hard man, and went round his male friends bullying them into buying tickets that bore Elena's number. It worked. She won, and spent the day chatting earnestly with her new boyfriend. Years later, the Party's propagandists would transform the event into a huge rally where the heroic young communist, Elena, was elected 'Miss Working Class', on account of her beauty and her dedication to the cause.

More jail terms followed for Nicolae, some for fighting, others for leafleting and protests. Contemporaries said he had little genuine interest in politics and might easily have chosen the Green Shirts of Codreanu's Iron Guard. But Nicolae Ceauşescu wanted to meet girls and some of his friends had told him the prettiest were in the YCL.

Ceauşescu was moved from jail to jail – Jilava, Caransebeş and the Târgu Jiu internment camp. Each time he was freed, he returned to the arms of his faithful Elena. There had been no one else. Elena was his first and his last. The two muddled through the war years together, though largely apart. They finally married on 23 December 1947, the year after the communists seized power. Ceauşescu's rise through the Party hierarchy saw his new wife offered a secretarial post in the foreign office. Within a short time, her bosses despaired. She showed no aptitude for written work, bridled at taking orders and was catty towards female colleagues. Elena was 'let go'.

She turned her attention to family matters. The Ceauşescus' first son, Valentin, was born not long after their wedding, in February 1948. A quiet, sensitive boy who preferred books to sport, he did well at the prestigious Lyceum 24, a school in the Primăverii district where most of the nomenklatura sent their offspring. A daughter, Zoia, arrived the following year. She attended the same school and showed some promise in mathematics, though her diligence was laced with a rebellious streak. A third child, Nicu, arrived in 1951. From an early age, Nicu was disruptive and challenging. Teachers were too afraid to discipline him. He did as he liked, threatening them with his father's retribution or even that of the Securitate. Smoking, truancy, fighting – naturally Nicu was destined for a career in politics.

Whilst Nicolae Ceauşescu spent long hours at Central Committee meetings, Elena raised the children. By the time her husband was elevated to the Politburo in 1954, she was juggling motherhood with a college course. She took evening classes in chemistry and hoped it would be a chance to gain some respect independent of Nicolae. The tutors were tolerant of Elena's near illiteracy until she was caught cheating in her exams and expelled. It hardly mattered. By 1960, with Nicolae's career flourishing, she was awarded a job at the Central Institute for Chemical Research. Although just a junior technician, it was a prestigious position and Elena's appointment caused resentment amongst the bona fide scientists. Five years later, those who had complained found themselves in an uneasy predicament. Elena suddenly became their boss. Without any formal qualifications, she was elevated to the position of the Institute's Director.

It was a tricky role for someone with no expertise in science. Her employees would put in requests for ethyl alcohol to carry out experiments and Elena would turn them down. 'You only want it to make home brew,' she would chide them. But when the same researchers asked for ethyl alcohol using its chemical formula, she would grant her approval. Elena soon learned it was better to avoid conversations with proper chemists after becoming confused about how to pronounce CO_2. Unfamiliar with even the simplest of chemical symbols, she referred to it as 'co-two' – in Romanian 'co-doi'. From then on, her staff knew her as 'Codoi', Romanian for 'Big tail'.

Elena concentrated, like her husband, on procedure and organization instead of research, showing herself to be a nit-picking and niggardly boss. She made it her mission to save money, personally examining all staff expenses and scrapping the telephone exchange at the Institute so that calls became a bureaucratic nightmare. Socially she struggled. Elena was a loner. When she was forced to mix with other Politburo wives, she could come across as cold and uninterested. Her impoverished background and lack of schooling made her suspicious of the more confident, easy-going women in the circle, while any female with good looks was regarded as a rival.

The Politburo wives were a conventional bunch – rarely photographed and seemingly content with domestic chores and raising children, they were a world away from the likes of Ana Pauker and the cosmopolitan, revolutionary young women of the early days of the movement. The traditional female roles they brought with them from the countryside seemed to infuriate Elena Ceaușescu. But by the spring of 1965, the wives noticed a change in her demeanour. Elena began inviting them round for drinks. She laughed politely at their jokes and complimented them on their handbags and shoes. Her charm offensive just happened to coincide with the terminal illness of Gheorghiu-Dej.

A succession of black limousines crunched along the deep gravel driveway of the general secretary's lakeside villa in March 1965, depositing their occupants in front of the grand white stucco entrance where they were greeted by footmen and ushered inside. Gheorghiu-Dej's lung cancer had been kept secret from the public but on 5 March, the sixty-three-year-old made a pre-recorded television address at his home and the producers were alarmed by his gaunt expression and faltering voice. They needed to re-record the segment several times. Word spread that Gheorghiu-Dej was seriously ill.

A Harley Street doctor flew in from London on 6 March and pronounced that Gheorghiu-Dej had only a short time to live. Members of the Politburo began keeping a close eye on his daily medical bulletins and an even closer eye on who among them was visiting Gheorghiu-Dej the most, in case they were trying to steal a march.

The list of possible successors was short. The nine-member Politburo was hardly overburdened with talent. Five of them had barely completed elementary school and three were former rail workers from Gheorghiu-Dej's union days who had been elevated for loyalty not literacy. Not only had Gheorghiu-Dej purged the upper echelons of the Party, he'd impoverished the entire country with his anti-intellectual policies. Children of political detainees were denied a university education. Their extended families were considered 'stigmatized'. Schools were barred from teaching critical thought. Academics were regularly arrested and detained. All this was designed to eradicate opposition but had inadvertently starved the RWP of even moderately capable minds.

Any potential successor would need to be of 'pure' Romanian blood. Even a foreign-born parent might debar them from office. The only Politburo member with a degree, Prime Minister Ion Gheorghe Maurer, was thus removed from the field of play, his father being of German extraction. Sharp-witted Soviet spy Emil Bodnăraş was also out of the running due to his father's Ukrainian roots. These two men had been the most senior members of the Politburo. Whatever measure one employed, Nicolae Ceauşescu was never more than fifth in line.

But in those final days of Gheorghiu-Dej's life, Ceauşescu was working industriously behind the scenes. As the Central Committee's Secretary for Organization and Cadres over the past decade, he had gradually come to monopolize decisions over structures, rules and, crucially, Party appointments, exerting pedantic authority over other Politburo members who underestimated the potential power of the role. They should have seen it coming. An almost identical sequence of events had occurred in Moscow forty years earlier, when a rough, ambitious young Marxist was overlooked for a ministerial role by Vladimir Lenin and was instead given an ostensibly dull, organization job in the Central Committee. His name was Joseph Stalin.

Ceauşescu was now able to take control of the medical management of Gheorghiu-Dej's rapidly deteriorating health, and also the momentous, looming decision. Always fussy about procedure, Ceauşescu put himself in charge of organizing visits to Gheorghiu-Dej's bedside, something that antagonized his rivals as they competed for a final squeeze of the hand or some barely perceptible gesture that might confirm their right to succession. Even Gheorghiu-Dej himself had been worried by his young protégé's 'feverish manoeuvrings' and told aides that Ceauşescu was too volatile and impulsive for the top job.[2] Again, there were echoes of Stalin, who Lenin described as 'too coarse', 'intolerant', 'capricious' and 'not intelligent' enough to succeed him. This was history repeating itself as farce.

We can imagine Ceauşescu standing sentry at the door of Gheorghiu-Dej's bedroom, a check-list of visitors in hand, solemnly explaining that the boss was deteriorating, that political discussion might weaken him further and that a few minutes each was all they were allowed.

Prime Minister Maurer visited Gheorghiu-Dej every day. Thick-set, with the creased, tanned face of a sunflower-picker and a shock of black-and-white badger hair, Maurer was actually the closest the Politburo had to a bourgeois intellectual. A lawyer who had helped defend Ana Pauker at her Craiova trial in 1936, he was an old-school Leninist, an authentic veteran whose ambition was quiet and selfless. We can see him perched beside his old comrade, Gheorghiu-Dej, lowering his voice so as not to be heard by the patrolling Ceauşescu. One version of events has it that Gheorghiu-Dej, now muted by cancer, motioned for a pen and paper and wrote, in violet ink: 'It is my final wish that Comrade Maurer be my successor.'[3] Apparently overcome with emotion, Maurer tried to splutter a few words of gratitude but by this time Gheorghiu-Dej's eyes were closing. He was slipping away.

Inevitably, others claim that Gheorghiu-Dej still found the strength to see them. The deputy prime minister, Gheorghe Apostol – a headstrong trade unionist with a deep loathing for Nicolae Ceauşescu – had stood in for Gheorghiu-Dej as general secretary on several occasions, and now headed to his master's deathbed for confirmation of his right of succession. A former foundry-worker, Apostol was as fiery as the molten metal he used to pour. We can envisage him pushing past Ceauşescu's clipboard and planting himself defiantly on the chair beside Gheorghiu-Dej's bed. Apparently, Maurer had turned down the offer of leadership – probably accepting that his German heritage would be unpalatable – and now Gheorghiu-Dej invited Apostol to be his successor. Apostol expected nothing less. One of his first tasks was likely to be the purging of that upstart Nicolae Ceauşescu from the Politburo.

Whatever the ailing Gheorghiu-Dej managed to say or, indeed, write in those final days, one thing is certain – he did not mean Nicolae Ceauşescu to be the next leader of Romania. But Ceauşescu was not seeking Gheorghiu-Dej's approval. The field, he knew, was already overcrowded. While Elena entertained the wives at their home near the lake on Zhdanov Avenue, Ceauşescu shifted his attention away from Gheorghiu-Dej's bedside to the corridors of the Central Committee building. Aware that Maurer had already counted himself out of the race, Ceauşescu's omniscience in organizational matters began to pay off. He learned that Maurer and Apostol had fallen out. It was time, he decided, to make Maurer an offer. If Maurer were to propose him as general secretary after Gheorghiu-Dej's death, he would support Maurer's continuation as prime minister. It was an appealing suggestion, and not necessarily for the reasons Ceaușescu intended.

As Maurer shuttled back and forth between the Central Committee and Gheorghiu-Dej's deathbed in mid-March 1965, Ceaușescu must have seemed to him a short, stammering, unprepossessing young man; an obedient apparatchik who had scuttled around Gheorghiu-Dej quietly and effectively, parroting whatever views his master proclaimed. With Gheorghiu-Dej gone, Ceaușescu would be a blank canvas and Maurer and Bodnăraș, the two big beasts, could apply whatever brush strokes they required. The more they thought about it, the more appealing Ceaușescu became.

There were, however, two other candidates ahead of him. The first was Chivu Stoica – senior in terms of age but particularly low on intellectual ability, even in such an arid landscape. Stoica had run away from home at the age of twelve to work on the railways, and was another Gheorghiu-Dej placeman. He was bought off with the title 'President of the State Council', officially President of Romania, although it would be largely a ceremonial title. The real power lay with the general secretary. That left the cadaver-like Alexandru Drăghici, minister of the interior and head of the Securitate, who had orchestrated the trial and execution of Pătrășcanu. Few in the Politburo were without blood on their hands but even to these hardened apparatchiks, Drăghici's insouciant use of torture and murder was disturbing. The more that Maurer and Bodnăraș examined the line-up, the more Ceaușescu shone weakly from the darkness.

On 18 March 1965, Gheorghiu-Dej received a telegram of good wishes from Mao Tse-tung, leader of the People's Republic of China, his newest and most valued friend. Gheorghiu-Dej had steered Romania towards China in recent years, with the same enthusiasm that he had reversed away from Moscow. It had been an astute strategic decision, born out of Gheorghiu-Dej's desire to escape Soviet domination but also to free Romania from a regional milieu that had seen it conquered and exploited by successive 'big power' neighbours through the centuries: the Austro-Hungarians, Ottomans and Russians. China might have been culturally and geographically remote but that was part of its attraction. There was no historical baggage. The arrival of the Sino-Soviet split – the dramatic rupture in relations between the two communist giants – had presented Gheorghiu-Dej with an ideal opportunity to help create a Red axis outside Russia's sphere of influence. His ill health had come just as China and Russia were gathering troops along their common border. As conflict loomed, all Eastern Bloc countries had scurried obediently to Moscow's side, offering unconditional support while decrying the Chinese 'aggressors'; all, that is, apart from Gheorghiu-Dej and Albania's Enver Hoxha. They were the only dissenting voices – both refusing to condemn China, much to Moscow's fury. That is why Mao had sent him deathbed good wishes.

The next day, 19 March, just after 4 p.m., Gheorghiu-Dej fell into a coma. There were already rumours that his fast-spreading cancer had somehow been irradiated into him by the Russians as punishment for his disloyalty. It was nonsense but tells us something about the deep distrust the average Romanian felt for their Eastern neighbour. Just before 6 p.m. that evening, Gheorghiu-Dej died. The succession had already been arranged. The new man in the top job would be Nicolae Ceaușescu.

*

That summer, Bucharest sweltered in a heat wave. The lawns outside the Central Committee building turned nicotine-yellow in the drought. In the exclusive Primăverii neighbourhood, members of the nomenklatura wandered along the banks of

Lake Herăstrău trying to keep cool beneath the linden trees and willows. At Gheorghiu-Dej's grand stucco-fronted villa, ornate Rococo furniture was discreetly removed from his private quarters. The palace was now available to the new general secretary but Ceaușescu told colleagues he considered the house 'unproletarian'.

In July, a Party Congress was organized, the first to be held without Gheorghiu-Dej since the war. Fleets of bullet-proof limousines ferried dignitaries from the airport to Palace Hall, a vast Frisbee-shaped building decorated with acres of tangerine-coloured timber. A team of Chinese bodyguards escorted a slow-moving vehicle right up to the building's main doors. From the rear seat emerged Den Xiaoping, number four in the Chinese Communist Party. It was a rare visit to the Soviet bloc by a senior Chinese official during the Sino-Soviet split. His presence in Romania said much about the role Ceaușescu was expected to play – not in the traditional Cold War arena of East versus West, but between the two competing giants of communism.

From the perspective of the Soviet Union, the communist world had always been a single strategic entity led by Moscow. Its European neighbours were subordinate 'brotherly' satellites that were dependant on the Kremlin for security, trade and loans. Soviet superiority was incontestable. Moscow had always assumed that China was part of the same system and would accept the same pattern of Soviet dominance.

But Peking was not only geographically and culturally distant, it disagreed profoundly with Moscow on interpretations of communist doctrine, particularly with Khrushchev's reforms. The Soviet leader's denunciation of Stalin precipitated a rancorous fall-out, Peking accusing Moscow of having 'discarded' the 'sword of Stalin', and implying that the Kremlin was moving back to its bourgeois past. In contrast, Mao had held onto the old ways, remaining Stalinist and refusing to support Khrushchev's push for a new 'peaceful co-existence' with the West. In a startling rebuke to his Soviet comrades, the Chinese leader had made a speech in which he ridiculed Moscow for seeking nuclear non-proliferation with the United States. 'We shouldn't be afraid of atomic bombs and missiles,' he told a Moscow conference in 1957, 'no matter what kind of war breaks out – conventional or thermonuclear – we'll win. As for China, if the imperialists unleash war on us, we may lose more than three hundred million people. So what? War is war. The years will pass and we will get to work producing more babies than ever before.'[4] European delegates had laughed uneasily at Mao's apocalyptic humour. Khrushchev had found the speech 'deeply disturbing'. From then on, the needling between China and the Soviet Union became increasingly surreal.

The following year, Mao received Khrushchev on an ill-fated trip to Peking, where he insisted on conducting one of their meetings in a swimming pool. Mao knew that Khrushchev could not swim, so the Soviet leader had been obliged to put on water wings. They paddled along together up and down the pool, their translators following along the sides. Finally, humiliated and exhausted, Khrushchev hauled himself out of the water and sat with his legs dangling so that, 'I was now on top, and he was swimming below.'[5]

By the time of Ceaușescu's July Congress in 1965, the two giants seemed poised for war, with China positioning 1.5 million men on its side of the Sino-Soviet border, and the Soviets facing them with a quarter of a million troops and 200 aircraft.

The Moscow contingent arrived in Bucharest headed by the new general secretary of the Communist Party of the Soviet Union, Leonid Brezhnev. Romania was still, formally, a Soviet satellite and still a member of the Warsaw Pact. But its mantra was one of independence. Ceaușescu viewed Moscow as an ideological ally but strategic adversary, while Brezhnev viewed Romania as 'deviationist'. Nevertheless, he had to accept the invitation to Ceaușescu's party. To refuse would be an admission that Moscow had lost Romania to China, with the possibility that other satellite states might follow suit and form an axis of dissident communist nations.

Once in Bucharest, the Chinese and the Soviets would have hoped to stay well clear of each other. Great care would have been taken to stage-manage the event so that there were no embarrassing encounters. On the opening day of the conference, Ceaușescu led a long line of officials into the hall in front of a mechanically applauding crowd. Dressed in a tailored dark-grey suit buttoned tightly over a pink silk tie, his unruly wire-hair razored and styled, a shining red star on his lapel, the transformation from organizer to leader seemed complete. Ceaușescu strode confidently to the platform, gripping a sheaf of papers. He opened congress with a solemn appeal for a moment of silence in memory of Gheorghiu-Dej, and then he began to show that everything had changed.

Reading hesitantly from his notes but with more verve than in the past, he announced that there was going to be a vote. The Central Committee had agreed that the Romanian Workers' Party should revert to its original name – the Romanian Communist Party (RCP), as it had been before 1944 – and now Congress would be asked to give its blessing to the decision. It might sound like inconsequential fiddling but this was a notice of intent, the realignment of the Party with its supposedly heroic and glorious roots, a return to the days before Gheorghiu-Dej. The Party Congresses would also be re-numbered, another seismic moment for procedural purists; instead of the Fourth RWP Congress, this would be the Ninth RCP Congress, re-establishing the lineage that had been broken just after the war by Gheorghiu-Dej and setting Romania on a corrected path.

'Are there any opinions on these proposals, Comrades?' asked Ceaușescu, peering into the eerily silent hall where 4,000 expressionless delegates sat, row after row, in identical ink-black suits. He paused for a moment. 'None?' he confirmed flatly. 'Let's vote then… who is in favour of changing the name of our Party?… raise your hands.' The entire audience raised their arms in unison. 'Anyone against?' Ceaușescu squinted into the vast room, eyes narrowing as if there might be a rogue hand somewhere that wished to have its owner identified in front of the nation. There was none. 'The Congress has unanimously approved changing the name to the Communist Party,' announced Ceaușescu. On the stage behind him, Central Committee members rose from their seats to lead thunderous applause.

In fact, the former Gheorghiu-Dej barons were uneasy. What they were witnessing was a mini-coup. The cult of Gheorghiu-Dej, of which they thought Ceaușescu was a member, was being pushed to one side by dull but malevolent procedural remodelling. Ceaușescu then announced a further change, something he had decided without even consulting his senior comrades. The Politburo was to be replaced by two new bodies: a permanent presidium and an executive committee. Even the old guard struggled to understand the significance of this but it turned out to be a procedural masterstroke.

Ceaușescu had been keen to avoid any messy sackings or purges. Instead, he was able to flood the two new bodies with his former subordinates from the organizational branch of the Central Committee, diluting the power of the Gheorghiu-Dej-era barons and guaranteeing himself a reliable majority on both bodies. Under the patronage of Ceaușescu, the new guard promised years of unconditional support. But the Ninth Party Congress went down in Romanian history not for its Byzantine off-stage struggles and bureaucratic manoeuvring, but rather for its unexpected medley of liberal-sounding reforms.

Ceaușescu announced that relations with Western communist parties were to be improved, particularly those of Spain and Italy. Poets, writers and artists were to be given new freedoms to question and examine political issues, although criticism would need to be 'committed, revolutionary, and within the confines of Socialist Humanism' – in other words, there could be no questioning of the omnipotence of the Party. The RCP's censorship of newspapers would be loosened and, indeed, for a while Western newspapers and journals, Western books and even Hollywood movies flooded across the Iron Curtain into Bucharest. Most significantly, Ceaușescu spoke of a new emphasis on legality and justice, an acknowledgement that the past had delivered neither.

At the same time, the old Romanian trope of nationalism was to be pursued with more vigour, resurrecting the true architects of Romanian greatness: Roman Emperor Trajan, Stephen the Great and Vlad Dracula.

Ceaușescu's speech at the Ninth Party Congress was his 'Khrushchev moment', a public rejection of his mentor and proclamation of a new era. It lacked the drama of Khrushchev's speech. No one fainted. But in his own low-key manner, and without mentioning Gheorghiu-Dej by name, Ceaușescu introduced a series of distinctly non-Stalinist reforms.

In the audience, the unreconstructed Stalinist, Den Xiaoping, would not have been greatly concerned. What mattered to Peking was less Ceaușescu's Stalinist credentials than his determination to chart an independent course from that of Moscow. A fascinating photograph survives from the day. Ceaușescu is walking his two most distinguished guests out of Palace Hall. The boyish Den Xiaoping is to his right, dressed in a Chairman Mao-style, high-collared suit, relaxed and beaming broadly. To Ceaușescu's left is the usually imperious Brezhnev, looking distinctly uncomfortable. But it is Ceaușescu whose demeanour is of note. Just four months into his job, the forty-eight-year-old leader of a country with just 19 million people has spread his wing-like arms around the two communist giants – who between them led a population of 1 billion – as if he were a protective parent telling them to go outside and play nicely.

Later, Ceaușescu held a private meeting with the Chinese, and the exchanges suggest he was far more comfortable with them than his crotchety old comrades in Moscow. A mood of almost gossipy excitement infused proceedings. After Den Xiaoping told Ceaușescu how pleased he was that 'you have strengthened the leading role of the Party in the state' and made provisions for 'more intense centralization', he and his aides took a few catty swipes at Moscow. One of them, the Chinese intelligence chief and Secretariat member, Kang Sheng, complained: 'The Soviets do not respect the sovereignty of our country; in order to discuss [the Vietnam War] with us, they sent only their embassy's counsellor. They look upon our country as a province of the Soviet Union.' Then Den Xiaoping weighed in, lambasting Moscow for trying to find common cause with the Americans in Vietnam. The Kremlin's intention, he declared to Ceaușescu, was to 'isolate China'.[6]

Even as the Romanians saw off their guests at the airport, Ceaușescu, buoyed by the reception to his reforms, was already devising a secret plan to do away with any rivals. Over the coming months, he would appoint a commission to begin investigating the Party's Stalinist atrocities of the 1950s, with instructions to find out exactly who was responsible. His priority was to re-examine the show-trial and execution of the former minister of law, Lucrețiu Pătrășcanu. Ceaușescu, of course, knew very well who was responsible.

*

On the final, exuberant bend of the Danube river, before it turns inexorably eastwards towards the Black Sea, appears a futuristic city of gleaming tubular pipes, freshly tarmacked roads, iron-girded factories, dormitories, canteens and towers so tall they seem to touch the sky. As Ceaușescu's cavalcade approached the site on a misty morning in September 1966, steam and smoke billowed from every roof and every gaping chimney, smothering the area in a blanket of low white clouds. Ceaușescu stepped from his black Mercedes 600 to greet a knot of officials, pursued by his official photographer. The Galați steel works, the largest in Romania, throbbed with energy and promise.

Construction of the plant, on scrubland and marshes, had begun when Stalin was insisting Romania should stick to growing wheat and vegetables to feed their more advanced 'brothers' in the Eastern Bloc. The factory was Gheorghiu-Dej's idea, a provocative display of defiance situated just ten miles from the Soviet border. Now it belonged to Ceaușescu. His vision of a new Romania would be built on heavy industry; steel factories, oil refineries, turbine halls, smelting plants – an industrial revolution a century behind that of the West. It represented a social contract with the working classes, the creation of a support base for communism and his regime. They gave him their backing, he provided them with free, modern housing and a regular income. Forty thousand workers moved into Galați. Many hundreds of thousands more migrated from the countryside to other towns and cities. Under Gheorghiu-Dej, industrial output had risen by 650 per cent in two decades, and now, under Ceaușescu, the rate would accelerate. His Tito-style reforms were entirely in the social sphere. When it came to heavy industry, the Romanian leader was still avowedly Stalinist.

Ceaușescu was escorted to a scale model of Galați in a giant glass display case, where architects pointed to the plant's salient features. The new leader's appetite for reading and digesting technical data often impressed the experts. Whether it was knowing the temperature of the blast furnaces or the factory's projected monthly output, he had a prodigious memory and would fire back reams of data. Although Ceaușescu suffered from huge lacunae in his general knowledge, heavy industry and technology were areas he thought he could master. He would have known that, splendid as Galați appeared, there was already a problem. Romania did not have enough iron ore to keep the plant working at full capacity. Previously, the lion's share of raw materials had been imported from the Soviet Union but, politically, that was now out of the question. Ceaușescu needed to look further afield, to the capitalist West.

Later that afternoon, he was given a hard-hat and posed with a pair of scissors ready to cut a long red ribbon and declare Galați officially open. The photographs show him relaxed, smiling and in control. Elena would have loved it. As director of the Central Institute of Chemical Research, she would have had every reason to be there. But her public appearances were still confined to that of 'accompanying wife', her potential as a politician still untapped. Meanwhile, Ceaușescu switched from displaying his pre-leadership morose face to sporting a camera-friendly lop-sided grin. With an eye on Western politicians, he had begun to understand the importance of image. From now on, his appearances would be more carefully stage-managed to bring him face to face with the masses. He adopted some of the techniques used by US presidential candidates, prioritizing photo-opportunities over committee meetings, attending sporting events and even kissing babies.

But some dangerous elements in the newly constituted Politburo were seething at his popularity. In the summer of 1967, Ceaușescu was walking down a corridor of the Central Committee building when he bumped into his old adversary, Alexandru Drăghici. The murderous interior minister was still influential amongst the Gheorghiu-Dej barons. Ceaușescu had a suggestion. Perhaps Drăghici would like to take a holiday? The whole of June promised to be sunny. He should leave immediately for Western Europe, perhaps take his family to see the Eiffel Tower and the Colosseum. Drăghici must have been puzzled by his boss's sudden generosity but he agreed nonetheless. As soon as his plane was safely in the air, Ceaușescu called a Central Committee Plenum.

A tanned and healthy Drăghici returned at the end of June just as Ceaușescu was preparing to reveal the Central Committee's decisions. The announcement would take place at the ministry of the interior, which oversaw the Securitate of which Drăghici was boss. Standing behind a pedestal, notes in hand, Ceaușescu announced that 'in the early years', the Securitate had 'lacked experience and ability' and had taken 'erroneous' guidance. The word 'erroneous' was one of his favourites. Everyone knew what it meant but no one dared say, as if de-coding was in itself a crime. 'Erroneous' was a euphemism for 'Soviet', once the highest of accolades, now sufficient for denunciation.

With Drăghici sitting awkwardly by his side, Ceaușescu went on speaking. The Securitate had committed 'abuses of Socialist legality', he said. Instead of discussing disagreements internally, their agents had 'interfered in Party life' – a euphemism for arresting and torturing innocent people. It could not be allowed to continue, said Ceaușescu; 'no citizen could be arrested without a grounded and proven reason'. The solution was to reduce the power of Drăghici's ministry and bring it firmly under Party control – a euphemism for the control of Ceaușescu.

He had not finished, however. The conclusion of his thoughts on Drăghici, and indeed on all the Gheorghiu-Dej loyalists, would be laid out in astonishing, un-euphemistic detail at a plenum of the Central Committee the following April. Hiding at the bottom of the agenda at that meeting was an item entitled 'The Rehabilitation of Certain RCP Activists'. Drăghici would have read it with a sense of foreboding. This was the result of the inquiry into how Lucrețiu Pătrășcanu had ended up being tried and executed. It amounted to a detailed chronology of a vindictive campaign against the former minister of law going back more than a decade. Drăghici listened intently as he was accused of setting up a team 'to get, at any cost, evidence to justify the assertion that Lucrețiu Pătrășcanu had allegedly been an agent of the Siguranța [the king's secret police] and an Anglo-American spy.'[7] He was, said the report, guilty of organizing the trial of Pătrășcanu and his sixteen co-defendants in contravention of the most 'elementary procedural guarantees'. We can only image Drăghici's face as his previously stammering rival turned into a vengeful judge and jury, reciting without emotion charge after career-ending charge.

The allegations then moved on to other senior Party figures. The late Gheorghiu-Dej was next. Under his stewardship, declared Ceaușescu, the Party had regarded differences of opinion as criminal offences rather than matters for discussion. The former leader, he said, was directly responsible for 'intervening in the inquiry [into Pătrășcanu]... and adding notes to the reports on interrogations.' This was electrifying stuff. Ceaușescu was unpicking the defining purges of the previous regime, accusing Gheorghiu-Dej and his henchmen of dishonesty and conspiracy to murder.

Next on the agenda was the fate of the Party's former general secretary, Ștefan Foriș. He had been bludgeoned to death with a crowbar in the foyer of Party headquarters in 1946. His assassination was motivated by unfounded evidence, said Ceaușescu. Gheorghiu-Dej and his entire Central Committee were culpable. The assassin himself, Gheorghe Pintilie, the first director of the Securitate, had acted outside any legal bounds.

At the end of the plenum, Pătrășcanu was 'rehabilitated' – communist-speak for a pardon in order that a new leader could punish his rivals. Pătrășcanu was no longer an enemy, but a victim. Everything had been turned on its head. The men responsible for this 'foul' and 'monstrous' frame-up were, by implication, the new enemies. Ștefan Foriș, whose battered corpse had never been found, was also rehabilitated. So were several of the old guard who were executed in Moscow during Stalin's purges. Marcel Pauker was among them. His wife, Ana Pauker, an earlier scapegoat for the 'excesses' of the regime, was not. Ceaușescu's personal dislike of her ran too deep. Pauker aside, Ceaușescu mythologized his links to the founders of the movement, skipping the post-war generation, reaching back to a period of revolutionary purity uncorrupted by power.

As for Drăghici, he was dismissed from all his posts and, days later, expelled from the Party. The man who had once been Gheorghiu-Dej's chosen successor – Gheorghe Apostol – soon followed Drăghici into forced retirement, as did several other members of the old guard. Ceaușescu's own lack of culpability hinged on a highly fortuitous quirk in the timeline. Although he had been one of Gheorghiu-Dej's inner circle himself, he had not become a member of the Politburo until precisely forty-eight hours *after* Pătrășcanu's death, meaning that he could not have contributed to the conspiracy.

The ousting of Chivu Stoica (president of the State Council, and a rival for the leadership) came next, during the same wave of purges, and freed up an inviting new role for Ceaușescu. The State Council was the supreme executive body of the Socialist Republic of Romania, a fifteen-man assembly that implemented laws, controlled the budget and could even appoint and dismiss ministers. Crucially, it was separate from the Party in order to prevent the potential abuse of power. Ceaușescu himself had criticized Gheorghiu-Dej for merging the two and leading both. One of his first decisions as general secretary had been to separate state and Party, in an apparent eagerness to re-introduce collective leadership. But in December 1967, with Stoica gone, Ceaușescu dropped the charade and became undisputed leader of both.

By 1969, only two former members of Gheorghiu-Dej's Politburo remained: Ion Gheorghe Maurer and Emil Bodnăraș – the two who had proposed and seconded Ceaușescu for the leadership. The rest were disgraced but allowed to keep their freedom. Drăghici was put in charge of a state-run agricultural company outside Bucharest, and outlived Ceaușescu. His final years were spent living with his daughter in Hungary from where he fought a Romanian extradition request to put him on trial for assassination and torture. He died in 1993. Chivu Stoica committed suicide in 1975 by shooting himself in the head with a hunting rifle. Other former Gheorghiu-Dej loyalists went quietly, apart from Gheorghe Apostol who departed in a final display of near-suicidal pyrotechnics.

After the plenum, Apostol sat down in the drawing room of his villa in Primăverii and began writing a lengthy letter to the Party newspaper, *Scînteia*. The covering note set the tone. 'I send you this article with a request that you publish it... If, indeed, freedom of the press exists, let us see if you can publish articles that express personal opinions.' Apostol then began setting out his various grievances. He acknowledged that Gheorghiu-Dej and other 'beloved leaders' could be 'firmly placed in the category of assassins', but then lambasted Ceaușescu for blaming everything on Drăghici, who, he said, had never been afforded a proper defence. The Party, said the former foundry-worker, was run by 'shepherds and railway men' who went around trampling on non-Party members with impunity. Public debate was 'a farce', he continued, there was no real freedom of the press and everyone mechanically followed the views of the leaders, who he described as 'two or three imbeciles'. With one final – and, we can imagine, rather satisfying – flourish, Apostol wrote of Ceaușescu: 'As long as the biggest zero, the man who thinks his opinion is infallible, is there at the top, as long as his deputies in the assembly are robots... we will do nothing with pleasure, and what we do will be done with disgust and dissimulation.'[8]

It was a roaring, and largely accurate, rebuke of the leadership, one that under the former regime would have led to a prison cell. The editor of *Scînteia* was clearly not tempted by a barnstorming scoop, not even in these supposedly enlightened times. He read the letter and decided not to publish. Instead, its contents were passed to Emil Bodnăraș, by now the Party's veteran peacemaker, who persuaded Apostol that his future probably lay some distance from Bucharest. In Buenos Aires, to be precise, where he became ambassador. It was another benign outcome, evidence of Ceaușescu's growing confidence that critics and former rivals could pose no threat to his leadership. The big zero was now running Romania unopposed, happily soaking up the fawning compliments of his Standing Presidium and beginning to believe that he was truly a leader of exceptional talent.

To congratulate him for his newly discovered liberalism, an unexpected visitor arrived from America. Richard Nixon had no official position at the time. The former US vice-president was a private individual practising law but was on the verge of announcing his candidacy for the 1968 presidential elections. He had flown to Moscow in the hope of starting informal discussions with Brezhnev but had been snubbed, and boarded a plane for Bucharest instead, hoping to meet the much-talked about young communist leader courageously pulling his country away from Russia. Ceauşescu rolled out the red carpet. It was an astonishing meeting, under the circumstances. Here was an Eastern Bloc leader entertaining a Republican Cold-Warrior, parading him around the capital in open-top cars in a manner supposed to be reserved for visiting Soviet dignitaries. Ceauşescu was thumbing his nose at Moscow, strutting his independence and even presenting himself as a potential bridge between the US and his allies in China. His warm reception for the holidaying presidential candidate would prove to be time and money well spent.

*

The ancient pine forests around the Polish border with Czechoslovakia were quiet at night but for the howling of wolves and the occasionally noisy foraging of wild boar. If a lone villager had been out that way on 20 August 1968, he would have seen a line of yellow headlights flashing through the trees on the Polish side, west of the city of Legnica, moving slowly towards the checkpoint which was a mere 120 miles from Prague. Had he waited, he would have heard the growl of diesel engines as a column of hunter-green military vehicles swept by, canvas sides flapping to reveal seated rows of anxious soldiers. There were similar scenes on the forested border with the Soviet Union to the east, and on the Hungarian border in the south. Troops were moving into Czechoslovakia from all neighbouring Warsaw Pact countries.

At 11.10 p.m. that evening, Western security forces realized something was afoot. They had lost radio contact with Prague.

Telephone signals were jammed. Over in Moscow, dozens of armed An-12 transporter planes taxied on the runway. One by one, they took off westwards carrying artillery and several hundred light tanks.

Moments later, the Russian ambassador to Czechoslovakia, Stepan Chervonenko, arrived in his limousine at Prague Castle with an important message for the Czech president. Just before midnight, the contents were passed on to an all-night sitting of the Politburo of the Czech Communist Party. The room fell silent. The Kremlin was informing Czechoslovakia that 'allied troops' were entering its territory. A Soviet-led invasion was underway.

The first secretary of the Czech Communist Party, Alexander Dubček, knew that his reforms were the reason for this intervention. Three years younger than Ceaușescu, Dubček could not have been more different. Charismatic, naturally gregarious and politically flexible, he seemed more like a democratically elected Western politician than a communist trained in Moscow. Dubček had taken over from the widely loathed hard-line Stalinist, Antonin Novotny, seven months earlier and was guiding his country through genuine liberal reforms. Throughout the spring of 1968, censorship was lifted. The powers of the secret police were dramatically curtailed. Consumer goods were the new mantra of Czechoslovakian economists, and Dubček was even mooting the possibility of multi-party elections. For his rejoicing citizens, the Prague Spring was 'socialism with a human face'; to Brezhnev, watching closely from his office in the Kremlin, it was a direct threat to Moscow's imperial authority. If allowed to flourish, Prague's sweeping reforms might become contagious and spread to the rest of the Eastern Bloc.

At 1.30 a.m., Dubček and his Politburo colleagues voted 7–4 to condemn the invasion (a Stalinist rump still existed in the Party that welcomed Soviet 'assistance', but the rest were reformers). Within half an hour, a proclamation was issued over Czech radio, calling on all citizens to remain calm while condemning the Soviet invasion as 'contravening all principles governing relations between socialist states'. At 9 a.m., with Soviet fighter aircraft roaring overhead, Russian officers arrived at Dubček's office, arrested him and several others, and spirited them off to Moscow. By lunchtime, tanks blocked the Charles Bridge beneath Prague Castle. Traffic came to a standstill, and an invasion force of 200,000 soldiers was occupying Czechoslovakia. The Russians had taken over their miscreant satellite state and were re-imposing Kremlin rules.

In Bucharest, Ceauşescu had received word of a possible invasion of Czechoslovakia several days earlier, through a source in the Warsaw Pact command. The Romanians had not been invited to take part. Neither had the reformist Tito in Yugoslavia or the unreformed Stalinist, Enver Hoxha, in Albania. All were kept in the dark, while five core members of the Warsaw Pact contributed troops to the operation: the Soviet Union, Bulgaria, Poland, East Germany and Hungary.

On the morning of 21 August, Romanian TV and radio announced a rally in Republic Square, where Ceauşescu would address crowds from the balcony of the Central Committee building. He bounded out like a prize-fighter, hands held aloft, punching the air in time to the roars of the crowd. 100,000 people surged along Bucharest's main thoroughfare, Calea Victoriei, past King Carol's former palace and all the way up to the Athénée Palace Hotel; students in berets and black sunglasses, fashionable men in turtle-neck sweaters, women in cream-coloured raincoats and knee-high boots. It was hardly London or Paris in terms of fashionable attire but these crowds were very different from the monochrome masses of the Gheorghiu-Dej era. The applause was deafening and spontaneous. There was no orchestration, no threats from the Securitate. These were high-spirited Romanian youths on the cusp of joining a world that they had only read about in the newly liberated press; the Beatles, American jeans, cowboy boots, Steve McQueen, Marlboro cigarettes – all seemed within reach.

Ceaușescu was followed onto the balcony by Emil Bodnăraș and Ion Gheorghe Maurer, and then by more than seventy senior Party figures, all wearing summer suits and skinny ties, enjoying wave after wave of public adulation. Microphone cables spilled over the balcony to huge mobile amplifiers. TV cameras were positioned on top of buses and rooftops. Spectators hung from trees. Ceaușescu surveyed the scene for a moment and then began. 'Dear Comrades... the Central Committee... the state and government... representatives of state organizations... all the unions... have decided unanimously... to express their full solidarity... with the Czech people and the Czech Communist Party.' The crowd's acclamation sounded like the roar of a jet fighter. Ceaușescu paused and then continued. 'Dear Comrades and citizens of Romania... the invasion of Czechoslovakia by troops of five nation states is a grave mistake...' There were more cheers. Some stared at the balcony, mesmerized. '...it is a danger to the peace of Europe... and to the future of Socialism.' Ceaușescu had notes in his hand but he did not consult them. He was rolling with the crowd, discovering a new mint-cool clarity. He seemed free from his stammer, from procedure, from Party etiquette and careful language. This was what leadership felt like. He was taking on Moscow. 'It is inconceivable that a country has to raise arms', he began gently, 'to defend its independence, its equality of rights...' – his voice was rising towards a bellowing crescendo – 'for one socialist state to infringe the liberty of another.' Now he was gesturing wildly, emphasizing every word by bringing down his outstretched arm as if he was chopping invisible logs. 'No country', he thundered, 'can call themselves "advisor" on the manner in which socialism should be constructed... it is the business of each individual nation!'

What became known as 'the balcony speech' was courageous, pointed and enormously popular with the crowd. It was the best

Ceaușescu would ever deliver. He had explicitly condemned Moscow and the so-called Brezhnev Doctrine by which Pact members could intervene to put a stop to any perceived threat to Socialist rule – or, as they put it, to supply 'brotherly protection', and had done so on a very public stage. Moscow viewed his defiance as a threat to the unity of the Warsaw Pact, and therefore an act of ideological vandalism against communism itself. The Kremlin could not afford for such disobedience to become contagious. Romania needed to be taught a lesson.

Soon after the rally, Ceaușescu sent reinforcements all along his vulnerable border with the Soviet Union. In towns and villages, he created guerrilla units, mobilizing the masses in preparation to defend the country – and, therefore, the Party – from Soviet imperialism. From now on, Party, state and indeed Ceaușescu himself would be one and the same. Anyone disagreeing with the Party was placing the security and independence of Romania at risk. Any perceived lack of unity was a weakness that might be exploited by the Soviet aggressor. Any dissenter was a traitor. The 'balcony speech' represented the high-water mark of Ceaușescu's popularity and his best opportunity to create genuine unity behind his leadership. Unlike Czechoslovakia, if Moscow attacked Romania, Ceaușescu was going to resist.

*

President Richard Milhous Nixon was standing on board the deck of the USS *Hornet*, 900 miles south-west of Hawaii, with a pair of powerful binoculars pressed to his eyes. It was the summer of 1969 and he was hoping to spot a silver capsule hurtling through the skies of the South Pacific on the last leg of a journey that had taken it to the moon and back. At 12.50 p.m. on 24 July, Commander Neil Armstrong and the crew of Apollo 11 splashed down close to Nixon's ship, having beaten the Soviets to the lunar surface. They were scooped out of the water and placed in a silver quarantine pod with a small window, through which

Nixon, basking in the lights of the television cameras, thanked them for an astonishing American feat. The Space Race had been driven by Cold War rivalries – it had its roots in the nuclear arms race – and the spectacular success of Apollo 11 was a much-needed boost for the West in a year when American casualties in Vietnam surpassed those of the Korean War. Hundreds of body bags were arriving at US airports each week. Nixon was looking for a face-saving way out of the conflict and would leave the USS *Hornet* for a tour of Asia in the hope of finding one.

The Chinese, he believed, were the key to peace, but America had not spoken to them for twenty years. After visiting the Philippines, Indonesia, Thailand and South Vietnam, Nixon flew half way around the world to meet someone who he knew was in regular touch with Peking and who might act as a go-between.

Crowds ten-deep lined the boulevards of central Bucharest, waving plastic American flags as Nixon and Ceaușescu swept by in an open-topped limousine. The date was 2 August 1969, just nine days after Apollo 11's splashdown, and excited Romanians sensed they were part of history. The fact that Nixon had chosen their country at this crucial time seemed to them evidence of the high regard held for their leader, and a signal that Romania could expect to enjoy increased prominence on the Western half of the world stage. The cavalcade sped along Calea Victoriei beneath giant communist-style portraits of both Ceaușescu and Nixon, circling the Arcul de Triumf, where the US president spontaneously leapt from his vehicle to meet the crowds. His security detail looked on with some disquiet as Nixon was swept away in the friendly melee and ended up dancing around the monument submerged in a sea of waving arms. This was the first state visit of an American president to a communist satellite state, and even Nixon's National Security Advisor, Henry Kissinger, admitted later that he was 'startled' when Nixon first suggested the idea. The crowd sensed Romania was at a fork in the road.

The timing, a year after the Soviet-led invasion of

Czechoslovakia, was also significant. Moscow had been piling the pressure on Romania for displays of loyalty and, with the threat of a Russian invasion still very much alive, Ceauşescu had tried to keep a low profile. Images of Nixon dancing in the streets of Bucharest were bound to stir things but Ceauşescu calculated that the Kremlin valued its 'peaceful co-existence' with America too much to risk marching into Romania. He was treading a thin line and, according to Nixon, doing so with 'consummate skill'.

From the street parade, Nixon and Ceauşescu went straight into private talks. Ceauşescu began by asking for more cooperation with America over science and technology. 'I have a chief in my home,' smiled the Romanian leader, 'who is Director of Chemistry.' Nixon had been well briefed. 'Your wife,' he nodded in agreement, and the two men laughed. A decision was made to send an American science mission to Romania.

Ceauşescu's main purpose was to secure US economic assistance, in the form of loans and increased trade, all of which could be achieved if Romania were to be granted Most Favoured Nation status (MFN). No Eastern Bloc country had been awarded such economic privilege by Washington, not even Western-leaning Yugoslavia, and to do so would cause a minor sensation on the world stage. Not only was Romania trading with Communist North Vietnam, which debarred it from qualifying, it would also be seen as incongruous for the headquarters of world capitalism to be bolstering the communist economy of a Soviet satellite in the midst of the Cold War. Nevertheless, Nixon promised he would look into it. Building bridges with Eastern Bloc states was an excellent way of eroding Soviet power, and Romania's constant quarrelling with Moscow meant that it was a favourite target.

'Tell me,' ventured Nixon, 'how far can our relations go without embarrassment to Romania or its president?' Ceauşescu spoke without consulting his aides, as he did in most of these meetings. It was his directness, his 'straight-from-the-shoulder exchanges' that Nixon admired. '… relations with the US cannot in any way impede relations with others,' replied Ceauşescu. 'It is true that our Soviet friends were slightly disturbed by your visit. We advised them thirty-six hours before it was announced. They never commented officially. The Soviet comrades find this difficult to accept. The Soviet Union was first in space. The US was first on the moon. Changes are taking place.'⁹

Then Nixon crept onto the subject of how to manoeuvre Russia and China – both of whom backed the communists of North Vietnam – into a situation where they would be prepared to negotiate peace. Ceauşescu's grasp of historical facts was impressive. He spoke sweepingly about remnants of the 'feudal' era in China and French support for the United States in the War of Independence, and gently chided Nixon for getting involved in Asia in the first place: 'In Vietnam, all your spending and support did not help to preserve the existing system. You spent about 25–30 billion dollars on the war. If you spend 2 billion dollars in Vietnam peacefully, you will have more development and will have made a friend.'¹⁰ It was all part of his over-arching philosophy of non-intervention, of leaving nation states well alone.

When Prime Minister Maurer was asked by Nixon to contribute to the discussion, Ceauşescu allowed him the floor for a moment and then interrupted sharply – 'I disagree with him' – before continuing to expound his own views. It has to be remembered just how remarkable this meeting was. On the rare occasions Gheorghiu-Dej spoke with American representatives, they were lowly US embassy staff who would grab him informally at the end of a conference somewhere in the Eastern Bloc. Talks sometimes amounted to little more than complaints about their respective embassy staff being tailed in Washington and Bucharest, and invariably there were Russian officials present. Romania could do nothing on its own. Gheorghiu-Dej had been affable enough and had built some bridges with the Americans, but Ceaușescu's summit with Nixon was of an entirely different order.

Nixon was impressed with Ceaușescu's unique access to all sides. The Romanian leader was speaking with representatives of the Vietcong, the communists' Provisional Revolutionary Government in South Vietnam, the Kremlin and, of course, Peking. 'Frankly,' ventured Nixon, 'if it serves your interest and the interest of your government, we would welcome your playing a mediating role between us and China.'

Instead of rushing in, Ceaușescu suggested they speak again over dinner and resume formal talks the next morning. So, how did Nicolae Ceaușescu, the barely literate shoe-maker's apprentice who had quietly navigated the backwaters of Communist Party committees and cadres, transform himself into what appeared to be a skilful and well-informed international negotiator? One of those who worked closely with him, the former Romanian ambassador to the United States, Silviu Brucan, described him as 'very smart, with a peasant's canny intelligence, and a prodigious memory'. Brucan later became one of Ceaușescu's chief critics but still marvelled at the 'prompt intellectual reactions' that enabled him to beat men like Nixon and Brezhnev to the punch.

'Although he had started with a vacuum of knowledge,' says Brucan, 'he learned fast, but did so with all the defects of a self-taught person – in his case, big gaps of knowledge in geography and history and, worse, in economics and technical sciences.' But, says Brucan, 'precisely because he was half-educated, he became the last encyclopaedist.'[11]

Some academics were less generous. Those who have studied Ceaușescu's diplomatic skills point out that he was merely reciting the same well-rehearsed arguments agreed by his entourage, a kind of 'groupthink' that he reflected back on whoever he spoke with. There was no analysis or questioning involved, just straightforward repetition. Ceaușescu had been marinated in austere Stalinist ideology all his adult life, and remembered phrases and thoughts that he could parrot back. Some of them he could apply to international events, such as the war in Vietnam or Russian attempts to subordinate Romania. In Marxist texts, for instance, imperial colonialism is supposed to be the highest stage of capitalism, something that Ceaușescu would have studied while in prison. As such, his mantra against Soviet imperialism and the territorial expansion of a country beyond its established borders were bread-and-butter maxims that he could repeat ad infinitum. Another point to bear in mind is that the notes taken in these diplomatic meetings would not necessarily convey the language used by Ceaușescu. Note-takers concentrated on capturing the ideas, not how the leader expressed them.

In Bucharest, Ceaușescu probed to find out whether Nixon would accept a broad-based coalition government in South Vietnam. He was relaying questions on behalf of the Vietcong, whose ambassador, he told the US president, he had spoken to just days before. Nixon suggested it might be possible but only if the Western-backed president, Nguyễn Văn Thiệu, were to be included in the plan. Ceaușescu recommended that Nixon be more flexible.

'I want to emphasize', said Nixon after a moment's reflection, 'why we cannot agree to a coalition... it is a hard word for us.' Quick as a flash, Ceaușescu invited the Duke University law scholar to try a little harder with his vocabulary. 'Change the word, then,' said Ceaușescu. Nixon did as requested. For the rest of the meeting he used the term 'mixed commission' instead.

In the end, the Romanian leader agreed to relay US messages to Chairman Mao in Peking, making him aware that Nixon's White House wanted to talk. 'We shall tell our opinion to the Chinese, and your opinion of this problem,' said Ceaușescu. 'We shall act to establish relations on the basis of mutual understanding.' His reward, if all went well, would be American loans and trade to help Romania's heavy industry flourish according to his unyielding Stalinist economic doctrine.

*

In a locked office in a quiet corner of the Bucharest Faculty of Chemistry, a middle-aged woman sat waiting to prove her academic brilliance. Sharp-featured, with a long masculine nose and eyes that she habitually narrowed to communicate her suspicion of others, for Elena Ceaușescu this was a momentous day. She was about to present her PhD thesis, 'The Stereospecific Polymerization of Isoprene', to a board of examiners in order to be confirmed a Doctor of Chemistry.

Oral examinations were, by tradition, open to the public in Bucharest. One brave and curious soul, a subordinate of Elena at the Chemical Institute called Mircea Corciovei, turned up that day to watch. The time and room were displayed on a notice board but the door was not only locked, it seemed that no one was inside. When Corciovei inquired, he was informed that the meeting had happened 'in camera' earlier that morning.[12] Of course, no one knows whether the meeting really happened or not. No one knows whether Elena Ceaușescu was even there. It was just as likely that she sent a minion to pick up her certificate. The thesis Elena submitted had been stolen from the Petrochemical Institute in Ploiești. The researcher who had written it vanished a few days later and was not seen in the city again.[13]

By the following day, the now Doctor Elena Ceaușescu was back behind her desk at the Institute, promptly as always at 10.30 a.m. Just around the corner from the location of Elena's alleged examination was the Engineering faculty which, in an era of unprecedented industrial expansion, was one of the most popular at Bucharest University. Among the students that year was a young dreamer called Gheorghe Iosifescu, a skinny youth with coarse yellow hair, high cheekbones that seemed Slavic in origin, and blue eyes that stared intensely from behind newly acquired John Lennon-style glasses. Gheorghe had been raised in the oil city of Ploiești, which had suffered the worst bombing in Romania during the war. The city's streets were perpetually filled with builders and heavy machinery, the population scarred with distrust of foreign leaders and domestic politicians alike. Gheorghe had buried himself in bootlegged Western music and books, much against his parents' wishes. 'What is the point in literature and the arts?' they would say. 'You cannot feed yourself on a plate of words.' So, when Gheorghe went to university, it was to study metallurgy with an eye on the futuristic steel plant at Galați and the promise of scientific trips abroad.

There had been some excitement in the dorm on the morning of 21 August 1968, when students had heard Ceaușescu was about to make his historic 'balcony speech'. But while his colleagues rushed to Republic Square, Gheorghe stayed behind. He'd managed to buy himself a tape-to-tape recording machine with a small hand-held microphone. There was just one Romanian record label at the time, Electrecord, which made poor quality copies of Western rock bands and sold them in coffee bars around the university. The recordings cracked and hissed. Gheorghe preferred recording directly from pirate radio stations, like Radio Luxembourg, waiting for the DJ to announce The Beatles or The Animals and then quickly pressing the large plastic buttons that started the spools turning.

Ceaușescu's liberalization of literature and the arts coincided precisely with Gheorghe Iosifescu's arrival in Bucharest, and gathered momentum during the events of the Prague Spring. Suddenly, some Western books and films were available, though most of them were years out of date and edited to remove 'pornographic' content. Cowboy films were the favourite, posing no threat to Party ideology and rarely featuring nudity. *Stagecoach* became one of the most watched movies of 1967, John Ford's Western making its debut in Bucharest twenty-eight years after opening in London and New York. *Gone with the Wind* was the smash hit of 1970, a mere thirty-one years after its release in the West. The British horror film, *Dracula: Prince of Darkness*, starring Christopher Lee and released in 1966, was banned though. Ceauşescu regarded it as a slur on his nationalist hero.

Exhilarated by the new openness, Gheorghe Iosifescu set his heart on becoming a theatre critic. He assumed Bucharest was moving towards the cultural freedom enjoyed in Paris or London, and that Moscow was fading from view.

Other liberal intellectuals felt the same. Many were so invigorated by events in the summer of 1968 that despite being opposed to communism, they joined the Party. Twenty-three well-known writers signed a public letter in the *Literary Gazette* declaring their 'complete agreement with the position of the Party and of the Romanian government, as defined by Comrade Ceauşescu'.[14] It was an important step for the RCP, to gain the support and trust of the normally critical intelligentsia. But Gheorghe Iosifescu refused to believe Ceauşescu was sincere. I know this because Gheorghe was my father-in-law, the son of Victoria Angelescu, who spoke to me often about the early days of Ceauşescu. He spent that summer trying to find himself a pair of authentic American jeans and learning the chords for Simon and Garfunkel's 'Sound of Silence'. He would need to be quick about it. That summer was to be the high-water mark of Ceauşescu's reforms, a brief glimpse of hope before the leader decided to row back into the darkness and the cold. Meanwhile, he had an illicit money-making scheme to organise.

*

There was an unusual chicken farm in the little village of Periş near Bucharest. It didn't look like much from the outside, just a row of metal warehouses at the end of a single-track road, but inside was a state-of-the-art facility, its clucking inhabitants lifted into the air by robotic arms, beheaded, plucked and packed in a matter of minutes. It was positively futuristic in comparison with other livestock farms in Romania, and was actually the product of a rare collaboration with Israel. But this wasn't about chickens at all. The entire construction was really a secret payment, as part of an outrageous scheme aimed at boosting the country's cash-starved economy through an international trade in human beings.

We must go back to the 1950s and Gheorghiu-Dej in order to understand the project's genesis. Something like 375,000 Romanian Jews had survived the Second World War (approximately half the pre-war population) and the then Romanian leader found himself on the horns of a dilemma. If he granted Jews the right to leave Romania and settle in the newly-created State of Israel, he would be accused by Arab states of supplying Israel with soldiers. If, on the other hand, he prevented them from leaving, Israel and its Western allies would accuse him of trampling on their human rights. And so Gheorghiu-Dej oscillated. When he announced a sudden lifting of emigration restrictions in 1958, queues a mile long formed outside the visa office in Bucharest, with 100,000 Jews eager to leave for the Middle East. Gheorghiu-Dej was furious at what he considered their 'disloyalty', but an idea gradually began to take shape. If Jews were so keen to leave the country, then a ransom fee would have to paid.

The sale of Romanian Jews was brokered through an innovative British-Jewish businessman called Henry Jakober, who lived in a grand property at 55 Park Lane in London. A refugee from Hungary, Jakober was an entrepreneur with imaginative ways of doing business and a plethora of contacts among spy agencies in Britain and Romania. In the beginning, his scheme to buy the freedom of Jews from Communist Romania was limited to a few private deals. It worked like this: Jakober would be approached at 55 Park Lane by wealthy relatives and friends of Romanian Jews – some of whom were being held in labour camps, others who were simply eager to leave a country that had treated their ancestors so deplorably. The names of the ransomed individuals would be handed over to Romanian intelligence, and a fee would be calculated for their release. Jakober would then deposit the agreed sum in a Swiss bank account, to be paid to the Romanian authorities when the Jewish refugees had safely arrived in the West.

The trade soon attracted the attention of Mossad, Israel's foreign intelligence service. Apparently sceptical at first, on moral grounds, the Israeli state soon became actively involved, as a way of freeing Jews and contributing to the growth of Israel. But Gheorghiu-Dej was worried. If all this became public, there would be an international outcry. The Soviet leader, Khrushchev, reassured him. Whilst on a visit to Bucharest in 1958, he urged Gheorghiu-Dej to continue the scheme but with a more discreet method of payment; trading Jews in return for merchandise would be far easier to hide. Soon, construction of the hi-tech chicken farm was underway (organized by Jakober) and in return, 500 Romanian Jews were heading for Israel.

Buoyed by the scheme's success, Gheorghiu-Dej's government decided that trading Jews was an excellent way of raising finance for various other agricultural schemes. Several pig farms were built with Israeli money, along with turkey farms, sheep farms and five more chicken farms. Exports from these facilities earned $8–10 million a year, which is said to have been placed in secret bank accounts controlled exclusively by Gheorghiu-Dej.[15] By 1965, Romania's annual authorization of exit visas was dependent on eggs, chickens, turkey, beef, and even corn flakes. At one point, Bucharest demanded the means to breed the best cows in the world, and soon diplomatic pouches were being sent to Romania weighed down with bull sperm in return for Jews.[16]

It was only after Gheorghiu-Dej's death that Ceaușescu was informed about the secret trade. On learning of what became known as the 'Jakober affair', it is said Ceaușescu had a kind of 'nuclear explosion', declaring that it would destroy Romania's image abroad. But two years later, he turned to an aide and asked, 'Is this man Jakober still alive?'

Under Ceauşescu's stewardship in the 1970s, the trade in Jews became even more elaborate and far more lucrative. Financing animal farms was no longer adequate, Ceauşescu was prepared to throw caution to the wind and demand direct cash payments in exchange for Jewish exit visas.

The ransom money was to be calculated according to a sliding scale. At the lower end were unemployed Jews and children, who were considered 'Category D' and required a ransom fee of around $2,000. More well-educated Jews were deemed 'Category A' and could only be released from the country for a fee of $6,000. In exceptional cases, that rose to $250,000.

Communist Romania 'sold' many tens of thousands of Jews to Israel. Between 1958 and 1965 (under Gheorghiu-Dej) the number granted exit visas was 107,540. Between 1965 and 1989 (under Ceauşescu) it was 58,817. Not all required a ransom fee but many thousands did, and the sums that Romania stood to gain were enormous.

The secret trade in Jews provided an important source of income for Ceauşescu. He never drew an official salary and, in fact, never actually earned a penny in his life, having worked in exchange for food and lodging when he was an apprentice shoe-maker. The ransom money constituted an emergency slush fund. He kept it in secret bank accounts alongside the proceeds from other covert operations carried out by his foreign intelligence services – the 'Departamentul de Informatii Externe' (or DIE). According to the former chief of the DIE, Ion Pacepa, these accounts contained around $400 million by the mid-1970s. They were used to buy Western motorcars for Ceauşescu's children and custom-built armoured Mercedes limousines for the leader and his wife, along with new acquisitions for Elena's expanding collection of diamonds. The First Lady was notorious for purchasing jewels while on trips abroad but on most occasions her aides persuaded the foreign hosts to present her with expensive 'gifts'. 'This is for a rainy day,' Ceauşescu would whisper to Pacepa as they discussed the slush fund while walking along the moonlit pathways around his villa. But everything in Ceaușescu's life was paid for by the state. He only ever managed to spend a fraction of his ransom monies – according to Pacepa, about $4 million.[17]

Meanwhile, Ceaușescu's apparent magnanimity towards the Jews was playing well on the international stage. The Americans, in particular, were impressed. Free movement of people was a pre-condition of US loans and trade (as was ending exports to North Vietnam) and Ceaușescu's granting of exit visas to Israel was used to help smooth the way to Most Favoured Nation status. 'As a result of a carefully negotiated understanding,' concluded a White House briefing, 'Romania permits a small emigration of Jews to Israel, which satisfies the letter of the law.'[18]

To the West, Ceaușescu was a rare beacon of light in a cold and unresponsive communist world. Nixon and Kissinger pointed admiringly to his continued relations with Israel after the Six-Day War in 1967, Romania being the only Eastern Bloc state to remain an ally. Another piece of deft footwork allowed him to remain friends with the major Arab nations at the same time. He soon offered a channel of communication between Israel, Palestine, the Arabs and the US, and even tried to host his own Middle East peace talks in Bucharest (although the Americans called his plan 'rather naïve' and none of the Arab nations turned up). Still, Romania at the end of the 1960s was punching well above its weight in the arena of international affairs.

*

It was a warm wind that greeted Nicolae Ceaușescu as his Russian-made plane touched down on the tarmac of Los Angeles International Airport in October 1970. He and Elena paused, smiling, at the top of the steps, before greeting a short line of dignitaries and heading off for their first night on American soil. The Ceaușescus were booked into the Disneyland Hotel.

Romanian President Greets 'Animals' at Disneyland.

President Nicolae Ceauşescu of Romania established informal diplomatic relations today with Mickey Mouse.

The Party was escorted to Disneyland's City Hall, where Mr Ceauşescu, a broad smile on his customary sober countenance, shook hands with Mickey Mouse and was presented with the official Disneyland flag. Mrs Ceauşescu received a Mickey Mouse wrist watch.

Mr Ceauşescu then took a "jungle cruise"... during which he was snapped at by animated crocodiles, saw elephants bathing in waterfalls, and was "attacked" by spear-carrying Africans.

Mr Ceauşescu also visited the Haunted Mansion and the Disneyland version of the United States atomic submarine, Triton.

The New York Times, 16 October 1970

Happily reinvigorated by the charms of Western capitalism, the Ceauşescus flew to San Francisco in a US presidential aircraft, equipped with a bedroom and office, where they were entertained by the directors of the Bank of America. They sailed in a yacht around San Francisco Bay before heading east to spend a night at colonial Williamsburg in Virginia, and then north to see Niagara Falls. Ceauşescu had never visited a department store before and when they arrived in New York, Elena persuaded him to accept an invitation to Macy's on Herald Square. The couple were overcome with the variety of luxury merchandise on display and could hardly fail to have been impressed when comparing it with the meagre offerings in Bucharest, even in shops reserved for the Party elite. One Romanian official reported that Ceauşescu thought Macy's was putting on a show on behalf of the US government, cramming the shelves with extravagant goods that were never normally available in order to mislead him about the achievements of capitalism. In Romania, it was not uncommon for shops to do precisely that for visiting dignitaries, so perhaps Ceaușescu did, indeed, suspect some kind of consumer-themed Potemkin village, but it seems more likely the couple were genuinely impressed. It was during this visit that Elena developed her life-long passion for extravagant fur coats, designer shoes and expensive handbags.[19]

The trip was organized around the ten-day celebrations of the 25th anniversary of the United Nations, and again, Ceaușescu's attendance had ruffled Moscow's feathers. Brezhnev had ordered that no Warsaw Pact head of state attend because of sharpening differences with the US over the Middle East, but Ceaușescu ignored him. He spoke at the UN of 'national independence' and of the need for all countries to withdraw their armed forces from foreign lands, an emphatic rebuke of Brezhnev's policy of intervention into the affairs of 'misbehaving' satellites. When he visited the White House at the end of the tour, Ceaușescu was the first Romanian head of state to do so.

On 26 October 1970, hundreds of US dignitaries lined up on the White House lawn, hoping for their first glimpse of a communist leader. A Marine band played a dramatic drum roll to coincide with Ceaușescu stepping from his limousine, like the build-up to a breathtaking magic trick, and out he came, on cue, into the autumn sunlight, followed by an immaculately dressed Elena in a designer lilac suit.

Later, standing beside Nixon on an outdoor platform in front of America's political elite, Ceaușescu appeared less comfortable than he had in Disneyland. These were the kind of people he had spent his career railing against and now they represented his first line of defence against Moscow. He would have recognized the irony: capitalists were now helping secure Communist Romania's independence.

Later, in the Oval Office, the talk was of Vietnam, and how China and Russia still held the key to peace. Since his last meeting with Nixon, Ceaușescu had sent his prime minister, Ion Gheorghe Maurer, to Peking, on the way back from Ho Chi Minh's funeral. Maurer had relayed Nixon's eagerness to re-establish diplomatic channels and now Ceaușescu wanted to claim his reward. 'I remember with satisfaction', said Ceaușescu, 'that you said that the problems [of achieving Most Favoured Nation status] could be solved in the not-too-distant future.' Nixon had bad news. There were still obstacles, he said. The US Congress would not allow MFN status while Romania continued trading with Communist North Korea. Perhaps, suggested Nixon, they could arrange something via the back door, under a different agreement, to sneak it through.

'To be very frank,' Ceaușescu confided, 'at present the Romanian economy is running a balance of payments deficit of $300 million... Romania would welcome credits from America under favourable terms.' The sum was the equivalent of $2 billion in today's money, a huge amount for a developing country desperately trying to find new trade partners to replace its former backers in Moscow. The admission provides a startling insight into a looming economic disaster that would plague Romania for the next two decades, condemning the entire nation to dire poverty, rationing, and forced labour.

There was more work for Ceaușescu as a go-between. Now he would need to help prepare the ground for a possible meeting between Nixon and Mao.[20] If it happened, it would signal an historic breakthrough and might result in what Kissinger called the 'rebalancing of the global equilibrium'. Ceaușescu was bearing a heavy responsibility.

CHAPTER FIFTEEN

It is true, we shall be monsters, cut off from all the world; but on that account we shall be more attached to one another.

Frankenstein, Mary Shelley

Nicolae Ceaușescu's plane flew eastwards across the Black Sea, high above the majestic mountains of the Georgian Soviet Socialist Republic, across the arid plains of Soviet Azerbaijan and the dark, still waters of the Caspian Sea. Soviet 'oil cities' stretched out beneath him, clusters of bright orange lights floating in the dark. Gas flares burned like a thousand lit torches. He had flown 2,000 miles from Bucharest and was still only a third of the way across the Soviet Union. Everything beneath him was controlled by Brezhnev, the man still intimidating Romania with military manoeuvres on its shared 800-mile border. An assault by Russian troops against Romania was still possible at any moment.

As Ceaușescu left Soviet air space in June 1971 and flew over China, the border was quiet but militarized and tense. Twenty months earlier, fighting had broken out between the Chinese People's Liberation Army and Soviet border guards at Zhenbao Island, leaving 300 dead. It represented the height of the Sino-Soviet conflict and relations were still on a knife edge. Ceaușescu's flourishing friendship with Peking was regarded by Moscow as treachery.

He landed in the Chinese capital on 1 June 1971, accompanied by Elena and half a dozen of his closest circle, including Prime Minister Maurer. Ceaușescu was already the most well-travelled leader in the Eastern Bloc. In Iran, he had been paraded in a horse-drawn carriage through the streets of Tehran, before discussing oil with the Shah. In India, pretty girls had placed garlands of jasmine around his neck, after he and Indira Gandhi discussed the importation of iron ore for Romania's huge steel plant at Galați. In Africa, Ceaușescu had dipped into the mineral markets of Joseph Mobutu's Congo and Jean-Bédel Bokassa's Central African Republic – a country whose rich diamond fields lit the imagination of Elena Ceaușescu. On all these foreign trips, Ceaușescu received the pomp normally afforded to a visiting head of state. But nothing could have prepared him for China.

As Ceaușescu's hundred-car cavalcade turned the corner into Tiananmen Square, he was greeted by thousands of cheering pioneer children, dressed in red neckerchiefs and gleaming patent leather shoes, shaking pompoms in perfect unison. Armies of dungaree-wearing workers pounded drums and clashed symbols. Peasant women danced with red silk sashes and bouquets of flowers, pirouetting and bowing in time with flutes and trumpets. The air was shrill with soprano voices from the Peking opera, blasted at high volume through loud speakers that lined the route. Ceaușescu's car slid past regiments of saluting soldiers from the People's Liberation Army, at which point thousands of balloons were released into the air. At one stage, the opera stopped and crowds chanted slogans, presumably scripted by a People's committee that cared little for pith and more for completeness; 'Firmly support the Romanian people's just struggle to persist in maintaining independence and keeping the initiative in their own hands,' they shouted. They were on safer ground with the old favourites: 'People of the world unite,' they chanted, 'to defeat the US aggressors and all their running dogs!'

Walking beside Chairman Mao at an official function later, Ceaușescu was the young apprentice at the feet of the master.

The two were ideologically close and had followed a similarly Stalinist path. Just like Ceaușescu, Mao had transformed China from an agrarian to an industrialized society with the help of Soviet investment and expertise. The Chinese, of course, achieved it with the Great Leap Forward, a near-apocalyptic campaign that resulted in 35–45 million deaths. But Ceaușescu viewed the terrible human suffering as a misfortune caused by drought and bad harvests, rather than by the crimes of Chairman Mao.

The Chinese leader had later cooled towards Moscow and pulled away, just like Ceaușescu had done. Now, with Mao's Cultural Revolution in full swing and industrial growth soaring, the economy had re-balanced and, as Ceaușescu could see, Mao's relentlessly imposed monolithic unity had driven his people to achieve levels of production unrivalled anywhere else in the communist world. The Romanian leader observed the obedient crowds, the faultlessly choreographed scenes of adulation and the deification of Mao, and compared it with the glum, weather-beaten faces back home in Bucharest.

That evening there was a grand banquet, during which the Chinese prime minister, Zhou Enlai, and Ceaușescu spoke about their 'special relationship' and their shared determination to resist 'big power chauvinism' – by which they meant Russia. Chinese newspapers were filled with fawning tributes to the Romanian leader, congratulating him on Romania's 'glorious August 23rd Armed Uprising' – the one that took place in 1944 against Antonescu's fascists. They neglected to mention, though, that it had been led by the most blue-blooded of the capitalist class, King Michael, and that the only communist present on the night in question, Lucrețiu Pătrășcanu, had since been executed.

The following morning, 2 June, Ceaușescu was taken to Qing-Hwa University where, again, he was met with lavish singing and dancing. Officials explained how they synthesized education and production, rejecting traditional subjects such as literature, history and philosophy, and forcing students to learn practical skills instead. Chinese graduates, they said, would go straight into factory jobs. Ceaușescu was so thrilled that he linked arms with the students and danced around the campus.

Again, what impressed the Romanian leader was the centralized decision-making process that allowed all this to happen. In Bucharest, he reflected, the whole process was painfully slow and bureaucratic, something Ceaușescu put down to his excessive power-sharing. He had allowed other Politburo members to have a say. There was debate. Prime Minister Maurer was constantly butting in. Yes, he would cut people off if they diverged too much but all this discussion was choking the system.

In Shanghai, Nicolae and Elena attended a performance of a Chinese opera entitled The White-Haired Girl. In its original form, it was a folk story about a young peasant girl who lost her family and turned feral in the countryside, only to be caught by local people and grotesquely assaulted for being a witch. But Chinese Party officials had re-engineered the tale to make it communist-friendly. Now the girl was a beautiful young peasant, whose father was a tenant farmer exploited by the wicked, land-owning bourgeoisie. The family was forced to run away to escape the forces of unfettered capitalism. Eventually, the girl's dashing fiancé, a member of the National Revolutionary Army, returns with his comrades, overthrows the landlord, and, naturally, redistributes the land to the peasants.

The White-Haired Girl was one of China's so-called 'Model Operas', the re-writing of which was overseen by Mao's powerful fourth wife, Jiang Qing. Nicolae and Elena Ceaușescu left the theatre struck by the endless possibilities it presented for the arts in Romania. On the last day of the visit, Chairman Mao welcomed Ceaușescu into his private quarters, along with a retinue of aides. Ceaușescu began by formally thanking Mao for his warm welcome but moved quickly away from the script. He was clearly overcome with what China had taught him. 'We saw hundreds of thousands of people,' he stuttered. '... we were impressed by the positive attitude and the joy of living... we were impressed by the pre-occupation with perfect education, to tie it to production, to life, to the construction of Socialism.'[1]

Mao nodded beatifically. The extravagant welcome had done the trick. Ceaușescu had found his place among fellow-travellers in the East, away from geographical captivity in the hands of the Russians. From China, the Romanian delegation travelled to Pyongyang in North Korea, where the reception made Peking seem almost restrained by comparison. Perfectly choreographed dancers floated across a huge metal rainbow, releasing white doves into the sky. Ballet dancers glided like swans beside the road. In Kim Il-Sung Square, 100,000 candyfloss pompoms waved in undulating pink, yellow, and pastel blue, like fields of spring blossom. Feather fans fluttered admiringly as Ceaușescu's car slid by. 'Lifting up the banner of independence, we always go together', the crowd sang to specially composed music. 'Praise Pyongyang and Bucharest, Dear Ceaușescu!' The Romanian leader was driven into a sports stadium where the entire audience rippled in yellow and red costumes, transforming themselves into the image of a giant rising sun. 'Welcome Ceaușescu, Even though your country is far away, you are always close to our hearts, Dear Ceaușescu! Dear Ceaușescu!' Kim Il-Sung took Ceaușescu's hand and raised it slowly into the air, as if he were a teacher showing how to respond to true adulation. Ceaușescu's disorientated face slowly turned into a broad smile. 'Dear Ceaușescu! Dear Ceaușescu!' the stadium sang ever louder. He had finally found his place, in that June of 1971, looking down on adoring crowds from his platform above the sun.

Four days after his return to Bucharest, Ceaușescu hurried into a meeting of the Central Committee and demanded everyone's attention. His aides had already written up his observations from the trip but now Ceaușescu wanted to share his excitement with the rest. In China, he began, 'what impresses from the beginning is that people are well-dressed – of course, in a modest manner

– which is different from town to town; in Beijing one can see more overalls and military uniforms, in Shanghai you see silk dresses... So, if you give them only a pair of overalls and a pair of shoes...' Ceaușescu lost his line of thought but seemed to be marvelling at how little the masses required in exchange for such unconditional devotion. 'Well,' he continued, struggling to find the right words, 'it is really something.'

'The supply of clothes is good', he went on, 'and this for 800 million people!' He looked around the room. 'They have a wide variety of cloths and fabrics... we keep going to Italy [for imports].' Then he snapped, 'The things we make of cotton are repulsive!'

He had visited a chemical plant, he told them. Everything was built in China. A ship yard: 'They build nuclear submarines and ships *themselves*!' Soya-bean packaging... ceramic cauldrons... lathes... sickles... ploughs...all built by Chinese workers. North Korea did the same. 'They build a factory in a year,' he declared, 'they build heavy machinery that we import from the USA and Germany, machines that can process parts 22–25 meters long!' Exasperated, and probably pounding his fist on the table as he did whenever he was losing his temper, Ceaușescu suddenly announced: 'I will not approve any imports any longer!'

The secret was mass mobilization, he said. The masses should not demand money as an incentive to work but be moved to contribute for the good of the nation, for Socialism. In China, everyone worked with a smile, 'from children to old people, all are mobilized, and tasks are assigned to them – to learn, to work; no one idles'. Ceaușescu wanted to complete the next Five-Year Plan in four and a half years, he said. It was all about getting people to believe in the Party, in the leader. If they believed strongly enough, the wheels of industry would be whirring.

Then he turned on certain members of the delegation. During the trip, he said, they had locked themselves in their rooms and refused to come out. 'It is true, Prime Minister Maurer was ill, but frankly speaking he was exaggerating it, and this made a bad impression.' Then there was the shopping. Ceaușescu's comrades had loaded two tonnes of furniture and luxuries onto the plane when they were leaving. Ceaușescu was beside himself. 'This means that people went there to buy furniture, this means that we give [these people] too much hard currency. This has already become a problem, everybody struggles to stay abroad for as long as possible, to buy the devil knows what incredible things there.' The room fell silent, no one daring to point out that they shopped abroad because there were so few consumer goods available at home. Heavy industry had been pursued at the expense of all else. 'This is disorder,' barked Ceaușescu. 'I have just learned that our staff in Ulaanbaatar [Mongolia] bought meat in Beijing... whatever for?' A comrade raised his hand. 'We bought only 60 kg of lamb and chicken,' he explained weakly, 'and it was intended for the plane journey.' Ceaușescu was unconvinced. 'You do not disgrace *yourself,* you disgrace the homeland, the people.' He surveyed the humiliated faces of his secret shoppers. 'What conclusions will our hosts reach?' he sighed. 'When there was an opportunity to buy something, they all rushed into the shops... they will think we are boyars, revisionists who have become bourgeois' – and with that, the meeting ended after a mere three hours and ten minutes.[2]

Ceaușescu spent the following two weeks working with his aides on his grandly entitled 'July Thesis'. Completed in short order, the details were received in astonished silence by the Executive Committee of the Romanian Communist Party on 6 July 1971. From now on, Ceaușescu announced, there was to be mass political mobilization. Children would be involved in patriotic work. Schools would educate their pupils in ideological purity. Universities would train students for factory work. In the arts, propaganda would be unleashed from every conceivable outlet: radio, television, films, theatre, books, paintings, opera, ballet – all would be a vehicle for revolutionary re-education.

Foreign and cosmopolitan influences would be neutered. Lists of outlawed books and authors would be re-drawn. From now on, factory production would be increased through patriotism, dedication to the Party and love for the *Conducător*, as Ceaușescu now chose to style himself – a title last used by Marshal Antonescu.

So where was Elena in all of this? She had spent her first days back in Romania day-dreaming about Chairman Mao's glamorous and powerful wife, Jiang Qing, the 'Great Flag-bearer of the Proletarian Revolution'. Madame Mao was ill during the Ceaușescus' visit but had managed to accompany Elena to her production of *The White-Haired Girl*, as well as cocktails at a reception. The plain, frumpish Elena had been dazzled by Madame Mao's style. She was a former actress, elegant in cocktail dress or figure-hugging fatigues, pretty, balletic, self-confident, famous, and a diva. Rumour had it that her staff were ordered to walk barefoot so as not to disturb her. Madame Mao had been elevated to the Politburo without any political base and now directed state propaganda and oversaw the Dear Leader's personality cult.

Elena began hectoring her husband for a more prominent role in public life. Shortly after the 'July Thesis', her photograph appeared in *Scinteia* seated around a conference table with a group of financial experts. It was a meeting of the National Commission of Economic Forecasting, the body that analysed future aggregate developments such as the evolution of prices and output. 'Dr-Engineer Elena Ceaușescu', as the caption identified her, was now contributing her apparent econometric expertise on how to improve the country's Marxist-Leninist push for rapid industrialization.

On a summer evening in 1972, the Frisbee-shaped Palace Hall in the centre of Bucharest hosted Party delegates from around the country. They filed out into the torpid heat, searching for kiosks that might sell cold black beer or shots of plum brandy with crushed ice. Their conference had just made an important decision: to increase the size of the Central Committee, the most powerful organ in the Party (other than the Party Congress, which only met once every five years). Ceauşescu told them they needed to infuse the Committee with new blood and new energy. He'd handpicked twenty loyal followers from lowly factory jobs, men and women who would always owe him patronage. But there was one other new member with a notable pedigree. Ceauşescu had selected his wife. The Chinese model was being scrupulously applied.

*

The spring of 1973 arrived with much promise in the Primăverii district of Bucharest. On the lake, herons could be seen wading in the shallows. The first storks were arriving from the south, building huge nests at the top of lamp posts and trees. Adjacent to the lake, on the grandest street of all, teams of designers and architects had moved in. Renewal was in the air.

Ceauşescu felt his old house was far too modest for a leader of his status. He wanted to impress with silk wallpapers and jade ornaments of the sort he'd seen in Mao's palace; Murano glass mirrors and baroque furniture like those in Italian palazzos; oil paintings, marble and chandeliers similar to those in the Élysée Palace; and a swimming pool decorated with mosaics of rainbows and fantastical fish. That last one was Ceauşescu's own kitsch creation, his take on the bath houses of ancient Rome. The property was to have three storeys of eighty spacious rooms, a summer house, Jacuzzi and lawns where peacocks would wander. It would be known as the Spring Palace.

Once finished, Ceauşescu's favourite room was his private cinema, where he would retire in the evening with Elena and his aides. Just like Stalin, who watched endless cowboy movies and episodes of *Tarzan* with his entourage, Ceauşescu's tastes were all American. His favourite series was the New York police drama,

Kojak, of which he never tired. He and Elena would position themselves on two deep seats at the front of the auditorium, Ceaușescu in his turtle-neck sweater clasping his favourite 'Odobesti Yellow' wine, Elena often sleepy and dressed in a velvet dressing gown. '*Kojak* is excellent,' he would whisper, 'he shoots first and asks questions later!'

One person who attended Ceaușescu's movie nights regularly was a discreet, owlish young man with a large domed head and a tiny, apologetic body that was so anonymous, so near to being invisible, that he could move around social gatherings as if he were a ghost. It was a skill that came naturally to Lieutenant-General Ion Pacepa and helped him rise to the top of his chosen profession. Pacepa had been recruited as a counter-intelligence officer of the Securitate while at university. By the time Ceaușescu's mini-Cultural Revolution was underway, in 1972, he had been promoted to deputy chief of Romania's foreign intelligence service and a close advisor to the leader. In official photos, he is seen standing in the shadows close to Ceaușescu, expressionless, noticeable only for an oversize pair of black-rimmed spectacles that covered a third of his face.

Pacepa's department was called Departamentul de Informatii Externe, or DIE for short, and was responsible for gathering intelligence on foreign governments and personnel, as well as overseeing operations to neutralize perceived opponents abroad. DIE was an arm of Romania's all-pervasive security apparatus, enhanced under Ceaușescu and centred around the Department for State Security (DSS) – the powerful secret police, better-known as the Securitate. A brief glance at the various departments created the year after Ceaușescu's China trip gives an idea of just how omnipotent and oppressive the agency had become. In addition to the standard security directorates of Domestic Intelligence, Counter-espionage and Military Counter-espionage, there was the 'Fifth Directorate' (whose sole task was to install security and surveillance devices), Directorate IX (whose officers listened into the conversations of everyone from cleaners to members of the Politburo), the Sixth Directorate (which rooted out 'clandestine writing') and the Special Radio Transmission and Counter-Information Unit (which filled the airwaves with propaganda and blocked any foreign stations).

Pacepa's DIE was among the most important, as it maintained the illusion in the West that Ceaușescu was popular with the Romanian masses, that his economy was booming and that he was therefore a worthy recipient of loans and trade. While Pacepa was breaking bread with the Americans and the Chinese, he was also on the look-out for business with 'outsider regimes', those who declined Cold War involvement and perceived themselves 'independent' like Ceaușescu himself. It was a search that transported Pacepa and his presidential charge into new territory, that of the African 'Big Men'.

When Pacepa and Ceaușescu arrived in the dusty heat of Tripoli's airport in February 1974, they were following in the footsteps of men such as Carlos the Jackal, Abu Nidal, and Joe Cahill (chief of staff or the Irish Republican Army). All had beaten a path to the door of Muammar Gaddafi to beg for money and arms for 'anti-imperialist' paramilitary operations, and all had been generously received. Gaddafi had set himself up as a sponsor of international terror, a multi-billionaire dictator armed to the teeth with Soviet-built missiles, who was busy weaponizing his massive reserves of oil to take on the old world order.

The door of the plane swung open and Ceaușescu waited for the customary band to strike up. He was disappointed. Just desert wind and the distant call to prayer. He descended the plane's steps accompanied by Ion Pacepa, and was greeted by a bunch of soldiers who half-heartedly pointed to a waiting military vehicle. Where is Gaddafi? Ceaușescu asked. The question was received with a shrug.

On paper, the two leaders should never have got along.

Colonel Muammar Gaddafi had come to power in Libya in the revolution of 1969, four years after Ceaușescu, overthrowing a Western-sponsored king in a military coup that he reputedly missed by oversleeping. He was twenty-seven years old at the time and the Libyan people quickly took him to their hearts. But he was fiercely opposed to communism because of its denial of religion and its centralization of power, and he had always refused to entertain a Warsaw Pact leader.

Nevertheless, Gaddafi saw something of himself in Ceaușescu – the Eastern Bloc's *enfant terrible* who refused to be defined by conventional political labels. The visit was a chance to tweak Moscow's nose, denying the Kremlin a foothold in his country while welcoming its errant son. As for Ceaușescu, he believed Gaddafi was a perfect fit. He, too, had come to power at a young age forty-eight was considered almost adolescent in Eastern Bloc terms – and was insistently 'independent'. He also fancied himself leading a new world order and enjoyed playing Washington off against Moscow.

The Romanian delegation was driven straight to a meeting in the centre of town. A few of Gaddafi's aides plodded uninterestedly around the venue. Their leader was not there, they muttered. They would send a search party to find him. Ceaușescu could not have failed to notice the enormous murals of Gaddafi on public buildings around Tripoli. His host was in the midst of his own Cultural Revolution. After being swept to power on a wave of pan-Arab Socialism, he had redrawn his philosophy into an anarchic blend of people-power and authoritarianism, held together by a fearsome personality cult. Ceaușescu was intrigued. There were lessons to be learned.

When Gaddafi finally turned up, Ceaușescu and Pacepa were ushered into a conference room to meet him. Gaddafi caught sight of his two guests and, without uttering a word, abruptly got up and walked in the opposite direction. Ordinarily, Ceaușescu would have struggled to disguise his irritation but there was too much at stake in Libya. He smiled indulgently and waited. Gaddafi knelt down in the far corner of the room and began to pray.

The following morning, Ceaușescu arrived for their meeting holding a large, antique silver box. Reaching inside, he produced a very old, handwritten book and explained to the curious Gaddafi that it was 'the original manuscript of the first translation of the Koran into the Romanian language'. As Gaddafi carefully leafed through the document, Ceaușescu announced: 'We have only this one copy, but I have only one real brother. It is for you to keep.'³

Ceaușescu's sacrifice of an irreplaceable piece of Romanian history seems to have done the trick. Later, the two men struck an oil deal. This was at the tail end of the global oil crisis of 1973–4, when Arab oil producers had pushed world prices up an astonishing 400 per cent in a matter of months and imposed a complete embargo on America as punishment for its support of Israel in the Arab–Israeli war. Gaddafi was a key architect of the price hike and had benefitted to the tune of countless billions of dollars. Romania could also have taken advantage of the soaring prices, had it not been for Ceaușescu's staggering mismanagement of his country's most precious resource.

In his blind determination for industrial supremacy, Ceaușescu had overreached himself. His expensive Western-built machinery and equipment required volumes of oil that Romania simply did not have. He had ignored the warning signs – the unprecedented shortfall in world oil, the sudden need to import – and had instead constructed even more refineries. Now Romania had a capacity well beyond its needs. The result was refineries standing idle and an inability to pay back the loans taken out to build them in the first place. Romania needed to import oil just as world prices were rocketing.

Gaddafi was an ideal source. The two men sipped mint tea in the Libyan leader's tent and thrashed out a mutually beneficial deal. Libya would pay $400 million, in cash, to use Romania's spare refining capacity. The product would then be sold as 'Romanian oil' rather than Libyan. It would provide Gaddafi with a safety-valve, should the West decide to impose a boycott on Libyan oil. The profits from selling Libyan oil under the radar would then be split fifty-fifty.

Soon, the two dictators deepened their economic ties. For Gaddafi, the Romanian channel was, indeed, a way around the sanctions soon to be imposed by the West. He sent crude oil to Romania's Black Sea ports in exchange for hard currency, military equipment, the construction of schools, roads, ports and even Romania's help in building Gaddafi's hugely ambitious legacy project, his Great Man-Made River.

Whenever Ceaușescu was abroad, the Romanian public were fed images that appeared to put their leader at the top table of world affairs; Ceaușescu grinning beside Arafat in some garish, baroque-themed room; Ceaușescu embracing Castro while being cheered by gun-toting revolutionaries in Havana; Ceaușescu welcoming the British prime minister, Harold Wilson, to Bucharest; Ceaușescu in the Congo with the cane-swinging Mobutu. How could anyone complain about a leader who was lauded by both America and China, by Arabs and Jews, a man who was trusted by all sides? His foreign hosts did not know it but they were providing nourishment for Ceaușescu's fast-growing demonic personality cult. Meanwhile, his globe-trotting diplomacy was reaping rewards.

In 1971, Romania was welcomed into the General Agreement on Tariffs and Trade (GATT). In 1972, it joined the International Monetary Fund and World Bank. The following year, the country was granted a preferential trade deal with the European Common Market, and in 1975, Romania finally received the biggest financial prize of all, becoming the first Eastern Bloc country to be granted Most Favoured Nation status by the US. American banks threw open their doors to Romanian business and Ceaușescu waded in.

When General Ion Pacepa arrived back from his foreign trips, he invariably received a buzz on his car's radio-telephone. 'Sixty-two, report to Zero One,' the voice would say, and his driver would make a U-turn, tyres screeching, before heading back across town to the Spring Palace. 'Sixty-two' was Pacepa's code name, 'Zero One' was that of Ceauşescu.

The two would walk through the palace rose gardens together, the only place Ceauşescu felt safe from Russian surveillance and bugging devices. The area twinkled with hundreds of tiny lights, hidden among the ferns and fountains, picking out the shapes of peacocks strutting around the lush lawns. 'What's new?' Ceauşescu would ask, and Pacepa would brief him about the latest developments with DIE officers around the world. Frequently on those evenings, they walked by an empty bench, to which Ceauşescu would turn and say, 'Good evening.' There was never anyone there but he always made the same gesture. Years before, an elderly woman had sat on that bench, wearing a black mourning shawl around her shoulders and a black kerchief around her head. Ceauşescu always ignored her, pre-occupied by his own thoughts. His evening greeting had only begun after she passed away. The elderly woman was his own mother, Alexandrina, widowed when his alcoholic father died in 1969. Ceauşescu had built her an elegant property in his grounds and filled it with servants, but he rarely paid her any attention. Now she was gone, his sombre gesture each evening was the only display of emotional vulnerability Pacepa ever saw.

*

On Ceauşescu's fifty-fifth birthday on 23 January 1973, the most celebrated artists of the day fell over themselves to compose 'homage' portraits for the great occasion. The 'cosmic romanticist', Sabin Balasa, painted Ceauşescu floating amongst child-angels in the heavens, Elena by his side dressed in a ghostly nightdress, pre-Raphaelite orange curls falling delicately around her throat.

Other birthday portraits included Ceaușescu striding through sunlit fields attended by beaming child 'pioneers'; Ceaușescu alongside Stephen the Great, Vlad the Impaler and Michael the Brave; Ceaușescu in a Mao-style suit guarded by ranks of stony-faced soldiers.

'Poetic' works were anthologized for the occasion under the title 'Omagiu' – 'Homage'. 'We gaze with esteem, with respect, at the harmony of his family life', began one. 'We attach special ethical significance to the fact that his life – together with that of his life comrade – Heroine of Socialist Labour, scientist, Member of the Central Committee of the RCP, Comrade Elena Ceaușescu, offers an exemplary image of the destinies of two communists.' The praise became more extravagant by the year. Newspapers printed odes and letters to the couple. TV stations cleared their schedules. Bookshops sold nothing but texts 'authored' by Ceaușescu, expounding his views on art, architecture, science and even interior design. School children made greetings cards carrying photographs of Ceaușescu in heroic poses. The favourite for his fifty-fifth birthday was a lantern-jawed Ceaușescu armed with a hunting rifle, standing beside a dead brown bear.

None of these artists or writers were forced to work for Ceaușescu but they knew that by pandering to his narcissism, they would be granted special privileges: the use of ski lodges and seaside apartments, the issuing of travel visas – like gold dust, even among the elite – and access to Party shops. As for senior members of the Party, they were only too happy to feed the Ceaușescu myth. By strengthening him, they strengthened themselves. Narcissism came to apply to the whole group. They shared his glory and relied on his patronage. They could only progress by raising him higher. And all the time, at these epic events, plain-clothes Securitate patrolled the crowds to ensure the only emotion expressed was one of apparent happiness.

The spring of 1974 arrived, stormy and inclement. Trees were late to blossom. Snow stuck to the highest Carpathian peaks right into April. The cold winds of a global recession were brewing and Bucharest was ill-prepared for what promised to be an economically blustery summer.

Imports of crude oil were creeping up, exports inching down. More than 100,000 barrels a day were arriving at Romania's Black Sea ports to keep Romania's heavy industry moving. By the end of the 1970s, that would turn into a budget-sapping 320,000 barrels a day. It was an economic crime for a country that boasted the largest reserves in Europe to now be a net importer. Romania was on its way to acquiring an oil trade deficit of $1.5 billion.

At the same time, neglect of agriculture meant that the one-time 'breadbasket' of Eastern Europe was having to import basic foodstuffs. Food imports rose by 600 per cent during the 1970s, another economic crime brought about by ideological dogma. But what about those loans, the ones upon which Romania's teetering growth was built? In 1974, they were still comparable with the rest of the Eastern Bloc but signs of distress were starting to show. The massive steel plants that had required farmers to retire their ploughs and move to the cities needed huge supplies of raw materials that Romania simply did not have. Instead, Ceaușescu needed to shop abroad.

Romania was starting to lose money hand over fist. In order to pay back creditors, Ceaușescu borrowed more and more. He was paying off loans with loans. Currency debt was spiralling. What had begun as an unfortunate but manageable $3 billion deficit in 1974 would turn into a crippling $10.2 billion deficit by 1981.

In the autumn of 1974, Ceaușescu decided that Elena should be 'elected' to the powerful, fifteen-strong Executive Committee of the Communist Party. Of course, it was not really a 'committee' at all, not in the orthodox sense of the word. Meetings had been cleansed of all but trifling disagreements. There were no meaningful votes. Whenever Ceaușescu spoke, Elena interjected on his behalf, while hectoring and theatrically groaning at the sound of anyone else. Her arrival signalled a change in her husband's comportment. Previously, he had at least given the impression of listening to other members but now he became sarcastic and patronizing. If a member tried to deliver one of their, admittedly long and dreary, reports, Elena would throw a withering look at Nicolae and he would intervene. 'We need to eliminate the poetry,' he would say, or, 'Novels are to be done in one's free time.' Soon he began to address the others as 'draga', or 'dear', as if he were speaking to a class of naïve school children.[4]

*

Gheorghe Iosifescu's chances of becoming a theatre critic had been incinerated in the bonfire of freedoms lit by Ceaușescu's 'July Thesis' of 1971. There would be no independent art or literature to criticize anymore. Instead, Gheorghe turned his attention to the new and expanding field of cybernetics, returning to university to take a second degree in the abstract concepts of black boxes, mechanical evolution and robotics. It included the obscure new science of computers, a technology whose potential caused intrigue and alarm in equal measure among Party leaders. If harnessed by the organs of the state, it promised imaginative new ways of exerting power. If mastered by opponents, the potential threat to the regime was incalculable.

Gheorghe, the man who would one day become my father-in-law, took a job at the state-controlled Centrul de Calcul (Centre for Calculus) in 1976, an organization tasked with trying to develop the country's cyber-technology capabilities. He had just married a Hungarian woman, Margaret, and was thus deemed a potential security risk.

His new office was in his hometown, the oil city of Ploiești, a bright, modern building with tubular furniture and laboratory-white décor. One day, he arrived to find someone had pulled up a chair beside his. The stranger seemed an odd addition to the team, with a pot-belly, crumpled suit and bovine features.

Gheorghe offered a greeting and introduced himself. His new

desk-mate turned but said nothing. '… and your name?' inquired Gheorghe, politely. The man looked at him and studied his face but remained silent. As Gheorghe sat down, the newcomer drew his chair closer. On the desk was an early computer, the size of a small fridge. Gheorghe switched it on and heard the reassuring whirr of fans and circuitry. The screen flickered lime green and a cursor appeared, inviting a code. 'What do you want to see?' asked Gheorghe. The man said nothing.

They sat for a while, the odour of stale tobacco emanating from the stranger's clothing. 'So, what project are you working on?' asked Gheorghe. Nothing.

'Do you want your own desk?' Nothing.

At the end of the day, Gheorghe packed his documents and placed them in his satchel. The stranger stood too. He had no papers but he waited and then followed Gheorghe down the stairs and out onto the street. Gheorghe said goodbye and the man turned, silently, and walked in the other direction.

He re-appeared the next day, and the next. Occasionally, he would write notes in a pad. Sometimes he disappeared for a cigarette and then returned to watch Gheorghe's screen. He never said a word. After several weeks, Gheorghe began conducting imaginary exchanges, playing the part of his new desk-mate with a chirping familiarity. 'How are you this morning?' he would inquire. 'Oh, I am great,' he responded to himself. 'And you?'… 'Yes'… 'Going on holiday?' … 'Yes, to the mountains. And you?'… And on it would go.

The man sat in the same chair, staring at Gheorghe's screen, not just for weeks or months but for thirteen years. Romanians called such a man a 'Bulă'. It was close to the word 'Pulă', which meant 'dick', but was far richer and more expressive than a mere curse. A Bulă described every dumb petty official with a bit of power. A Bulă was coarse, often vindictive, usually a peasant type, who worked unquestioningly for the Party, inflating his lowly role into one of considerable importance while operating as little more than a grass. Bulăs were such an identifiable type that they took on a life of their own. They became a stock character for anti-communist jokes when Romanians dared criticize the Party apparatus. 'A Bulă enters a bar...'

The Bulă watching Gheorghe Iosifescu belonged to the Securitate. Under Ceauşescu, the role of the much-feared secret police had changed. The mass arrests and internal deportations of the Gheorghiu-Dej era had come to an end and had been replaced with mass surveillance and monitoring. The Securitate's job was to reach into the lives of every Romanian, to know their habits, movements, even thoughts. There were still disappearances. Still beatings. But the Securitate's purpose was no longer physical, but mental terror. Gheorghiu-Dej had inflicted scars so deep that Ceauşescu had only to play on the memory. Terror might still be fired up and re-applied at any time. But, for now, it was fear that infected the Romanian people, fear that was so pervasive, so toxic, it was as if it rose like an invisible gas from the drains. Fear of speaking on the phone, in case the Securitate were listening. Fear of meeting friends, in case the Securitate deemed them enemies. Fear of having friends, in case they worked for the Securitate. Fear that any independent thought might be betrayed by an unguarded comment, or a look, or even the absence of a look. No one could live their lives outside the reach of the Securitate's hidden microphones and armies of informants. All free thought, all individuality had been removed from the system. There were no individuals anymore, only the nation, and the nation was the Party, and the Party was Ceauşescu.

At the Athénée Palace Hotel, where Western diplomats and foreign businessmen stayed, the manager was a colonel in the Securitate's counter-espionage directorate. Housekeeping photographed every scrap of paper in guests' rooms. Telephone operators eavesdropped on conversations. Elegant young ladies in the bar worked as honey-traps. Microphones were installed in ashtrays and flower arrangements. The whole establishment was a front for the combined espionage of Ion Pacepa's DIE and the domestic security service.

Military barracks were bugged, as were the homes of military officers, union officials, ambassadors and even those occupying the highest positions in the Communist Party. According to Pacepa, Ceaușescu 'secretly ordered that new Politburo members and government ministers be covered by microphones in their offices and homes, from their first day until their removal'.[5] In 1965 the Romanian security forces possessed just one KGB-designed electronic monitoring centre in Bucharest, and eleven others around the country. By 1978, the scale of the operation had increased exponentially. The capital had ten monitoring centres, the regions 248 and there were 1,000 'portable units', designed to eavesdrop on holiday resorts and remote villages.

Elena Ceaușescu took a particular interest in monitoring the Politburo wives. Starting in 1974, Pacepa visited the First Lady regularly on Friday mornings to give her news from the microphones. Elena had two offices: one at the Chemical Institute, the other at the Central Committee Building. The latter was almost as large as that of Ceaușescu, whose image dominated the wall facing Elena's desk in the form of a life-size portrait. Her bookshelves were lined with row after row of Ceaușescu's speeches, all bound in sumptuous red leather. There was no paperwork on the desk, nothing in the drawers, no evidence of any work. The only clue that the room belonged to Elena were the rows of framed certificates on the wall. It had been Pacepa's job to harangue prestigious international institutions around the world to acknowledge Elena's 'genius'. She had an honorary doctorate from the Philippines (her husband had been awarded an honorary PhD in law from the same institution), a commemorative medal from Iran, and a Dame Grand Cross from Italy. Her latest campaign was to secure herself a Nobel Prize.

'What's new with Violeta?' asked Elena one day. She was

referring to the glamorous young actress-wife of the foreign minister, Stefan Andrei. According to Pacepa, Elena once asked 'What do you think Violeta sounds like when she's making love?' The young woman was rumoured to have lots of discreet visitors when her husband was out of town, and Elena wanted evidence. Some weeks later, Pacepa placed a cassette on the First Lady's desk. Elena listened again and again, laughing and making crude observations. Pacepa says she would collect tapes of other Politburo wives in compromising situations and then taunt them with cryptic comments. Such was her excitement about their bedroom antics, she would rush back from foreign trips in order to find out the latest, as if she were following episodes of her favourite soap.

Even Elena's own family were not safe from surveillance. She ordered that her daughter, Zoia, be bugged to see if she had a boyfriend. A young man called Mihai was identified, and his family targeted. Elena watched videos of the boy's mother. 'Look at her bow legs and fat ass,' she remarked, and concluded that the family were 'too insignificant, uneducated, and unstylish' for a relationship with her daughter to continue.[6]

It was often said that, in Ceaușescu's Romania, one in three people worked for the Securitate. In fact, the organization was relatively compact in terms of salaried employees. By the end of Ceaușescu's rule, it had 38,682 operatives, fewer than half of the East German Stasi. But it was the use of informants that made Ceaușescu's secret police such an all-pervasive and suffocating organization. They were everywhere – taxi drivers, receptionists, foremen, waiters, butchers, anyone whose life brought them into regular contact with others. The number of informants was staggering, four times that of the Stasi. 400,000 Romanians were informers out of a population of 22 million. That was where the real psychological damage was done. Every floor of every block in the country had its own Securitate informer.[7]

*

Deep beneath the forested valleys of the western Carpathian Mountains, in the Jiu Valley of Transylvania, coal miners crawled along on their hands and knees through unstable tunnels, lamps strapped to their heads, in temperatures up to 60 degrees Celsius. They were less worried about Securitate informants than the frequent roof collapses and the lung disease. When miners retired at the age of fifty, they were lucky to survive another decade.

Day and night, the wail of pre-war, Siemens-built motors could be heard across the countryside. Lifts plunged downwards at dizzying speeds, transporting men a kilometre beneath the surface, where they drilled more than a million tonnes of coal each year. Romanian coal miners were considered the engine room of communism, the worker-ants digging selflessly to keep the people warm and the machines turning. Ceaușescu's court artists depicted them in heroic poses, square-jawed, handsome, loyal. Yet they lived in near-medieval conditions, without heat or running water, their families squeezed into single-room wooden huts. Ceaușescu needed to tread carefully. If he ever lost the goodwill of the miners, he would lose the country. The first threat to his leadership surfaced unexpectedly from the coal yards of the Jiu Valley on a summer day in 1977.

On 3 August that year, a telephone call was put through to the President's personal line. 'Please come immediately,' said a terrified voice, 'the situation is serious.' It was the first vice-president of the Council of Ministers, Ilie Verdeț. A group of miners had taken him hostage.

35,000 soot-faced miners crammed into the courtyard between the coal sheds and the administrative offices at Lupeni mine, shouting at managers and demanding reform. They had gone on strike three days earlier, after the authorities announced that their retirement age would be increased from fifty to fifty-five years of age, and that the working day would be extended. What began as a spirited but manageable disagreement had taken an unexpected turn on 2 August, with threats of violence and demands for Ceaușescu himself to address the work force. It was then that they had kidnapped Verdeț.

Ceaușescu and his aides set off for the Jiu Valley straight away, and arrived later that afternoon in a convoy of black limousines. But the miners refused to let their president pass. Ceaușescu climbed from his car, ashen-faced. It was the first time he had encountered any sort of defiance. A witness described his eyes, darting backwards and forwards, and said he was visibly 'shaken'. Someone handed him a microphone. 'Comrades, this is not the way...' he began, 'this is a disgrace for the entire nation, a disgrace.'

Then, in an apparent panic, he declared that there had been a misunderstanding, that the Party leadership had already resolved to *reduce* working hours. He and his ministers were not the ones at fault, he said, it was the miners themselves who were resisting. The crowd was not taken in. 'Bandits, thieves!' they began to heckle. Ceaușescu tried to backtrack, suggesting that shorter working hours would be introduced gradually. The miners were not having it. 'A six-hour day from tomorrow,' they chanted. For several moments, Ceaușescu was paralyzed, a look of incomprehension settling over his face. Then he snapped out of it and chose a different approach. 'If you do not go back to work,' he threatened, 'we'll have to stop pussyfooting around...' There were boos and jeers.

Finally, the most daring chant of all rose from the crowds, louder and louder. The scowling President was now flanked by officers from the Securitate. 'Down with Ceaușescu,' bellowed the miners. 'Down with Ceaușescu.'

The following day, the Jiu Valley was declared 'a restricted zone'. Soldiers were sent in and 4,000 miners forcibly removed from the region.

Such was the Party's control over the media, not a word was written about the Jiu Valley strike. It was a feature of Ceaușescu's regime that no 'harmful' information ever leaked out. No one knew that there was unrest and so no one could show their solidarity. With no opposition reported, individuals assumed none existed. They withdrew into their shells, and tried to get on with life as best they could.

*

There was a goldfish in a spherical bowl on a shelf in Gheorghe Iosifescu's apartment. It looked like a tiny segment of peach hanging almost motionless in the water. He collected some coloured pebbles from outside to provide a marine landscape, and sprinkled a few breadcrumbs on the surface, and the fish slowly grew in strength and curiosity. His family had no idea where it came from. 'Someone in the street,' he would say, and they had an image of an elderly man in a raincoat, pockets full of polythene bags containing little golden fish. There were few pets in Romania. Cats were almost unheard of. Dogs were too much of a strain on a family's budget. A fish was ideal.

Gheorghe Iosifescu had bought it for his two-year-old daughter, Flavia. There were no toy shops in the oil city of Ploieşti, no dolls or dressing-up boxes, no colouring books or games. The fish was her sole source of entertainment. Sometimes the bowl was brought down from the shelf and placed on the floor, where Flavia gazed through the sides and watched the fish swim in endless circles. It became her 'suzetă', a pacifier that kept the little girl quiet, enchanted, and content.

On 4 March 1977, the water in the bowl began to stir. Tiny vibrations pricked its surface. Gheorghe Iosifescu was just putting Flavia to bed. The water began to shake, as if the bowl was sitting on a car engine. A clatter came from the kitchen. Cutlery slipped from the table. Then a rumble, like a jet engine, from deep beneath the foundations of the block. The light in the middle of the ceiling began to swing. Glasses rattled in kitchen cabinets. One by one, the books jostled to the edge of the shelf.

Gheorghe Iosifescu was frozen to the spot. Waiting. Holding on to his child.

When the goldfish bowl fell, it burst like a pricked balloon. Broken crockery, glass, water, pots and pans, everything was on the floor. Iosifescu tried to scoop up the fish but it was slippery, peach-like. He ran into the kitchen and grabbed a bucket but there was no water. Just a trickle from the taps. The fish flapped on the rug. Flavia was crying. Shouts came from behind the walls. Neighbours were running out onto Boulevard Republicii in their pyjamas. Some buildings had completely collapsed, burying their occupants under piles of rubble.

The earthquake measured 7.2 on the Richter scale. Its epicentre was in the eastern county of Vrancea but the shockwaves reached across the Balkans. In Bucharest, twenty-three poorly-built communist blocks were destroyed, killing more than a thousand residents. The Central Committee building was damaged, as was the former king's palace and City Hall. Much of the capital's surviving classical architecture was razed to the ground or damaged beyond repair: old Parisian-style villas, seventeenth-century Orthodox churches, synagogues, grand Ottoman houses, all destroyed.

Ceaușescu toured the ruins and declared a 'state of necessity'. The cost of repairs was estimated at $2 billion, a crippling sum that would almost double the national debt. His foreign minister wired Jimmy Carter's administration in Washington and asked for emergency funding. It would help Romania maintain its independence from the Soviet Union, he said. But, within a week, Ceaușescu had changed his tone. He still required the money but this was no longer about re-building, it was about creating a new Romania. The destruction had provided an opportunity to start again, to reconstruct the capital and, indeed, the nation in whatever manner he chose.

As soldiers and students picked through the rubble for bodies, Ceaușescu called an emergency meeting of the Executive

Committee and declared: 'We shall not hesitate about certain demolitions... we will work as if on an empty space.' There would be large-scale architectural intervention and a new style of building work. He called together the country's leading designers and lectured them on how Bucharest should look, with grids of symmetrical roads, identical apartment blocks and a vast 'Civic Centre' at its heart.

The problem was, the earthquake had not cleared enough space for what he desired. 'If we demolish all of Bucharest,' said the President, 'it will be nice', and he proceeded to order a programme of mass destruction, even of buildings untouched by the quake.[8] In the months and years that followed, he tore down churches, 'bourgeois' buildings and 'foreign-influenced' architecture. His planned 'Civic Centre' became particularly ambitious. Whole neighbourhoods needed to be cleared, hundreds of families evicted. The time frame was generous. He wanted it finished by 1984. But the Civic Centre would soon morph into a single vast building, a grotesquely dominant piece of architecture that would serve as Ceaușescu's palace. With twelve floors, more than 1,000 rooms and corridors wide enough to race cars along, the work was to be overseen by the visionary himself. It would become the biggest civilian building in the world.

*

'I want that yacht!' blurted Elena as she walked along the Jordanian beach with Nicolae and spy chief Ion Pacepa. They were staying with King Hussein at his residence in the Gulf of Aqaba and, after dinner, the trio were invited onto the king's private yacht. Elena was overcome. She waited until they finished eating and then began nagging Nicolae for a similar luxury craft in which to holiday on the Black Sea coast. 'I won't leave without it,' she said, and became so insistent that she burst into tears. The next morning, King Hussein was approached to ask if the boat was for sale. It was not. It had been a present to his third wife, Alia, and it must stay in her possession. However, said the king, he would have his aides call the yacht-builders to see if they would make a similar craft for the Ceauşescus.

With Elena's appetite whetted by a single evening's sailing, she persuaded her husband to purchase not one yacht, but three. One was moored on Lake Snagov, beside their summer villa that had originally been built for the brother of King Carol II. The second they used to cruise up and down the Danube. The third was the most luxurious of all; four decks painted cream and sparkling turquoise, cocktail terraces, banqueting rooms and a gymnasium. It was moored on the Black Sea and named *Mircea Cel Mare*, after the grandfather of Vlad Dracula.

Servicing Elena's insatiable appetite for luxury items soon became a significant task for the Securitate. Ion Pacepa was regularly ordered to phone ahead to foreign dignitaries to make sure that they had gifts of fur coats, black pearls and diamonds waiting in Elena's room. She would change the schedules of her trips to suit her shopping habits, insisting that high-class jewellers close their stores to the public and give her private viewings. She 'borrowed' items of diamond jewellery from fashion houses and then refused to hand them back. Her shoe and handbag collection became as extravagant as that of the infamous First Lady of the Philippines, Imelda Marcos. But Elena was not content with priceless jewels, luxury yachts, five palaces and a travelling band of servants she referred to as 'the idiots'. She wanted her own personality cult.

The opportunity arrived on 7 January 1979, the occasion of her sixtieth birthday. In fact, even that was a lie. It was actually her sixty-third but Elena insisted that three years be knocked off her age, so that she would appear younger than her husband. *Scînteia* reported that she was sixty and was celebrating forty years of 'revolutionary life'. Court artists were summoned, depicting the plain, acidic-looking Elena as an ever-young beauty, with lustrous auburn hair, clear, intelligent eyes and a wrinkle-free, tanned complexion. Her long, pointed nose was censored and replaced with a petite, feminine button. Her suspicious glare was smoothed into a benevolent smile. All around her were rays of sunshine and doves of peace. Photographers were ordered to stand well back and shoot her from a distance. Never side-on, again to avoid the nose. Every photo was inspected and sanctioned before being published. The true appearance and personality of the First Lady became lost in the fug of propaganda.

On each subsequent birthday, TV stations aired extravagant homages to Elena. Documentaries were made about her scientific achievements, along with choreographed song-and-dance extravaganzas. By the mid-1980s, the TV schedules on 7 January were cleared of anything other than programmes dedicated to Elena Ceauşescu's 'greatness' and 'self-sacrifice'.

Her personality cult blossomed and gradually began pulling away from that of her husband, the two becoming separate but complementary. Elena's did, however, rankle with most Romanians. Whereas Nicolae Ceauşescu had at least shown some merit, some commitment to the nation, climbing the Party hierarchy with a degree of legitimacy, Elena had not. She was a parvenue, a vulgarian, a character entirely manufactured by Party propagandists. The idea that Ceauşescu was force-feeding his wife to the nation undermined his own candle-weak credibility. He was taking them for fools. And there was another power-hungry Ceauşescu waiting in the wings. The First Couple's debauched, playboy son, Nicu, was being groomed for greatness.

There are many colourful stories about the excesses of Nicu Ceauşescu, most of which involve heavy drinking, drugs, high-speed car accidents and the near rape of young girls. But an account by spy chief Ion Pacepa stands out for the casual nature of Nicu's depravity.

The scene was a VIP party in March 1978 to celebrate the birthday of Pacepa's old friend, the gentle and unusually well-educated Stefan Andrei, who Ceauşescu had just promoted to foreign minister. It was held at the Party's guesthouse for foreign communist dignitaries, a large red-brick building in the middle of a beautifully manicured park on Boulevard Kiseleff. By the time Pacepa arrived, it was past midnight and most of the attendees were unsteady on their feet.

Nicu was twenty-seven years old at the time, already portrayed by Ceaușescu propagandists as a 'scientist of international repute' and the alleged author of several volumes on nuclear physics. He would soon become the first secretary of the Communist Youth, at whose conferences crowds would chant: 'Ceaușescu junior, our next Conducător!' That was the way his father had engineered things, to begin a dynasty, Elena taking over first and then Nicu. For ambitious Party officials it meant that, not only did they have to fawn over the witless and demanding Elena, but over Nicu too. And so it was that Nicu was on the guest list for all the important parties.

The new foreign minister had mentored Nicu during his teens, trying to give him the rudiments of a decent education, but Nicu had skived off and followed his own path. Nevertheless, when there was drink and food to be had, Nicu would appear promptly. 'A spy among us,' announced Nicu as General Ion Pacepa pushed his way into the party. 'Let me kiss our master spy.'[9] The men were sitting around a banqueting table and Nicu was in high spirits. 'Oysters for the General!' he shouted, smashing a plate to attract the waiter's attention. 'Four dozen, on ice. Where are you, you scum?' It seems that Nicu picked up his vulgarity from his mother, rather than his father.

Ceaușescu Snr had many ugly habits. He ate like an uneducated peasant, biting into tomatoes as if they were apples, spraying pips and juice across his guests, but he was careful with his language, almost puritanical, and at least made attempts to appear refined. It was Elena who cursed and swore indiscriminately, and from whom Nicu acquired the habit. On the night in question, he apparently threw a glass at the waiter to speed him on his way.

Pacepa, according to his own account, then gave a toast, which was spoiled by interventions from Nicu, who lurched behind Stefan Andrei's chair and burst into a raucous rendition of 'Happy Birthday', before pouring Scotch over his host's head. Andrei then attempted to make a speech of thanks, during which the waiter arrived with a silver platter full of oysters. 'Put it here in the middle of the table,' Nicu is said to have shouted. 'Is there any seasoning on them?

'They are just fresh and raw, Comrade Nicu,' the waiter replied, at which point Nicu exploded. 'They need seasoning, you idiot. This isn't a cat house, it's a VIP club.' Pacepa says that Nicu then climbed onto the table, unzipped his flies and began urinating over the oysters, carefully 'seasoning' every one of them.

Nicu was wrestled from the table and forced back into his chair, but he had not finished. 'Who doesn't like my seasoning?' he shouted. 'Nobody?' Grabbing a syphon from the table, he began squirting the oysters, and the guests, with fizzy water. According to Pacepa, when everyone finally left, Nicu remained and was last seen pushing a waitress towards the edge of the table while removing her blouse.

The following autumn, the RCP's Twelfth Congress was held. Nicu was selected as a candidate member of the Central Committee. The dynasty was starting to take shape. Elena's rise was occurring in tandem and at an even greater velocity. In 1978, she was appointed first deputy prime minister, second only to Ceaușescu himself. That summer, she packed her most expensive dresses and most eye-catching handbags. She and Nicolae had an invitation they'd wanted for years. In June, they boarded a flight for London for an official state visit. A nervous letter had already been sent ahead from the British embassy in Bucharest, explaining: 'Mrs Ceaușescu would be pleased to receive some kind of academic distinction.' A further briefing letter also arrived, warning of Ceaușescu's nastiness. 'He is as absolute a dictator as can be found in the world today,' wrote British ambassador Reggie Secondé. Elena Ceaușescu was 'a viper' who liked shopping and their children were all 'feckless'. There was also a warning from French President Giscard d'Estaing, who reported that on a recent visit to Paris the Ceaușescus had looted their quarters and even hacked holes in the walls looking for bugging devices.[10] Wherever they stayed, said d'Estaing, all silver brushes should be removed from the dressing tables or they would 'pinch the lot'. The Ceaușescus were accommodated in the centre of London, in a building that was, perhaps, a little too modest for their tastes. They were to be guests of the queen at Buckingham Palace.

CHAPTER SIXTEEN

The sky was vast and the world endless, but man's life was turning inside a courtyard like in a prison. Deep and bright was the sky, but down there was a house surrounded with a fence and man's soul was struggling, darkened and blind.

Morometii (Volume 1), Marin Preda

It was morning rush hour on Tuesday, 13 June 1978 and London's hot, summer streets were packed with commuters and tourists. In Leicester Square, queues were already forming outside the Odeon cinema, where huge posters of John Travolta beckoned them into a lunchtime showing of *Saturday Night Fever*. Around the corner, near the Mall, a small group of Romanian dissidents had gathered with placards bearing the word 'DICTATOR'. Moments later, police arrived and moved them on. Those who refused were arrested and taken away in a Black Maria. Above them, dipping beneath the thin, milky summer clouds, was a presidential plane descending steadily towards Heathrow.

At Victoria Station, Nicolae Ceaușescu almost skipped from the train, followed by Elena, who clomped, horse-like, behind him. They were greeted by the queen in a cherry-red coat, then by Prince Philip and the young Prince Charles. The Romanians stood beside Queen Elizabeth II on the station platform as the Grenadier Guards saluted and the national anthem played. A gilded horse-drawn carriage then whisked them up the Mall, where Ceauşescu appeared overcome by the cheers and the flags. A rare smile lit his face. He leaned forward excitedly and waved like a foppish prince on the way to his castle. This was the adulation he craved, and the British were laying it on with style and pomp. Gifts awaited them at Buckingham Palace – a hunting rifle with telescopic sights for Nicolae, a gold brooch for Elena.

Ceauşescu was the first Warsaw Pact leader to be granted a state visit to the United Kingdom. He was not, though, the first Romanian leader to set foot in Buckingham Palace. It is unlikely to have crossed Ceauşescu's mind, but a little girl called Marie had once played in the gardens, accompanied by her grandmother, Queen Victoria, before crossing the snow-covered Carpathians as a seventeen-year-old princess to marry King Ferdinand of Romania and become the country's much-loved queen. Ceauşescu's comrades had evicted Marie's offspring from the Romanian throne and he was now lapping up the hospitality of her English cousins.

That night, Buckingham Palace hosted a state banquet, to which Elena arrived in sparkling diamonds and pink silk. Nicolae wore a tailored dark suit, smiling broadly, as if he had finally found his place. In a rare departure from habit, Ceauşescu chose to leave his food-taster at home, trusting the British security services to protect him from potential Russian poisoners. Ceauşescu was reportedly well behaved. He did not stuff the British lamb and potato into his mouth all at once, and did not once wipe his hands on the tablecloth. The silver cutlery was all accounted for. At the end of the meal, the queen praised his 'heroic struggle' against Russian hegemony, and said how much Britain had been impressed by 'the resolute stand' he had taken to 'sustain the independence of Romania'.

The following day in Bucharest, photographs of the visit were splashed across the front cover of *Scînteia*. Romanians greeted them with sorrow and disgust. Britain, a country many considered the most sophisticated and fair-minded of democracies, was playing along with the Ceaușescu myth, strengthening his grip on power. How could anyone now raise a murmur of discontent, when the Queen of England had endorsed him in such resounding terms? That same day, Elena was driven by limousine to Burlington House in Piccadilly. Her fiercely scraped-back hair was replaced by a luxuriant bouffant in the style of Margaret Thatcher – the then leader of the opposition who had also shaken hands with the visiting Ceaușescus. Elena had a date at the Royal Institute of Chemistry.

In front of an enthusiastic crowd of leading academicians, she was applauded onto stage beside the institution's president, Professor Sir Richard Norman. He spoke in exuberant terms about her 'distinguished' contributions to the field of macromolecular experimental chemistry and her brilliant work for 'the benefit of mankind'. Elena listened with an expression of haughty self-regard, as the esteemed Sir Richard turned and bestowed upon her a Fellowship of the Institute.

'Academician Doctor Engineer Elena Ceaușescu', as she liked to be known, was then driven to the Polytechnic of Central London for another presentation. After being praised for steering her son, Nicu, into the field of nuclear physics, the self-appointed Tsarina of Romanian science was awarded a professorship *honoris causa*, the first such title presented by the institution to a foreigner. When the Romanian public saw photos of their much-despised First Lady accepting scrolls in scholarly British gowns, they whispered to each other, '*S-a suit scroafa-n copac*'. It is an old Romanian saying that means 'the sow has climbed the tree'.

The real purpose of the visit, however, was played out in discreet panelled rooms around Whitehall. Britain was serenading Ceaușescu's officials in the hope of securing a major aviation deal. British Aerospace and Rolls-Royce – both nationalized at the time – were on the hunt for a co-producer of engines and aircraft, and Romania was keen to strike a partnership. By the end of the visit, civil servants at the department of industry were toasting a lucrative deal. The Romanians had agreed to pay £300 million for the licences, designs and machinery. The fact that Ceaușescu had no money, and that his economy was in deeper debt than anywhere else in Europe, hardly seemed to matter.

Back at Buckingham Palace, Nicolae and Elena were enjoying playing king and queen, wandering around the lake and the lush gardens, and pointing out the architectural features they might use in a palace of their own. The queen was no stranger to controversial foreign guests. She had entertained Zaire's Joseph Mobutu on a state visit five years before, but she knew enough about Ceaușescu's dictatorial excesses to find his presence in her home particularly unpleasant. She was out walking her corgis in the palace gardens when she saw the Romanian President and his wife approaching, and had just enough time to jump behind a bush and hide.[1] Nevertheless, etiquette and a successful aviation deal meant that Ceaușescu received more than just a gun and some jewellery to take back to Bucharest. He left London with an honorary knighthood.

The Romanian government eventually fell behind with its payments to Rolls-Royce and, in 1985, the British foreign secretary, Geoffrey Howe, was dispatched to Bucharest to try to retrieve the arrears, a task that he pursued with only moderate success.[2] It was Ceaușescu's chief spy, the owlish, bespectacled Lieutenant-General Ion Pacepa, who had been instrumental in organizing the London trip, but even as the presidential party arrived back home in Bucharest, he knew that an unprecedented political storm was brewing.

The seed had been planted some years before, on a humid August evening in 1976, when Pacepa and his former boss at DIE, Major General Eugen Luchian, were walking with Ceaușescu in the rose gardens of the Spring Palace. As they strolled past the floodlit pagodas and the ornate white marble fountains,

Ceaușescu suddenly declared: 'Emil Georgescu must be silenced forever... He should have his jaws, teeth and arms broken so that he will never be able to speak or write again.'[3] The two spies glanced at each other uneasily and said nothing. Emil Georgescu did not even live in the country anymore and a Mafia-style hit in a foreign country was always plagued with problems.

Georgescu was everything Ceaușescu despised: a defector who was not content with simply having escaped the country but persisted in taunting the President from afar. He was a journalist at the US-funded Radio Free Europe (RFE), the crusading anti-communist radio station that reached millions across Eastern Europe, employing dissident writers to broadcast uncensored news to all Soviet satellites from the safety of its offices in Munich. Although banned in Romania, it had become a firm favourite with the country's educated classes who huddled around their transistor radios at night, sliding the dial through the hisses and pops until they came upon the familiar jingles and the acerbic deconstruction of Ceaușescu's leadership by Emil Georgescu or one of the other journalists working for the station.

Ceaușescu tried repeatedly to jam the frequencies, but the German engineers were always one step ahead. Hence his plan to rid the airwaves of Emil Georgescu by other means. Ceaușescu concluded that assassination was the best option and explained to his spy chiefs that they should hire foreign mercenaries without any connections to the homeland. Pacepa was not persuaded and reminded the President what had happened last time.

Just a few months before, in August 1976, Ceaușescu had ordered the murder of an émigré priest called Vasile Zapartan, who'd been criticizing the Romanian president from his pulpit in West Germany. Ceaușescu had exploded with rage when he heard how Zapartan described him as a dictator. 'Kill him without attribution,' yelled Ceaușescu (according to Pacepa), banging his fist on the table. Zapartan was killed in a car crash soon afterwards. No questions were asked; it was just a very unfortunate accident. The West German authorities did not even investigate the death. Ceaușescu was congratulating himself on a job well done, when his urbane former prime minister, Ion Gheorghe Maurer, dropped by. Ceaușescu was always a little suspicious of Maurer, not just for his superior intellect but for his apparent possession of some sort of moral code. 'Nick,' said Maurer, 'as Romania's supreme leader, you can do anything. Good or evil. But one thing you don't do. Don't give the order to kill. That's first-degree murder. It doesn't matter if the one giving the order is a beggar or a king.'[4]

Ceaușescu made some small talk and waved Maurer away. The advice did not sink in. A few weeks later, the RFE journalist, Emil Georgescu, was driving along in Munich when he too was involved in a serious car accident. The operation was less successful than the last. Georgescu suffered serious injuries but managed to survive. He was back behind the microphone within six months.

His listening public were delighted and Radio Free Europe became even more popular. Romanians began writing to the station, thanking it for having the courage to tell the truth. Ceaușescu had the letters intercepted. His plan was to track down the authors and have them arrested. But the Romanian public had lived with the Securitate long enough. They understood that all letters sent abroad were likely to be scrutinized. When Securitate officers began the job of trawling through those addressed to 'RFE, Munich', they discovered that none had been signed. All were anonymous.

'I'll give you three months', Ceaușescu announced to his aides, 'to collect handwriting samples from the whole Romanian population.' Students were to have their essays removed from schools and universities and placed with the Securitate. Employers were to insist that all workers submit a hand-written CV for writing analysis and logging. Ceaușescu's aides remained unconvinced. 'What about retirees, and the unemployed?' asked one. Ceauşescu exploded. 'Invent some kind of new form,' he bellowed, 'something they will have to fill in... Use your head. Do I have to teach you how to do it?'

From then on, every state-owned typewriter had to be registered, with samples of their typeface filed away by the Securitate. When not in use, their custodians were instructed that the machines must be locked and sealed. Anyone possessing a private typewriter must inform the Securitate and ask for authorization. Again, samples of the typeface were required, a sort of fingerprinting so that any subversive material might be traced to the culprit. Some Romanians buried their typewriters beneath the earth outside their apartment blocks or in neighbouring fields, retrieving them under cover of night for a few brief hours, and then returning them to the ground before sunrise. A more eloquent symbol of the death of free speech, literature, and art is difficult to imagine.

Meanwhile, Radio Free Europe continued to grow in popularity, particularly its Romanian service. For Ceauşescu, destroying it became an obsession. In 1978, shortly before the London visit, he called his spy chief, Ion Pacepa, to his office. This time there were to be no mistakes, said the President. He wanted the 'neutralization' of RFE's Romanian service director, Noel Bernard, the man whose regular ten-minute slots dismantled Ceauşescu's personality cult in bleak, unsparing language. By this time, Ceauşescu refused to even speak the radio station's name, referring to it, simply, as 'Chatterbox'. Bernard, its boss, had to be eliminated, said the President. '... And Georgescu!' interjected Elena. Ceauşescu nodded his ascent, leaning over to Pacepa and saying: 'The DIE should take over Georgescu, and finish with him.'

Pacepa was forty-nine years old. His career as Ceauşescu's spy chief had inevitably inflicted death and human suffering. But there was something about receiving a casual, cold-blooded command from Elena Ceauşescu that sickened him. On 22 July 1978 – a month after Nicolae and Elena returned from

Buckingham Palace – he arrived home from his regular meeting with the President sometime after midnight. The road outside 28 Zoia Avenue in Primăverii was quiet. Once inside, he took out his prized violin and played a few bars of Dvorak's 'Humoresque', in front of a portrait of his deceased mother. Then he bent down, removed part of the parquet flooring and prised out a small envelope. Inside was a membership card for the 'Association of Young Friends of the United States', an organization that the Communist Party had declared 'traitorous'. The next morning, Pacepa took a scheduled flight to Frankfurt for a business meeting with Romanian embassy staff. After lunch at a castle outside the city, he made his excuses and retired to his suite at the Intercontinental Hotel in Cologne, promising to meet up again the next day. At dawn, he caught a train to Bonn and made his way to the sprawling United States embassy beside the Rhine.

Under the lime trees at the rear of 28 Zoia Avenue, brightly coloured dragonflies dipped into the swimming pool. A deckchair sat empty. It was 35 degrees in the shade, but the owlish man with the huge spectacles was not there. No one had seen Lieutenant-General Ion Pacepa for several days.

Washington received a call from its embassy in Bonn, stating that a mysterious middle-aged man claiming to be Ceaușescu's spy chief had walked through the door and asked for political asylum in America. After a brief interview, in which Pacepa was able to prove his identity, the White House sent a United States Air Force Hercules to West Germany, and Pacepa was whisked off to the airport under armed guard. In the plane's belly, a wooden cabin had been constructed containing a dining and sleeping area, so that the former spy could rest without being disturbed. The plane's commander came to shake his hand. 'Welcome to freedom, Sir,' he said, and Pacepa burst into tears. It was the first time anyone had addressed him as anything other than Comrade for years.

When Ceaușescu heard about Pacepa's defection, he was

taken ill. He cancelled all public engagements and disappeared from view. Pacepa had been so visible at Ceaușescu's side that it was almost impossible, even for the President's most talented propagandists, to pretend nothing had happened. The potential for damage was huge, not only in the secrets Pacepa was certain to divulge to the West but the sheer reputational damage of losing a spy chief in the middle of the Cold War.

At the White House, the mood was one of barely restrained glee. This was the most high-ranking defection from a communist regime since the war. 'The Romanians will be upset over the Pacepa case for some time,' confided the US State Department in a secret memo. 'Ceaușescu's image as a man in control of his internal affairs is shaken, and his natural paranoia about his advisers is heightened.'[5]

But in Bucharest, the President was soon off his sick bed and back at work, filled with his usual energy. The headquarters of the Central Committee building and the Spring Palace were placed under heavy guard. Security troops patrolled Bucharest day and night. The government indicted Pacepa for high treason and condemned him to death. They placed a bounty on his head of $2 million.

Even today, when I contacted the 91-year-old Pacepa in the United States, he replied that he was happy to talk by email but that he could never meet up because he was still worried about assassination.[6]

Pacepa's defection sparked the greatest political purge in post-war Romania. A third of the ruling Council of Ministers were demoted. Romanian ambassadors and their staff were recalled to Bucharest. Some seized the opportunity and defected. Children of foreign officials were taken out of classrooms and interviewed about their fathers' activities. The Romanian foreign intelligence service was totally destroyed. The task of recreating it fell not to Ceaușescu, but to his wife. It was Elena who would now be in charge of overseeing the country's foreign spying.

Radio Free Europe reported the details of Pacepa's defection with some relish. When Ceaușescu heard they were mocking him, he resolved to follow through the assassination plan that Pacepa had failed to execute. 'Oh Deformed One,' began the letter to car-crash survivor Emil Georgescu, 'we have heard that you have begun to bark at us, you mangy Judas... If you do not shut your Jewish trap, we'll see to it that you will be gripping clay underground along with other contaminated monsters... Be careful viper, otherwise we will be cutting off your venomous tongue.'[7]

Georgescu had little choice but to brush off the warnings. By 1981 he was still suffering ill-health from the assassination attempt. Then one day in July of that year, he left his Munich apartment at 8 a.m. and came across a stranger waiting in the stairwell. Speaking in French, the man asked Georgescu to confirm his identity. Georgescu began screaming. Immediately, the stranger produced a knife and began stabbing him. Georgescu fought back, using his attaché case as a shield. 'Why, why?' shouted the journalist, at which point his breathless assailant is said to have shouted: 'So that you will never write again!'

The attack was eventually interrupted by Georgescu's wife, who'd heard the commotion from upstairs. As the assailant fled to a waiting vehicle, she managed to scribble down the number plate. Beside her, on the concrete floor, lay the blood-soaked body of her husband. Georgescu had been stabbed twenty-five times, yet as she knelt down beside him, she realized he was still breathing.

At a Munich courtroom the following year, a twenty-five-year-old Frenchman called Freddy Layani, and his driver, Claude Cottenceau, were brought before the jury in handcuffs. They admitted the knife attack but said they had been recruited by common criminals in Paris 'to beat Georgescu and return with money and jewellery'. Unlikely as the story was, they stuck to it under stiff cross-examination. This was a robbery that had gone wrong. The stabbing was never intended. It was self-defence. When the crucial question of involvement by Romania's security services was raised, Freddy Layani looked puzzled. No, there was no such plan. He had no idea what the prosecutor was talking about.

And, indeed, the evidence was all circumstantial, just as Ceauşescu intended. Nothing could ever be proved. Layani was convicted of attempted manslaughter and jailed for eleven years, while his co-defendant received four-and-a-half. The West German authorities were less circumspect. It was 'an assassination attempt', announced the German interior minister, and warned that the seriously ill Georgescu faced further attempts on his life.[8]

Georgescu died the following year, of lung cancer. But even his death was not without suspicion. Another RFE broadcaster, Vlad Georgescu, had died of a brain tumour at the age of fifty-one. The head of the Romanian Service, Noel Bernard, who Ceauşescu had ordered Pacepa to kill, passed away from unspecified cancer at the age of fifty-six. It could all be bad luck, of course, but many informed and sensible Romanian journalists believe that Ceauşescu's agents were poisoning the regime's critics with radioactive powder slipped into drinks. Ion Pacepa has since said that Ceauşescu regularly used poisons and radioactive substances, and had given such attacks a nickname: 'Radu', short for radiation. As far-fetched as it might seem, Bernard's death offers a fragment of potential evidence. After the fall of communism, his widow went to Securitate headquarters and found a strange attachment on his file. Pinned to the paperwork was a newspaper article concerning Bernard's cancer surgery. Beside it, a Securitate agent had written, 'the measures undertaken by us are starting to have an effect'.[9]

*

The graph of Romania's rising debt resembled a topographical study of a tall Carpathian peak, beginning with a gentle incline in the mid-1970s, climbing through challenging foothills in the latter years of the decade and then soaring into a sheer, dizzying rock face in 1981. By the end of that year, the country had accumulated $10.2 billion of debt, and banks across the world wanted it back. The interest alone was costing Romania $1.5 billion a year. Unpaid bills were mounting. Finally, and with great reluctance, Ceaușescu was forced to approach the International Monetary Fund for a rescheduling.

Ahead of him lay a world of disciplinary horror that he had never before encountered. Suddenly, capitalists in grey suits were telling him how to run his country. Young men at IMF headquarters in Washington set new performance criteria for the Romanian economy and dictated actions on exchange rates, prices and interest. Ceaușescu was smarting. This was his economy, his workforce. He refused to equip the IMF with the necessary data and was obstructive when they requested policy change. By 1983, he had had enough. In a storm of rage, he reversed IMF-imposed decisions, denounced the whole organization as 'meddling' and declared that from this point on, Romania would 'go it alone'.

Ceaușescu vowed to teach these scoundrel capitalists an economic lesson. His Greater Romania would pay back all its debts in full before the end of the decade, and he would never rely on outside help again. The world would watch and learn as his loyal subjects scrimped and saved to defy the laws of gravity, lifting Romania out of debt by the sheer force of their self-sacrifice.

The challenge was to boost exports while at the same time ending all but the most crucial of imports. It was primitive stuff. But once the economy was running at a surplus, Ceaușescu could then start skimming off hard currency to pay back the debts. That was the theory, anyway. Ceaușescu's problem was that he needed huge imports of fuel and iron ore to supply his heavy industry, so neither could be reduced. Instead, cuts would have to be made in consumer goods and agriculture, and in particular, food. Since Ceaușescu had neglected domestic food production for a decade, the country had become heavily dependent on the foreign markets. So, when during 1981–2 he cut food imports by two-thirds, the consequences for the vast majority of Romanians were catastrophic.

Supermarket shelves emptied. Securitate men and the militia took control of food distribution, ensuring that Party bosses were kept well supplied while the rest of the population began queuing for scarce meat, vegetables and bread. Chickens and cows were slaughtered before maturity to hurry them to the plate. Livestock was reared on poor diets so that their meat lacked nourishment. People tried to grow their own food but with much of the population now relocated into cities, they had no land to cultivate. In the 1970s, the shops had been reasonably well stocked but few people had possessed enough money to buy the goods on offer. By 1983, the problem was upended; people had the money but there was no food to buy.

The plunge in imports was matched by a vigorous push for exports. For a time, Ceaușescu did manage to increase Romania's foreign trade but only by volume, not value. In Arad, in western Romania, railway carriages were produced for the international market, but the lathes required frequent repairs and Ceaușescu had stopped the importation of spare parts. It meant that foreign clients were supplied with carriages literally falling apart at the seams. Romania tried to export TV sets but entire consignments were sent back, rejected as dangerous because of poor electrics. The Chinese announced that their barter arrangements could not continue because the rudimentary machinery that the Romanians were supplying in exchange for oil was too shoddy. Romanian-produced cars were returned because of the low-quality steel used to make them, but instead of improving the product, factories patched them up using even larger quantities of the same low-quality metal, which had the effect of adding weight to the vehicles and making them undriveable.[10] On one occasion, the French decided that machinery imported from Romania was of such low quality, it made more economic sense to melt it down into sheet metal.

In the winter of 1983, my father-in-law, Gheorghe Iosifescu, left the state-controlled Centrul de Calcul at lunchtime, waved sarcastically to the Securitate agent who monitored him and caught the tram home through the freezing streets of Ploiești. When he arrived at Block 32, Apartment 7, Boulevard Republicii, his living room had the familiar stuffy warmth obtained by trapping heat in a room and sealing the doors with blankets and cushions. Ceaușescu had ordered that all heating be centrally controlled, to prevent wastage. The pipes would belch into life for an hour each morning, providing a quick burst of warmth, and then shut down. The trick was to stop it from escaping. Hot water was a similar challenge. It was available only one day a week. The rest of the time, a twist of the tap would produce a hiss of stale air. Baths were made with pans of water boiled on the hob.

As he entered the apartment, Gheorghe was greeted by a rush of activity. His nine-year-old daughter, Flavia, was racing around trying to find her medals. Everything else was ready: the military-style white shirt with epaulettes, the black skirt and red neckerchief, the sash of golden braid. Like every girl and boy in Romania, she had been inducted into the Pioneers at the age of seven. But Flavia was special because she had been voted '*Pionier de frunte*' – Leading Pioneer – by her classmates, a prestigious position that came with dreaded responsibility. Part of the job was collecting evidence of the alleged misdemeanours of others, and then standing before class once a week to name the offenders and their crimes. Fighting, swearing, cheating – all must be recorded and listed. Regular school denunciations were the regime's way of preparing youngsters for life under the Securitate.

Her father found her medals on the pine bookcase and Flavia pinned them to her shirt pocket, ready for inspection.

The date was 18 December 1983 and she was about to represent her school at an historic event. Outside the block, women stood mummified in layers of coats and blankets, exhaling clouds of air into the chill Ploieşti afternoon. On a fringe of frozen earth beside the block sat a dozen Dacia 1300s in various states of decay. Anyone fortunate enough to have a car in Romania had a Dacia, named patriotically after the ancient land upon which the country was built. They were manufactured largely in primary blue or red, giving the streets a dull uniformity broken only by the appearance of the occasional racing-green Skoda or exotic mustard-coloured Trabant. The Dacia was really a Renault 12, its parts imported from France, and then reconstituted as a cheap family car for the domestic market. But when the French-made parts ran out and Romania was left to produce its own, the factories tried to make them out of the country's notoriously low-quality steel. Gheorghe Iosifescu's Dacia was so unreliable that he carried the battery with him into his apartment each evening, wrapped in an old blanket to keep it warm and functioning.

At the town's football stadium, lines of Pioneers stood to attention on the terraces. Despite the freezing temperatures, none were allowed to wear coats or jackets. Uniformity was all part of the spectacle. A group of teachers distributed placards to every tenth child. Some carried slogans, such as 'Long Live Our Beloved Leader'. Others were portraits of the President and his wife when they were young.

The children waited two hours. No one was allowed to move. Flavia crouched occasionally to get the blood flowing. The cold was intense. Then a cheer erupted, a sound so loud and sudden that the children looked at each other startled. In through a gate beneath the main stand drove a cavalcade of black limousines. The leader had arrived. They could see him standing in the back of a long, shining, black car. He waved, and they waved. Round the track the vehicles went, in slow procession. Placards were raised in unison. The cheers and applause were deafening, yet when Flavia looked around, her colleagues were so cold that their little hands could hardly have been making a sound. The national anthem struck up. The convoy turned the corner at the top of the pitch and made its way back around, the fur-coated figure of Ceaușescu waving his gloved hand, his black Persian lamb hat pulled low over his head. Then he was gone.

It was only later, in her parents' apartment, that Flavia learned that the cheers were recordings played through loudspeakers and that it would hardly have mattered if no one had clapped at all. Every year, on 18 December, the Pioneers were expected to celebrate the anniversary of Stalin's birth in 1878.

In the early 1980s, Romania withdrew itself from the world. To those outside, it was preserved in aspic as the plucky communist state that defied the Russians in '68, and then set out on its own independent course. To those inside, it became a prison, a dark social experiment from which there seemed no escape. Few had any interest in what was going on behind its heavily guarded borders. The Cold War was heating up once again. President Ronald Reagan was accelerating the reversal of detente, building up US military strength and attacking the Soviet Union's 'evil empire'. He needed Romania on his side and Ceaușescu seemed immune from Western criticism, even to a US administration that allegedly found communism morally repugnant. On any ideological or human rights measurement, Ceaușescu's regressive Stalinism was the most morally repugnant of all, but Cold War realpolitik meant that the West continued to indulge him. Before Ceaușescu broke with the IMF, and within eighteen months of Pacepa's defection, the White House offered him yet another multi-million-dollar loan, and even agreed the export of US-manufactured munitions to Bucharest.[11] As late as 1984, when Romania was deep within the most suffocating and oppressive years of Ceaușescu's rule, the US vice-president, George H. W. Bush – a devout Christian who recoiled from any form of

Socialism – lauded the Romanian leader as one of Europe's 'good communists'.

Inside the country, amid the cold and the hunger, the soul of a man could be bought with even the most trifling of bribes. A cut of fatty bacon. A box of oranges from China. A banana. Children had never seen a banana. Give a man a bag of chicken thighs and he would do anything. A bag of chicken thighs was currency. Securitate agents and Party workers were awarded chicken thighs for years of unquestioning obedience. Teachers were given chicken thighs by determined mothers in exchange for favourable grades. Doctors, who were paid the same as factory workers, would demand a bag of chicken thighs in return for a bottle of Western medicine.

The kind of people who attended Party congresses thought chicken thighs rather beneath them. Chicken thighs were for the lower orders. These people had access to chicken *breast*, a part of the bird's anatomy that most people had not tasted for several years. They were the communist elite, the men and women who existed on a higher plane, who had tasted the sweet, alpine air of unconstrained corruption. They would have started out working on some hopeless factory floor. Perhaps they compiled a report on a trouble-maker. Maybe they pointed out the slackers or the thieves or the merely suspicious to the Securitate. And then a few portions of chicken thighs might have come their way. Something with which to bribe an official for more petrol or cooking oil or the use of a cabin by the beach. And then the game really began. More 'monitoring' on behalf of the Securitate. More chicken. More favours in return. What about a role in the local Party? From there it was an easy reach into the coffers of a state-run farm. And then you were really motoring. Diverting meat and eggs to your own family and friends. You could supply food to officers at the port in exchange for crates of foreign goods. You could then channel those foreign goods to a planning officer in exchange for a new apartment. And in that new apartment, you could entertain police chiefs, mayors, party officials and even Ceaușescu's aides.

The process was so central to Romanian life that they had a word for it: *pile* (pronounced pee-ley), the use of connections and bribery to progress through the system, either by using the Party or the Securitate. *Pile* was not so much a process as a state of mind, and was deeply ingrained in the country's psyche. Nothing was done on merit. Going to university, getting a job, securing an apartment – all required *pile*. It was Ottoman in origin, a form of baksheesh, and it had continued – indeed, flourished – under communism because the official, centralized, state-controlled system was supposed to enforce equality, yet human nature insisted on so much more. And in Romania, where many of the population had next to nothing, more meant just a bag of chicken thighs.

This nucleus of corrupt men and women represented Ceaușescu's extended court, the modern-day boyars who lorded it over the masses in a communist order that had become a grotesque replica of Romania's feudal past. The Party had been set up to end the very thing it now mimicked. The only difference was that it was no longer the bourgeoisie and the educated who governed, but the most ignorant and expertly corrupt. The old boyar council had been replaced by the Central Committee. Boyar banquets were now Party congresses. The ruling prince was, of course, Ceaușescu.

On a dark autumn afternoon in 1984, delegates streamed into the tangerine-coloured auditorium of Palace Hall in Bucharest for the Thirteenth Congress of the Romanian Communist Party, to play out a scene that had more in common with Ionesco's Theatre of the Absurd than any political rally. The Party elite fell over themselves to heap praise on Ceaușescu, even as their countrymen queued outside for scraps of food.

'The unprecedented achievements in the economy, education and culture,' began Petru Enache, a former lathe-worker whose mastery of *pile* had taken him to the top, 'lend our time the image of an impressive renaissance.' Enache was secretary in charge of ideology, a rotund, red-faced individual whose extravagant homages to Ceauşescu had made him a popular act. 'The great victories won in these years,' yelled Enache, 'have been possible due to... Nicolae Ceauşescu, the politician who is constantly concerned with fervent patriotism, the destiny of his people, and acting towards the constant progress of his homeland, and who has also asserted himself as a great thinker and present-day strategist.'[12]

In fact, the destiny of Ceauşescu's people had, for three years now, been dominated by wartime-like rationing of bread, milk, cooking oil, meat, and petrol. Food imports had been cut again that very year, with Ceauşescu pretending it was all part of a government health drive to improve people's diets. He called it his 'scientific plan' for 'rational eating'. Each person was restricted to just 39 kg of meat a year – equivalent to one and a half chickens a month. But even that was misleading. By the time most people reached the front of the queue, all that was left was chicken feet and necks, along with occasional pig feet and tails. These portions were known as 'the patriots', because they remained in Romania, while the prime cuts were exported abroad.

The audience cheered as Petru Enache sat down. He was the darling of the Congress, perhaps even a leader himself one day, should anything unexpected happen to Ceauşescu. But popularity within the Party came at a price. Elena Ceauşescu was suspicious of Enache. She was preparing her son, Nicu, to be Ceauşescu's successor, and Enache was an irritant.

Three years later, Enache would start to moderate his views and become an unlikely admirer of the new Soviet leader, Mikhail Gorbachev, and his epoch-changing reforms of Perestroika (restructuring) and Glasnost (openness). Such wayward sympathies would, in the eyes of Ceauşescu, make him a dangerous deviant and a possible rival. Enache would later die in mysterious circumstances at the age of fifty-three. Some say he had an argument with Elena and that his body was later found in a pool of blood on his bathroom floor. Others say that the overweight Enache died of a heart attack. The mystery is kept alive by the presence of a death certificate that seems to give Enache's cause of death the day before he actually died.[13]

That was all for later. For now, at the Thirteenth Party Congress, it was the turn of little Ana Mureșan, the ultra-loyalist with the moon-shaped glasses and a distinctive waddle brought about by years of over-indulgence. Mureșan looked like an unnervingly over-indulgent aunt who might lace her cookies with a sprig of deadly nightshade. She was a candidate member of the powerful Executive Committee, and she needed Elena's backing to confirm her position. 'With feelings of great esteem and love,' she began, 'we want to convey our appreciation and recognition to Comrade Elena Ceaușescu.' She proceeded to thank the First Lady for her selfless work in 'developing scientific research, education and culture' and for her 'generosity and devotion' to all Romanians. The auditorium erupted once again.

They were no longer cheering Elena, but an *impression* of Elena, an idealized version of a First Lady who was both brilliant and humane. They had superimposed onto her whatever qualities they desired. Her photos, her qualifications, her achievements, all were false. But it did not matter. Collectively, they had established a new truth, one that suited everyone. The old Elena, the near illiterate peasant with the acid tongue and the bovine features, receded into the past. The new one, with the academic scrolls and crocodile-skin shoes, strode monstrously into the future. Her greatness was constrained only by their own imaginations, and they imagined Elena as their idol.

A new painting by Gheorghe Pirvu showed her floating in the heavens dressed in shimmering white, the sleeves of her dress billowing into the shape of angel wings. Child Pioneers stood beneath her with uplifted arms, as if she were an apparition. For the purposes of the painting, Elena appeared to be a teenager.

And yet the 'Mother of the Nation', as she styled herself, had shown anything but kindness and understanding to the nation's children. The Ceauşescus had been concerned by a drop in the country's birth rate. For them, it signalled a potential long-term fall in productivity and they responded by launching a drive for reproduction. All married girls, from the age of just fifteen, must breed. Months before the Congress, the President announced it was a woman's 'patriotic duty' and that the target was ten children per couple. Medals would be available for each child delivered. There were to be tax breaks for so-called 'Heroine Mothers' and financial penalties for married women over the age of twenty-five who remained childless. The breeding drive would be bolstered by the banning of contraceptives and the continuation of the ban on abortions, which had begun shortly after Ceauşescu became leader. Most disturbing was an act of enforcement that was unique in the communist world. In factories and offices across the country, women of child-bearing age were subjected to random gynaecological examinations to check that they were not breaking the law by using contraceptive devices.[14] The birth rate did rise between 1986 and 1988, but the measures led to tragedy. Romania saw a dramatic increase in back-street and self-induced abortions. During Ceauşescu's dictatorship, 10,000 otherwise healthy women died after unsafe abortions, most of them from post-abortion haemorrhage and blood poisoning.[15]

This was the set of policies that helped create the country's 170,000 orphans, who would later represent the defining image of post-revolutionary Romania. They only came to light when Western journalists, covering the revolution in 1989, ventured out of the capital into the countryside. There, they stumbled upon dungeon-style rooms of malnourished children chained to beds, some of them rocking back and forth like caged animals, others diseased and lying in their own excrement.

Nevertheless, at the Thirteenth Party Congress, delegates showered Elena with praise. They cheered again when her mentally unstable son, Nicu, was made a candidate member of the Executive Committee, to sit alongside his mother and father on the most powerful body in the land. Nicu's wife, Poliana Cristescu, was already head of the Pioneer Organization, and was now 'elected' a full member of the Central Committee. Other members of the Ceauşescu family began slotting into senior roles around them. The President's younger brother, Ilie, was appointed deputy minister of defence. Another brother, Nicolae, became lieutenant-general in the ministry of the interior. A third, Ion, became minister-secretary of state for planning. A fourth, Marin, was given a position in foreign trade. A fifth became a member of staff at the Party paper, *Scînteia*. Ceauşescu's sister became deputy minister of education. None were capable individuals. They paraded their celebrity and their status, while a whole generation of talent was lost, either to labour camps or to obscure menial jobs. Romanian society was turned on its head. Cleverness, originality, and wit were all viewed as sins. Brilliant academics worked as porters in railway stations. Writers became cleaners. Priests were reduced to performing exorcisms in return for a few morsels of food.

Meanwhile, there was malnutrition on the streets of what people had once called Little Paris. People were dying of lung disease brought on by cold and lack of nutrition. Vitamins were in such short supply that hospitals gave blood transfusions to children in lieu of fresh food. The needles were often dirty and the use of contaminated blood led to an AIDS epidemic, something the puritanical Ceauşescu denied and therefore worsened. Romania's health system was ill-equipped to respond. At the time of the Thirteenth Party Congress, new-born babies were dying in hospital incubators because of government-ordered power cuts. In 1983, infant mortality rates were among the highest in Eastern Europe, at 26.8 per 1,000 children. At the same time, pensioners were viewed as obsolete units of production who consumed precious supplies of food and energy without giving anything back. They were expendable. Anyone over the age of sixty was routinely denied medicine or hospital treatment. Many suffered painful winter deaths in their own homes. Meanwhile, at the conclusion of the Thirteenth Party Congress, the sixty-six-year-old Ceaușescu – who was rumoured to be having needless blood transfusions abroad in order to keep him young – was cheered rapturously and lauded for having achieved 'the richest accomplishments' in all Romania's history.

*

An ancient Byzantine church rolled past the residential blocks of Unirii Square in the winter of 1985 – slowly, of course, as was befitting a church of its age and grandeur. Residents living on the top floors of neighbouring blocks looked out of their windows and saw three ornate towers pass by, each crowned with a high metal cross and coated with a dusting of snow. 'The Mihai Voda Church', they yelled. 'Look, it's on the move!' 9,000 tonnes of masonry trundled by, heading eastwards towards Sapienței Street, followed by its teetering sixteenth-century tower. Other churches had also been seen moving through the narrow streets of old Bucharest that year, but Mihai Voda was the biggest and the most important; a gem of ecclesiastical architecture founded in 1594 by the Romanian national hero, Michael the Brave.

A young engineer called Eugeniu Iordăchescu had come up with the idea of moving the capital's ancient churches after learning that a whole neighbourhood was about to be demolished to make way for Ceaușescu's rebuilding plans. The earthquake of 1977 had failed to destroy sufficient acreage to accommodate the President's megalomaniac dream of a city centre built to his own extravagant design, and so bulldozers were now tearing down perfectly good and, in many cases, historically significant buildings to free up the space. Iordăchescu was horrified and devised a plan that involved lifting the churches onto specially made tracks and rolling them to new locations outside the destruction zone.

No government official would formally sign off the idea, in case it was unpopular with Ceaușescu. So, Iordăchescu and his colleagues started the project with just a nod and a great deal of nerve. They dug beneath the first church, the tiny Schitul Maicilor, inserted large reinforced concrete supports, severed the foundations, and then levered it onto tracks and pushed it away. Amazingly, the church rolled along without even cracking. Then they moved on to the next, always in a race against Ceaușescu's wrecking balls. The Mihai Voda church was rolled 289 metres down a 6-metre incline, before being deposited in a position where it remains to this day, hemmed in by grim communist blocks.

Gradually, the team became more daring, moving entire residential buildings while they were still connected to mains water and electricity, and, on one occasion, while Iordăchescu stood on the balcony as if he were the captain of a brick galleon desperately trying to flee Ceaușescu's stone-smashing armada. Another time, a block had to be moved in such a hurry that it happened while the residents were still in bed. They had been told to pack up and leave at 10 a.m., but the operation began at 6 a.m. instead and when they ventured downstairs, their residence had already moved 2 metres down the street.

They were the fortunate ones. This bustling quarter of Bucharest, known as Dealul Spirii, was home to 60,000 people. It was at the very heart of the city, replete with grand public buildings, an ancient monastery, schools, tramlines, shops, and twenty-two churches. Now the entire population was turfed out, sacrificed for some warped architectural homage to the President that would fill an area twice the size of the financial district of London.

On a bright summer day in June 1984, with the destruction well underway, three figures were seen picking their way across the flattened earth. It must have been a surreal sight: the President dressed in his smart suit, trying to unfold a huge architectural plan while barking orders; Elena hobbling in her kitten heels, berating her aides for all the mud and dust; and behind them, a wide-eyed young woman barely out of university, with a bobbing pony-tail and an anxious expression. Anca Petrescu had been at architecture school when a competition was launched to design the new 'People's Palace'. She had entered with little hope of beating the country's established practitioners but had cleverly played to Ceaușescu's incoherent grandiose tastes, producing a spectacular papier-mâché model of a palace that fused French neo-classical with Pyongyang brutalism. Its frontage would measure an astonishing 200 metres – twice as long as Buckingham Palace – with views along 'Victory of Socialism Avenue', a sterile corridor of fountains and pools lined with ten-storey tower blocks from whose mean little windows residents could stare out at other mean little windows all the way along its unchanging 3.5 kilometres of concrete despair.

Anca Petrescu won the competition. At the age of just twenty-eight, she became chief architect for the rebuilding of central Bucharest. Every Saturday morning, the Ceaușescus would appear on site to check on her progress. Nicolae always made a show of shaking hands with the labourers while haughtily ignoring the 700 architects assisting Petrescu. He had his own ideas about how the buildings should look, but architecture, like medicine, is a dangerous field for amateurs. Ceaușescu, it turned out, was unable to gauge the effect of a column or a door, even when Petrescu showed him a scale model. She ended up having to build life-size replicas in papier-mâché. Her assistance just added to the confusion. Ceaușescu switched from Doric columns to Ionic, and then back again. The roof looked good flat but what about a dome? Wouldn't that be better? His biggest problem was understanding scale and perspective. Because the project grew and grew, the spaces around the palace also grew, leaving a confused Ceaușescu thinking the palace looked too small. He wanted it bigger. At one point, he insisted on adding another two storeys and then ranted and raved after discovering that the ceilings of the additional floors were low and the rooms dark. He ordered more windows to be built to let in natural light, and when they were constructed, changed his mind and wanted them rectangular rather than arched.

So it went on, month after chaotic month. Marble was trucked down from Transylvania, almost an entire mountain's-worth for the countless bathrooms and freeway-style corridors. Entire hillsides of oak forest were felled for the parquet floors. Crystal glass for the chandeliers weighed 4,000 tonnes, the equivalent of hanging 2,000 Dacia cars from the ceilings. Not only were there twelve storeys above ground, there were at least eight beneath. It would have taken the Ceaușescus too long to walk from one end to the other, so they had a two-person underground railway built. We can imagine the couple squeezed beside one another, Elena wrapped in one of her huge mink coats, Nicolae with his black lambswool hat askew over his eyes as their Disney-style railcar rattled them through the dark tunnels beneath their palace of horrors.

Dracula had done the same, building tunnels beneath his fortified homes so that he could spirit himself away from any conspiring boyars, or more likely from an Ottoman attack. He would take great pleasure in appearing, as if from nowhere, at the rear of his private church to greet boyars who had seen him just moments before in his study. It played to his assumed aura of divinity.

Ceaușescu's escape tunnels ran from his palace into the sewers, partly to hide him from a Russian invasion but also from his own people, should they ever begin to organize. Other Romanian cities were also bulldozed, relieved of their *fin de siècle* architecture, their bustling alleyways, their French-style boulevards and shaded pavement-cafes where men and women once sat beneath lime trees sipping Turkish coffee sweetened with a dollop of marmalade. All of it was swept away. In the oil city of Ploiești, where my in-laws lived, orchards of apples and apricots were destroyed, as were the botanical gardens, the popular Art Deco cinema, the little zoo and the entire central district where Byzantine and French neo-classical villas had jostled for space around a busy market square. Communist blocks were thrown up in a matter of months. Each apartment had a tiny concrete balcony the size of a mat, although balcony was the wrong word. That would suggest leisure, sunshine, deckchairs. In Romania there was no leisure, no private space away from the prying eyes of the Securitate. A 'balcony' was for cold storage. Flagons of pickled vegetables were stacked up on makeshift shelves. Dogs were pushed out onto those tiny patches of concrete to relieve themselves, their pee dripping down onto the balconies below.

This was architecture as a form of control. There was no joy to be had, no aesthetic pleasure derived from the cement walls or ill-fitting windows. These were human coops, factories of conformity, soulless dwellings for a people reduced to units of production.

At Block 32, Flat No. 7, Boulevard Republicii, a young woman would arrive twice a week, scarf pulled over her face, the collar of her coat pulled high around her ears. Local Securitate informants would head her off before she reached the lift, asking where she was from and what business she had entering the block. She was visiting family, she would report. She was aunt to a little girl, Flavia Iosifescu, who lived on the seventh floor. They would watch her, doubtfully, as she entered the tiny lift and pulled the sheet metal door shut behind her.

In fact, this was no aunt at all, but Flavia's secret English teacher, Nicoletta Matei. In Romania, the study of languages was frowned upon. Speaking anything but the mother tongue was seen as an attempt to pursue a line of contact with the outside world, to understand banned books and newspapers, to rebel. Learning English, in particular, was profoundly subversive. It signified an intent to escape, to defect to the West. That is why lessons had to be organized secretly. These twice-weekly visits were also an opportunity to learn something about the world beyond the Iron Curtain, a place that, for most Romanian children, was receding into obscurity. America and Britain seemed distant, almost mythical lands, portrayed by the government as debauched and immoral, while at the same time parents whispered about dreamlike places where shops were full of food and young people danced endlessly on warm summer nights, to The Beatles and The Rolling Stones. For a child, the secrecy surrounding the West merely added to the allure.

Their own history, on the other hand, was bewildering for its anxious avoidance of the actual past. School books removed any references to Romania's long period of fascism or to the royal family. History began with the Communist Party. There was nothing before the Second World War, just mystifying empty years during which Ceaușescu and his wife had allegedly been doing popular and brave things against a blank backdrop. Before that, there was nothing, all the way back through the centuries, until students encountered a crackle of life around Stephen the Great, Michael the Brave and Dracula, and then nothing again, all the way back to the Romans, at which point the text books erupted into life and colour. It was the creation of Roman Dacia by Emperor Trajan in the second century AD that Ceaușescu insisted was their true heritage. Romanians were, in fact, Romans by blood, brave survivors of a lost world. Food shortages and cold were nothing for the hardy descendants of centurions. He was their Caesar, guiding them through the hostile forests of a conspiring world. They needed to stay separate, to remain uncontaminated by Western consumerism or the Slavic hordes.

Flavia sat at the living-room table with Miss Matei, learning her English grammar and phonetics by candlelight. The power cuts were now a daily occurrence. Out in the fields, there were candles too, flickering in the glassless windows of concrete huts where guards took shelter from the October wind. Beyond, in the muddy fields, were long regimented lines of hunched figures, their faces lit occasionally by yellow flashlights. Each had a sack to fill. They dug through the mud with forks and spades in search of potatoes. But these were not hired hands. Earlier that morning, a fleet of old buses had turned up at the Centrul de Calcul, where Gheorghe Iosifescu worked, and at other offices around the city, disgorging Securitate officers who commandeered every able-bodied man and woman for forced labour in the fields. 'Patriotic Work', as the authorities liked to call it, soon became a regular thing. Judges worked shoulder-to-shoulder with convicts. Priests picked corn alongside plumbers and welders. No one was spared, other than those with impressive reserves of *pile* who could buy their absence by producing false medical certificates.

School children were viewed as a resource, picked up from school and bussed to the fields, although their work was lighter than that of their parents. Head Pioneer Flavia Iosifescu picked cherries with her classmates, monitored by local Party officials. The children climbed into the lower branches and filled punnets with as many fruits as they could grab. Hiding in the thick leaves, they filled their mouths too – thrilling mischief for children who rarely saw fruit in the shops. When they left, each child was searched. Even a single cherry at the bottom of a pocket would be confiscated. The harvest was not for Romanians, it was for export. The potatoes, corn, wheat, cherries – all were sent abroad.

Flavia Iosifescu was the girl I would later marry. To this day, she remembers the forced labour and the terrible anxiety when security officers checked her satchel for stolen fruit. Ceaușescu was still obsessed with paying off his foreign debt and teaching a lesson to those who humiliated him at the IMF and World Bank. While the rest of Eastern Europe channelled every penny they could muster into welfare and consumer products as popular discontent began to surface across the region, Ceaușescu did not concern himself with public opinion at all. Using his people as a vast supply of forced labour, everything he squeezed from the economy was pumped into heavy industry and debt elimination. Vital services were abandoned. In the four years up to 1985, investment in education and health fell by 59 per cent, municipal services by 37 per cent. Without investment, city-centre roads were cratered with potholes. Cars and trucks became damaged and un-roadworthy. Ceaușescu's refusal to import spares meant that vehicles were cannibalized for fan belts and pistons. A third of state-owned delivery lorries were off the road by 1985. Officials shifted goods to trains instead, but all the best railcars had been exported.

Ceaușescu then tried to take a grip of the country's faltering agriculture himself, micromanaging in a fashion that a secret CIA report described as 'bizarre'.[16] He dictated everything from the size of food rations for hogs, through to production goals for bees. Between 1981 and 1984, he increased the price of beef by 100 per cent, pork by 83 per cent, coffee by 106 per cent. He told farmers which varieties of wheat could be planted, how far apart to space their fruit trees, and then suddenly decided that all cooperative farms must produce 5 kg of silk worm cocoons a year. But none of that alleviated hunger. Meat and milk were in such short supply that the authorities gave up formal rationing. If anyone was fortunate enough to find either product, they were free to purchase in whatever quantities they could afford. The encouraging news was that this painful austerity had reduced Romania's debt by 30 per cent at the start of 1985. However, that still left a staggering $2 billion a year to pay on interest alone. The cost to the Romanian people continued to grow. Infant mortality was the highest in Europe. The overall death rate was accelerating faster than anywhere else in the Eastern Bloc. Even as Ceaușescu continued to build his new palace, he limited households to a single 15-watt light bulb and one appliance, with the militia entering homes and plastering over any additional electrical sockets to ensure there was no over-consumption.

*

Over in the far west of the country, near to the ancient Roman spa town of Herculane, discreet groups of young men and women hid in the thick forest in the summer of 1985. A glorious retreat in the days of Queen Marie, with baths of hot springs and domed palaces, the town had faded to near dereliction during the Ceaușescu years, possessing just one road in and one road out. The allure of Herculane was no longer its hot mineral baths but its proximity to Romania's western border, fifteen miles away along a heavily patrolled track and demarcated by the Danube. On the far bank lay the more liberal Yugoslavia. Herculane was a frontier town. Just getting there was a challenge, the road bristling with Securitate officers and army checkpoints. But the prize was a shot at the river crossing.

At its narrowest point, the Danube was a quarter of a mile wide and the currents were strong. If a crossing was attempted by a weak swimmer, there was every chance they would be dragged downstream to contend with the jaws of the huge Iron Gates hydroelectric dam.

People spent months training for the crossing. They lifted weights in their apartments, studied maps and currents, sewed camouflage tents in which to hide themselves in the Herculane forests. The psychological preparation was more testing. A notorious border unit patrolled the Romanian side of the river, equipped with rifles, sniffer dogs and speed boats. They were famously competitive about how many *frontieriști* they could neutralize. That was their name for border hoppers, 'frontier people' who would rather die than spend another day in Romania.

From 1985 the numbers of *frontieriști* spiked. This was the year that all contact with foreigners was banned. Romanians were no longer permitted to study abroad. Elena Ceaușescu purged the foreign ministry of anyone who spoke a foreign language. She even managed to find an ambassador for Paris who did not speak French. When scientists at the Academy Presidium complained that the ban on attending foreign conferences precluded them from doing their job, Elena replied: 'Nonsense comrades, I have never participated in foreign conferences, and look where I am!'

It is estimated that 16,000 people tried to cross the river near Herculane, more than those who crossed the more well-documented border between East and West Germany. *Frontieriști* would camp for days in the forest, waiting for a gap in patrols, and then lower themselves stealthily into the water, their meagre belongings strapped in plastic bags around their waists. Powerful torches would flash from the banks. If a swimmer was spotted, the Romanian soldiers opened fire. There was little mercy. Following particularly busy weekends, the Yugoslav authorities phoned their Romanian counterparts to complain that bodies were clogging the machinery of the dam.

On both sides of the river, rows of unmarked graves were dug. Even today, no one knows who occupies them. For those who made it to the other side, there were no guarantees. As they hauled themselves, breathless, up the far bank and into the Yugoslavian forests around Novi Sip, they would often be picked up by patrols, questioned and then returned to Romania, where they would face at least a beating and a spell in jail.

*

After 1985, there was a shift in power in Romania – from Nicolae Ceaușescu to Elena. Nicolae had developed diabetes and prostatitis, and the resulting physical discomfort made him even more irascible. Elena decided that she should protect him from the burden of daily decision-making by taking those decisions herself. The list of her husband's appointments had to be sent to Elena for approval first. There would be two cabinets: Cabinet One run by Nicolae, Cabinet Two run by Elena. She had her own parallel set of aides. Every set of paperwork would pass through Cabinet Two. It might be forwarded to Nicolae. It might not. She would decide. The result was a pantomime of advisors trying to reach Nicolae behind Elena's back. All of them resented the new procedures and considered Elena irrational, vindictive and stupid.

Her *bête noire* was the new Russian leader, Mikhail Gorbachev, and his epoch-changing reforms that promised to open the Soviet Union to the West and liberalize its institutions. Elena despised him, telling anyone who would listen that Nicolae had been the true reformer for two decades. Gorbachev, she said, was simply following Ceaușescu's lead, and she was mystified as to why anyone paid him attention. But there were queues at the Aeroflot offices in Bucharest where uncensored versions of Gorbachev's speeches had been made available. Even within the near hermetically sealed borders of Romania, people sensed that profound change was in the air. Gorbachev was visiting his East European neighbours and, unless Ceaușescu had something to fear, Bucharest was next on his list.

*

Soldiers and civilians were out early on Sunday, 24 May 1987, painting fences, sweeping streets, paving over unfinished roadworks. Lorries arrived at shops in Bucharest carrying curious deliveries of household items that onlookers had not seen for years. There was fine food too – prime cuts of beef, salami from Italy, even biscuits and cakes, all stacked in shop windows while the rest of the stores remained empty. Soldiers kept the crowds back. None of it was for consumption.

The following morning, a military guard stood to attention along the runway at Otopeni Airport as Mikhail Gorbachev stepped from his Ilyushin 62 Aeroflot plane. Elegant, tanned and relaxed in a grey lounge suit, he looked every inch like an American politician. Reminiscent, in fact, of Richard Nixon when he landed in Bucharest all those years before, at the start of Ceaușescu's odyssey into Washington's arms. Now Gorbachev was the West's bridge to the communist East. Ceaușescu was obsolete.

The Romanian was stony-faced as he greeted his Soviet counterpart, his over-oiled hair matted into unappetizing clumps, his skin grey and puffy. Gorbachev surveyed the crowd uneasily. 'Ceaușescu! Gorbachev!' the people chanted, again and again.

As they climbed into the motorcade, portraits of the two leaders were held aloft. Gorbachev was represented by a contemporary photograph, his coffee-stain birthmark clearly visible on the right side of his forehead; Ceaușescu by an image taken twenty years before, showing him as a young man. It was inadvertently poetic – the authentic face of reform in crisp, unforgiving celluloid, the great deceiver in a heavily worked blur that was more artistic impression than blood and bones.

Through the packed streets of central Bucharest they were driven, the pair's heads poking through the sunroof of a jeep, pavements lined with folk dancers in golden brocade, gymnasts balancing on each other's shoulders, pirouetting peasant women in identical lilac skirts. Ceaușescu had micromanaged every detail. It was an homage to the street scenes created by Mao in China. Gorbachev was not impressed. Later, he waded into the crowd and tried to strike up a conversation. It was unheard of in Bucharest since the visit of Nixon. They stood agape, nodding at everything he said, while looking around nervously for the Securitate.

On the third day of his visit, Gorbachev addressed the Central Committee and senior Party members in a speech that was broadcast live on Romanian television. He spoke of allowing limited private enterprise, of small businesses being the way to energize the economy, of allowing certain capitalist forces into the Eastern Bloc. Ceaușescu stood thunderous on the side-lines. It was, for him, 'rightist deviationism' and a personal attack on his own handling of the economy. Television viewers loved it.

But the most revealing account of Gorbachev's visit came a fortnight later, in a report to the Soviet Politburo on 4 June 1987 written by the Soviet leader himself. '... the [Romanian] people's situation is very difficult,' said Gorbachev, 'there are constant shortages of power, heat, food products, consumer goods, and Ceaușescu has been telling me all this time that he has already achieved everything... I look at him, and I feel like a fool.' The obedience of the Romanian crowds, he said, set his teeth on edge. They were like 'a wound-up musical box; "Ceaușescu, Gorbachev", "Ceaușescu, Peace"... it makes one's head burst... When I came closer to the people, I would ask them, "Do you know any other words?" Later I was told that these criers were brought there on a bus for this purpose.' He told his comrades that Romania was like no other country he'd witnessed in Eastern Europe, a place where 'human dignity has absolutely no value'.

Gorbachev reserved his most damning verdict for Ceaușescu himself. The Romanian leader was, he said, '... unbelievably impudent. His self-assurance and self-praise are absolutely monumental, comparable only with his attempts to teach and admonish everybody.'[17] The question was: how long could Ceaușescu isolate his people from the reforms sweeping the rest of the region?

*

László Tőkés had the countenance of a rugged, eighteenth-century explorer, the kind who marched across the tundra, shooting hares and swigging whisky. His domain was the blasted, wintry landscape around the western city of Timișoara, where, as a pastor of the Reformed Church, he conducted bracing outdoor services for famished peasants, preaching in farmyards and cemeteries, on hillsides and beside roaring communal fires. Wherever he was, his mainly Hungarian congregation was always anxious about a sudden visit from the secret police.

Tőkés was on the Securitate's radar. He was trouble. His sermons frequently contained a political theme. Specifically, he was critical of one of Ceaușescu's most megalomaniacal policies. It was known as 'systematization', an innocent word to describe a scheme of rare destructive power. Ceaușescu wanted to re-organize the very foundation of Romania's social history. He had decided to shut down villages and forcibly transfer their inhabitants to tower blocks in cities and towns. In his deluded vision of the future, the process represented a great advance in human development. The problem was that none of the ancient rural communities wanted to move.

In March 1987, Ceaușescu announced that half of Romania's 13,000 villages would be razed to the ground, their inhabitants re-housed in specially built 'agro-industrial' towns. Some were given just forty-eight hours to leave, and when the wrecking crews turned up they were offered a choice: either pay for the bulldozers or destroy your own homes with pick-axes and hammers. Many had no money and were forced to choose the latter. They were then photographed for propaganda purposes: 'excited' peasants loyally destroying their homes 'with a view to a better future'. The pictures did not convince a disbelieving outside world. Ceaușescu's systematization attracted international condemnation, including an unprecedented political intervention from Britain's Prince Charles, who backed a campaign to twin Romanian villages with European ones and then protest their destruction.

Ceaușescu was rattled by the sudden global attention and hit upon a chillingly inventive solution. Instead of clashing with peasants, he would smoke them out. Villages awoke to find their electricity and mains water supply cut off. Food shops were boarded up by the Securitate. Buses no longer passed through. These ancient communities were allowed to atrophy. Residents had little choice but to gather their belongings and traipse across the countryside to the nearest town. Half-starved peasants were herded into poorly built, overcrowded apartments, their humanity left buried beneath the rubble of their ancestral plots.

This was the policy that inspired László Tőkés to speak out. At first, he thought systematization was directed against ethnic-Hungarian villages in Transylvania, those which Ceaușescu believed were most hostile to his regime. But Tőkés soon realized that the scheme was indiscriminate, that ethnic Romanians and Hungarians would be affected in equal measure, and, crucially, he began to advocate solidarity between the two.

His repeated calls for resistance were punished by the fearsome presiding bishop, László Papp, who, under instruction from the department of cults and the Securitate, ordered Tőkés to stop preaching and relocated him to a remote rural parish in northern Transylvania. Tőkés refused to go. He was then informed that his eviction would be enforced on 15 December 1989.

The day dawned with the kind of sky Romanians call *tulbure* – murky like stirred ditch water, with tension and foreboding as if the heavens knew what was about to occur. A freezing wind blew in from the Carpathians. One by one, parishioners began to appear in the street beneath Tőkés's flat. They clasped one another's hands and began to form a human chain that stretched right around the building. Tőkés was inside with his pregnant wife and young child, waiting for the militia to appear. He leaned out of his window and thanked the crowds for their support, but suggested that it would be safer for them to return home. 'We won't leave!' yelled the crowd, and more began to gather.

By 7 p.m. on 16 December, more protestors had filled the dark streets around Tőkés's apartment. They demanded that the pastor show himself at the window, to prove he was still alive. He appeared, sporadically, waving and pleading with the protestors to leave. Each time, they shook their heads and assumed he was being put up to it by the Securitate.

Chants of 'Down with Ceaușescu' followed, and 'Down with Communism'. The crowd then wheeled around, crossed the bridge into the centre of town and attacked Party headquarters with stones. When soldiers turned up to disperse them, the ringleaders seized their water cannons, dismantled them and hurled them into the river. At the same time, Securitate agents took the opportunity to storm Tőkés's flat. They smashed down his door and charged inside just in time to see the pastor, dressed in yellow slippers and a black cape, slip down a ladder, into a courtyard below, following his heavily pregnant wife, Edit, young son, Maté, and two family friends. They took refuge in the church.

But there was no sanctuary in Ceaușescu's Romania. The door of the sacristy was quickly broken down and Tőkés was seized by a uniformed officer, who punched him repeatedly in the face and stomach. He was then led outside, staggering through the puddles, his face covered in blood.

It was 17 December 1989. News of the violent demonstration in Timișoara quickly reached the capital. Ceaușescu was being driven through the streets of Bucharest in his Mercedes 600, flanked by security vehicles and motorcycles, when he heard. He needed to act quickly to stop the protests from spreading.

The hours were counting down. Nicolae Ceaușescu had just eight days left to live.

CHAPTER SEVENTEEN

Listen to them, the children of the night. What music they make!
Dracula, Bram Stoker

The protests in Timișoara spread overnight on 16 December 1989, into the grand old city of Arad, just a few miles from the Hungarian border, and then across the Carpathians into the Transylvanian city of Cluj. Wild rumours quickly took hold. There were 4,000 dead in Timișoara, then 6,000. Some said 40,000.

The violence was the fault of Mikhail Gorbachev and George H. W. Bush, announced Ceaușescu to a hurried meeting of the Central Committee. The two leaders had met in the austere Cold War setting of American and Soviet battleships just off the coast of Malta at the start of December 1989, just a few weeks after the fall of the Berlin Wall, to discuss the rapid East–West thaw. They had emerged to make their historic announcement that the Cold War was over. The news hit Romania like a depth-charge, shaking Eastern Europe's hermit fiefdom and forcing Ceaușescu into an existential crisis. The Cold War was essential to his survival. Ceaușescu was at his strongest when tensions between East and West were drum-tight.

Across Ceaușescu's desk in the Central Committee building sat the defence minister, Lieutenant-General Vasile Milea, a square-jawed sixty-two-year-old whose avuncular style had made him a popular figure among rank-and-file soldiers but who was too soft for Ceaușescu's tastes. Milea was supposed to be in charge of putting down the protests in Timișoara. 'What did your officers do, Milea?' snapped Ceaușescu. 'Why didn't they intervene immediately, why didn't they fire? They should have fired to bring them down, to warn them, and then to fire at their legs... You don't put an enemy down with Sunday sermons, you have to burn him. Socialism is not constructed with false information and with devotion, but by fighting. At the moment in Europe there is a situation of capitulation, of signing pacts with imperialism in order to wipe out socialism.'

Milea replied, quietly, 'I did not give them ammunition.'

Ceaușescu thumped his fist on the table. 'I did not think you would shoot with blanks, that is like a rain shower.' His voice was hoarse with shouting. 'Those who entered the Party building should not leave the building alive. They've got to kill the hooligans, not just beat them.'

Ceaușescu then turned to his interior minister, Tudor Postelnicu, who bore a striking resemblance to the President himself. Another illiterate foundry-worker, famous for his poisonous campaigns against writers and intellectuals during his stint as head of the Securitate, Postelnicu later took the unusual step of denouncing himself as 'an idiot' during a genocide trial. Today, he stared impassively at the floor as Ceaușescu continued his withering assault. 'Where was the show of strength I ordered? My impression is [the interior ministry troops] were not armed?' Postelnicu shuffled uncomfortably in his seat and muttered in the affirmative.

Ceaușescu then summoned his Securitate chief, the unreadable General Iulian Vlad, who slipped into the room, his face half-obscured behind his customary yellow-tinted glasses. 'Why weren't they armed?' Ceaușescu bellowed.

Vlad was not easily flustered. 'I thought it wasn't necessary,' he replied flatly.

'Why didn't you report this and tell me?' spluttered Ceaușescu. 'I talked with you the whole night… Don't you know what "state of emergency" means?'

'Yes, Comrade, I know,' said Vlad. 'I gave the order.'

'Not even now are you telling the truth,' Ceaușescu shouted back. 'Had one of your men fired, the protestors would have fled like partridges.'

Elena spotted an opportunity to chip in. 'You should have fired on them,' she said, 'and, had they fallen, you should have taken them and shoved them into a cellar. Weren't you told that? Not one of them should have got out.'

Ceaușescu studied the faces of his three most important apparatchiks. Then he announced that they were all dismissed from their roles. From now on, he would take command of the army. 'Prepare a decree for me… we cannot carry on like this,' he shouted to his aides, and then, gesturing at Milea, Vlad and Postelnicu: 'All night I stood and talked to them every ten minutes, only afterwards did I realize they had not done what I ordered.'

The three men – 'the Holy Trinity of repression', as a former Party ideologue described them[1] – tried desperately to change Ceaușescu's mind. In a ritual of humiliating Marxist self-criticism, they each declared themselves, shamefully, to have failed. 'Please place your trust in me,' pleaded Milea. 'I did not appreciate the danger from the beginning.'

The normally cool General Vlad realized he was fighting for his career, if not his life. 'Hearing the tasks you have given to me,' he said, 'I will in future proceed in such a way as to merit your faith.'

There was silence. Ceaușescu stared bleakly at the reports from Timișoara on his desk and then had a change of heart. 'Good,' he said grudgingly. 'So, shall we try once more, Comrades?'

The three men filed solemnly from the room. In the meantime, Ceaușescu ordered his servants to pack his suitcases. He viewed the protests as local flare-ups, nothing sufficiently serious to warrant changing his schedule. Late on the night of Sunday, 17 December – with Timișoara, Arad and Cluj still rioting – he flew to Iran for a two-day official visit.

In Timișoara, the crowds outside local Party headquarters swelled to tens of thousands. Protestors broke in and seized secret paperwork and personal files and hurled them like confetti out of the broken windows. Piles of documents were burned in the main square. The First Army Command ordered its soldiers to implement an operation codenamed 'Radu the Handsome' after Dracula's brother, permitting actions 'designed to crush foreign aggression and to defend the country's revolutionary achievements and territorial integrity'.[2] It was a pre-existing emergency procedure, designed for repelling a Soviet invasion. There was no mention of how it should be implemented in peace time, and against Romania's own citizens.

At 4 p.m. that day, before he left for the airport, an order was given by Ceaușescu to shoot protestors in Timișoara. Militiamen and soldiers began arriving in the city in huge numbers. Plain-clothes Securitate officers stalked the streets in blue jeans, fur hats and parkas, brandishing machine guns. Soldiers sped along the central boulevard in TABs, Romanian-built armoured personnel carriers. Helicopters buzzed overhead. A column of men and women marched near to the opera house and heard a popping noise above. Some of the street lamps appeared to be exploding. Snipers had positioned themselves high up in commandeered apartments and were shooting from the windows. On the steps of the opera house lay a dead body. There were more bodies in a nearby street. Undaunted, the crowd began chanting to the army: 'Don't be afraid, join us!'

Elena was running the country in her husband's absence and there was growing unease among the generals about potential military defections. On 18 December, an order was issued from the Army Upper Political Council confiscating all personal radios, so that soldiers would have no means of finding out about the spread of violence.[3] Soon after, an order barred wives and relatives from entering any army premises, in case they should relay unhelpful information.

By the time Ceauşescu arrived back from Iran on 20 December, he realized for the first time the seriousness of the crisis facing him, but failed to grasp that he, and his Stalinist cronies, were the cause. He still blamed 'terrorists' inspired by ethnic Hungarians such as Tőkés. Ceauşescu had seen the news reports from across Eastern Europe throughout that year, showing neighbouring communist regimes being swept aside by popular democratic movements. The speed with which it happened had transfixed the world. In June, he saw Lech Wałęsa's Solidarity movement win the right to free elections in Poland. On 9 November he'd watched the fall of the Berlin Wall on television. But Ceauşescu was unmoved. Romania, he believed, was immune from global currents of change. Just to make sure, he decided to address his people with a patriotic speech that was supposed to rekindle memories of his famous unifying speech against the invasion of Czechoslovakia in 1968 – the high point of his career. To make the link clear, he would even present the speech from the same balcony. It would take place in Bucharest on 21 December 1989.

At 11 a.m. that morning, Palace Square was awash with banners, flags and the familiar ageless portraits of the ruling couple. Tens of thousands had been bussed in overnight, sleeping under Party supervision at factory barracks and guest houses. They crammed into the historic heart of the capital, between the former royal palace, the university, the Athenaeum concert hall and the Athénée Palace Hotel. A low morning sun, bathed the crowd in tepid, amber light.

After a while, a couple of Party officials appeared on the balcony of the Central Committee building, shouting Party slogans and trying to raise a cheer. This was the Ceauşescu warm-up act. Securitate agents had been assigned to each section of the audience, dressed in fur hats and long coats. They clapped ostentatiously, regularly checking around them to make sure others followed suit.

At 12.30, there was movement at the back of the balcony. A line of grim-faced men in bulky coats and fedora hats filed through the glass doors at the rear and took positions to either side of a battery of microphones. An announcement was made. It came from the mayor of Bucharest. Using the absurdly theatrical delivery of an American boxing promoter, he boomed through the public address system: 'Let me introduce to you… the much beloved and esteemed leader of the country… an eminent revolutionary patriot…' The mayor's voice rose through the gears, syllable after exaggerated syllable: '… who over three decades… has delivered… prosperity… freedom… the full independence of Socialist Romania… the General Secretary of the Party… our Comrade… Nicolae Ceaușescu!'

On cue, the crowd shouted 'Hurrah! Hurrah! Ceaușescu!', as he emerged dressed in a black woollen coat with generous fur lapels and a sleek fur hat. The television cameras zoomed into his pale, uncertain face. Whatever his public pronouncements, Ceaușescu's instincts would have told him that the reception was different from normal. The cheers were subdued, grudging even. Securitate agents were having to work hard to elicit any noise at all. He began his speech in a distinctly frail voice. 'First, I want to address you, the participants of this great popular meeting… warm greetings revolutionaries!' Only the Securitate officers stationed at the front could be seen applauding. 'I want also to address thanks to the organizers of this great event…'

Ceaușescu was one minute and seventeen seconds into his address, when he heard yells from somewhere near the back. Such an intervention was unprecedented. He glanced up and stumbled over his words: '… considering… it… is…' He began losing his way. The yells became louder. '… considering… it… is…' Jeers and whistles echoed around the square. Ceaușescu never finished his sentence. He did not have to. His audience was never there for his oratory. It was a moment frozen in time and in history. Ceaușescu stood with his mouth half open and his forehead creased with confusion. It became the abiding image of his final moments in charge of Romania; the leader reduced to the Biggest Zero.

Beneath him, Securitate agents attempted to wrestle the agitators to the ground but by now there were thousands of them. Militiamen detonated a few tear gas grenades and angry ripples spread through the crowd. Sensing an imminent invasion of the Central Committee building, sinister aides rushed around the balcony, hurrying each other through the escape doors to the rear. Ceaușescu remained. He raised a hesitant hand, like a lion-tamer stranded at the back of a cage, and the crowd roared louder. Elena, who was still standing at her husband's side, drowning in an oversize fur coat, shouted: 'Someone is shooting.' Then an official whispered in Ceaușescu's ear that he must move inside. Ceaușescu refused. 'Hello! Hello!' He tapped his microphone as if there were some technical malfunction. 'Silence!' shrieked Elena. 'Can't you hear me… Silence!' The tone she used was one of a shepherd trying to hush unruly animals.

Soon after, the couple were whisked into the safety of the Central Committee building while, outside, waves of protestors filled the square with impassioned cries. The vibrations from the stamping and the shouting reverberated like a tremor through the city. At 1.38 p.m., just an hour after Ceaușescu had begun his speech, an order was issued for the army to take positions around the square. Road blocks were quickly erected at each entrance, made up of ministry of interior troops, regiments of militiamen and lines of armoured vehicles. In front of the famous Intercontinental Hotel, demonstrators constructed their own barricades from tables and chairs that they had seized from the popular Dunarea Restaurant. Just after 10 p.m. they rolled lorries behind the barricades as reinforcement and set them alight. The army responded by sending in tanks, with platoons of soldiers shooting over the heads of the protestors.

Amazingly, Nicolae and Elena Ceauşescu remained in the Central Committee building. The time to flee by road was fast expiring. There was a chance, while the crowds were still poorly organized, but Ceauşescu did not want to be seen cowering in the back seat of a car, fleeing from his own people. He assumed that the military would prevail and that the square would be empty by the morning. The Ceauşescus could hear machine-gun fire and saw high flames licking the night sky. No one will ever know what they were thinking. Maybe they were still blind to the suffering of their people and the hatred that was filling the square. Astonishingly, they decided to bed down for the night in the Central Committee building.

At 7 a.m., Ceauşescu called a meeting of his Politburo. The streets outside were awash with protestors. Huge columns of well-organized workers were converging around the military road blocks, trying to persuade soldiers to join them. Ceauşescu sat before his diehard ministers, dishevelled, unshaven, unfed but lucid with adrenalin. He wanted details from every checkpoint: numbers of officers, weapons available, an immediate explanation as to why the protestors still dared defy the army. He summoned his popular defence minister, General Vasile Milea, and berated him for having failed to supply enough troops. The President wanted more and told Milea to give an order to open fire. Milea, who had been wavering for two days, now took an extraordinary decision. He would not follow orders. It was the first dissent from inside Ceauşescu's circle and it had far-reaching consequences.

An hour later, at 9.45, a voice crackled over military radios, instructing all units to obey orders *only* from the commander-in-chief – in other words, from Ceauşescu himself. Thirteen minutes later, a counter-order was despatched under the codename 'Rondo' – the sign of General Milea – which instructed troops not to fire on civilians. It effectively negated the previous order.

By this time, General Milea had taken a car through the crowds to the office of the Patriotic Guard. He arrived in a state of anxiety and asked an officer if he could borrow his belt-gun. Then he made his way to a colleague's office, unbuttoned his tunic, steadied the gun on a desk in front of him and blew a hole through the left side of his chest. The time was 10.40 a.m.

Twenty minutes later, when news of Milea's suicide reached soldiers outside the Central Committee building, some thought he must have been killed by Ceauşescu for refusing to obey orders. Soldiers from the 1st Armoured Division began to withdraw from their positions in protest, and drifted back to barracks. Inside a grand room in the Central Committee building, Ceauşescu's mind had turned to escape. He summoned a general with an unlikely pedigree. Victor Stănculescu was a rakish sixty-one-year-old with an aristocratic manner, a love of snooker and an affection for the English actor, James Mason. Stănculescu was also the country's deputy defence minister and, after Milea's death, set for promotion. Calm under pressure, the General urged the Ceauşescus to call for a helicopter. They ordered four, with a view to airlifting the whole government out. Three were mysteriously cancelled. The fourth began descending at 11.23 a.m., circling the building and sending protestors fleeing for cover.

The commander of the three-man crew was Lieutenant-Colonel Vasile Malutan – fastidious, cautious, unused to taking unnecessary risk. During his descent, he had nearly backed out of the mission. Aside from the chaos on the streets, there were too many helicopters in the sky. One was dropping sheaves of leaflets urging protestors not to be taken in by 'imperialist conspiracies' and to return home 'to enjoy the Christmas feast', a Marie Antoinette-style suggestion that inflamed protestors further. Malutan toyed with the idea of returning to base but had spotted Securitate sharpshooters on adjacent buildings and thought better of it. He landed precariously amid the aerials and masts, settling on the edge of the roof of the Central Committee building near to an emergency exit door.

At the same time, on the ground, an order was issued for all armoured cars to relocate to the front of the Central Committee building, to block the increasingly animated crowd. But the summoned units did the opposite, withdrawing completely and effectively inviting the crowds to stream inside. Pilot Malutan had been waiting for twenty minutes and was becoming desperate. 'Where are they, why don't they come?' he shouted to a Securitate official. The response was chilling. 'There are demonstrators inside the building.' Malutan radioed his base. 'Do I stay here?' he asked. The answer came back in the affirmative.

By now, protestors were spilling out onto the balcony from where Ceaușescu had tried to deliver his last speech. Others were already searching room to room. Bodyguards ushered the Ceaușescus out of their hiding place and helped them into an elevator. As the lift reached the top floor, the doors jammed. One of the guards smashed them open. The couple hurried onto the roof, breathless, exhausted and terrified. Ceaușescu looked like he was close to collapse. Assisting him was the aristocratic General Stănculescu, nominal defence minister for the sixty minutes since his boss had committed suicide. He waved them off and then retreated downstairs. By this time, one group of protestors had reached the top floor and were looking for a way to the roof. Ceaușescu was out in the open. Beneath him, in Palace Square, the crowd surged and yelled as the President's hunched figure ran alongside that of Elena towards the helicopter. Accompanying the presidential couple were two Securitate bodyguards. Then came the beanpole figure of the deputy prime minister, Manea Manescu, Ceaușescu's brother-in-law, followed by the morbidly obese prime minister, Emil Bobu, who waddled, walrus-like, to the rear.

Pilot Malutan shouted that there were far too many passengers to take off safely. They would never get off the ground.

The Ceauşescu party ignored him and tumbled inside, the two Securitate and two ministers squeezed into the rear seat, the Ceauşescus in the middle along with a crew member, while pilot Malutan and his assistant occupied the cockpit. At that moment, a line of protestors ran out onto the roof. Malutan had little choice. Grossly overloaded, he raised the helicopter at full throttle and barely cleared the edge of the building, dipping momentarily and struggling to remain airborne. The time was 11.47 a.m.

As the Ceauşescus banked above the crowds, Malutan turned to them and yelled 'Where to?' No one had any idea. There was no escape plan. Reaching the helicopter had been the goal. In huddled animation, shouting above the din of the blades, the Ceauşescus began exploring their options. The process was brief. Below them, the whole of Bucharest seemed to be on the move. 'To Snagov!' shouted Nicolae.

The picturesque rural settlement, twenty miles north of Bucharest, was the scene of Vlad Dracula's last battle and the site of his supposed burial at the ancient monastery on the lake. Ceauşescu had a summer house there, a former hunting lodge with grand stucco frontage and bucolic views. Their helicopter touched down on rolling lawns by the water's edge and disgorged the six passengers who crouched beneath the rotor blades and raced inside. Ceauşescu insisted that Malutan join them, secretly worried that he might fly off if left to his own devices.

Once inside, Ceauşescu began a round of desperate calls on his VIP phone, contacting district secretaries in region after region. 'What are things like in your area?... Is it calm?... Are the people quiet?' At one point, while talking to officials in Timişoara, he broke into what sounded like the continuation of his unfinished balcony speech. 'We must maintain our territorial integrity,' he thundered. 'We have sufficient comrade activists to serve the cause for another hundred years.'

As Malutan watched the extraordinary scene unfold, his mind turned to self-preservation. Over the helicopter radio he had heard chaotic reports from officers on the front line, and had arrived at a more realistic appraisal of the situation than the President. Solemnly, he informed Ceaușescu that the strain imposed by overloading the helicopter had damaged the engine. 'I cannot guarantee your safety,' he said. 'Why not allow me to return to base and come back with a safer craft?' It was, of course, a ruse but Ceaușescu began to consider the offer. Elena, on the other hand, was immediately suspicious.

'If you go away and leave us,' she said, 'we're done for... who else is with us?'⁴

'Alright,' said Malutan, 'I will take off, but not with everyone.'

He ran outside and ordered the helicopter crew to re-start the engines, telling them that if the Ceaușescus did not board immediately, they should take off without them, even if the Securitate officers began shooting. But as soon as the blades began turning, Elena heard the sound and came scurrying out, followed by Nicolae. The other two, Bobu and Manescu, kissed the President's hand as he buckled himself in, and waved goodbye. It was 1 p.m. The pale winter light already seemed to be fading.

The French-made Dauphin helicopter set out eastwards, high above frozen fields and empty lanes, towards Pitești, the city where the notorious prison experiments had taken place in 1950. That afternoon, it was quiet. The protests had not yet reached there. 'Don't tell anyone where we are going,' shouted Ceaușescu, by now afraid that his progress was being tracked via the helicopter's radio system. Malutan flew high in the hope of being picked up by radar, then plunged dramatically towards the ground. 'They've spotted us,' he lied. 'We could be shot down at any moment.' He landed the helicopter in a desolate field near to a road.

It must have been a surreal sight: Nicolae Ceaușescu still dressed in his elegant fur-lined coat, silk scarf and expensive leather shoes; Elena also in a fur, with a Hermès scarf and high heels, clambering around aimlessly in the frozen mud. The

President and his wife – who had once entertained Nixon and Mao and who had slept on goose-feather pillows in Buckingham Palace and been showered with marigolds in New Delhi – now ditched in a field of dead corn with two thick-necked minders.

Presently, a car appeared, a red Dacia. One of the minders stepped out, machine gun beneath his coat, and waved the vehicle down. Its driver was a local doctor, Nicolae Deca, who was astonished when he realized the identities of the bedraggled party. The Ceauşescus squeezed onto his rear seat and began debating noisily which way to go. Within minutes, they had arrived at a small village and Deca pretended he was running out of petrol.

The streets were empty, aside from a young man called Nicolae Petrisor, who was washing his black Dacia outside his home. The Ceauşescus decided to switch vehicles. As they climbed out of the doctor's car, Petrisor recognized them. 'They're here!' he shouted to his wife. 'It's them!' The Securitate agent, Florian Rat, strode over and flashed his gun, and Petrisor quietened down. Incredulous neighbours began to gather as the Ceauşescus requisitioned both him and his car, clambering into the back seat. One shouted: 'Nicolae, don't do it, they will kill you.' Others called their children and told them to take a good look at the fleeing 'tyrants'.[5]

Then began a darkly comic journey, with the Ceauşescus and their one remaining Securitate officer – the other had run away – trying to find a place of safety. They pinned their hopes on the city of Târgovişte, the ancient former capital of Wallachia, where Vlad Dracula had once built his home behind high stone walls and had watched men and women being impaled from the turret of his infamous Chindia Tower. The Ceauşescus sought sanctuary in a 'showcase' steel factory on the fringes of the city but were turned away at the gates. Amazingly, given that the country was still nominally under Ceauşescu's control, the workers began hurling stones at the presidential couple's car.

The next stop was Târgoviște's 'Plant Protection Centre', where the Ceaușescus were greeted by director Victor Seinescu, who allowed them inside and fussed around them. While they tried to explain their pressing need for armed assistance, the driver of their commandeered car seized the moment and drove away. It was 2 p.m., only an hour since they had left Snagov. Events were moving swiftly.

Ceaușescu knew that support from the army was haemorrhaging, having witnessed events in Palace Square. There was no point in phoning their local headquarters. But just down the road was the office of the ultra-loyal Securitate, which they shared with the Militia (police). Relations between the army and Securitate were often strained. Confronted with a domestic security breach of such magnitude, Ceaușescu calculated that it was the Securitate who would be more reliable. They'd fight to the death to protect him, even if it meant killing their military comrades in the process.

Ceaușescu's instincts were right, at least about the likelihood of a split between the two. In fact, at that very moment in the beautiful Transylvanian city of Sibiu – where his son Nicu was Party secretary – the army and the Securitate were engaged in a running battle, fighting each other from their respective headquarters on either side of the same road. Automatic gunfire echoed, as the Securitate tried to overrun the city's army HQ. Army cadets responded by advancing in an APC and opening fire on the Securitate buildings. More than fifty people were killed, eight of them soldiers, twenty-three Securitate, the rest civilians.

Back at the Plant Protection Centre in Târgoviște, it was 2.30 by the time two uniformed Securitate officers arrived to collect the presidential couple. By now the streets were swarming with protestors and the Ceaușescus' car was almost engulfed. It was a near miracle that no one saw them huddled on the back seat. Eventually, the danger was such that the driver had to pull down a dark side-street and wait. Headlights off, sunlight gone, the presidential couple were told not to make a noise. They lay there on the back seat for four hours, like fugitives.

It was a crucial period. Again Ceaușescu's instincts were partly correct. The local army HQ had, indeed, switched sides and were now supporting the protestors. But he was mistaken about the loyalty of the local Securitate. At their Târgoviște HQ, they had seen live coverage from Bucharest and concluded that the game was up. Late that afternoon, dozens of them abandoned their posts, leaving cars, weapons and munitions behind. When local army HQ heard about the exodus, they sent a fifty-man unit to take over the building.

And so it was that when the car transporting the Ceaușescus crawled into the Securitate complex at 6 p.m., they were not greeted by loyal Securitate at all, but by officers from the now oppositional Romanian army. Nicolae and Elena were bundled into the back of an ARO (the Romanian equivalent of a Land Rover) and whisked off to Army HQ down the road. The Ceaușescus were now prisoners.

Spool back, though, to 11.43 that morning, and the scene in Bucharest. This is where the decisive action was happening. As the Ceaușescus' helicopter receded northwards into the clouds, the imperious General Stănculescu, who had just helped them onto the roof, made his way back inside. He faced a pressing dilemma. The Ceaușescus might never be seen in Bucharest again but, then again, it was entirely possible they could rally military support in the regions and be back home for supper. A premature defection would risk his life. A delayed one, on the other hand, might leave him vulnerable to the whims of a score-settling successor. Agonizing about which path to take, Stănculescu took a car to Bucharest's military hospital, where he knew a doctor. He raced inside, made his way to his friend's office and asked for a plaster cast to be put on his leg. A full one, from ankle to knee so that he could hardly move. It was around 1 p.m. The Ceaușescus would have just been leaving their hunting lodge at Snagov.

At the same time, a disgraced former general happened to be strolling past the Central Committee building, drawn by the day's protests and eager to take a look. His name was Major General Stefan Kostyal, an aging Stalinist who had once shared a prison cell with the young Ceaușescu and later fallen out with him in spectacular style.

Kostyal lived under intense Securitate surveillance, his phone and apartment bugged, a Securitate car stationed outside his building twenty-four hours a day. The Securitate even had a key to his flat and would let themselves in to drink his plum brandy.[6] The reason for such heavy surveillance was that, in 1984, Kostyal had been suspected of being part of a plot to oust Ceaușescu.

In fact, there had been two such plots, involving a network of disgruntled past and present generals and a handful of politicians. Kostyal was a leading figure behind one of them. The second was headed by another former high-flying officer, General Nicolae Militaru, a career soldier accused by Ceaușescu of spying for the Russians in 1978 and dismissed from his post as head of the Bucharest military garrison. Brooding, solid and fearless enough to have contacted Gorbachev for assistance in ousting Ceaușescu, Militaru was also looking for revenge and was the first point of contact for anyone in the army planning a coup.

Significantly, this rather austere group of disaffected curmudgeons had the support of an unusually urbane and erudite young politician once viewed as Ceaușescu's heir apparent. Ion Iliescu had the same kind of sun-burst charisma and effortless style as the young John F. Kennedy. Polished, articulate, with an impulsive, mischievous grin, he wore sharp suits and skinny ties, and even made jokes in the middle of speeches. Iliescu shone brightly from behind the customary rows of stony-faced Party hacks, taking his first ministerial job in 1968 at the age of just thirty-seven. Of course, such uncontrived popularity had its price. Ceaușescu was envious and when he arrived home from his famous China and North Korea trip to find Iliescu less than enthusiastic about adopting a similar style of granite-hard totalitarianism, he had him side-lined. A series of anonymous jobs in the regions saw Iliescu effectively shut down for a decade and a half. Publicly, the young politician never complained but oppositional elements detected his openness to a potential plot. He was placed under heavy Securitate monitoring and made it clear to that small core of potential plotters that he could only be coaxed from the shadows by a professional, near foolproof plan.

These two groups of potential coup schemers merged in 1984 but the resulting plot – scheduled for when Ceauşescu was out of the country that summer – was so comically disorganized that it fell apart when the military units chosen to lead it were suddenly ordered to leave Bucharest for the countryside to carry out patriotic work. The fact that the plotters were unable to re-schedule suggests that they had a thin and unreliable base, and would almost certainly have failed.

By the winter of 1989, only the bones of the original plan survived: meeting points, how to commandeer the television network, and the names and contact details for like-minded coup enthusiasts. Vague as it was, this was the blueprint that General Kostyal followed after he had observed Ceauşescu's helicopter leave the Central Committee building that morning. He headed straight to the ministry of defence, where he expected to find his old friends and conspirators.

In fact, when he walked in, he found the insouciant General Stănculescu, fresh from hospital in his phoney leg plaster and presiding over a building full of people who seemed to think little had changed. 'Everything is calm,' said Stănculescu, addressing Kostyal as if he were his superior. 'The troops are back in barracks.' Kostyal was anxious. 'Where is General Ilie Ceauşescu [the President's brother]?' he inquired. Stănculescu seemed puzzled by all the fuss. 'Upstairs, in his office,' he replied.[7] Kostyal ran upstairs to discover it was true. Ceaușescu's brother was, indeed, sitting behind his desk, getting on with paperwork as if nothing had happened. 'Put that man under arrest,' thundered Kostyal. Stănculescu recoiled. 'We'll do it, by and by,' he said. 'No, you'll do it now,' shot back Kostyal, 'and you'll also send for Iliescu, Militaru and Corneliu Manescu [all part of the original plot] and bring them to the defence ministry.' Stănculescu stalled. He pointed to his prop – his heavily plastered leg. He was having trouble moving, he said, and was no good for organizing anything.

They needed Ion Iliescu above anyone. Almost sixty years old by now, his fashionable suits replaced by old jumpers, his face grooved with worry and a bad diet, Iliescu was the person least contaminated by links to Ceaușescu – although still part of the old apparatus. But at that moment he was on his way to a thirteen-storey block in the middle of Bucharest, a tower that contained the national television station. The streets were packed with people. Tear gas hung in the winter air. Gunfire rang out along downtown boulevards. Securitate sharpshooters were using guerrilla tactics, hiding in domestic apartments and constantly shifting position. Just like Iliescu, they too were moving towards the TV tower, suspecting it was a meeting point for the opposition and knowing that whoever controlled its broadcasts controlled the people. Iliescu arrived at 2.30 and made his way to Studio 4 on the eleventh floor, the place from where Ceaușescu's daily propaganda broadcasts were normally transmitted. He found a ragtag group of demonstrators crowded in front of a camera, some in their half-discarded military uniforms, others still breathless from the street. They cheered Iliescu as he entered and thrust him to the front. It was an astonishing moment. The images were flashed around the country. This diminutive, unremarkable-looking man, who many had never seen before, was the first person other than an RCP general secretary to address the Romanian people since the communists had terrorized their way into power half a century before.

'Dear comrades, friends and citizens,' he began, clearing his throat, 'I am too nervous and filled with emotion...' Up and down the land, Romanians watched enthralled on their televisions. They had no idea what had become of their president, but this was the most extraordinary broadcast in anyone's lifetime. Many thought it was just a surreal intermission, that Ceaușescu loyalists would rush the studio at any moment and their TV screens would go dead. Instead, they watched this passionate stranger speak with precision and luminosity.

'... no one would have expected that this regime, which wanted itself to be almighty, all-knowing, all-doing, which didn't even exhibit the minimum lucidity to understand the horror that Romanian people were suffering...' Iliescu's voice cracked with emotion. '... to show the calm to resolve the situation peacefully.' Families watched transfixed. They were more used to ramblings about tractor production and potato harvests. 'Ceaușescu is guilty of an odious crime against his own people,' continued Iliescu. '... this man without a heart, without a brain, without reason.'

In the studio, there was a cheer of delight. Iliescu announced that he had spoken to General Stănculescu twenty minutes earlier and that Stănculescu had ordered all remaining army units off the streets. The Securitate were a different matter, though. They were still out of control. By this point, the number of dead had reached 162. Over the next few days, it would rise to more than a thousand.

Iliescu glanced at his watch, announcing that it was a quarter to three in the afternoon, and said that anyone interested in being part of a 'committee for the salvation of the nation' should meet at the Central Committee building at 5 p.m. sharp. 'I spoke with Cabinet No. 1,' he said with a wry smile (a reference to Nicolae and Elena's separate cabinets), 'and the No. 1 person wasn't there, the secretary wasn't there... there was a comrade there... he asked who I was, he didn't know who I was...' 'You will be known soon,' shouted a crowd member. There were more cheers.[8]

Weaving through streets of abandoned tanks where Securitate sharpshooters were firing at anything that moved, Iliescu made his way to the ministry of defence. By this time, he was confidently trotting out the names of those with whom he wanted to govern. Many were unreformed Stalinists, crepuscular figures from another age, men who had taken part in purges and mass jailings, some of them from the Gheorghiu-Dej era, others who had been Ceauşescu loyalists until just hours before. Of course, it was hardly surprising that a system that had strangled dissent for half a century could provide no ready supply of liberal thinkers. Even so, the men beginning to surround Iliescu were a sulphurous brew.

At the defence ministry, he picked up two significant characters. One was Ceauşescu's ultra-loyal Securitate chief, General Vlad, inscrutable as ever behind his yellow lenses. At that very moment, Vlad's Securitate sharpshooters were firing on protestors and yet here was their boss, having apparently undergone a Damascene transformation, running off with the opposition. Crucially, Vlad had not given his men an order to stop shooting.

Also leaping into the convoy of vehicles bound for the 5 p.m. meeting was General Stănculescu, who now appeared miraculously mobile as he swung his plastered leg into a vehicle and headed off to the Central Committee building. At 5 p.m. that afternoon – Friday, 22 December – as the Ceauşescus hid in the back of a vehicle on their way to Securitate headquarters in Târgovişte, a chaotic meeting was convened in Bucharest. The proceedings were tape-recorded without the knowledge of the attendees. There was bedlam. Crammed into a room on the first floor were soldiers, opportunistic politicians, strays who had wandered in from the street, a poet, an army architect and even a famous actor.

At the height of the hubbub, a guard shouted that Gheorghe Apostol was at the door – the Gheorghiu-Dej loyalist who had called Ceauşescu 'the biggest zero' in 1968 and who had been *persona non grata* ever since. He was now seventy-six years old, and hardly a democrat. They did not let him in. The protestors had hoped the meeting would be dominated by street revolutionaries. One young man could be heard shouting out: 'The new government must include people who actually started and took part in the revolution.' He was quickly hustled out of the room.

Another voice was that of an unknown engineer called Petre Roman, a youngster whose parents had been communist aristocracy in the 1940s, but who was not a Party member himself. He had mysteriously arrived alongside Iliescu, who seemed to have taken the young firebrand under his wing. When Roman tried to speak, he was cut down to size. 'Nobody knows who you are!' someone heckled. But within days, everyone would. Roman was to become Iliescu's prime minister.

Just before midnight on 22 December, Iliescu appeared on television screens once more. He announced the creation of a transitory body called the National Salvation Front, which would take control of the country while elections were organized. Still, there was no word on the Ceaușescus.

*

Fifty miles away in Târgoviște, the President and his wife were settling down to a less than comfortable night on a makeshift bed in a converted military office.

Their room was divided into two cubicles separated by desks, with army beds and blankets. The Ceaușescus were to sleep on one side, a guard on the other. They would be watched twenty-four hours a day. In the corner was a large, hissing, porcelain stove. Water was supplied through a single cold tap positioned above a tiny washbasin. The ground floor wing of the barracks was immediately cordoned off, and only hand-picked officers and NCOs were allowed access.[9]

Ceaușescu had arrived in a flurry of confusion. 'Well, what's the situation? Give me your report,' he'd snapped, still believing he was Commander-in-Chief. His new status had taken a while to sink in. That first night, an officer delivered him a tray of army food – salami and salted cheese. Nicolae refused to eat it, indicating that the bread was stale. The officer felt bold enough to answer back. The army had been eating food like this for years, he said, these were standard rations. 'Don't give me that crap,' barked Ceaușescu, 'this area has the best bread in Romania.'

Elena complained about everything – the tea, the bed, the absence of clean clothing. She swung into terrifying fits of rage and constantly accused the guards of insolence. When the barracks captain addressed her husband, she snapped back: 'How dare you talk to the Commander-in-Chief like that?'

But there were also displays of tenderness between the two, intensely private moments laced with despair. They huddled together in their cot and lay in each other's arms. The officer monitoring them, Major Ion Secu, reported that 'they talked in whispers, and though they kept hugging each other, they also kept on bickering softly'. He heard Nicolae say: 'If you had only told me what was going on, I could have got rid of that Iliescu. I could have finished him off last summer. But you didn't let me. You knew about the plot and didn't let me touch them.' Elena whispered back: 'It's all your fault, we shouldn't have come here in the first place.'[10]

On Christmas morning of 1989, Nicolae and Elena were manhandled into the belly of an armoured vehicle, to hide them from on-going attacks by Securitate units that were still trying to rescue them. While the Ceaușescus were inside, three helicopters arrived from Bucharest. They were carrying military judges, prosecutors, a defence advocate, a doctor and an execution squad.

An hour or so later, the couple were assisted from the vehicle. Ceaușescu was shaking slightly and required the arm of a soldier to lean against. They were led back into the building, but not to their sleeping quarters. Instead, they were taken to a makeshift surgery. On the way, Ceaușescu bumped into General Stănculescu.

Last time the two were together, Stănculescu had helped him escape onto the roof of the Central Committee building. Now Ceaușescu assumed his loyal comrade had come to rescue him. In fact, it was Stănculescu who'd organized the trial that was about to take place.

There is extraordinary footage of Ceaușescu being examined by a doctor. His eyes dart around the room. Everything looks normal. A bed. A stethoscope. A doctor in a white coat. Ceaușescu is told to sit on a bed and remove his jacket. He does so immediately, rolling up his sleeve and offering his arm. His blood pressure is taken and Ceaușescu is transformed into an anxious patient, hoping that the readings are nothing to worry about. The doctor relays the figures to someone out of shot. They are not good. He glances at his patient. 'What do you want me to do?' Ceaușescu sighs and shrugs his shoulders. What can anyone do? But there is a flicker of relief. Not about the figures, but about the concern for his health. It suggests there can be no imminent danger. Perhaps he can think more long-term; a trial in Bucharest... an appeal if things go wrong... an intervention from world leaders to stop all this madness. He pulls on his overcoat, straightens his tie, wraps his silk scarf around his neck and leaves the surgery.

The next scene is a small schoolroom, located a little further down the corridor. It is airless and claustrophobic. Sixteen men are waiting behind primitive children's desks for Nicolae and Elena Ceaușescu to enter. Most are in full military regalia. This is supposed to be a military court but it conforms to no judicial convention. It is grubby, poorly lit and has a disused porcelain oven in the corner. The Ceaușescus are made to sit behind two wooden desks pushed together to create a makeshift dock. Nicolae is huddled in his thick black coat, his hands clasped on his knee. Elena is wearing the same honey-coloured fur coat and Hermès scarf she wore for her husband's last speech. In her hand is a small, flat, white package that contains insulin sent from

Bucharest to treat Nicolae's diabetes. At the door stands a soldier in a helmet. There are tears streaming down his face. Paratrooper Ionel Boeru has volunteered, like every other soldier in the room, to be part of the execution squad.

There is a hurry about the place. A need to have things done and be out before dark, before sharpshooters loyal to Ceauşescu discover what's happening and try to overrun the building. The charges are announced by one of three prosecutors. He looks ill-prepared, like he has been dragged out of bed. He is wearing an old jumper and jeans. Chin tucked into his neck, he mumbles: 'Genocide [in Timişoara]... attacks against their own people [during the revolution]... destruction of buildings and institutions... undermining the economy.' He glances up, before concluding: 'I plead, on behalf of the victims of these two tyrants, for the death sentence.'

Nicolae and Elena gaze around the room scornfully. 'Do you understand the charges?' asks the chief prosecutor. 'Have you understood them?'

'I do not answer,' replies Ceauşescu, trying to summon some authority. 'I will only answer questions before the Grand National Assembly. I do not recognize this court. The charges are incorrect, and I will not answer a single question here.'

The chief prosecutor wears a tired dark suit and thick glasses. When he motions extravagantly with his arms, he can nearly touch the Ceauşescus in their little makeshift dock. 'The situation is known,' he says. 'Every honest citizen knows that we do not have medicines, that you two have killed children and other people in this way, that there is nothing to eat, no heating, no electricity.'

Nicolae Ceauşescu is fidgeting with his lambswool hat. 'I do not answer,' he says.

'Who gave the order to shoot in Bucharest, for instance?' says the prosecutor.

'I do not answer,' says Ceauşescu.

'Who ordered the shooting into the crowd?'

Elena looks aghast. 'Forget about them,' she says to Nicolae. 'You see, there is no use talking to these people.'

'There is still shooting going on,' persists the prosecutor, 'fanatics… they are shooting at children, they are shooting randomly into apartments… are you paying them?'

Ceaușescu's voice is hoarse. 'I will not answer. Not a single shot was fired in Palace Square. Not a single shot. No one was shot.'

'By now there have been thirty-four casualties,'[11] says the prosecutor.

'Look,' shouts Elena in a mocking voice, 'and that they call genocide.'

Elena then whispers something into Nicolae's ear. The prosecutor sees an opportunity. 'Elena… ' he says, with some relish, '… has always been talkative, but she does not know much. I have observed that she is not even able to read correctly, but she calls herself a university graduate.'

Elena laughs dismissively. 'The intellectuals of this country should hear you, you and your colleagues,' she scoffs.

The prosecutor ignores her. 'Nicolae Ceaușescu should tell us why he does not answer our questions. What prevents him from doing so?'

'I will answer any questions, but only at the Grand National Assembly, before the representatives of the working class… all the world should know what is going on here. I only recognize the working class and the Grand National Assembly.'

The prosecutor lowers his voice and says firmly: 'The world already knows what has happened here.'

'I will not answer you putschists,' says Ceaușescu.

'The Grand National Assembly has been dissolved.'

Ceaușescu shakes his head and raises his voice. 'This is not possible at all. No one can dissolve the National Assembly.'

'We now have another leading organ. The National Salvation

Front is now our supreme body.'

'No one recognizes that,' snaps Ceaușescu. 'That is why the people are fighting all over the country.'

'Who do you think the people are fighting?'

Ceaușescu is weary with it. 'As I said before, the people are fighting for their freedoms and against this putsch, against this usurpation.... the putsch was organized abroad... I hope you do not work for the foreigners and for the destruction of Romania?'

The prosecutor ignores him and turns to counsel for the defence, who is also seated on a child's chair. He asks him to address his client and inquire whether he understands that he is no longer president of the country?

The defence lawyer is Nicu Teodorescu – elegant, though a little dishevelled in a charcoal grey pinstripe suit, and clearly enjoying the presence of the television camera. He rises with a theatrical flourish and asks Nicolae Ceaușescu if he understands that he has lost all functions.

Ceaușescu answers: 'I am President of Romania. I am Commander-in-Chief of the Romanian army. No one can deprive me of these functions.'

Since the Ceaușescus were captured, crowds have broken into their grandiose home. 'Now we finally saw your villa on television,' says the prosecutor, 'the golden plates from which you ate, the foodstuffs that you had imported... pictures from your luxurious celebrations.'

Elena interrupts. 'Incredible!' she snaps. 'We live in a normal apartment, just like every other citizen. We have ensured an apartment for every citizen through corresponding laws.' Whenever Elena has an outburst, Nicolae pats her arm to calm her down and comfort her.

'You had palaces,' insists the prosecutor.

'No, we had no palaces,' says Nicolae. 'The palaces belong to the people.'

'Children cannot even buy plain candy,' says the prosecutor, 'and you are living in the palaces of the people!' Then, changing tack, he turns to the defence team. 'Please ask Nicolae and Elena Ceaușescu whether they have ever had a mental illness.'

Nicolae stops fiddling with his hat. 'What! What should he ask us?'

'Whether you have had a mental illness,' responds the prosecutor calmly.

Nicolae is bridling. 'What an obscene provocation,' he gasps.

'You have never been able to hold a dialogue with the people,' persists the prosecutor. 'You were not used to talking to the people. You held monologues and the people had to applaud, like in the rituals of tribal people. And today you are acting in the same megalomaniac way.'

Nicolae responds that he does not recognize his court-appointed defence counsel. The prosecutor has all but finished. Gravely, he asks for the death penalty and for the impounding of all the Ceaușescus' property. He gives way to the defence and Mr Teodorescu takes the floor.

'Even though he, like her,' begins Teodorescu, gesturing at the Ceaușescus, 'committed insane acts, we want to defend them. We want a legal trial.' He then addresses them personally. 'You led the country to the verge of ruin and you will be convicted on the basis of the points contained in the bill of indictment. You are guilty of these offences even if you do not want to admit it. Despite this, I ask the court to make a decision which we will be able to justify later as well.' Teodorescu puts on a pair of thick glasses to read from some hastily scribbled notes. 'Finally, I would like to refer once more to the genocide, the numerous killings carried out during the past few days. Elena and Nicolae Ceaușescu must be held fully responsible for this. I now ask the court to pass a verdict on the basis of the law, because everybody must receive due punishment for the offences he has committed.'

It is a surprising defence. A plea in mitigation, in fact. A plea for justice to take its course. Moments later, the military judge rises, along with the rest of the court. The Ceaușescus refuse. They remain seated. Elena tries to interrupt. Nicolae reaches out and pats the back of her hand to silence her. The sentence is one of death. Annihilation. Zero.

They appear calm. Their defence counsel approaches and asks what they would like to do. The Ceaușescus wave him away. 'Whoever is responsible for this coup against the state,' remonstrates Nicolae, '… is a traitor, they are all traitors.' The military panel file out while he is shouting. A group of paratroopers surround the couple. There is an order to take them out and shoot them, separately. Elena is on her feet, shouting: 'If you want to kill us, kill us together.' Her voice becomes hysterical. The paratrooper who was earlier in tears tries to calm her, and asks his commanding officer to grant the Ceaușescus their last wish, to be shot together. Elena shouts: 'Together, together, we will always be together.'

Another paratrooper arrives with a length of rope. 'What kind of thing is this?' shouts Nicolae, as they try to tie his hands. 'Don't offend us!' Elena screams, trying to bat away their approaches. The young paratroopers are unsure what to do. The president of their country, the only one they have ever known, is ordering them to stop. Their commanding officer is telling them to tie the prisoners' hands. A more decisive colleague strides over and grabs Elena by the shoulder, spinning her round so they can get to her wrists.

The rope is thin, like twine. The kind used for wrapping parcels. They loop it around and pull it tight. 'Shame! Shame!' shouts Elena. 'I brought you up as a mother.' Everyone is shouting now, except Nicolae. He has put his hands behind his back obediently, without a fight. He allows them to tie him. He asks one of the soldiers to loosen his wife's binding. It is hurting her, he says.

Seconds later, they are manhandled down a stone corridor. Nicolae is tearful but Elena is raging. As they are pushed quickly along, Elena bumps into a soldier. 'Lady, you are in real trouble,' he shouts. 'You keep away from me, you motherfucker,' spits Elena.

There is weak sunshine in the yard. Stone flags. Thin leafless trees. Young soldiers, machine guns on automatic. The firing is uncontrollable. More than one hundred bullets pierce the Christmas Day air. Thick white smoke fills the yard. Powdered masonry falls from the blasted wall.

Then an order to stop, and the hesitant footsteps of the doctor – the one who examined Nicolae Ceauşescu barely an hour ago – picking his way across the stone in his white coat, stethoscope around his neck, crouching beside two prostrate bodies.

Silence in the yard as soldiers consider what they have done, silence and cautious smiles. And outside, the barking of stray dogs. Some say that the moon that night turned blood red.

EPILOGUE

What had begun as a bold and spontaneous uprising by a small group of daring non-conformists and students soon looked more like a coup d'état by Ion Iliescu and his closest associates. His National Salvation Front (NSF), founded on the first day of the Revolution, supposedly to facilitate an orderly transition to democracy, had little interest in involving authentic revolutionaries and street fighters. Its aim was to eliminate Ceauşescu and replace him with a more benevolent version of the same. The old system, give or take a few minor tweaks, was deemed perfectly serviceable. Indeed, Iliescu never renounced communism.

It was often said that whoever succeeded Ceauşescu would be the most popular leader in Romanian history, simply by way of comparison. Huge popularity awaited the new incumbent, even if all he achieved was a reliable supply of heat, light and food. The bar was depressingly low, and the level of political passivity depressingly high. For many, particularly in the countryside, centralized, authoritarian control remained a better option than the alien concept of liberal democracy, with all the individual responsibility that that entailed. Once Iliescu had taken the presidency in 1990, he didn't have to do much to stay in power. He quickly transformed the NSF into his own political party – despite undertakings to the contrary – and would come to dominate Romanian politics for the next decade.

Iliescu's ruling elite was recruited largely from former

Ceauşescu officials who had occupied a second tier under the old guard. They quickly rebranded themselves moderates, slipping seamlessly into the roles of their predecessors, and accruing vast personal fortunes from Iliescu's tentative privatization. Joining them were former members of the Securitate – now rebranded the 'information service' – whose agents had always been at the top of Romanian industry and who now became much-feared oligarchs, many of whom still dominate Romanian politics, sport and business today. The Securitate has never really gone away. 'Securitate hunters' dig through public records to expose the dirty secrets of wealthy public figures, and there is no shortage of these.

During Iliescu's leadership, old tropes of nationalism and isolationism re-emerged. There were scare stories about Hungarians trying to dismember Transylvania, ugly outbursts of anti-Semitism (which Iliescu roundly condemned), and efforts to rehabilitate wartime leader Marshal Antonescu. Authentic reformers saw their revolution slip away. They took to the streets demanding meaningful change, but the new regime responded just like the old. Mobs of ultra-loyal coal miners were summoned to Bucharest to act as Iliescu's shock troops, brutally crushing the pro-democracy protests on behalf of the government.

Today, many Romanians forgive Iliescu his mistakes, viewing him as the freedom-loving father of the Revolution. His intentions, they say, were pure, and he played a poor hand well. It is true that Iliescu never sought personal gain, and that he did introduce individual freedoms while loosening state control on the economy, but it was all glacially slow. Political rivals consider him a hard-line communist who grudgingly reformed as little as he could get away with. They still want his blood. Now in his nineties, Iliescu finds himself being prosecuted over the deaths of 862 people during the Revolution. His accusers say he and his close circle 'stole' the uprising from the people, transforming it into a coup d'état while retaining Ceauşescu's apparatus of power. They blame him and his associates for the deaths that occurred after his television address of 22 December 1989, when Ceaușescu had already fled Bucharest and Iliescu had announced the creation of the National Salvation Front. The days of continued fighting, they say, could have been prevented, but Iliescu and others encouraged disorder in order to promote their own political legitimacy. The case is likely to drag on for years.

More meaningful reform arrived after 2000, as Romania began preparations to join the European Union. Strict membership conditions required profound reform in the economy, the justice system, and human rights. An ambitious and controversial politician, Adrian Năstase, became prime minister, and accelerated the drive towards a market economy. There was economic growth, partnership with the West, and transparency in justice. Finally, Romania seemed to be blooming.

But politicians had found a new and cynical method of doing away with their opponents. It began during a well-meant drive for purity in public office. Politicians realized that, in the heat and confusion of privatization, many of their number had been engaged in business deals that were, at best, legally fuzzy. A succession of tit-for-tat prosecutions began. But soon the notion of having to find actual evidence became something of a chore, and politicians introduced a new catch-all offence known as 'abuse of office'. It covered anything from officials 'causing harm by not doing their jobs properly', to 'influence buying' and outright corruption. Huge numbers of high-profile public figures were sucked into its gravitational pull.

The conviction list includes leaders of political parties, countless senators, judges, MEPs, mayors, prosecutors, football club owners, and a chief of general staff of the Romanian army. Among them is the visionary prime minister, Adrian Năstase, who was sentenced to two years in prison for corruption in 2012, despite the fact many believe the charges politically motivated.

When the police turned up to take him away, Năstase shot himself in the throat. He survived, but was sentenced to more jail time later. Similarly high-profile was the jailing of the President of the Chamber of Deputies, Liviu Dragnea, sentenced to three and half years in 2019 for 'instigating to abuse of office'. Even the prosecutor in charge of investigating organized crime, Alina Bica, ended up being investigated by her own department, and convicted. She then went on the run to Costa Rica.

Some of these were genuine offences, but others were not. The law of 'abuse of office' was itself being mercilessly abused to dispose of political opponents. In the 1920s, fascist politicians had done something similar, organizing mass trials of communist opposition. The communists had then done the same against perceived fascists. The new law was now being hijacked to achieve the same result.

As I write this, in 2021, Romania has moved into a new and exciting phase. Its economy has one of the highest growth rates in Europe. Foreign investment is pouring in. The skyline of Bucharest is dominated by glass and steel skyscrapers full of smart, young graduates working for huge multinational computer companies such as Oracle, Microsoft, IBM and Google, as well as Amazon. The country leads the way in IT, and tech companies are queuing up to establish their European hubs in Bucharest, where talent is plentiful and costs low. Inside these offices, there's an exhilarating sense of new frontiers being conquered. Everyone seems under the age of forty. These are the children of the Revolution, young men and women who have elbowed their way into top jobs, and who wave away dismissively their flat-footed, complacent colleagues in America's Silicon Valley. The Romanian contingent are fleet of foot, uninterested in meetings and rule books. They are hungrier.

There's a new generation of ambitious young lawyers, too, who want to take the legal system out of the hands of politicians, making it transparent and fair. There's even brave talk, among some, of transforming the old Napoleonic code and introducing common-law style juries.

The collective trauma of communism, followed by revolution and then a decade of near darkness, has ignited in some a rare level of drive and inspiration. Up in the Transylvanian city of Cluj, a group of pioneering painters have caught the imagination of the art world with their wild and experimental styles, their loose application of paint, and their creation of haunting, sometimes brutal images of post-communist Romania. Members of the Cluj School are in their thirties and forties, working out of an abandoned communist brush factory in the city, while their canvases are exhibited in top galleries around the world. Many, such as Adrian Ghenie, Marius Bercea, and Bogdan Mihai Radu from neighbouring Sibiu, have become highly collectable. A painting by Ghenie sold at Christie's in 2016 for £7.1 million.

This is modern Romania, not the corruption and the toxic squabbles of the political class, but the young people who are getting on with their lives irrespective of what their leaders do. History has taught us that Romania's political leaders have never been the ones to follow.

ACKNOWLEDGEMENTS

This book was twenty-seven years in the writing. It has grown from experiences and encounters too numerous to mention, from formal dinners with esteemed Romanian diplomats to casual conversations with peasant farmers in Transylvania, and often boisterous debates with members of my own extended family. My wife, Flavia, was my inspiration, of course. She has never stopped teaching me about Romanian history, and encouraging me to read the works of Romanian playwrights, novelists and poets. Her father, Gheorghe, gave me valuable insights into a life lived under communism. He and I enjoyed many philosophical and political discussions over black beer, before he passed away in 2015. Flavia's brother, Claudiu Iosifescu, drove me around the country on relentless expeditions. As part of the new generation of successful tech professionals, Claudiu furnished me with insights into how young people view life in post-communist Romania.

I wrote much of the book at the London Library, in the same rooms where Bram Stoker researched and wrote *Dracula*, hoping that his spirit might somehow inspire me to a higher level of writing. Only you can judge whether he succeeded. The staff at the library were all endlessly supportive despite the building's closure, ferrying me hand-delivered books right through the coronavirus lockdown.

My thanks go to Dr Iulian Toader in Bucharest for his insights into Romania-US relations during the Cold War, and also to staff at the Richard Nixon Presidential Library and Museum in California. The Romanian National Archives and the National Library of Romania were also of great help, digging out documents throughout the pandemic.

The many excellent books by historian Dennis Deletant acted as an indispensible encyclopaedic guide throughout the writing process. My chapters on the Romanian Holocaust benefitted greatly from the diligent research of Radu Ioanid, Romania's ambassador to Israel and previous director of the Holocaust Memorial Museum in Washington. For Queen Marie, I made great use of original research by Hannah Pakula in her matchless book, *The Last Romantic*.

Thank you to Florin Dobrescu for his insights into the Legionaries of the Iron Guard, and to George (Gheorghe) Cuşa, survivor of the Piteşti Prison experiments, who was so generous with his time and his hospitality. Also thank you to Vlad Iacob for his insights into the politicians of modern-day Romania.

Finally, in London, special thanks to my editor Neil Belton, who was brilliant and who made the book better, and to my agent Georgina Capel without whose encouragement I might never have written it in the first place.

ENDNOTES

Chapter One

1   John Hunyadi and his ragtag army won an historic victory at the Siege of Belgrade. He was feted across Europe and toured the camps thanking his brave crusaders. During the celebrations, Hunyadi, now well into his sixties, suddenly fell ill. He died of plague on 11 August 1456. Mehmed, meanwhile, was struck by an arrow in the thigh. That night, the Ottoman army withdrew and returned to Constantinople.

    The main source for this chapter is *Dracula, Prince of Many Faces*, by Radu R. Florescu and Raymond T. McNally (Hachette Book Group, New York, 1989).

Chapter Two

1   Stoker divided his research time between the London Library and the Whitby subscription library on the north-east coast of England, where he spent his holidays. It seems he first came across William Wilkinson's *An Account of the Principalities of Wallachia and Moldavia* (1820) in the Whitby subscription library. He even gives a shelf mark in his notes, o.1097, but that copy has been lost. The London Library, where Stoker was a member, still has the copy they believe he consulted. The page is still folded over and Stoker appears to have marked other pages of interest.

2   Robert Levy, *Ana Pauker: The Rise and Fall of a Jewish Communist* (University of California Press, 2001), p. 19.

3   Philip G. Eidelberg, *The Great Rumanian Peasant Revolt of 1907*, (Leiden: EJ Brill, 1974) p. 207.

4   Hannah Pakula, *Queen of Roumania* (London: Eland, 1989) p. 180.
     All the quotes from Marie in this chapter are taken from Pakula's
     brilliant biography of Queen Marie.

Chapter Three

1   R. W. Seton-Watson, *A History of the Roumanians* (Cambridge
     University Press, 1934), p. 492.
2   'Reports by Sir John Norton-Griffiths on destruction of Romanian
     oilfields, machinery and grain in 1916'. National Archives, Kew: POWE
     33/266.
3   Iulian Simbeteanu, 'John Norton-Griffiths, the Englishman who
     destroyed the Romanian oil refineries and reserves (europecentenery.
     eu Sept 2018).
4   Glenn E. Torrey, *The Revolutionary Russian Army and Romania, 1917*
     (University of Pittsburgh, 1995), p. 1.
5   The son that Zizi had with Prince Carol was also named Carol. Later in
     life, he said he had only seen his father once, when he was five years old.
     In 1926, Zizi fought a ten-million-franc court case in Paris for damages
     incurred by grief over her divorce. To support her son, she resumed her
     life as a dancer, while he was educated at the Académie des Beaux Arts
     and trained as an artist. Zizi died in Paris in 1953. Her illegitimate son,
     Carol, died in 2006.
6   All the quotes from Marie in this chapter are taken from Pakula's
     brilliant biography of Queen Marie.

Chapter Four

1   This account of the event is based on Codreanu's own memories in
     his book, *For my Legionaries* (www.jrbooksonline.com/PDF_Books/
     For%20My%20Legionaries.pdf).
2   The so-called Twenty-one Conditions, officially the Conditions of
     Admission to the Communist International, refer to the conditions,
     most of which were suggested by Vladimir Lenin, for the adhesion of
     the socialist parties to the Third International.
3   Levy, p. 38.
4   The figure for Jewish students at the University of Iaşi was
     exaggerated by Codreanu and was closer to half.
5   The number of active RCP supporters left behind was less than 300 (in
     1927).

Chapter Five

1   Pakula, p. 296.
2   Rebecca Haynes, 'Work Camps, Commerce, and the Education of the "New Man" in the Romanian Legionary Movement' (*The Historical Journal*, Vol. 51, 4, Cambridge University Press, 2008), p. 960.
3   Codreanu, p. 109.
4   From the chapter 'A Year of Great Trials, May 1924–May 1925' in Codreanu, p. 115.
5   From the original newspaper article, *Universul*, 52, nr. 126, 8 iunie 1924; p. 1. 'Studenții de la Iași au fost bătuți' [The students of Iași were beaten]. In: *Universul*, 52, nr. 127, 9 iunie 1924, p. 3. Courtesy of the staff in the Special Collections Unit at the National Library of Romania.
6   Codreanu, p. 117.
7   Dennis Deletant, *Communist Terror in Romania* (St Martin's Press, 1999), p. 8.
8   Pakula, p. 335.
9   Pakula, p. 365.
10   Roland Clark, *Holy Legionary Youth: Fascist Activism in Interwar Romania* (New York, Cornell University Press, 2015), p. 55.

Chapter Six

1   Nicu Cracea, *Dezvaluiri Legionare Vol II* (Bucharest, Editura Fundatiei "Buna Vestire" 1995) p. 210.
2   Codreanu, p. 138.
3   Constantin Iordachi, 'Charisma, Politics, and Violence: The Legion of the Archangel Michael in Inter war Romania', *Trondheim Studies on East European Cultures and Society* (December 2004), p. 52.
4   Codreanu, p. 170.
5   Paul Quinlan, *The Playboy King: Carol II of Romania* (Greenwood Press, 1995), p. 83.
6   Quinlan, p. 96.
7   Pakula, p. 370.
8   Levy, p. 47.
9   Quinlan, p. 119.
10   Iordachi, p. 55.
11   G. Duca, *Too Long Was the Sadness* (Hoover Institution Archives, Stanford University, George I Duca Papers), p. 50.

Chapter 7

1   Iordachi, p. 94.

2   *The Argus Newspaper* (Melbourne, Victoria,), Jan 24, 1938, headline: 'Anti-Jewish Campaign'.

3   Ionuț Florin Biliuță, PhD Dissertation: 'The Archangel's Consecrated Servants: An Inquiry into the relationship between the Romanian Orthodox Church and the Iron Guard, 1930–41' (Central European University, Budapest, Hungary, 2013), p. 214.

4   Pakula, p. 406.

5   Minutes of an Interrogation of Ana Pauker at the Council of War, July 25, 1935, Dossier No. 12413–146 (31), pp. 2–3. Taken from Levy, p. 49.

6   Levy, p. 50.

7   The quote is from General Pétain; see Prof Dennis Deletant, *Hitler's Forgotten Ally* (Palgrave Macmillan, 2006), p. 38.

8   Jonathan A. Grant, *Between Depression and Disarmament: The International Armaments Business, 1919–39* (Cambridge University Press, 2018), p. 106.

9   Biliuță, p.251.

10 Rebecca Haynes, 'Reluctant Allies? Iuliu Maniu and Corneliu Zelea Codreanu against King Carol II of Romania', *The Slavonic and East European Review*, Vol. 85, No. 1, Jan. 2007 (Modern Humanities Research Association), p. 21.

11 Ibid, p. 22.

12 Deletant, *Hitler's Forgotten Ally*, p. 33.

13 Pakula, p. 410.

14 Eleanor Herman, *Sex with the Queen: 900 Years of Vile Kings, Virile Lovers, and Passionate Politics* (William Morrow Paperbacks, 2007), p. 267.

Chapter Eight

1   Alice-Leone Moats, *Lupescu: The Story of a Royal Love Affair* (Henry Holt and Co., 1955).

2   Lya Benjamin (ed.), *Evreii din România între anii 1940–1944, vol. 2, Problema evreiască in stenogramele Consiliului de Miniștri* (Hasefer, 1996), p. 31.

3   Iordachi, p. 81.

4   Ibid. p. 123.

5   Jewish Telegraphic Agency (27 May 1938).

6   'Iron Guard Trial', *The Times* (24 May 1938).

7   Galeazzo Ciano and Hugh Gibson (ed. and trans.), *The Ciano Diaries, 1939–1943* (Doubleday, 1946), p. 146.

8   Rebecca Haynes, 'Without the Captain: Iuliu Maniu and the Romanian Legionary Movement after the Death of Corneliu Zelea Codreanu', *The Slavonic and East European Review* (Modern Humanities Research Association, April 2019), p. 307.

9   R. G. Waldeck, *Athene Palace: Hitler's 'New Order' Comes to Rumania* (Constable, 1943), p. 58.

Chapter Nine

1   Horia Sima, *Sfârsitul Unei Domnii Sângeroase*, for a partial view on his illegal entry into Romania and subsequent cross-examination. p. 80-140.

2   Ibid. p. 155.

3   Deletant, *Hitler's Forgotten Ally*, p. 47.

4   Quinlan, p. 210.

5   Elie Wiesel, *The Report of the of the International Commission on the Holocaust in Romania* (Bucharest, 2004), p.79.

6   Deletant, *Hitler's Forgotten Ally*, p. 16.

7   Dr Hermann Neubacher, German Special Representative for Economic Problems, quoted from Waldeck, p. 137.

8   Deletant, *Hitler's Forgotten Ally*, p. 47.

9   Ciano, pp. 288–9.

10   The exact population breakdown for Northern Transylvania at the time depends on whose figures one believes. In the 1930 census, carried out by Romania, there were 1,176,900 Romanians compared with 912,000 Hungarians. The census of 1941, carried out by the Hungarians, found 1,344,000 Hungarians and 1,068,700 Romanians.

11   Waldeck, p. 177. He is referring to both Carol deserting his post to marry Lambrino, and to his general conduct over the preceding year.

12   This account is based on Waldeck's on-the-spot reporting of events, pp. 178-9.

Chapter Ten

1   After the revolution of 1989, Marie's heart was placed in the National History Museum in Bucharest, and then moved again, in 2015, to the

Golden Room at Pelisor Castle, the room in which she died.

2   Deletant, *Hitler's Forgotten Ally*, p. 57.

3   Matatias Carp and Gerda Tanner (trans.), *The Black Book: The Sufferings of the Jews from Romania 1940–1944* (The Socec & Co. S. A. R. Publishing House, 1946), p. 61.

4   Carp, p. 60.

5   Levy, p. 64.

6   Vilma Dragan (Kajesco) interview, Mircu, *Ana Pauker si altii*, p. 104 (taken from Levy, p. 53).

7   Edward Behr, *'Kiss the Hand You Cannot Bite': The Rise and Fall of the Ceauşescus* (Penguin, 1992), p. 56.

8   Deletant, *Hitler's Forgotten Ally*, p. 64.

9   Carp, p. 155.

10   Waldeck, p. 347.

Chapter Eleven

1   Deletant, *Hitler's Forgotten Ally*, p. 133.

2   Originally from statement of Aurel Totoiescu to public prosecutor A. Schreiber, 16 August 1945 (taken from Deletant, *Hitler's Forgotten Ally*, p. 135).

3   Deletant, *Hitler's Forgotten Ally*, p 137.

4   Ibid. p. 152.

5   Ibid. p. 146.

6   Radu Ioanid, *The Holocaust in Romania, The destruction of Jews and Gyspies under the Antonescu Regime, 1940–44* (Ivan R. Dee, 2000), p. 3890 (digital version).

7   Ioanid, p. 3926 (digital version).

8   Deletant, *Hitler's Forgotten Ally*, p. 173.

9   Ioanid, p. 5119 (digital version); originally from Raul Hilberg, *The Destruction of the European Jews*, Vol. 2 (Yale University Press, 1961), p. 784.

10   International Commission on the Holocaust in Romania, Final Report 2004 p. 89.

11   Deletant, *Hitler's Forgotten Ally*, p. 232.

Chapter Twelve

1   R. H. Markham, *Rumania under the Soviet Yoke* (Meador Publishing Co., 1947), p. 185.

2 Levy, p. 69.

3 Simon Sebag Montefiore, *Stalin: The Court of the Red Tsar* (W&N, 2003), p. 486.

4 Vlad Georgescu, *The Romanians, A History* (I. B. Tauris, 1991), p. 223.

5 Sebag Montefiore, p. 195.

6 Levy, p. 79.

7 Sebag Montefiore, p. 486.

8 'Antonescu's defence of his policy', *The Times* (Thursday, 16 May 1946), p. 3.

9 From Antonescu's final letter to his wife Maria, held in the archive of the Romanian Information Service (taken from Deletant, *Hitler's Forgotten Ally*, p. 260).

10 Markham, p. 297.

Chapter Thirteen

1 Vladimir Tismaneanu, *Stalinism For All Seasons* (University of California Press, 2003), p. 95.

2 *Time Magazine* (20 September 1948).

3 *Life Magazine* (3 January 1949), p. 73.

4 Testimony of Cornelius Stoian, student at the Polytechnic School in Bucharest, in *Evidence of violations of human rights provisions of the treaties of peace by Romania, Bulgaria and Hungary* (US Department of State, submitted to the UN, Nov 3, 1950) p. 152.

5 See Marius Oprea article in Deletant, *Communist Terror in Romania* (C. Hurst & Co, London, 1999), p. 121.

6 Tismaneanu, p. 115.

7 Silviu Brucan, *The Wasted Generation* (Routledge 1993), p. 2214 (e-edition).

8 Ibid. p. 1882.

9 Levy, p. 86.

10 Deletant, *Communist Terror in Romania*, p. 217.

11 Levy, p. 287 (note 162).

12 Levy, p. 201.

13 Remarks of Gheorghe Gheorghiu-Dej, Transcript of a Meeting of the Politburo of the R.W.P., November 29, 1961 (Executive Archive of the Central Committee of the R.C.P., pp. 4–6; taken from Levy, p. 203).

14 Another account – from the defector Ion Pacepa, former deputy head of the Romanian Intelligence Service – has it that Pătrășcanu was

shot in the back of the neck on Gheorghiu-Dej's orders the night before. See Ion Pacepa, *Red Horizons: Chronicles of a Communist Spy Chief* (Washington D.C.: Regnery Gateway, 1987).

15 This anecdote about Gheorghiu-Dej and Khrushchev is from interviews the author Dennis Deletant carried out with Romania's former deputy prime minister for planning issues, Alexandru Bârlădeanu, in 1996. Quoted from his book, *Communist Terror in Romania*, p. 282.

16 Johanna Granville, 'Dej-A-Vus: Early Roots of Romania's Independence', *East European Quarterly, XLII, Vol 4*, (Department of History, University of Colorado, January 2009), p. 389.

17 The process of collectivization in Romania was formally launched from 3–5 March 1949 at a Central Committee plenary. Robert Levy describes in detail how Pauker resisted the idea. During the first year, the policy was pursued with caution. There was no compulsion and the government waited for volunteers from peasant communities. Coercion only occurred once in 1949, remained rare in the first half of 1950 and reached 'massive proportions' in the latter part of that same year, with the involvement of the militia and the Securitate.

18 Levy, p. 224.

Chapter Fourteen

1 Henry Kissinger, *On China* (Allen Lane, 2011), p. 167.

2 William Taubman, *Khrushchev: The Man and His Era* (W. W. Norton, 2003), taken from Kissinger, p. 171.

3 Stenographic transcript of the discussions held with the delegation of the Chinese Communist Party which participated in the proceedings of the 9th Congress of the Romanian Communist Party, 26 July 1965 (translated and published by Parallel History Project on NATO and the Warsaw Pact [PHP], April 2004, *Romania and the Warsaw Pact, 1955–1989:* www.isn.ethz.ch/php).
Edited by Dennis Deletant, Mihail E. Ionescu and Anna Locher.

4 Khrushchev Remembers, p. 255, taken from p. 167, Kissinger, *On China*.

5 Taubman quoted in Kissinger, p. 171.

6 Stenographic transcript of the discussions held with the delegation of the Chinese Communist Party, 26 July 1965.

7   Private Meeting Between President Nixon and Ceaușescu, Bucharest, 2 August 1969. From the US Office of the Historian, Foreign Relations Of The United States, 1969–1976, Volume XXIX, Eastern Europe; Eastern Mediterranean, 1969–1972.

8   Deletant, *Communist Terror in Romania*, p. 295.

9   Private meeting between President Nixon and Ceaușescu, Bucharest, 2 August 1969.

10   Population figures for Jews in Romania vary. These are taken from the censuses of 1948 and 1966.

11   Brucan, p. 2211 (e-edition).

12   Ibid.

13   This is from the testimony of one of my own family members who was a chemical researcher at the same institute.

14   Figures from the Romanian censuses of 1930 and 1977.

15   Memorandum from the President's Assistant for National Security Affairs (Brzezinski) to President Carter, Washington, D. C., 22 February 1977. Meeting with Vasile Pungan (Romania). From the Office of the US Historian online.

16   Radu Ioanid, *The Ransom of the Jews* (Ivan R Dee, Chicago, 2005), p. 86.

17   Pacepa, p. 78.

18   Memorandum from the President's Assistant for National Security Affairs (Brzezinski) to President Carter, Washington, D. C., 22 February 1977.

19   Pacepa, p. 78.

20   Pakistan was passing similar messages from the Americans to Chairman Mao.

Chapter Fifteen

1   Minutes of the conversation between Nicolae Ceaușescu and Mao Tse-tung in Beijing, 3 June 1971, Wilson Centre Digital Archive. Viewed online at: https://digitalarchive.wilsoncenter.org/document/117763.

2   Quotes in this section are all from 'Minutes of the Romanian Politburo Meeting Concerning Nicolae Ceaușescu's Visit to China, North Korea, Mongolia, and Vietnam', 25 June 1971, History and Public Policy Program Digital Archive, ANIC, Central Committee of the Romanian Communist Party, Chancellery, File No.72/1971,

ff.10–58. Translated by Viorel Buta.

3   Pacepa, p. 100.

4   Ashby B. Crowder, MA Thesis: 'Legacies of 1968: Autonomy and Repression in Ceaușescu's Romania, 1965–1989' (Faculty of the College of Arts and Sciences of Ohio University, Ohio, August 2007), p. 115.

5   Pacepa, p. 131.

6   Pacepa, p. 54.

7   Historian Denis Deletant examined Securitate files and explores the figures in his book, *Ceaușescu and the Securitate: Coercion and Dissent in Romania, 1965–1989* (Routledge, London, 2015), p. xiv.

8   Emil-Sever Georgescu, 'New Archival Evidence on the 1977 Vrancea, Romania Earthquake and its Impact on Disaster Management and Seismic Risk' in *Seismic Hazard and Risk* (Springer, Cham, 2018), p. 24.

9   This story is based on Pacepa's account of the event in *Red Horizons*, p. 38. Critics of Pacepa will say it was embellished, and it may well have been. But Nicu's boorish behaviour is well known and this, it seems to me, gives a fair picture of his behaviour when drunk.

10   Robert Hardman, 'Trumped', *The Spectator* (1 June 2019).

Chapter Sixteen

1   'The Queen Once "Hid in a Bush" to Avoid Romanian Dictator Nicolae Ceaușescu', *The Independent* (23 May 2020).

2   Mark Percival, 'Britain's "Political Romance" with Romania in the 1970s', *Contemporary European History*, Vol. 4, No. 1 (March 1995), pp. 67–87.

3   Pacepa, p. 162. In writing his accounts of such conversations, Pacepa relies on memory rather than notes, and he has a fondness for over-colourizing events. Many academics steer clear of quoting him. I hold a slightly different opinion and believe that someone who spent so many years alongside Ceaușescu will be giving us a fair reflection of his tone and language. We know the essence of this story is true because of events that unfold later.

4   Ibid. p. 163.

5   Action Memorandum From the Assistant Secretary of State for European Affairs (Vest) to Acting Secretary of State Christopher, Washington, 18 August 1978.

6   Ion Pacepa died on 14 February 2021, apparently due to COVID-19.

He was ninety-two years old.

7   George R. Urban, *Radio Free Europe and the Pursuit of Democracy: My War Within the Cold War* (Yale University Press, 1997).

8   Richard H. Cummings, *Cold War Radio: The Dangerous History of American Broadcasting in Europe* (McFarland & Co., 2009), p. 166.

9   From Bernard's wife, Ioana Măgură Bernard, 28 April 2003, 'Europa Liberă – dosar incomplet'. Revista 22.

10   CIA intelligence analysis. Romania; Difficult Adjustment to the Financial Crisis, July 1986, p. 6.

11   Telegram From the Department of State to the Embassy in Bucharest, 30 July 1980: Joint State-Defense message. Subject: US Military Exports to Romania. From office of National Historian. Ref: Bucharest 5390.

12   Tismaneanu, p. 208.

13   The cause of Enache's death remains a mystery. There is a death certificate saying that he died of a heart attack but many think it is fabricated. One former aide to Ceaușescu, Nicolae Stan, described how Enache was 'found in the bathroom at night, covered in blood' in a statement in 2011. https://evenimentulistoric.ro/a-murit-dupa-o-cearta-cu-elena-Ceaușescu-sfarsitul-rivalului-pr.htm.

14   Deletant, *Ceaușescu and the Securitate*, p. 332.

15   Ibid. p. 333.

16   Romania: Difficult Adjustment to the Financial Crisis, CIA 1986. P. 16. https://www.cia.gov/library/readingroom/docs/CIA-RDP89T00295R000200200001-6.pdf.

17   Report on Mikhail Gorbachev's Visit to Romania, 4 June 1987 (Central European University Press). See: https://books.openedition.org/ceup/2779?lang=en.

Chapter Seventeen

1   Brucan, p, 168.

2   Deletant, *Ceaușescu and the Securitate*, p. 353.

3   Ibid, p. 353.

4   Behr, p. 7.

5   Ibid. p. 11.

6   Ibid. p. 225.

7   Ibid. p. 227.

8   A criminal prosecution was launched against Iliescu and what the

lawyers called his 'dissident, pro-Soviet plotting group' for alleged crimes against humanity in the days after the Ceaușescus fled, focusing on events from 22–25 December 1989. The allegation is, in short, that they stoked the flames of the revolution unnecessarily and were therefore responsible for the deaths that followed. Even thirty-one years after the revolution, Romanian history never sleeps.

9   Behr, p. 13.

10   Ibid. p. 14.

11   In the chaos, they did not know the real figure. The total number of deaths in the Romanian Revolution was 1,104, of which 162 were in the protests that led to the overthrow of Ceaușescu (16–22 December 1989) and 942 in the fighting that occurred after the seizure of power by the National Salvation Front.

IMAGE CREDITS

1. Photo 12/Universal Images Group/Getty Images.
2. Fusion of Horizons/Flickr.
3. Keystone-France/Gamma-Keystone/Getty Images.
4. © National Archives of Romania, SANIC, Photographic Documents Collection, I, 7528-19.
5. © John Frost Newspapers/Mary Evans Picture Library.
6. © National Archives of Romania, SANIC, Photographic Documents Collection.
7. Sueddeutsche Zeitung Photo/Alamy.
8. © National Archives of Romania, SANIC, Photographic Documents Collection, no. 1073; I, 3350-3.
9. © National Portrait Gallery, London.
10. Universal History Archive/UIG/Getty Images.
11. ullstein bild/Getty Images.
12. Granger Historical Picture Archive/Alamy.
13. Keystone-France/Gamma-Keystone/Getty Images.
14. © Centre for Analysis of the Radical Right.
15. © Central European University Press, 2006. http://books. openedition.org/ccup/docannexe/image/2418/img-1.jpg.
16. Keystone-France/Gamma-Keystone/Getty Images.
17. Keystone-France/Gamma-Keystone/Getty Images.
18. Heinrich Hoffmann/ullstein bild/Getty Images.
19. CORBIS/Getty Images.
20. Heinrich Hoffmann/ullstein bild/Getty Images.
21. © akg-images.
22. © US Holocaust Memorial Museum, Washington.
23. Wikimedia.

24. Online Communism Photo Collection/National Archives of Romania/Photo #E025.

25. Wikimedia.

26. Online Communism Photo Collection/National Archives of Romania/Photo #EA086.

27. Online Communism Photo Collection/National Archives of Romania/Photo #E345.

28. Wikimedia.

29. Patrick ROBERT/Sygma/Getty Images.

30. Bettmann/Getty Images.

31. Mike Stephens/Central Press/Getty Images.

32. Patrick Durand/Sygma/Getty Images.

33. Collection Joinville/akg-images.

34. REUTERS/Alamy.

35. AFP/Getty Images.

INDEX

ABOUT THE AUTHOR

PAUL KENYON has been exploring Romania for two decades. He is a distinguished BBC correspondent, BAFTA award-winning journalist and author of the bestselling *Dictatorland*.